# The Story of the
# **Tour de France**

*How a Newspaper Promotion Became
the Greatest Sporting Event in the World*

Volume 2: 1965–2007

By Bill and Carol McGann

First published by Dog Ear Publishing
4010 W. 86th Street, Ste H
Indianapolis, IN 46268
www.dogearpublishing.net

ISBN: 978-159858-608-4

This book is printed on acid-free paper.


Printed in the United States of America

# Table of Contents

# Acknowledgements and explanations

Our acknowledgments are this volume's first page of text because the unselfish assistance we received from so many kind people was crucial to the writing of this book. If this book has merit, it is because of their help.

Three men were particularly important to this enterprise. Two of them are familiar to any reader of cycling history: Owen Mulholland and Les Woodland. Both of these erudite men have put their profound knowledge of cycling, history and general culture at our disposal. They are generous men who made it clear that we were not to be shy about asking them for help. We took them at their word and as we noted in the first volume, we were rewarded with endless valuable insights and countless little-known facts, nearly all of which have been included in this work. Both allowed us to quote from their books and both gave us much needed advice. They have been good and kind friends.

Mr. Mulholland not only fielded countless questions, he reviewed the text and made many excellent suggestions.

The third man, James Witherell, won't be known to the reader, but we hope that someday he will be. He has written a yet unpublished *magnum opus* on the history of the Tour, *When Heroes Were Giants*. We hope the fruit of his extraordinary knowledge of the Tour de France will soon see the light of day. Out of the blue, Mr. Witherell sent us a letter noting a couple of errors in the on-line version of this history. We entered into a correspondence that yielded his very gracious offer to review the text of this volume. He joyfully tackled the huge task of fact-checking our text as if it were his own book. We are extremely grateful to this bighearted man.

Scott Gibb and Mary Lou Roberts also scrutinized the text, making sure that people with varying levels of familiarity with the subject and jargon of cycling would understand the story. We ended up incorporating almost all of their suggestions.

Francesca Paoletti drew the map of France at the beginning of the book. We needed a map that was drawn specifically for a Tour de France history and Francesca has done a wonderful job.

Antonio and Mauro Mondonico and Valeria Paoletti also lent invaluable help. Our gratitude to them and the many others, listed in the bibliography, is profound.

Special thanks are due to Joël Godaert, Robert Janssens and Guido Cammaert, authors of the *Tour Encyclopedie*. In their words, they researched the results of each and every Tour like archeologists. I depended heavily upon their work, which is now largely posted on www.memoire-du-cyclisme.net. The *Memoire* site is a wonderful storehouse of information that was an essential tool in completing this story. The prodigious work the contributors to the site performed is a valuable service that has earned my deep gratitude.

Any errors are our own.

# A couple of explanations

Doping has always been a part of cycle racing. In the early years riders used strychnine, ether, cocaine, brandy and a host of other drugs, anything to dull the pain and allow them to get through the ordeal of the impossibly long races of the early twentieth century. As time and technology progressed, the drugs and their efficacy improved. Out of this grew a riders' doping culture that became almost formalized with its own code of behavior. Almost no rider, even in retirement, spoke about doping to the press. A code of silence as effective as the *omerta* of the Mafia was imposed. As doping grew in sophistication and cost, the riders continued to behave as if they had a right to dope and intimidated anyone who spoke out. The management of teams by ex-riders has exacerbated the institutionalization of doping in cycle racing. Team management of doping programs described in the latter chapters of this volume was a natural outgrowth of this process.

Modern performance enhancing drugs are so effective that many riders have felt forced to either turn to them in order to remain competitive, or retire. The constant, ongoing drug scandals of the last decade make this sad fact apparent. Clearly, drugs are an important part of our story.

For us, the problem is how to handle the accusations and suspicions of drug use. Several riders have noted that it is virtually impossible for a rider to prove the negative, that is, that he didn't use drugs. At the same time, recent cases have demonstrated that a rider can take drugs and evade even the most advanced and sophisticated tests. The defense that a rider is clean because he has been tested often is meaningless. Yet for an innocent rider, what other defense can he have?

Because of this problem, we assume for the purposes of this text that a rider is clean unless he has had a positive dope test, has had a court conviction for drug use or transport, or has confessed to using drugs. If events require that we note inconclusive evidence or accusations about doping in our narrative, we have done so. But again, barring our 3 tests of proof, the rider remains innocent.

Any writer delving into the history of the Tour finds himself in a morass of errors and self-serving propaganda. Since some of these fables are now part of the lore of the Tour, I have retold them anyway, pointing out where I believe they depart from fact.

A note on names. Many racers' names, especially Flemish ones, either have several possible spellings or their names were changed by French reporters. Often this French rendition is the way we know them. Jozef becomes Joseph. Ferdy Kübler becomes Ferdi Kübler. I have tried to use the names that the racers were either born with or at least as they were used by their countrymen. When following this rule would create more confusion, I have ignored it. For example, the Buysse brothers (Lucien was the winner of the 1926 Tour) were officially surnamed Buyze. Nowhere in the literature of the Tour have I found them so referenced, so Buysse they shall remain.

Please join us as we continue the wonderful story of the Tour de France, the greatest sporting event in the world.

# Map of France

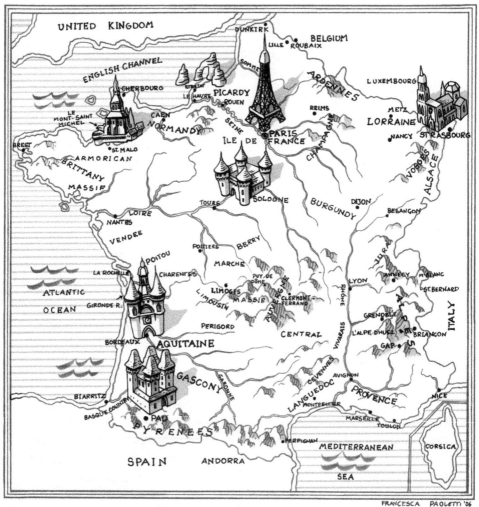

FRANCESCA  PAOLETTI '06

# Preface by Les Woodland

I think of myself, with conceited ease, as an *Eminence Grise* of cycle-racing. There are a great many of us, of course. Here in France we hold informal reunions in village bars, and over glasses of Pelforth we crystallise the advice we will entrust to the riders of the Tour de France.

It isn't easy to condense strategy into the few words that a cyclist can hear while negotiating a traffic chicane at 50kmh. It isn't easy to drown out the radio ranting of some has-been team director who, for heaven's sake, can never have the clarity of vision that we in the bar can have.

That, I think, is why no Frenchman has won the Tour de France for 20 years. These guys almost deliberately don't listen.

But are we discouraged? No we are not. We shall be there again this summer, Dédé, Bernard, Jacques, Jean-Yves and me. We shall wait for the caravan as though it were some heavenly host and then we shall fight to retrieve the cheap key rings, leaking packets of coffee and silly cardboard hats that seem at that moment so important.

We will count and compare our booty and we will go home knowing our place in the pecking order of the cycling roost. And then our wives will ask what we've brought that rubbish home for and the whole lot will go in the bin.

Except for riders' bottles. There is no greater prize than a rider's bottle. Men who run international marketing conglomerates, men who plan naval manoeuvres, men who extract sick hearts... such people will fight in the gutter rather than let someone else go off with a bottle.

Does it matter that you could buy an exactly similar bottle—except that it's clean, not rimed with riders' flob and not scuffed from its collision with the ground—for two euros? No it doesn't. Naturally it doesn't.

Of course, not all Frenchmen like the Tour de France. I know a man called Delmas who views its fairground subtlety with the loftiness of a man who spent his working life professoring at the Sorbonne. He would be embarrassed if anyone assumed he knew the name of a single rider. To him, the Tour de France is Jerry Springer, but for a month. And you can't turn it off.

But do the rest of us care? Of course we don't. For four weeks we own France. We own the world. And we drink beer and shout our advice and then we go home and watch a Frenchman come thirty-second.

# Introduction: Our Story so Far

The first volume of our Tour de France history explains the Tour's origins in 1902 and tells the story of the Tour through 1964, when Jacques Anquetil became the first man to win the Tour 5 times. In this volume we begin the story *in medias res*, jumping right in with the Tour's 1965 edition.

If the reader hasn't read the first volume, the following synopsis of the Tour's first 62 years will help make the narrative that follows understandable.

In the nineteenth century newspapers used a multitude of devices to increase their sales. Much of what both Charles Dickens and Alexandre Dumas wrote was serialized in newspapers. People breathlessly bought the next day's edition to learn how the 3 Musketeers or Oliver Twist would get out of the fix the authors left them in at the end of the last installment. In the U.S. Darwin and Hattie McIlrath, sponsored by the *Chicago Inter Ocean* newspaper, went on a 3-year trip around the world by bicycle while the paper printed weekly reports of their progress. Newspapers would often create their own news, for which they were the only suppliers in an era before radio and television.

Around 1862 Frenchman Pierre Lallement had the inspiration to connect pedals to a crank and the crank to a wheel and with that brilliant invention the bicycle was born. In 1867 Pierre Micheaux began manufacturing bicycles in Paris. Almost from that moment, the newspapers understood the magical appeal of men crossing great distances on these wonderful new machines and began promoting bicycle races. In 1869 *Le Vélocipède Illustré* sponsored the 130-kilometer Paris–Rouen race. Other papers jumped in and soon Europe was covered with races as people along the race routes eagerly bought papers that told the story of the race and listed the results. Both cycle racing and the papers thrived under this symbiosis.

In 1902 Henri Desgrange, the editor of the French sports newspaper, *L'Auto*, was desperately searching for some way to drive his competitor Pierre Giffard, and his newspaper *Le Vélo*, out of business. Desgrange's paper was the creation of right-wing industrialists who were upset with both the liberal politics and high-priced advertising that characterized Giffard's paper.

At the suggestion of one of his writers, Desgrange took the audacious step of promoting a month-long bicycle race around France, a plan much grander than the 1-day races that were the norm. His race would have the competitors ride 6 separate races, with rest days in between each race, in a grand tour of France. He then added up each rider's accumulated time for each race, or stage, with the winner being the rider with the lowest total elapsed time. This kind of multiple-race competition is called a stage race. This is the most glamorous and prestigious type of bicycle road racing and we can credit Desgrange and his staff with its invention and refinement.

The first running of this Tour de France in 1903 was a smashing success. *L'Auto's* sales soared, driving *Le Vélo* out of business. Despite a few missteps, Desgrange and his Tour (and believe me, it was his Tour) went on to become first a French and then an international institution. Of the 12 Tours run before the First World War, 4 were won by foreigners.

The Tour was almost killed by its success and the passions the race generated. Rampant cheating and spectator hooliganism marred the second Tour. To gain control of his race, Desgrange made several changes. The most important was that he altered the way the way the standings, called the General Classification, were calculated. In 1903 and 1904 it had been based on elapsed time. He switched to adding up the riders' placings, or points. In a 20-stage race, if a rider won all 20 stages he would have 20 points. This was much easier to measure and minimized cheating. But, it made for dull racing because if a rider came in second, 5 minutes or 2 hours behind first place, it was all the same. He also shortened the stages and increased their number. The 1905 edition took 11 stages to get around France.

In 1912 Eugène Christophe finished second in the Tour's General Classification, even though he had a lower elapsed time. In a move that characterized Desgrange's nimble and adaptable way of managing the Tour, he went back to using time to calculate the winner.

In 1905 the Tour also started to include mountains. At first the more modest of the Vosges and Alpine ascents were used. Because this was so well-liked, in 1910 Desgrange was talked into running the Tour over the high Pyrenees. Although he feared that this was asking more of the riders than they could do, they were up to the task and the drama of the mountains stages made the Tour even more popular.

Desgrange developed a very complicated rulebook. The most striking difference between the early Tours and today's was the requirement that a rider perform all of his own repairs. The most fabled story involving this rule was that of Eugène Christophe. In 1913 he broke his fork on a mountain descent and was forced to hike to the next town with his bike over his shoulder. Working at the blacksmith's forge for 3 hours, he fixed the fork and resumed the race. Because earlier that day the Tour's leader had abandoned, Christophe had been first in the General Classification when his fork broke. But with that catastrophe, his hopes of winning were dashed.

Over the next half-century the regulations regarding rider assistance were gradually relaxed. This amelioration reduced the effect a mechanical failure could have on the race's outcome. Several worthy riders lost probable Tour victories in the Tour's first 25 years because of the harshness of this rule. In spite of Desgrange's early rules that caused equipment failures to make the results seem to be the working of capricious chance, Belgian rider Philippe Thys won 3 Tours, 1913, 1914 and 1920. He would probably have won in 1922 except for a broken wheel. His feat would not be repeated until 1956.

Desgrange wanted his race to be inhumanly difficult. He wanted it to be a primitive test of a man's endurance, strength and character. He did all he could to make it an individual effort, but failed because in the end, bicycle racing is a sport contested by teams and won by individuals.

When Desgrange became convinced that Belgian teams colluded to help a sickly Maurice de Waele win the 1929 Tour, he had had enough. Desgrange hated teams and he hated sponsors. He couldn't do away with teams. The natural tendency of man, the social animal, to work together overcame all of Desgrange's efforts to isolate the competitors. But he could do something about the sponsors.

Until 1930, bicycle companies were the primary sponsors of the teams contesting the Tour. Boldly, Desgrange scrapped the trade team system and formed the teams along national lines. There was a team from France, one from Italy, etc. If he couldn't come up with enough national teams, he would add French regional teams. To help pay for the increased cost of supporting the riders during the Tour, since the sponsors couldn't be expected to, Desgrange charged a fee to firms who wanted to drive their logo'd cars and trucks along the Tour route. The publicity caravan is still with us and is an important part of the color and excitement of the Tour.

The public loved the national team system as much as the bicycle companies loathed it. For them, it was a 3-week publicity blackout. The system gave France 5 straight victories in the early 1930s after a long period of Belgian domination.

Seeing that the cycling fans liked the Grand Prix des Nations individual time trial promoted by one of his newspaper competitors, Desgrange included the first individual time trial in the 1934 Tour. This gave big-gear men a chance to take back time from the smaller mountain climbing specialists. It gave the Tour a new balance and a new interest.

The conditions under which the first Tour riders competed were appalling by our standards. The bikes were single speed, the roads were mostly unpaved. In the mountains, the word "road" could be generous. Often the way over the high mountains was little more than a path. Even though bikes with gear changing systems were available before the First World War, Desgrange forbade the use of derailleurs. Desgrange's successor, Jacques Goddet, bowed to the force of change and finally allowed their use in the 1937 Tour.

The Tour was suspended during both World Wars. *L'Auto*, which had continued printing during the German occupation of the Second World War, was shuttered by the authorities after the war was over. Goddet formed a new newspaper, *L'Équipe*, and staged the first postwar Tour in 1947.

By 1951, the Tour had taken on the form we know today. Over the first 3 decades Desgrange had gradually increased the number of stages. By 1925 the Tour was run in 18 stages, close to our current 20 or so. The racing slowly moved from an emphasis on the endurance required to complete the Tour's early stages that could approach 500 kilometers. By shortening the stages, the racing became more exciting as speed became an important element in the competition.

For the first half-century, the Tour's ever-changing routes had traced the hexagonal outline of France. In 1951 the Tour went inland into the hilly Massif Central for the first time. In 1951 the only major elements missing from a current Tour were the Prologue individual time trial and the resumption of trade teams.

In the post-war years France was rich with cycling talent. But because the French riders were unable to unite behind 1 designated leader, the Italians and the Swiss dominated the Tour. In 1953 Louison Bobet convinced the French National Team to race for him. With the help and protection of his teammates, Bobet won 3 straight Tours.

In 1957, Jacques Anquetil won the first of his 5 Tour victories. Anquetil had a unique style. He was a master time-trialist. He would stay with the climbers in the mountains, preventing their gaining any time on him. He would then destroy his competitors with a stunning time trial. His defensive riding style tended to alienate the public, but Anquetil cared only about winning and winning with the minimum effort. His duels with Raymond Poulidor, nicknamed "The Eternal Second", enlivened the Tours of the early 1960s. Poulidor was almost always second-best in competitions with Anquetil.

In the early 1960s the Parisian publisher Émilion Amaury became more financially involved with the Tour and promoted one of his writers, Félix Lévitan, to co-organizer of The Tour. Goddet remained the director of the Tour's sporting side and Lévitan became responsible for the race's finances. In 1962, bowing to pressure from bike manufacturers, the Tour reverted to using trade teams.

We concluded Volume 1 with a titanic battle between Anquetil and Poulidor when they raced up Puy de Dôme, a dead volcano. Poulidor won the climb, but was unable to gain enough time that day to take the leadership of the 1964 Tour from Anquetil. With that Anquetil became the first man in Tour history to win the Tour 5 times.

And now, the 1965 Tour de France.

# Chapter 1

## 1965–1968. A troubled time for the Tour with a riders' strike, a tragic death and a reversion to national teams

**1965.** Émilion Amaury, the publisher and World War Two resistance fighter who had influenced the French cycling federation's decision to award the Tour to Jacques Goddet after the war, purchased Goddet's *L'Équipe* sports newspaper and the Tour de France itself. Félix Lévitan—because of his friendship with Amaury—now had greater power and influence in running the Tour. To this day the Amaury organization still owns the Tour, several important Classics including Paris–Roubaix, and *L'Équipe*.

Anquetil didn't ride the Tour in 1965. A large percentage of a racer's income could be derived from appearance money in the post-Tour criteriums, and Anquetil didn't believe that a sixth Tour win would earn him still higher fees. He did see a downside to losing, fearing that a failed attempt to win the Tour would decrease his value to the criterium promoters. The reader should not think that Anquetil had decided to miss the Tour because he was not in top form. Anquetil's spring was magnificent. He won the Dauphiné Libéré, and then that afternoon flew to the midnight start of Bordeaux–Paris, which he also won. He was the victor in Paris–Nice, the Critérium National, and was third in the French National Championships.

With Anquetil out Poulidor felt he had a good chance. Yet by now it had become obvious that, while Poulidor possessed a wonderful engine, his regular tactical lapses were looking less like bad fortune and more the product of his own lack of racing savvy. His spring was one of close calls with second places in the Vuelta a España, the Dauphiné Libéré, the Critérium National and the French Championships.

Italy had 2 standouts to send to the Tour, Vittorio Adorni, winner of that spring's Giro and Tour of Romandie, and Gianni Motta, fifth as a neo-pro in the Giro the year before.

Adorni's Salvarani team brought along a young rider, Felice Gimondi, to help Adorni whenever he could. The year before, Gimondi had won the Tour de l'Avenir—sometimes called the "Junior Tour de France"—an important stage race for racers under 25 years old. Just weeks before the start of the 1965 Tour, Gimondi, only 22 years old and in his first year as a professional, had taken an astonishing third to Adorni's first place in the Giro d'Italia. In 2004 we had the privilege of talking with Signor Gimondi at length about the 1965 Tour, and we've included some of his comments in our story.

Gimondi was a last-minute inclusion in the Salvarani Tour team. Being young and having just finished 1 Grand Tour, he made it seem that he was reluctant to ride the Tour de France. He probably wouldn't have been asked to ride if several of the Salvarani riders who intended to ride the Tour hadn't fallen ill. Pressed into service by the team's director, Luciano Pezzi, Gimondi agreed to start the Tour. But he insisted upon having a 1966 contract signed before starting. He said he was afraid that if he failed to complete the Tour he would be washed-up and no one would want him as a team member. The 1966 4-million lire contract with Salvarani was his insurance. Yet, for the seeming reluctance that is usually written about Gimondi's entry into the 1965 Tour, he knew that he could do it. He told us that as the Giro progressed he could feel that he was getting stronger and stronger. "Deep inside I knew I wanted to race the Tour!…the thought of the Tour made me really enthusiastic," he said. He knew he had a real talent for stage racing.

The 1965 edition was counter-clockwise (Pyrenees first) and for the first time in Tour history, started in Germany. Rik van Looy won the Cologne–Liège stage and the year's first Yellow Jersey. That afternoon was the team time trial and van Looy's Solo-Superia team's third place was only 18 seconds behind Ford-Gitane, allowing him to spend the night with the *Maillot Jaune*.

The second stage from Liège to Roubaix started to upset the apple-cart. 3 riders, Bernard Vandekerkhove, Felice Gimondi and Victor van Schil, got a 14-second gap on the field at the finish line. That gap plus the time bonuses put Vandekerkhove in Yellow and Gimondi—who initiated the day's winning attack on the northern European cobbles—in second place, only 53 seconds behind. Gimondi showed surprising maturity, handling the cobbles of the stage like a Belgian veteran. The next day's run-in to Rouen in Normandy was enlivened by constant aggression including escape attempts by top pros Ferdi Bracke and Julien Stevens. With about 8 kilometers to go the field had been brought back together when Roger Pingeon attacked. He was immediately followed by Gimondi, André Darrigade, Michael Wright, Bracke and several others. Their lead was tenuous as they raced for the finish line. Darrigade was one of the most skilled field sprinters alive. He was particularly dangerous since he was looking to tie the career 25 stage win record of another André, André Leducq.

Here is Gimondi's description of the final kilometers, "I was in a break with others, only 10 seconds ahead of the peloton and we could not slow down. We were all redlined. Before leaving that day I had written some numbers on my doeskin gloves: on one glove I had written the numbers corresponding to the sprinters and on the other I had written the numbers of the riders racing for the General Classification. In this way I had things under control. You know I didn't know all the riders yet. Knowing that Darrigade, who was in the break with me, was a dangerous man in the sprints I tried an escape with 1 km to go and I won with a 4-5 second lead."

This was the first professional race Gimondi had ever won, a stage in the Tour that resulted in his ownership of the Yellow Jersey. He was the first Italian to wear the Yellow Jersey since Gastone Nencini had won the Tour in 1960. The press wrote that this was a wonderful exploit and that it augured well for team leader Adorni's chances because the team had such a fine domestique. Adorni was now sitting in eighth place, 2 minutes, 16 seconds behind Gimondi. Gimondi came to the Tour with no particular pressure from his sponsor, being told to just ride from day to day. As he started to accumulate high placings and then the Yellow Jersey, he began to place pressure on himself. And now that the team had the lead, the protection the team gave to its best rider partially switched to Gimondi as the sponsor wanted to keep the lead as long as possible. At this point Gimondi was 3 minutes, 23 seconds ahead of Poulidor.

The next real test was stage 5b, a 26.7-kilometer individual time trial in Chateaulin. Poulidor won it, but damn, that kid was there in second place, only 7 seconds behind. Motta was third at 19 seconds. Gimondi's captain Adorni was fifth, 30 seconds slower than Poulidor. Gimondi remembers, "Chateaulin is in Brittany. This is an area that really loves bicycle racing. I remember 30,000-40,000 people yelling for their idols in a village whose shape made it very much like a big, natural stadium. So it was more difficult for me, being an Italian."

After the time trial the General Classification stood thus:

1. Felice Gimondi
2. Bernard Vandekerkhove @ 2 minutes 20 seconds
3. Vittorio Adorni @ 2 minutes 49 seconds
4. Ferdinand Bracke @ 2 minutes 57 seconds
5. Raymond Poulidor @ 3 minutes 6 seconds

Adorni crashed in stage 7. Gimondi waited for him with the rest of the Salvarani team, and so lost the Yellow Jersey to Vandekerkhove. When asked if this were not odd for the Tour leader to wait for another rider, Gimondi gave a reply that shows all the confidence of youth, "I knew there would be more chances for me to get it back."

Gimondi's first such chance came in stage 9, from Dax to Bagnères de Bigorre in the Pyrenees. In terrible heat the riders had to climb the Aubisque and the Tourmalet. In the front of the race Spanish climber Julio Jimenez was the first over both mountains. But in the back there was a bigger drama. 3 kilometers into the Aubisque Adorni climbed off his bike and grabbed his stomach in agony. Others were also quitting: Lucien Aimar, Peter Post, Julien Stevens, and the Yellow Jersey, Vandekerkhove. In all, 11 riders abandoned that day. Federico Bahamontes lost over 37 minutes and abandoned the next day. Suspicions were voiced about doping that went wrong much like in 1962 when the Wiels team had "bad fish" at a restaurant that had no fish on the menu. Nothing was ever proved.

Poulidor had trouble that day but when Gimondi flatted on the descent of the Tourmalet and had to wait for his follow car, Poulidor was able to make contact. Gimondi remembers the day: "It was a hard stage. On the Tourmalet I was in a break of 5 or 6, including [Julio] Jimenez, [Gianni] Motta and Poulidor. A little behind us there was [teammate Arnaldo] Pambianco. He saw the easy way I was pedaling and he beckoned me to attack…I accelerated a little and Jimenez counter-attacked immediately. He was not dangerous for the Overall so at the top of the Tourmalet he was first and Motta and I just followed him…[After I got my flat repaired] Poulidor passed me and then reached Motta. But then I flew on the descent and I caught them with 5 kilometers to go [he must have meant that Poulidor caught Esteban Martin and Guido de Rosso; Motta was 1 minute up the road]." The days in the Pyrenees were so hot that the asphalt melted. Gimondi remembers seeing the imprint the bicycle tires left in the pavement as they rode.

After stage 9 Gimondi was again the Yellow Jersey, and with the abandonment of Adorni he became the undisputed leader of his team. Poulidor was second now, 3 minutes, 12 seconds behind the Italian.

The remaining 2 days in the Pyrenees produced no fireworks or challenges to the existing order in the General Classification with all the top names finishing together. After stage 11 and the Pyrenees finished, here's how things stood:

1. Felice Gimondi

2. Raymond Poulidor @ 3 minutes 12 seconds

3. André Foucher @ 4 minutes 23 seconds

4. Gianni Motta @ 4 minutes 32 seconds

Poulidor knew he had to make a move and after consulting his manager, Antonin Magne, announced that he would attack on Mont Ventoux. At this point it was still thought that the young Gimondi would be incapable of maintaining his lead. The real opposition would surely come from Motta in the Alps. It certainly was not unreasonable to believe that the inexperienced young rider was vulnerable. In the 2 stages leading up to Mont Ventoux Poulidor slid to third place but remained 3 minutes, 12 seconds behind Gimondi.

Stage 14 started in Montpellier and finished at the top of Mont Ventoux. At the base of the climb the Spanish climbers Joaquin Galera and Julio Jimenez took off, then Henry Anglade escaped with a couple of others. Poulidor and Gimondi were hot on their tails. Early on the climb Motta was in trouble. Poulidor and Jimenez pulled away while Gimondi, after being initially dropped, made it back up to Galera and

Anglade. Anglade eventually dropped them and Gimondi finished between Anglade and Galera.

Poulidor won the stage, but not by a large margin. Gimondi came in fourth, only 1 minute, 38 seconds behind. With the time bonus for winning the stage, Poulidor pulled to within 34 seconds of

Felice Gimondi ascends the Izoard

the young Italian. Gimondi had narrowly saved his Yellow Jersey. Gianni Motta finished fourteenth, over 4 minutes back, his quest for Yellow effectively over. Poulidor had shown his climbing prowess. Could he repeat this performance in the coming Alpine stages?

Astonishingly, through the Alps the gap between Poulidor and Gimondi remained unchanged. Even though they crossed the Izoard, the Vars and the Lautaret, the situation remained static.

Stage 18 was a 26.9-kilometer time trial up Mont Revard. Again Poulidor announced his intention to take the Yellow. Again Gimondi flew. Against all expectations, Gimondi won the stage, and with that stage victory took the 20-second time bonus. And this win came despite a problem with the 19-tooth rear cog he had intended to use, with a 42 sprocket up front. He was forced to use the 18. But that day Gimondi said he had the legs. To make sure there was no unnecessary drag Gimondi opened up the front brake quick release, knowing there would be no braking on an uphill race. He was there to win the Tour de France. Poulidor came in second, 23 seconds slower.

While everyone expected that Poulidor would win the stage, Gimondi tells of his confidence. "Mont Revard is not far from Italy so that day there were many Italians and even [my sponsor] 'Patron' Salvarani watching. They were there to console me. They thought Poulidor would beat me for sure because he was a specialist in that kind of stage. I told them to wait and see what happens because I had been able to beat hill climb time trial specialists in the past."

There was a bonus of 20 seconds for first place, 10 for second. That put Gimondi 1 minute, 12 seconds ahead of Poulidor. Third place Motta was over 8 minutes behind. It was now a 2-man race with only the final 37.8 kilometer Versailles–Paris time trial left to influence the outcome. Gimondi was a bit nervous because he knew Poulidor was excellent against the clock and that if he had a good day the 72-second lead could be wiped out.

Gimondi won the final stage, with Poulidor third, 1 minute, 8 seconds behind. The 1965 Tour was Felice Gimondi's first stage race victory.

"I thought it would be much harder than it was," Gimondi said. At 22, it might have been easy, but he would never win the Tour again.

Final 1965 Tour de France General Classification:
1. Felice Gimondi (Salvarani): 116 hours 42 minutes 6 seconds
2. Raymond Poulidor (Mercier-BP) @ 2 minutes 40 seconds
3. Gianni Motta (Molteni) @ 9 minutes 18 seconds
4. Henry Anglade (Pelforth) @ 12 minutes 43 seconds
5. Jean-Claude Lebaube (Ford-France) @ 12 minutes 56 seconds

Climbers' Competition:
1. Julio Jimenez: 133 points
2. Frans Brands: 73 points
3. Joaquin Galera: 68 points

Points Competition:
1. Jan Janssen: 144 points
2. Guido Reybrouck: 130 points
3. Felice Gimondi: 124 points

**1966**. The 1966 Tour was a 4,329-kilometer counter-clockwise affair that made 2 passes through the Massif Central. The first one was after the Pyrenees, and then after the Alps the riders had to suffer through the hilly terrain before an almost due north shot up to Paris. There were 2 individual time trials totaling 71.3 kilometers, normal in this era, plus a 20.8-kilometer team time trial.

Cycling was starting to grapple with a problem that had been part of the culture of racing almost from the very start of the sport: doping. The first races in the nineteenth century were staggeringly long affairs that tested the limits of human endurance. Stages in the early Tour could take over 17 hours to complete. From the beginning riders took various substances to allow them to complete their ordeals. When the Pélissier brothers withdrew from the 1924 Tour and gave their famous interview to Albert Londres they described the long list of drugs they took. "We run on dynamite," Henri Pélissier said.

As the years progressed nothing changed except the brand of dynamite. Just before World War Two amphetamines were synthesized and athletes immediately understood the advantage they gave. Through the fifties the evidence that bike racers were doping was obvious to most observers. There were pictures of racers with dried foam on their faces or of riders driven mad by a combination of heat and amphetamines stopping in the middle of a race to find relief in a fountain. Because a writer can't make an outright accusation of doping without having a positive test to back him up, and testing was not instituted until the mid-1960s, journalists would use a shorthand that was designed to hint at a rider's possible drug use. The cycling literature of the age abounds with references to "fleck-stained mouths" and faces covered with dried foaming spit. Sometimes racers would ride until they slowed and fell off their bikes, their body's safety mechanisms overridden by the dope. After riding until he collapsed Jean Malléjac lay on the ground still strapped to his bike, his legs convulsively pumping the pedals. Others would remount their bikes and go the wrong way. Sometimes one could almost follow the route of a race by the trail of syringes left by the side of the road. Roger Rivière crashed in 1960 because he had taken so much of the opiate Palfium to kill the pain in his legs that he couldn't feel the brake levers. Bahamontes said that he loved a good hot day in the mountains because the riders juiced up on amphetamines couldn't take the heat.

Marcel Bidot, the French Team manager during the 1950s, thought that three-quarters of the peloton was doped. The result of this long history of drug use by professional riders is that doping became part of the DNA of the peloton. It wasn't something that was used by just a few under extraordinary circumstances. Both Coppi and Anquetil were remarkably frank and open about their regular use of drugs. These men were professionals and they knew that these substances helped them go faster, longer, or at the very least killed the pain and reduced the suffering that the sport brought to the body. The racers felt that they had a right, a license that went above and beyond whatever rules the cycling federations may promulgate to prevent the use of these substances. When drug testing began, and still to this day, the vast majority of racers saw nothing wrong with using drugs and evading tests. It's just part of the job. If this were not true the modern code of silence about their use by riders would not be so complete. And the *omerta* is so powerful it keeps the riders silent about the subject even after they have retired.

Knowing that something had to be done to control the completely out of hand drug situation, the Belgian federation started drug testing in 1965. Also in 1965, after Tour doctor Pierre Dumas had done extensive research on the subject, France passed a law against doping in sport. Racers in Belgium had been subjected to searches and tests in 1965 and French riders could see that these new rules would come to no good as far as they were concerned.

Jacques Anquetil, after sitting out the 1965 Tour, decided to give it another shot after all. Ill, neither Gimondi nor Adorni came. Only 2 Italian teams were entered, Filotex with Franco Bitossi and Molteni with Rudi Altig, Tommaso Da Pra and Albertus Geldermans. It was said that the Italian reluctance to ride the Tour was caused by the new French anti-doping laws.

The relationship between Anquetil and Poulidor had actually deteriorated during the spring. Poulidor had been leading Paris–Nice for 2 stages but unlike Anquetil, he failed to get in the winning break of the final stage. Anquetil won the stage and the overall race, relegating Poulidor to second place by 47 seconds. Poulidor was bitter and accused Anquetil of working with other teams to win. This is a strange accusation to render by an experienced pro as this happens every day in every race. The effect of Poulidor's public complaints was to deepen the acrimony between the 2.

On the surface the Tour appeared to be a Poulidor-Anquetil fight. But Raphaël Géminiani, the director of the Ford-France team, planned to use a man he considered to be extremely talented but hugely underestimated. Lucien Aimar had been the team's hope for the 1965 Tour but the young pro had to abandon on the infamous hot ninth stage. Before the start of the 1966 Tour Géminiani told Anquetil that if he had not soundly defeated Poulidor by the start of the climbing Aimar would be the designated team leader.

Both Anquetil and Poulidor had formidable claims to being the top contender. Anquetil had won Paris–Nice as well as Liège–Bastogne–Liège. He came in third in the Giro. There he showed a rare vulnerability in an individual time trial when Vittorio Adorni beat him by 27 seconds.

Poulidor came in second in that Paris–Nice and won the Dauphiné Libéré and the Critérium National.

The account between Poulidor and Anquetil was opened on the second stage when Poulidor crashed and Anquetil attacked. Poulidor was forced to chase hard. He was able to rejoin but he was fuming. Again he publicly complained. Anquetil didn't care and called Poulidor a cry-baby.

Rudi Altig won the first stage. As the Tour circled across northern France and then headed south through Bordeaux, Altig kept a slim lead of just about a minute. At the end of stage 9, with the climbing in the Pyrenees to begin the next day, the General Classification stood thus:

1. Rudi Altig
2. Albert van Vlierberghe @ 47 seconds
3. Edward Sels @ 52 seconds
4. Guido Reybroeck @ same time
5. Jan Janssen @ same time

It had been rumored in the peloton that there would be a drug raid by the police at some point during the Tour. The racers' intelligence further said that the place and time would be after stage 8 in Bordeaux, before the Pyrenees. As it was predicted, so it came to pass. Since the riders were expecting the police they made sure they weren't in their hotel rooms when the inspectors arrived. Almost all of them, that is. Poulidor, apparently unaware of the impending raid, was walking down the corridor of his hotel and was stopped by several officers who had him give a urine sample. Poulidor noted at the time that there were problems that rendered the whole affair dubious. There was no system for guaranteeing the chain of custody or for making sure that the sample would remain uncontaminated. Further, the rider could not really know that the sample that was attributed to him when it was tested was indeed his. Eventually Altig and several others were found and gave samples. A couple of the riders who were met by the police simply refused to give specimens.

The reaction of the riders was intense. As the racers felt that doping was a necessary part of their profession, almost an entitlement, they were deeply angered over this new intrusion. Led by Anquetil they staged a strike by riding their bikes for 5 kilometers then dismounting and walking, arguing with the officials before resuming the race.

Altig still had the Yellow Jersey, a fact that did not displease the major contenders. He was not going to be able to keep the lead once the major climbing started but until then his Molteni team controlled the race and kept things in order, saving the other riders from expending energy.

Stage 10, the day after the strike, was the first Pyrenean stage with the Soulor and the Aubisque climbs, ending in Pau.

The facts of the stage are strange. It should have been an aggressive, hard-fought day since the race was still tight, with 41 riders within 2 minutes of Altig in the General Classification. Early on 9 riders escaped, including domestiques of both Anquetil and Poulidor plus one of Altig's teammates, Tommaso Da Pra. After a bit more than 100 kilometers of the stage had been ridden, another 26 riders escaped in various small sorties, including Anquetil's teammate Lucien Aimar. Meanwhile the big names, Anquetil, Poulidor, Tom Simpson and the others stayed together showing no tendency to race hard or chase the breakaway riders. Da Pra won the stage and the Yellow Jersey, beating the field containing Anquetil and Poulidor by 9 minutes. A group of 20 had formed out of the various escaping waves of riders and they finished 7 minutes ahead of the Anquetil/Poulidor main pack. Among the 20 leaders were some very dangerous riders: Lucien Aimar, Jan Janssen and Raymond Delisle.

So why the go-slow when it is obvious that the top riders could have caught the lesser racers who just rode away? There are several interpretations, none is completely satisfactory. One is that this was a slow down to continue the protest against the dope testing. If that were so, the riders did not make their intentions clear.

Perhaps it is also true that Anquetil had no intention of riding the 1966 Tour to win. He was there to act as a spoiler, to make sure Poulidor did not win. With his teammate Aimar up the road he was fulfilling his mission and had no need to chase down his own man. And Poulidor? Again he mystified his manager Antonin Magne. Poulidor said he had only 3 teammates with him on the Aubisque and none of the other riders would go with him. In all probability his attention was transfixed to Anquetil and with Anquetil in sight, he saw no reason to do anything. For all intents and purposes the Tour for both men was over. They now had a deficit of 7 minutes on many superb contenders. Again Poulidor had, through a tactical lapse, given away the Tour. The day's racing drew only angry contempt from both the spectators and journalists.

Franco Bitossi, who was riding in the Anquetil/Poulidor group, talked to us about that stage. "Anquetil knew he could not win. Therefore he worked to control Poulidor, trying to keep him from catching

Aimar. I think [Poulidor] underestimated the consequences that this break would have for the overall General Classification. Maybe he thought that Anquetil would chase Da Pra and he was waiting for a reaction from him. But Anquetil decided to help Aimar since he knew he didn't have any hope of winning the Tour that year."

The racing started in earnest the next day with a climb new to the Tour, the Col de Menté, sandwiched between the Ares and the Portillon. When Delisle and Pingeon attacked to chase an earlier break, Poulidor and Anquetil answered the call and raced after them. The speeds in the mountains that day were too much for a rider of Da Pra's class, costing him 7 minutes. Another fortunate rider in the previous day's break who could also stay with Poulidor and Anquetil this day, Jean-Claude Lebaube, was the new leader. But the contenders had been too complacent too long and the gap to the leading General Classification men was huge. Anquetil was sitting in fifteenth place, still over 7 minutes back.

The final day in the Pyrenees, stage 12 with the Ares and Portet d'Aspet, cost Lebaube 30 seconds and the lead. Now a Peugeot rider, Karl-Heinz Kunde was the Yellow Jersey, the third leader in 3 days.

Here were the standings at this point:

1. Karl-Heinz Kunde
2. Jean-Claude Lebaube @ 27 seconds
3. Marcello Mugnaini @ 44 seconds
4. Jan Janssen @ 1 minute 6 seconds
5. Lucien Aimar @ 1 minute 56 seconds
6. Raymond Delisle @ 2 minutes 24 seconds

Both Aimar and Janssen had been vigilant and had made sure they were in all of the important moves as the Tour had progressed.

The stage 14b time trial gave Poulidor a small chance at redemption. He won the stage with Anquetil second, only 7 seconds behind. This lifted Poulidor to thirteenth place, still almost 6 minutes behind Kunde. But more interestingly, Aimar and Janssen had also turned in excellent rides. Janssen was now in second place at 32 seconds and Aimar was sitting in third, 52 seconds back.

The first alpine stage, number 15, had some climbing and showed how Poulidor and Anquetil viewed their relative positions.

Poulidor took terrible chances descending in atrocious weather to try to gain some time on his rivals. Anquetil, having mentally conceded the race and seeing no reason to endanger his skin during what was probably his final Tour, let Poulidor go. Poulidor did take back a minute from Anquetil, but more importantly he was only able to get a half-minute closer to Aimar and Janssen.

Stage 16 with its crossings of the Croix de Fer, the Télégraphe and the Galibier promised hard racing. The top 9 places were still filled with the riders who escaped in stage 10. Bitossi says the action was hot almost from the gun, saying *"Pronti, via!"* (ready, go!) about the day's start. Kunde tried to join the front group but showed signs of tiredness early on. Joaquin Galera was first over the Croix de Fer with Bitossi and Julio Jimenez right behind him. After the top of the Croix de Fer a group of 15 formed with Bitossi, Aimar, Poulidor, Altig, Janssen and Anquetil constituting the main firepower.

Here's how Bitossi remembers it. "After the Croix de Fer, Simpson took off on the long descent. I stayed with the others [Anquetil, Poulidor, Pingeon, Janssen and Altig] and we found him later coming out of a ravine, a little bruised. But after a few curves he attacked again and Jimenez took off on the Télégraphe climb to catch him. Poulidor and Anquetil attacked later on the Galibier to catch them. I remember that they went incredibly fast. I remained behind and Mugnaini [a teammate high in the standings] was a little ahead. I caught Simpson just before the tunnel of the Galibier (that year we didn't climb all the way to the pass; instead we rode through the tunnel). I passed Simpson. He seemed tired but then, after a few curves on the descent he passed me again. He did 2 curves in front of me and then he crashed for a second time! I passed him once more and at the end of the curves, just before the finish he passed me again. There was a beautiful sun but I felt some drops hitting me. He was not drinking so it could not be water. He was very focused on speeding up on the descent! So I thought it was sweat. Then at the finish my masseur asked me if I had crashed…I was covered with blood! Simpson's blood…I still can't get that day out of my mind." One cannot read Bitossi's story of Simpson's descent without being struck by Simpson's almost manic riding and his indifference to the effects of 2 crashes. Nor can one escape the conclusion that Simpson was probably drugged that day. Jimenez won the stage, Anquetil followed 2 minutes, 25 seconds later with Poulidor right with him. By finishing second Anquetil denied Poulidor the second-place time bonus.

The racing was so hard that day that 27 riders were eliminated. Included in the list of racers who could not make the time cutoff were Rik van Looy, Tommaso Da Pra, Guido Carlesi and Vin Densen. Aimar and Janssen continued their upward march in the standings.

1. Jan Janssen
2. Lucien Aimar @ 27 seconds
3. Marcello Mugnaini @ 1 minute 48 seconds
4. Jose-Antonio Momene @ 2 minutes 42 seconds
5. Karl-Heinz Kunde @ 3 minutes 15 seconds
6. Raymond Poulidor @ 3 minutes 36 seconds
7. Jacques Anquetil @ 4 minutes 44 seconds

Stage 17 determined the outcome of the race. The Coletta was the penultimate of the 4 climbs the racers had to pass that day on the way to the finish in Turin. Franco Bitossi and several others, including Domingo Perurena, were off the front. Poulidor and Janssen were in a chase group of 5. Aimar was dropped and Anquetil had to nurse him up to the Poulidor group. As they crested the mountain, Anquetil told Aimar to attack on the descent. Aimar possessed truly formidable descending skills—he said that he had been clocked at 140 km/hr descending Mont Ventoux. Bitossi told us that Aimar was counted among that elite group of descenders that included Gastone Nencini, Rini Wagtmans and Francesco Moser. Were Poulidor and Janssen aware that Aimar could drop down a technical descent like a stone? I don't know, but Poulidor didn't react and Janssen says he was further back in the group talking with Anquetil and did not see the move. Aimar steamed down the mountain and managed to catch up with Perurena as they went over the final climb. From then on, it was a time trial to Turin. Bitossi won the stage, his second stage win that Tour. Aimar came in 1 minute, 40 seconds after Bitossi and became the Tour leader. Poulidor came in almost 2 minutes after Aimar. Another tactical lapse had cost Poulidor another chance to win the Tour. Later Aimar asked his friend Bitossi why he didn't wait for him. This was the era before earphones. Bitossi told Aimar that he had no idea what was going on behind him. Janssen said he found out about Aimar's escape from

Televizier team rider Henk Nijdam. He went to the front, found Bitossi and Aimar were gone, and set about chasing for all he was worth. As we know, he never closed the gap. Janssen says that his director, Maurice De Muer, drove up to him and told him that he didn't know about Aimar's flight, claiming that the Tour radio (reports broadcast by the Tour, not the modern 2-way communications systems used by teams today) wasn't working at the time. Janssen says he doubts De Muer's story.

The new General Classification:

1. Lucien Aimar
2. Jan Janssen @ 1 minute 35 seconds
3. Marcello Mugnaini @ 3 minutes 23 seconds
4. Jose-Antonio Momene @ 4 minutes 17 seconds
5. Karl-Heinz Kunde @ 4 minutes 50 seconds
6. Raymond Poulidor @ 5 minutes 11 seconds

Stage 18 from Ivrea to Chamonix gave Poulidor yet one more chance with climbs over the Grand St. Bernard, the Forclaz and the Montets. Poulidor waited until the final 4 kilometers of the Forclaz to attack. Bitossi tells us what happened. "On the Forclaz climb there was a battle and Aimar was dropped by Poulidor and Pingeon. Mugnaini, who was third in General Classification, was in difficulty too. That day I was feeling good, so I waited and helped Mugnaini on the climb. At the same time Anquetil helped Aimar. After the Forclaz climb there was another little climb and then 20 kilometers to Chamonix. In the final part of that stage I remember Anquetil's working for Aimar and my working for Mugnaini. We did 20 kilometers as if it were a team time trial. Aimar and Mugnaini sat behind Anquetil and me."

Poulidor had escaped with Luxembourg rider Edy Schutz. Acting the gentleman, Poulidor let Schutz take the stage win. In the chase Anquetil, Bitossi and Janssen rode like fiends and limited Poulidor's time gain to 49 seconds.

The nineteenth stage was ridden in stormy, cold weather. 50 kilometers after the start Jacques Anquetil, suffering terribly from what would later be diagnosed as acute bronchitis, got off his bike and never rode another kilometer in the Tour de France.

The final chance for the riders to affect the outcome of the Tour was the last stage, a 51.3-kilometer time trial into Paris. Poulidor was too far down to take the overall win but Janssen was an excellent time trialist and probably dreamed of erasing the fragile 95 seconds that separated him from Aimar.

Poulidor did well, coming in third. Janssen took about a half-minute out of Aimar, not enough to win.

The final General Classification for the 1966 Tour de France:

1. Lucien Aimar (Ford-France): 117 hours 34 minutes 21 seconds
2. Jan Janssen (Pelforth) @ 1 minute 7 seconds
3. Raymond Poulidor (Mercier-BP) @ 2 minutes 2 seconds
4. José-Antonio Momene (KAS) @ 5 minutes 19 seconds
5. Marcello Mugnaini (Filotex) @ 5 minutes 27 seconds

Climbers' Competition:

1. Julio Jimenez: 123 points
2. Joaquin Galera: 98 points
3. Aurelio Gonzalez: 51 points

Points Competition:

1. Willy Planckaert: 211 points
2. Gerben Karstens: 189 points
3. Edward Sels: 178 points

A few post-Tour notes:

One serious consequence of the 1966 rider's strike was the reversion to national teams for 1967 and 1968. Tour co-boss Félix Lévitan thought the sponsors were behind the strike and wanted to remove their influence.

Even though Holland is a major cycling nation, Jan Janssen's second place was the first time a Dutchman had made it to the podium in the Tour.

The 2 minutes, 2 seconds that Poulidor lost to Aimar in the seventeenth stage to Turin turned out to be exactly the same as his margin of defeat in the final General Classification.

Since this was the final Tour for Anquetil, let's take another look at this brilliant, enigmatic, fascinating man. He was first and foremost the finest, most elegant pedaling machine of his time, maybe of all time. His economical style, cleanly stroking a monster gear with his toes pointed down, his back flat and motionless, defined him. In addition to winning the Tour 5 times, 4 of the wins sequential, he won the unofficial world time trial championship, the Grand Prix des Nations, an incredible 9 times. He continued to race professionally until 1969. After that he was a team director and a radio commentator. He was always frustrated that the French public loved Poulidor but remained cold to him. His conservative, calculating racing style coupled with a shyness that was mistaken for arrogance prevented any sort of real connection with the public. His friends and teammates never exactly understood him, but they all found him generous to a fault.

He was said to be haunted by his father's early death at 56. Anquetil was always afraid that he too would be the victim of an early death. And so he was: Anquetil died of stomach cancer at 53.

By any normal standard his private life was disordered. He had an affair with a doctor's wife that had enough sordid details for another book. The wife, Jeanine, divorced the doctor and married Anquetil. After retiring Anquetil started to dream of having a child, a gift Jeanine could not give him. Anquetil, always the thinker and master strategist, came up with a solution. Jeanine had an adult daughter fathered by the doctor. Anquetil suggested that he bed Jeanine's daughter, Annie, so that he could have a child. The 2 women agreed, and a daughter, Sophie, was born.

Annie and Jeanine began to fight over Jacques and eventually Annie moved out. Then Jeanine invited her son and his wife, Dominique, to move in to the Anquetil mansion. Anquetil then seduced Dominique and a son Christopher was produced. Jeanine divorced Anquetil while Dominique remained.

Poulidor and Anquetil, bitter enemies during Anquetil's professional life, became friends after Anquetil retired. Anquetil's daughter Sophie was the lever that caused the reconciliation. Of all the riders in the world, Sophie chose Poulidor to be her hero. Poulidor was in a hotel room and was surprised to have Anquetil visit him. To Anquetil's substantial irritation Sophie wanted some sort of souvenir of Poulidor's. Being a devoted father, Anquetil asked Poulidor for a couple of his cycling caps. "You're still pissing me off," Anquetil told him.

Anquetil was always known to have an acute sense of time and an intuitive understanding of math. In racing he used these skills to his advantage in order to exactly manage his efforts, never wanting to waste a watt of energy. The full extent of his ability in this area is astonishing. Poulidor tells the story of an evening drive on a road that Anquetil had never been on before. The road had a series of traffic lights that were timed, not triggered by car sensors. After going through 2 intersections Anquetil said, "Raymond, drive at exactly 57 kilometers an hour." They did and were met by a green light at every intersection.

Poulidor and Anquetil grew so close that Poulidor said that when Anquetil died, he felt as if he had lost a brother. When Poulidor visited Anquetil during his final days "Master Jacques" had not lost his sense of humor. "I'm sorry Raymond, but you're going to finish second again."

The story is a beautiful farewell and is repeated over and over but it is not true.

Poulidor's last meeting was at the hospital after Anquetil had had most of his stomach removed and later that evening at Anquetil's house. They had dinner together but Anquetil ate the meal without pleasure and retired early. Poulidor later spoke to him on the phone when Anquetil told him that he felt terrible on that famous day on the Puy de Dôme in 1964 when Anquetil and Poulidor dueled, and now he always had that same bad feeling. Jacques Anquetil died November 18, 1987.

**1967**. Félix Lévitan was convinced that the team sponsors had been responsible for the riders' walking strike in the 1966 Tour. He also believed that Desgrange had shown understanding and wisdom when the Tour went to the national team formula in 1930. Lévitan further believed that the underlying problem of the team sponsors being a corrupting influence on the Tour remained as true in 1967 as it was in 1930. The Tour went back to the national team format. While the reasoning Lévitan gave sounds high-minded, I believe the real reason Lévitan wanted to switch was that he was a proud man and was deeply offended by the challenge the strike presented. There wasn't any commanding or dire necessity to go to national teams. I think Lévitan did it because he could.

To accommodate all the fine riders from the major cycling nations there had to be 3 French teams (the secondary teams were "Bleuets" and "Coqs") and 2 each from Spain, Italy, and Belgium. The second Belgian team was called the "Red Devils", and was hardly a secondary group considering the quality of its riders, which included Bernard Vandekerkhove, Victor van Schil, and Walter Godefroot. The French team contained 1966 winner Lucien Aimar, Raymond Poulidor and a strange, perhaps even weird, but hugely talented rider named Roger Pingeon. Pingeon was an erratic rider who generally lacked the force of will needed to win a race. He had retired from racing the year before but decided to race the 1967 season. He retired again in the early spring but returned to competition and by summer he was showing good form. Riding for Peugeot he was generally unhappy about being a domestique for Tom Simpson. With the change to the national team format Pingeon wouldn't have to worry about that, Simpson would be riding on the British team. But Marcel Bidot, faced with a team bursting with talent, decided that there would be 3 protected riders on the team: Poulidor, Aimar and to the surprise of most, Pingeon.

With the entry of the Dutch team's Jan Janssen, who missed winning the 1966 Tour by 67 seconds, the Spanish team's Julio Jimenez and Italians Felice Gimondi and Franco Balmamion the 1967 Tour entry list was filled with great riders.

The race jumped in distance to 4,779 kilometers, reversing the slow trend towards shorter Tours. With 25 stages the average stage length was 199 kilometers. The average speed for the 1967 Tour ended up being nearly 2 kilometers an hour slower than the year before. The longer stages had to have had a part in this. It was clockwise with trips into the Vosges and Chartreuse mountains before the Alps. The Pyrenees followed with a trip up the Puy de Dôme being the last climbing stage.

The Tour constantly renewed itself through change and adaptation. Not only did the Tour change to national teams, it introduced the Prologue, a short time trial before the first stage. Poulidor showed his usual bad luck by taking a very close second to Spanish rider José-Maria Errandonea in the Prologue. If he had been able to go just 6 seconds faster and win the Prologue, he would have had the Yellow Jersey for the first time in his career. It was not ever to be.

As the Tour made its way across the roads of northern France the Yellow Jersey changed hands regularly. The narrow time differences among the top riders in the early stages made for a volatile podium. By stage 5 the Tour had arrived in Belgium. A group of about 14 riders broke away at about the sixtieth kilometer. French team member Jean Stablinski saw that Rik van Looy and several other Belgians were in the escaping group and knew that they would want to win on their home turf. He told Pingeon to bridge the gap up to them, which Pingeon easily did. Stablinski knew Pingeon was in superb shape but that he needed encouragement to overcome his lack of self-confidence. By kilometer 120 the van Looy/Pingeon group had arrived at the Belgian city of Thuin with its steep cobbled hill, with a gap of $3^1/_2$ minutes on the field. On the hill Pingeon just applied a bit of pressure and dropped his breakaway companions. Pingeon kept going and rode an epic solo 60 kilometers to victory in the city of Jambes. He beat the chasers by almost $1^1/_2$ minutes and the field by almost $6^1/_2$ minutes. Pingeon had so little confidence that it was said he rode as if at any moment both of his tires would explode and his derailleur would go into the spokes. This man was now in Yellow.

That afternoon was the 17-kilometer team time trial. The French lost only 13 seconds to the Belgians, cementing Pingeon's position. The British team came in last, surprising no one, indicating that if Simpson were to be a serious factor in the Tour he would be largely on his own.

Stage 7 took the Tour into the Vosges Mountains. A small break that included Pingeon's teammate Raymond Riotte, who had been in the stage 5 break into Jambes, took a minute and a half out of Pingeon and the rest of the field. Riotte now found himself the leader.

On the eighth stage, a much harder day in the Vosges with 4 rated climbs—the last being the Ballon d'Alsace—Poulidor had hoped to improve his situation. Instead it was a day of terrible misfortune for him. He had flat tires, crashes and mechanical problems. On the descent of the penultimate mountain he fell and had to watch his competitors escape while he waited for his delayed team car. Poulidor finished sixty-eighth that day, 11 minutes, 42 seconds behind winner Lucien Aimar. Poulidor's chances were ruined. He announced that he was now riding as a domestique for Pingeon who had reclaimed the lead.

The first major alpine stage was the tenth with the Tamié, the Télégraphe and the Galibier. Poulidor was true to his word and shepherded Pingeon over the series of climbs finishing 3 minutes behind the day's winner, Felice Gimondi. Pingeon's lead was now 4 minutes over Désiré Letort, a rider on the secondary France-Bleuets team.

The next 2 days changed little. So, at the end of stage 12, the General Classification showed Pingeon's firm grip:

1. Roger Pingeon
2. Désiré Letort @ 4 minutes 2 seconds
3. Julio Jimenez @ 4 minutes 57 seconds
4. Franco Balmamion @ 5 minutes 48 seconds
5. Felice Gimondi @ 6 minutes 15 seconds
6. Lucien Aimar @ 7 minutes 2 seconds
7. Tom Simpson @ 8 minutes 20 seconds
8. Jan Janssen @ 8 minutes 39 seconds

It was on stage 13, 211.5 kilometers from Marseille to Carpentras with the climb up Mont Ventoux that tragedy struck. That morning, before the start of the stage, Tour doctor Pierre Dumas looked at the weather and worried. Given the heat that was promised for the day, he thought that a racer who went too far in doping himself for the stage could die.

Tom Simpson was a very well regarded racer. The reversion back to national teams was a terrible handicap but also a sort of blessing for him because while there were not enough good Britons to form a high quality team to help Simpson win the Tour, he didn't have to worry about competing with Pingeon for the leadership of the team. Winning the Tour was his aim. His agent had put him under terrible pressure to come up with good results because his 1966 season had been devoid of big wins. Simpson knew he had to deliver.

Before continuing, let's look at Simpson's record, because today all we remember about him is that fateful day in Provence.

Tour de France, 7 participations:
1960: twenty-ninth overall
1961: did not finish (DNF)
1962: sixth overall and a day in Yellow (first Englishman to do so)
1964: fourteenth overall
1965: DNF
1966: DNF
1967: DNF

His other results show that he was a very good racer: wins in the Tour of Flanders, Paris–Nice, Bordeaux–Paris, Milan–San Remo, Tour of Lombardy and the Brussels 6-Day with Peter Post as his partner. Also, in 1965 he won the World Pro Road Championships.

But wait. Let me have Owen Mulholland tell Simpson's story:

"As always, the Tour loomed as the centerpiece of Tom's season, and he wasn't enthralled when the organizers decided to revert to the old-time formula of national teams. All through the season riders compete for their trade team sponsors, in Tom's case, Peugeot. Now the riders were supposed to forget all about those commitments and race for their respective countries. A small group of home grown English pros with almost no continental experience were all Tom could look to for teammates. He knew he would be on his own.

"His game plan, therefore, was to ride cautiously on the flat and save himself for the mountains where the big time gaps would make all the difference. The 1967 Tour followed a clockwise direction across northern France before dropping south through the Vosges and Alps. Simpson survived these tests fairly well, although he'd had to put down the hammer very hard on several occasions.

"July 13 began in Marseille, and as he awaited the call to the line a Belgian journalist noted that Tom looked tired and asked if it was the heat. 'No, it's not the heat.' Tom replied. 'It's the Tour.' As events were to prove, this was a telling comment.

"Still the heat could not be ignored. Already it was approaching 80°F in the old port city, and many riders winced at the thought of what lay before them. 100° was quite possible, and there was no protection whatsoever on the rocky face of Mt. Ventoux which they were scheduled to tackle around 2:00 in the afternoon.

"The long approach slope to the base of the 'Giant of Provence' (as Mt. Ventoux is known locally) served to shred the field and leave the big guns clustered at the front. Simpson, as expected, was the only member of his team to be in this group. After 7 miles of grueling toil Tom began to slip back to a group of chasers about a minute behind. In that group was Lucien Aimar, the '66 Tour winner. He remembered how Tom hadn't been content to sit in the group, but kept trying to bridge the gap back up to the front bunch. But no matter how hard he tried, Tom simply could not maintain the tempo necessary to move up.

Tom Simpson, left foreground, in crisis on Mont Ventoux

"Suddenly Tom dropped from his little cluster of riders. Barely able to turn the pedals he began to weave across the road. In a hundred yards he collapsed. Immediately he was surrounded by spectators.

"The well-meaning fans lifted him onto the saddle and got him going with a good push. When the momentum dwindled in a few feet Simpson began his former zigzag course. Another hundred yards and Tom again tottered from the bike, this time utterly spent. He immediately lapsed into a coma and nothing the Tour doctor or a local hospital (where he was taken by helicopter) could do brought relief. In 3 hours Tom Simpson was dead, victim of his own indomitable will and the sorcery of his supposedly magical pills."

In the hospital, Simpson's jersey pockets were found to contain amphetamine pills. Blood tests showed amphetamines and alcohol, which increases the effect of the stimulants, in his system. He suffered heart failure from the heat and severe dehydration. The drugs had made it possible for Simpson to ignore his body's screaming signals that it was in danger.

It is usually written that Simpson's last words were, "Put me back on my bike." They make compelling, seductive drama, which is why they are repeated in every story about Mont Ventoux. But it's not true. When he fell the first time he told the British team mechanic Harry Hall, "Get me up, get me up. I want to go on. Get me up, get me straight." As we know he continued up the hot mountain and then collapsed just before the summit. An editor put what had been intended as a reporter's paraphrase in quotes, and from then on the words have been part of cycling lore.

History records and the public little cares that Jan Janssen won the stage.

It has been said that a man's virtues are his own and his faults are those of his times. It was never more true than in the case of Simpson. He was charming, possessed a fine sense of humor and was well liked by his fellow riders. Gimondi, who was to be his teammate the following year, wept when he learned of Simpson's death. Simpson was brave and driven, willing to take terrible chances. He was suffering from terrible diarrhea (his mechanics had to hose his bike down before working on it) at that point in the Tour, a condition that surely contributed to his dehydration. To make things still worse Tour management made it hard for the riders to get enough water, making hand-ups from team cars illegal. They feared that the riders would get a free tow while holding on to the bottle. The riders often finished the stages terribly dehydrated. Despite his illness and exhaustion Simpson not only had no intention of quitting, he was intent upon getting a high placing that day. Franco Bitossi says Simpson would not have died today because the riders are more carefully monitored. At the earliest signs of trouble he would have been pulled from the race. Also, he probably would have been able to get enough water.

When Simpson's ambitious mentality met the drug-culture of professional cycling of the 1960s it was as if he had walked into the first scene of a Greek tragedy where the outcome is already known by the audience.

Was he a bad person or a hero? He was neither. Like thousands of other men he accepted the terms that continental racing dictated. Riding without dope would probably have meant failure. At least that's the way most of the riders saw it. It might not have been true. Franco Bitossi's heart problems forced him to ride clean because death was a probable side-effect of amphetamines. He still won 147 races with his prodigious talent. However, a look at his career wins shows that some of cycling's greatest titles just eluded him.

The next day the peloton agreed to ride if one of Simpson's British teammates would be allowed a ceremonial stage victory to honor Simpson's memory. The continentals rode slowly and Barry Hoban came across the line alone.

The 2 days in the Pyrenees, stages 16 and 17, let Julio Jimenez close to within 2 minutes of Pingeon. The stage 20 climb up Puy de Dôme put Jimenez even closer to Pingeon at 1 minute, 39 seconds. That was as close as he could get. The final time trial was won by Poulidor with Pingeon third, 45 seconds slower. Much like Gimondi in 1965, this was Pingeon's first major professional victory. Race wins were rare in his career, but given his physical talent, they should have been a common and regular occurrence. Pingeon had a long, ungainly appearance. But I have seen a film of him riding. Pingeon was a gloriously elegant rider with a beautiful, economical style. I have never seen anyone look better on a bike.

This was the last Tour to finish in the *Parc des Princes* velodrome where Tour winners had finished since 1903. It was demolished after Pingeon's victory.

"If it takes ten to kill me, I'll take nine and win" – Tom Simpson.


Final Tour de France General Classification for 1967:

1. Roger Pingeon (France): 136 hours 53 minutes 50 seconds
2. Julio Jimenez (Spain) @ 3 minutes 40 seconds
3. Franco Balmamion (Italy) @ 7 minutes 23 seconds
4. Désiré Letort (France-Bleuets) @ 8 minutes 18 seconds
5. Jan Janssen (Holland) @ 9 minutes 47 seconds
6. Lucien Aimar (France) @ same time
7. Felice Gimondi (Italy) @ 10 minutes 14 seconds
8. Jozef Huysmans (Belgium) @ 16 minutes 45 seconds
9. Raymond Poulidor (France) @ 18 minutes 18 seconds

Climbers' Competition:

1. Julio Jimenez: 122 points
2. Franco Balmamion: 68 points
3. Raymond Poulidor: 53 points

Points Competition:

1. Jan Janssen: 154 points
2. Guido Reybrouck: 119 points
3. Georges Vandenberghe: 111 points

**1968**. The Tour continued to be run with national teams for 1968. With the death of Tom Simpson the previous year doping controls had to become mandatory. The government made it clear that if rigorous, transparent, effective testing was not instituted the government would do the testing itself. Under that threat, the riders and sponsors gave up their resistance to the idea. The winner of each stage was now tested by the Tour organization. The Giro had instituted testing and the result was a series of disqualifications that almost reads like a Who's Who of cycling: Raymond Delisle, Gianni Motta, Peter Abt, Franco Bodero, Franco Balmamion, Victor van Schil, Joaquin Galera, Felice Gimondi and Mariano Diaz. The riders at this point had not learned how to outrun the testers. It was a skill they would soon perfect.

In addition, from now on the riders would be able to get water from their team cars. The sport was finally recognizing that dehydration was not a sign of toughness but a terrible danger to athletes riding at the very edge of human tolerance. Rest days were reinstituted. Tour boss Goddet wanted the Tour to remain "inhuman" in its difficulty but he did have to respect the physiological needs of his racers.

The Tour was hungry for revenue as its financial condition and its status started to fall. A new competition was instituted and hence a new sponsorship. The "Combine" winner would be the rider whose overall performance in all 3 categories—General Classification, Points and Climbers—was calculated to be the best in aggregate and would be awarded a White Jersey. To attract and satisfy a sponsor the Points Jersey was changed from Green to Red for just this year. Points winner Bitossi said his jersey was really orange.

To signal the Tour's good intentions, it called itself "*le Tour de la santé*", or Tour of good health.

The French were split into 3 teams, 'A', 'B' and 'C'. Poulidor, Pingeon and former world champion Jean Stablinski were on the 'A' squad. Lucien Aimar and journeyman pro Charly Grosskost were on the 'B' team. The 'C' team was made up of lesser riders, the majority of whom did not make it to Paris.

The Italian team had Franco Bitossi who was now riding at the zenith of his powers as well as Silvano Schiavon and Italo Zilioli. But the other great pillars of Italian cycling, Felice Gimondi, Vittorio Adorni (second in the Giro that year and World Champion that fall) and Gianni Motta did not enter.

Belgium's 'A' team had the outstanding Herman van Springel, and the new World Hour Record holder Ferdi Bracke was on Belgium 'B'. Eddy Merckx, winner of the Giro that year wasn't ready yet to try his hand at the Tour. Dutch entrant Jan Janssen had been knocking on the door of Tour success with second place in 1966 and Points Jerseys in 1964, 1965 and 1967, as well as winning the 1964 World Championship. He was a versatile rider whom Franco Bitossi described as a cycling artist who could do anything on a bike.

Grosskost won the Prologue in Vittel but most of the favorites were clustered within a few seconds of him: Janssen at 2 seconds, Poulidor at 5, Bitossi at 13 and Bracke at 14. Grosskost also won the second stage and was able to keep the Yellow Jersey until the third stage, when he lost it to the Belgian team time trial bulldozer. The times of the stage counted only for the team competition but the rules awarded 20-second and 10-second time bonuses to the members of the first and second place teams. Complicated stuff. Van Springel was now the leader.

With all of the stages leading to the Pyrenees having been mass sprints, the narrow lead changed a couple of times and landed on the shoulders of Belgian rider Georges Vandenberghe after stage 5. The only truly notable event during that week was the positive dope test of French 'A' team rider José Samyn after stage 8. He has the dubious distinction of being the first rider to be booted from the Tour because he failed the dope controls.

Vandenberghe was on the Belgian 'B' team. Ferdi Bracke, Eric Leman, Walter Godefroot, and Eric de Vlaeminck were his teammates and worked hard to keep his lead safe. By the time the Tour arrived at the base of the Pyrenees at the end of stage 11, the Dutch had suffered several abandons and were down to just 7 riders. Here were the standings:

1. Georges Vandenberghe
2. Bernard Guyot @ 2 minutes 29 seconds
3. Adriano Passuello @ 3 minutes 26 seconds
4. Jean-Pierre Genet @ 3 minutes 27 seconds

Stage 12 was the first major day of climbing with the Aubisque and the Tourmalet. It was thought that Vandenberghe would surely lose the lead as the angels took flight up the mountains. He surprised the experts with his fine riding through the stormy weather, finishing with Pingeon, Bitossi and Janssen and keeping the lead. Poulidor and Bracke did themselves a lot of good by coming in with the lead group, $2^{1}/_{2}$ minutes in front of the Vandenberghe bunch. But this stage cost Janssen 3 more teammates, leaving him with only 3 domestiques. He lost 2 minutes, 29 seconds to Poulidor and was feeling terribly tired. The other riders noticed and Janssen heard some Italians say that he was dead. That fired the Dutchman up. He became determined to come back.

The next day with the Port and Envalira climbs Vandenberghe again was able to stay with the fancied contenders and keep his lead, at this point 1 minute, 34 seconds over Schiavon. Poulidor was fifth at 4 minutes, 13 seconds. Nothing changed the next day, the final stage in the Pyrenees. Vandenberghe had survived the first real test. But Poulidor could reasonably think this Tour was within reach given that the 4 men ahead of him were not in his class.

Janssen won stage 15 and picked up the time bonus, but he was still sitting in thirteenth place, almost 6 minutes back.

On stage 15 Poulidor's luck held true to form. Highlighting the tensions that often plague national teams, Pingeon, on Poulidor's France 'A' team, attacked and rode a 193-kilometer solo breakaway to win the stage. A motorcycle following Poulidor's group found its way blocked by spectators. Swerving, he caught Poulidor's handlebars and brought the unlucky Frenchman down. Poulidor remounted, his nose broken and his face bloody from the crash. He chased with help of teammates, but the race (Janssen, van Springel, Aimar, Bitossi) was riding away from him. Poulidor's smashed-face heroic ride brought him to the finish only 1 minute, 5 seconds behind the big group of potential winners and 4 minutes, 3 seconds behind the soloing Pingeon.

Vandenberghe's Yellow dream came to an end on stage 16. Aimar (France 'B'), specifically looking to destroy Pingeon's General Classification hopes, attacked while Pingeon slowed to drink. 12 of the best riders got clear. Bitossi and German team leader Rolf Wolfshohl escaped together, with Bitossi getting his second stage win of the Tour. A minute behind them was the rest of the Aimar break (less Aimar who came in 135 seconds later): Godefroot, Janssen, van Springel, Bracke and Gandarias. Vandenberghe finished 9 minutes later in a large group that also contained Pingeon and Poulidor, who was suffering terribly from his crash.

Franco Bitossi recalls the stage, "There was a rivalry between the France 'A' team (with Pingeon and Poulidor) and the France 'B' team (with Aimar). Pingeon broke away for 190 kilometers and went like a motorcycle [stage 15], while Poulidor crashed 10 kilometers before the finish and had to abandon a few days later. So the next day Aimar said, 'Pingeon is tired, Poulidor is in bad shape. We are going to get rid of both of them.' And in fact the day after, in the stage 16 from Albi to Aurillac, we agreed to attack Pingeon when he slowed to drink. Everybody knew that there was to be an attack immediately after the feed area. Poulidor was unable to react. Pingeon couldn't catch up and lost his chance to win the Tour."

The cream was starting to float to the top. Here were the standings after stage 16:

1. Rolf Wolfshohl
2. Gregorio San Miguel @ 50 seconds
3. Franco Bitossi @ 1 minute 17 seconds
4. Herman van Springel @ 2 minutes 9 seconds
5. Ferdi Bracke @ 2 minutes 10 seconds
6. Andrés Gandarias @ 2 minutes 18 seconds
7. Jan Janssen @ 2 minutes 21 seconds

Jean Stablinski failed a dope test and was kicked out of the Tour. Both the French and the Dutch teams were suffering terrible luck. The French had effectively lost Poulidor at this point (he retired the next day) and had 2 of their riders tossed for doping. The French had no one who was in a position to compete for the General Classification. Janssen had lost several of his Dutchmen in the Pyrenees and now had only 3 teammates.

Pingeon rode another of his giant breakaway rides. Stage 18 went from the Massif Central into the Alps and by the end of that hard day Pingeon had salvaged a bit of pride for the French with a stage win and re-entry into the top 10 in the General Classification. Franco Bitossi rode with him partway but now deeply regrets the adventure. "As I said, my mistake in that Tour was breaking away with Pingeon in Grenoble (stage 18). I was second in General Classification after Wolfshohl and I felt some pressure from the journalists for the Yellow Jersey. If I had been patient and had stayed with the peloton I would have worn the Yellow Jersey at the end of the stage. Instead I wanted to go with Pingeon and attack. I had a crisis on the last climb and I lost 6 minutes."

After stage 18 the race was very tight with the top 8 riders within about 2 minutes of the new Yellow Jersey, Spaniard Gregorio San Miguel. San Miguel lost the lead the next day in stage 19 to van Springel. It was a very hard day with 4 major climbs. Janssen says that this was the day he went for the Tour win. He figured that if he could stay with van Springel all day, he would be in a good position to finish him off in the final time trial. He achieved his goal, finishing just 4 seconds behind van Springel.

Janssen was in a position much like 1966 when he was about a minute and a half behind Aimar but could not close the gap. Now with the climbing completed he was only 16 seconds behind van Springel. In the stages leading to Paris the standings remained static.

Here was the General Classification going into the final stage, a 55.2-kilometer individual time trial:

1. Herman van Springel
2. Gregorio San Miguel @ 12 seconds
3. Jan Janssen @ 16 seconds
4. Franco Bitossi @ 58 seconds
5. Andrés Gandarias @ 1 minute 15 seconds
6. Lucien Aimar @ 1 minute 38 seconds
7. Ferdi Bracke @ 1 minute 56 seconds
8. Rolf Wolfshohl @ 2 minutes 12 seconds

9. Roger Pingeon @ 2 minutes 28 seconds

10. Antonio Gomez del Moral @ 3 minutes 38 seconds

This was an extraordinary situation. Crowded into the top 10 were 2 former Tour winners (Aimar and Pingeon), the World Hour Record Holder (Bracke), former World Road Champion and 3-time winner of the Green Sprinter's Jersey (Janssen) and a powerful rider of superb abilities who had the Red Sprinter's Jersey sewn up (Bitossi). On this final day any of them could win the Tour. Bracke was the finest time trialist of the leading group and was thought to be the favorite but van Springel was also very good against the clock.

The day was windy and the course sinuous. In the end, van Springel just could not muster the power he needed to keep the lead. He started strongly but faded in the last 12 kilometers. Jan Janssen rode a superb chrono with lots of strength left for the final kilometers. Here's how it played out:

1. Jan Janssen: 55.2 kilometers in 1 hour 20 minutes 9 seconds

2. Herman van Springel @ 54 seconds

3. Roger Pingeon @ 1 minute 17 seconds

4. Ferdi Bracke @ 1 minute 23 seconds

5. Rolf Wolfshohl @ 1 minute 50 seconds

13. Franco Bitossi @ 4 minutes 17 seconds

Bitossi started the time trial just in front of Janssen. He recalls, "Every time I rode a time trial, I always had the best rider starting immediately behind me. That year Janssen started right after me. When he passed me he was going so fast that I thought it was Merckx. He was flying!" When we asked him why he didn't have a better result that day he explained, "I was tired at the end, I didn't have the legs anymore. But in that Tour I really worked hard for the Points Jersey. I never placed worse than twelfth in any stage."

Janssen won the Tour by only 38 seconds. In so winning, he became the first Dutchman to win the Tour. It was the closest Tour in history and the closest ever until Greg LeMond beat Laurent Fignon in 1989 by only 8 seconds.

Bitossi had a terrific Tour. He won the Combine and the Points classifications, came in eighth in the General Classification and came in second in the King of the Mountains. We asked him about the Points Competition, thinking he had it wrapped up earlier in the Tour. "No. It was a battle with [Walter] Godefroot, who came in second in the Points Competition. At the end of the Tour he came to me and said, 'You should have told me before that you wanted this jersey so much! I would have let you have it and maybe you would have allowed me to win at least 1 stage!' I had shadowed him everywhere during the entire Tour. It was a draining fight. Yet, in order to win a Grand Tour you have to ride economically and use your energy only when really necessary."

Journalists wrote that this Tour was flat and that the riders didn't display their normal combativity. Bitossi says it was ferocious from the first day. There is one telling statistic that proves Bitossi's point. Of the 110 starters there were only 63 riders left in the Tour at the end.

Final 1968 Tour de France General Classification:

1. Jan Janssen (Holland): 133 hours 49 minutes 42 seconds
2. Herman van Springel (Belgium) @ 38 seconds
3. Ferdinand Bracke (Belgium) @ 3 minutes 3 seconds
4. Gregorio San Miguel (Spain) @ 3 minutes 17 seconds
5. Roger Pingeon (France 'A') @ 3 minutes 29 seconds
6. Rolf Wolfshohl (Germany) @ 3 minutes 46 seconds
7. Lucien Aimar (France 'B') @ 4 minutes 44 seconds
8. Franco Bitossi (Italy) @ 4 minutes 59 seconds

Climbers' Competition:

1. Aurelio Gonzalez: 96 points
2. Franco Bitossi: 84 points
3. Julio Jimenez: 72 points

Points Competition:

1. Franco Bitossi: 241 points
2. Walter Godefroot: 219 points
3. Jan Janssen: 200 points

# Chapter 2

## 1969–1975. The Merckx years. The greatest bicycle racer of all time dominates the Tour

**1969**. After the 2-year test the Tour reverted to trade teams. The national team system, while popular with the public, was not without problems. The Tour organization was responsible for the transport, feeding and lodging of the athletes and this was no small expense at a time when the Tour had little to spare.

Additionally, the sponsors detested the system because they suffered a virtual 3-week publicity blackout while their riders rode the most popular event in the cycling calendar. Worse, most of the sponsors had to watch their riders act as domestiques for the riders of other teams. Raymond Poulidor, riding for Mercier the rest of the year, did his best to help Peugeot rider Roger Pingeon win the 1968 Tour. This cannot be what Mercier planned when they sponsored Poulidor. Moreover the riders could not be counted on to forget their trade team loyalties during the Tour when their trade sponsors were the true source of their living. The result was confusion, ambiguity and friction. Given that there were no commanding reasons for the change to national teams in 1967 it is not surprising that the Tour counted its centimes, listened to the cycling industry, and went back to trade teams.

The Tour organization continued to search for revenue. Cycling's and the Tour's fortunes were hitting a period of low ebb. In 1969, for the first time, the Yellow Jersey had an official sponsor, 2 actually. In 1967 the clothing company Le Coq Sportif acquired the right to put their logo on the Yellow Jersey. In 1969 the synthetic dairy products company Virlux paid to have its name placed on the upper left breast of the Yellow Jersey. Until then the initials of Tour founder Henri Desgrange had been placed somewhere on the front of the Jersey. To make room for the new advertising (including the Yellow Jersey holder's principal sponsor), Desgrange's initials were placed on both shoulders.

At 4,117 kilometers the 1969 Tour was the shortest since Desgrange went from 11 to 13 stages in 1906. With 25 stages (counting the Prologue) the average stage was now only 158 kilometers, a dramatic drop from the nearly 200-kilometer average stage length of the mid-1960's. This doesn't mean that the riders were getting an easier time of it. 3 of the days had split stages. The riders hated the days with 2 stages. They had to get up very early in the morning in order to eat enough and digest their food before the racing started. After the first stage of the day was completed they would wait around in the sweltering July heat, sometimes in tents, before being forced to race again. The return of the split stages was another symptom of the Tour's financial troubles. Cities paid the organization a fat fee to be a start or finish city. By crowding 2 stages in a day the Tour reaped a financial windfall. Still worse for the riders, there were no rest days in 1969. 1968's "Tour of good health" was a thing of the past.

It was a clockwise Tour starting in Roubaix and heading into Belgium, then Holland. The Vosges Mountains were the first serious climbing, followed by the Alps, the Pyrenees and finally the Massif Central with a trip up Puy de Dôme. From there it was a straight shot north to Paris. This Tour avoided the roads of both Brittany and Normandy for the first time since the beginning in 1903.

The Tour's entry list of contenders had depth: Jan Janssen (riding for BIC), Herman van Springel (Mann), Joaquim Agostinho (De Gribaldy), Roger Pingeon (Peugeot), Andres Gandarias (KAS), Raymond Poulidor (Mercier), Felice Gimondi and Rudi Altig (Salvarani). Also, there was some new talent riding the Tour for the first time who would shake things up in later years: Lucien van Impe (this Tour was his second race as a pro), Luis Ocaña and Roger de Vlaeminck.

But the 500-pound gorilla was Eddy Merckx. There was no question that he was the most complete and capable rider alive. Merckx won the World Amateur Road Championships in 1964. He turned pro in April 1965 and from there his record of wins is without parallel. He won Milan–San Remo the next year, the first of 7 such victories. In 1967 he won the Professional World Road Championship plus Milan–San Remo, Ghent–Wevelgem, Flèche Wallonne and rode his first Grand Tour, the Giro, coming in ninth. In 1968 he won 32 races including the Giro and Paris–Roubaix.

His 1969 was even more stunning with a total of 43 victories including Paris–Nice, Milan–San Remo, Tour of Flanders and Liège–Bastogne–Liège. He planned to do the Giro-Tour double and was leading the Giro after taking the Pink Jersey on stage 14. It was after stage 16 that he was given the news that he had tested positive for amphetamines. His Pink Jersey was taken from him and he was ejected from the Giro. The new leader of the Giro was Felice Gimondi who went on to take the final victory.

Merckx has maintained to this day that this was a setup to allow an Italian to win the Giro. He says that bribes were offered to him to let an Italian win and when that failed he was set up. He furthermore argues that the stage where he tested positive was so easy that that was no reason to dope. The circumstances around the testing were anything but clear. Given the cloudy nature of the entire affair, I believe Merckx should be considered innocent. If they had the goods on him, the various questionable oddities which reek of a frame-up that surrounded the affair probably would not have happened.

Seething with rage over the miscarriage of justice and seeking redemption, Merckx came to the Tour with a fury and a will to win that was powerful by even Merckxian standards. Further motivation came from a deep seated desire of his countrymen to see a Belgian again in Yellow. The previous year the Belgians had come close when their Herman van Springel lost the Tour to Jan Janssen by only 38 seconds in the final stage. Janssen says that the Belgians were furious at him and still tell him to this day, "You stole the Tour from our Herman van Springel." No Belgian had won the Tour since Sylvère Maes in 1939.

Decided by lot, members of Merckx's team were the first riders to ride the Prologue individual time trial. In a show of bravado Merckx's director, Guillaume Driessens, had Merckx go first. Usually the protected rider goes as late as possible so that he will have riders up the road to chase. Driessens justified the unusual move by saying that the sooner Merckx got his ride finished the sooner he could begin resting for the next day's competition which involved the first of the split stages. Rudi

Altig won the Prologue with Merckx in second place, 7 seconds behind. The early riders faced a headwind that calmed down as the later riders finished the course.

Stage 1b was a 15.6-kilometer team time trial in the Belgian city of Woluwe-St. Pierre and passed in front of Merckx's parents' grocery store. Of course Merckx's Faema squad won the stage. While the times of the teams didn't affect the rider's individual General Classification standings, the riders of the fastest 3 teams got 20-, 10- and 5-second time bonuses. By virtue of that 20-second bonification Merckx was in Yellow in his home town. Altig was second at 8 seconds and 1968 Tour winner Jan Janssen was third, 20 seconds back.

It wasn't Merckx's intent to keep the Yellow Jersey all the way to the end. He was pleased when his domestique, Julien Stevens, won the next day's sprint and the lead. Merckx wouldn't relax, but he could save some energy until the race entered the Vosges Mountains. Stevens kept the lead as the Tour went through the Argonne region but lost the Yellow Jersey on first day of climbing in stage 5. All the big guns finished together, 18 seconds behind the stage winner, Joaquim Agostinho. One of Pingeon's domestiques Désiré Letort, found himself the new Yellow Jersey, 9 seconds ahead of Merckx.

It was on stage 6 the Merckx made it clear what sort of race this was to be. The race did 3 climbs, culminating in the Ballon d'Alsace, one of the first climbs ever included in the Tour back in 1905. Over the course of the stage, while the others suffered from both bad luck (Gimondi flatted, Poulidor had a mechanical), crashes (Roger de Vlaeminck) and plain fatigue, Merckx simply rode them off his wheel. The group of riders who hoped to control Merckx in this Tour (particularly Pingeon, Poulidor, Gimondi, Aimar and Gandarias) finished 4 minutes, 21 seconds after the Belgian had soloed to the finish. Galera and Altig had limited their losses to "only" 55 seconds and 115 seconds respectively. It was an extraordinary performance and the high mountains were yet to come.

The General Classification after stage 6:

1. Eddy Merckx
2. Rudi Altig @ 2 minutes 3 seconds
3. Jan Janssen @ 4 minutes 41 seconds
4. Felice Gimondi @ 4 minutes 50 seconds
5. Raymond Poulidor @ 4 minutes 56 seconds

Stage 8a was an individual time trial only 8.8 kilometers long, luckily for the riders in the Tour who weren't named Merckx. He was able to increase his lead slightly, only 2 seconds on Altig but he took a quarter of a minute out of Pingeon and Poulidor.

The Tour hit the first of the high Alps on stage 9, with the Forclaz and Montets ascents. Pingeon was showing a rare bout of self-confidence, believing that Merckx was manageable. The 2 of them escaped on the Forclaz and rode together to the end of the stage. Merckx let the Frenchman go first over both summits and take the sprint. This was a rare bit of charity by Merckx that won't be repeated very often in this book.

The effect of the stage was to bury Janssen, Poulidor and Gimondi and lift Pingeon to second place, a distant 5 minutes, 21 seconds behind Merckx.

The next day's stage, number 10, with the Madeleine, Télégraphe and Galibier climbs was made still harder by terrible weather. Herman van Springel got away successfully on the run-in to Briançon and Merckx led in Wagtmans, Gimondi and Pingeon 2 minutes later. 111 riders had started the stage, but only 97 finished this hard day, making for 14 abandons. 57 of the stage 10 finishers came in over a half hour after van Springel.

Each day Merckx seemed to take a bite out of his competitors, sometimes a big one, sometimes a smaller one. The fact was that the time lost to Merckx while he was in this indominatable state was irrecoverable. Stage 11 with the Vars and Allos put Pingeon another 22 seconds back when Merckx and Gimondi finished together. No charity given to Gimondi here, Merckx won the stage. Stage 12 brought the Tour into Provence with a final minor climb, the Espigoulier. Merckx and one of his lieutenants, Victor van Schil, broke away with Gandarias and Gimondi, who won the stage. Another chunk of time taken out of the riders who couldn't get into the winning move, this day it was 1 minute, 23 seconds.

After the Alps Merckx had an enviable lead:

1. Eddy Merckx
2. Roger Pingeon @ 7 minutes 11 seconds
3. Felice Gimondi @ 7 minutes 14 seconds
4. Raymond Poulidor @ 11 minutes 9 seconds
5. Andres Gandarias @ 12 minutes 11 seconds

As the Tour cruised through Provence and Languedoc on the way to the Pyrenees, 15-minute penalties were given to Rudi Altig, Pierre Matignon and Bernard Guyot after stage 14 for testing positive for dope.

For the rest of the riders the bad news from stage 15 was that Merckx was showing no signs of tiring. He won the 18.5-kilometer time trial handily, relegating Pingeon, Poulidor and Altig about another minute further back while Gimondi lost 93 seconds.

Stages 16 and 17 were the Pyrenean stages. Stage 16's results looked unremarkable even though it had 3 major climbs when Merckx finished fourth behind winner Raymond Delisle, Jan Janssen and Wladimiro Panizza. The important story of the stage was that he had inflicted more of his terrible math upon his real competitors. Pingeon lost 20 seconds and Gimondi about 30.

It was on stage 17 that Eddy Merckx etched his name on the granite wall of Tour de France history.

At the start of the stage, here was the General Classification:

1. Eddy Merckx
2. Roger Pingeon @ 8 minutes 21 seconds
3. Felice Gimondi @ 9 minutes 29 seconds
4. Raymond Poulidor @ 12 minutes 46 seconds

With such a substantial lead, Merckx could easily ride Anquetil- or Indurain-style: just keep the dangermen in sight and preserve and defend the advantage.

The age of Anquetil was over. This was the age of Merckx.

Stage 17 was a 214.5-kilometer epic stage with the Peyresourde, the Aspin, the Tourmalet and the Aubisque. Over the first 2 mountains, Merckx was content to let Joaquin Galera be first over the top.

On the ascent of the Tourmalet with most of the would-be contenders for company, Merckx attacked. Only his teammate and the tallest man in the pro peloton, Martin Vandenbossche, could go with him. The others could only watch.

Over the top of the Tourmalet his lead over his chasers was only a few seconds. On the descent Merckx again showed what a complete rider he was, descending far faster than his chasers. He arrived at the bottom of the Tourmalet alone and a minute ahead of the chasing group. Given the commanding lead Merckx had in the General

Classification and the fact that there were still 140 kilometers and the Aubisque left in the stage, the others felt that it was unlikely that Merckx would continue to press his advantage. The initial motivation to drop (actually spank) Vandenbossche and continue alone was Merckx's resentment that Vandenbossche had accepted a contract with another team, Molteni, for the coming year. Vandenbossche was now back in that lead group of chasers, loyally working to protect Merckx.

With 105 kilometers left, Merckx took on food and continued to forge ahead. He later told *L'Équipe* "I was just 'walking', and when I heard the time gap I decided I had to carry on."

At the top of the Aubisque, wondering if he should wait for help, he was told that he now had a lead of 7 minutes. He decided to keep on with his breakaway. Merckx flew down the hill and over the rolling countryside that stood between him and the finish line.

He crossed that line 7 hours, 4 minutes, 28 seconds after he started. The second rider to finish was Michele Dancelli, 7 minutes, 57 seconds in arrears. Pingeon and Poulidor were right behind Dancelli. In a single day Merckx had about doubled his lead.

Coming in at 14 minutes, 49 seconds was the major group containing Gimondi, van Impe and Agostinho. Taking into account the narrowing differences between riders' abilities that has steadily occurred over the past 100 years, Merckx's 1969 stage 17 ride has to be one of the few Tour exploits that can be considered on par with Coppi's 1952 stage 11 victory.

The new standings showed how Merckx had shattered his rivals:

1. Eddy Merckx
2. Roger Pingeon @ 16 minutes 18 seconds
3. Raymond Poulidor @ 20 minutes 43 seconds
4. Felice Gimondi @ 24 minutes 18 seconds
5. Andres Gandarias @ 29 minutes 35 seconds

When the race climbed Puy de Dôme in stage 20 Merckx would have liked to have won the stage but he woke up too late to realize that a man sitting at the bottom of the standings had taken off on a solo quest to win one of the Tour's most prestigious stages. Aroused, Merckx took off after the now tiring Pierre Matignon (who lost 15 minutes in a doping penalty earlier in the Tour). Utterly exhausted Matignon crossed the line 85 seconds ahead of the flying Belgian. The effect of Merckx's tyrannical attempt to squash a poor flea was to leave the other contenders scattered behind.

That left only the final time trial in Paris and of course it was another Merckx victory. Over 36.8 kilometers he put the day's second-place Poulidor a minute back and cost Pingeon, the year's best challenger, 74 seconds.

Here is the final General Classification of the 1969 Tour de France. Merckx won by the largest margin in 17 years. One has to go back to Fausto Coppi's 28-minute lead over Stan Ockers in the 1952 Tour to find a greater gap.

1. Eddy Merckx: 116 hours 16 minutes 2 seconds
2. Roger Pingeon @ 17 minutes 54 seconds
3. Raymond Poulidor @ 22 minutes 13 seconds
4. Felice Gimondi @ 29 minutes 24 seconds
5. Andres Gandarias @ 33 minutes 4 seconds

Merckx also won all the other Tour competitions including the "Combine" classification.

Climbers' Competition:

1. Eddy Merckx: 155 points
2. Roger Pingeon: 94 points
3. Joaquin Galera: 80 points

Points Competition:

1. Eddy Merckx: 244 points
2. Jan Janssen: 149 points
3. Marinus Wagtmans: 136 points

Merckx's team, Faema, won the Team General Classification.

Eddy Merckx's domination of the 1969 Tour de France was utter and complete. In an interview in *L'Équipe*, Merckx said, "I'd love to ride the 1969 Tour again, my first. I'd ride it the same way. It is my most beautiful memory, by a long way."

No doubt.

**1970**. Lévitan continued to look for more money. The 1970 Tour was about 250 kilometers longer than the year before but now those 4,369 kilometers were, counting the Prologue, divided into 29 stages. 5 days had 2 stages and, like 1969, there were no rest days. In addition to looking for revenue from cities wanting to be a start or finish point, the Tour created a new competition, which of course required a new sponsor. This time a special jersey was to be awarded to the best young rider. Even little things were not beyond the Tour in its hunt for lucre. Merckx's racing number was "51" to give publicity to a candy called "Pastis 51".

The 1970 edition was clockwise, starting in Limoges, almost in the geographical center of France. From there it went to La Rochelle on the western coast and circled northward to Brittany, eastward to Normandy and then into Belgium. It scraped the edge of Germany on the way south to the Alps, then the Pyrenees before heading back up to Paris. It was a punishing schedule but the smoldering riders wouldn't erupt into rebellion until 1978.

The public could be forgiven if they expected Merckx to repeat his 1969 Tour victory. His spring had been magnificent. Riding for Faemino, he won the Het Volk, Paris–Roubaix, Paris–Nice and the Giro d'Italia. He came to the Tour sporting his new Belgian Road Champion's jersey, the only one the great man was ever able to win.

Yet, Merckx said that he was never again the rider he was in 1969. Late in the 1969 season he had a terrible crash in a derny-paced race on the velodrome in Blois, France. It was at night, under the lights. The electricity went out momentarily and both Merckx and his derny pacer crashed. The driver, Ferdinand Wambst, died and Merckx suffered a cracked vertebra. Merckx said he never healed correctly and that he always suffered back pains after the crash. Occasionally you can see photographs and movies of Merckx adjusting his saddle in the middle of a race, sometimes on the fly, as he tried to find some relief from the pain. Merckx said that before the crash, climbing was a pleasure. After it, he was always in pain.

He may have lost a little of his edge, but it didn't show in the Prologue time trial. Merckx won it.

It was the second stage from La Rochelle to Angers that is so interesting and sheds some light on Merckx's psychology and his need to win.

Local boy Roland Berland on Luis Ocaña's BIC team took off, wanting to give a little greeting to his wife, who was waiting up the road. This is a common practice among professional riders, a courtesy usually freely given. Instead of a solo trip up the road to get a quick kiss Berland found himself in the company of 7 others, including Rolf Wolfshohl and Ernesto Jotti. After a few kilometers 2 lieutenants from Merckx's Faemino squad, Italo Zilioli and Georges Vandenberghe, as well as Walter Godefroot of Salvarani bridged the gap. Because they were protecting Merckx's lead, the 2 Faeminos didn't do any work in the break. This was especially prudent since Godefroot and Wolfshohl were 2 of the best riders in the world.

BIC's director Maurice De Muer drove up to the break and told Berland not to work too hard because that would give the freeloading Faeminos a gift of a likely stage win.

Then, Faemino's director, Guillaume Driessens, drove up to his 2 riders in the break and gave them surprising directions. He told them to pour on the gas and take the breakaway home.

Italo Zilioli, one of the Faemino breakaways, was an almost frighteningly slender rider who looked too frail to compete in sports. His lanky body earned him the nickname "Coppino" (Little Coppi). Yet, he had extraordinary power in those skinny limbs and was one of the finest stage racers of his age, having come in second in the Giro 3 times. Merckx knew what he was doing when he asked Zilioli, whose career seemed to be in its twilight, to join his team.

The break with the 2 Merckx domestiques along with Godefroot and the others leaped ahead of the field and managed to gain a gap of 6 minutes on the peloton.

The peloton reacted. The pack was strung out as the chase was engaged. But who was leading the pack?

Eddy Merckx.

He was chasing the lead group which was riding at the express direction of Merckx's team director. It was Driessens' plan to do the usual, let another member of his team take the lead and take the pressure of defending the jersey off of Merckx's shoulders. It's an old strategy. With the ensuing high speeds, Delepine, Jotti and Wolfshohl were dropped from the break. Zilioli kept hammering away with his team captain chasing. The gap fell under the pressure of the chase. The peloton spit out riders who couldn't stand the pace set by Merckx and the other teams.

At 4 kilometers to go, the gap was still 35 seconds.

Because of a crash, the 2 breakaway Faeminos were alone together with Godefroot and Berland 250 meters behind.

Zilioli won the stage with a furiously chasing Godefroot only 2 seconds behind the winning pair. The de Vlaeminck brothers, Eric and Roger led in the field containing Merckx 24 seconds later. Italo Zilioli was in Yellow, 4 seconds ahead of Merckx.

When Merckx was asked why he had chased down his own team-mates, he said he wanted to get away from Roger Pingeon and Raymond Poulidor who were having mechanical trouble. I think he wanted to keep the jersey from start to finish and had no intention of letting Zilioli borrow "his" Yellow Jersey.

Merckx also complained that with a team time trial coming up, his 2 men should not be working that hard. Driessens countered that the effect was to make the other teams with no riders in the break work hard and furthermore he was the boss of the team, not Merckx.

Perhaps Driessens was right. Faemino won the team time trial by over a minute.

On the sixth stage, Merckx got into a breakaway and took the lead back from Zilioli.

There was another telling incident in this sixth stage. Zilioli was still the Yellow Jersey. When he suffered a flat tire, not one Faemino rider stayed to help him. They were all up front helping Merckx. Zilioli, leading the Tour de France in the fabled Yellow Jersey, was on his own. He was a domestique of Merckx first, the Yellow Jersey second.

The General Classification after stage 6:

1. Eddy Merckx
2. Walter Godefroot @ 5 seconds
3. Roger De Vlaeminck @ 11 seconds
4. Jan Janssen @ 18 seconds
5. Herman van Springel @ 42 seconds
6. Italo Zilioli @ 57 seconds
7. Raymond Poulidor @ 1 minute 2 seconds
8. Joop Zoetemelk @ 1 minute 3 seconds

The Tour was now in the Brussels suburb of Forest in Belgium. The afternoon's short time trial produced a surprise. The champion of Spain, Jose Gonzales-Linares, beat Merckx by 3 seconds on the 7.2-kilometer course. Merckx had the Yellow, but he was denied the victory on his Belgian home turf.

The ninth stage, from Saarluis in Germany to Mulhouse back in France, produced a strange day of racing. On the Grand Ballon, the final ascent of the day, Mogens Frey and Joaquim Agostinho—both members of the same Frimatic team—broke away. Frey had escaped earlier and Agostinho had bridged up to him. They descended together and for a while traded pace, relaying each other during the final 20 kilometers. Then Frey stopped working and just sat on Agostinho's wheel. The team manager drove up and told Frey to work. Perhaps the Dane did not understand any French. In any case, Frey refused to help and stayed glued to Agostinho's wheel, keeping his nose out of the wind.

When it came time for the sprint Agostinho, thinking it would be a show sprint that his teammate Frey wouldn't contest, started to wind it out. To Agostinho's astonishment Frey started to come around him. Furious, Agostinho rode his bike to the side of the road to force Frey to go the long way around. Frey kept coming so Agostinho put his hands out to try to block him. Angry and desperate he finally grabbed Frey's handlebars and managed to cross the line first.

The band at the finish line played the Portuguese national anthem in celebration of Agostinho's victory. Agostinho was sure of both his win and the force of justice and did a victory lap. The race jury didn't think that was how a race should be won and awarded the stage to Frey, relegating Agostinho to second.

Agostinho said that Frey had made signs (they didn't speak a common language) that Frey would not contest the sprint and felt cheated by Frey's cheap attempt to win the stage. Later Frey explained that he had broken away first and that Agostinho had no business bridging up to him, potentially bringing other riders along. Team owner De Gribaldy, unhappy with the mess, made the 2 share the same hotel room that night.

As one of the transition stages before the Alps, stage 10 traveled south through the limestone highlands of the French Jura in baking heat. Displaying his usual aggression, Merckx won the stage in a 4-man break. The result was to put all of the contenders except Zoetemelk (who was with Merckx) another 3 minutes back. Since Merckx had done so much of the work in the break his superiority was clear to all. Both Zoetemelk and Poulidor effectively capitulated in the press, Zoetemelk saying he would work to defend his second place.

The eleventh stage time trial was another short, flat one of only 8.8 kilometers. Merckx reversed the finish of the earlier chrono and showed that the previous day's efforts had diminished neither his strength nor his desire to win when he beat Gonzales-Linares by 9 seconds. Before the start of stage 12, which took the Tour into the Chartreuse and signaled the beginning of the serious climbing here was the General Classification:

1. Eddy Merckx
2. Joop Zoetemelk @ 3 minutes
3. Georges Pintens @ 4 minutes 24 seconds
4. Gosta Petterson @ 7 minutes 57 seconds
5. Herman van Springel @ 8 minutes 28 seconds
6. Raymond Poulidor @ 8 minutes 56 seconds
7. Italo Zilioli @ 9 minutes 14 seconds

Through the Alps Merckx increased his lead, first by winning stage 12 with its 5 tough climbs, then leaving most of his competition over 3 minutes behind when he came in fourth in stage 13. Merckx's lead over second-place Zoetemelk was now 6 minutes, 39 seconds.

Stage 14 was a tough 170-kilometer ride from Gap to the top of Mont Ventoux. This was the Tour's first visit to the "Giant of Provence" since 1967, the tragic year of Tom Simpson's death. It was also Merckx's first race up the legendary slopes. Back in June he had expressed his feeling that Mont Ventoux was not a particularly difficult ascent.

It was a terribly hot day which, as in 1967, boded ill for the racers who would climb up the unprotected roads of the mountain. The stage was started late so that the riders could avoid the worst heat of the day. The Tour wanted no more Tom Simpsons.

Merckx attacked early on the climb and only Agostinho could go with him. Halfway up the mountain Merckx had about a 1-minute lead on a chase group of Poulidor, Aimar, Zilioli and Zoetemelk. 10 kilometers from the top Merckx dropped Agostinho (who claimed derailleur trouble and said he could have stayed with the Belgian) and was now out on the steep slopes alone. When he passed the monument to Simpson Merckx took off his cycling cap and made a sign of the cross. With just a half-kilometer to go Merckx cracked. Merckx could barely turn the cranks as he struggled to complete the final few meters. The man did have his limits. He won the stage followed by his former teammate Vandenbossche who came in over a minute later. The rest of the best came in starting at about 1 minute, 30 seconds. While answering questions from reporters Merckx's head slumped and he collapsed. Vandenbossche was also on the edge of foundering from the effort. Oxygen from an ambulance was brought in order to revive them. As the easiest and quickest way off the mountain Merckx rode in the ambulance down to Carpentras where the next day's stage would start. Merckx later wrote that he was hyper-oxygenated and that the rescue efforts almost caused a catastrophe. Merckx's Mont Ventoux win was his sixth stage win so far this Tour.

After the Alps and Mont Ventoux, the General Classification stood thus:

1. Eddy Merckx
2. Joop Zoetemelk @ 9 minutes 26 seconds
3. Gosta Petterson @ 12 minutes 21 seconds
4. Rini Wagtmans @ 12 minutes 29 seconds
5. Raymond Poulidor @ 14 minutes 6 seconds

Merckx didn't win either of the Pyrenean stages. The first was a mammoth day that took in the Col de Menté, the Peyresourde, the Aspin and a final ascent to La Mongie, a ski station about 300 meters below the summit of the Tourmalet. The effects of his velodrome crash the previous autumn seemed to have badly affected Merckx that day. He could never get comfortable (he was also suffering from stomach troubles) and changed his bike a couple of times. Bernard Thévenet, 22 years old and riding in his first Tour, went clear with 8 kilometers to go on the final ascent to La Mongie. He held the gap and won the stage. Merckx was dropped but none of the 3 riders in front of him, Thévenet, van Impe or Vandenbossche were threats to his overall position. Even when he was having a bad day Merckx was extending his lead.

The next day the riders climbed all the way to the top of the Tourmalet. Spanish rider Andres Gandarias escaped but because the road was wet from fog he took the descent with care, allowing Merckx and a couple of other riders to make contact. With the Aubisque facing the quartet and then another 90 kilometers of descent and rolling roads to the finish Merckx decided to take it a little easier. Other riders joined them to make a big group that broke up towards the end with no effect upon the standings.

After the Pyrenees:

1. Eddy Merckx
2. Joop Zoetemelk @ 9 minutes 57 seconds
3. Gosta Petterson @ 13 minutes 21 seconds
4. Rini Wagtmans @ 14 minutes 2 seconds
5. Martin Vandenbossche @ 14 minutes 52 seconds

There were 2 time trials left. Stage 20b in Bordeaux was another Merckx victory, in which he beat the other Petterson brother, Tomas, by 12 seconds. The final time trial from Versailles to Paris put the icing on the Merckx victory cake. Luis Ocaña, who had been thought to be a serious challenger to Merckx, suffered from bronchitis for the first 2 weeks of the Tour and was riding on courage and determination. In the final week he recovered enough to win a stage and get second to Merckx in the final time trial, losing 1 minute, 47 seconds over the 54-kilometer course.

For his 1970 Tour confirmation, Merckx had won 8 stages.

Final 1970 Tour de France General Classification:

1. Eddy Merckx (Faema-Faemino): 119 hours 31 minutes 49 seconds
2. Joop Zoetemelk (Mars-Flandria) @ 12 minutes 41 seconds
3. Gosta Petterson (Ferretti) @ 15 minutes 54 seconds
4. Martin Vandenbossche (Molteni) @ 18 minutes 53 seconds
5. Marinus "Rini" Wagtmans (Willem II) @ 19 minutes 54 seconds
6. Lucien van Impe (Sonolor) @ 20 minutes 34 seconds
7. Raymond Poulidor (Fagor-Mercier) @ 20 minutes 35 seconds
13. Italo Zilioli (Faemino) @ 26 minutes 17 seconds

Climbers' Competition:

1. Eddy Merckx: 128 points
2. Andres Gandarias: 94 points
3. Martin Vandenbossche: 85 points

Points Competition:

1. Walter Godefroot: 212 points
2. Eddy Merckx: 207 points
3. Marino Basso: 161 points

The gap to second place was "only" about 13 minutes compared to the huge 18 minutes he had inflicted the year before. Although Merckx said he was nervous the entire Tour, feeling as Magne had almost 2 generations ago that the race wasn't won until the last pedal crank was turned, he rode the 1970 Tour differently. He wasn't consumed with the rage that had propelled him to tyrannical excess in 1969. British writer J. B. Wadley noted that after the Mont Ventoux stage Merckx had basically ceased his offensive efforts. If he had been so inclined he could have easily taken more time out of Tour freshman Joop Zoetemelk. By winning the 1970 Giro and Tour, Merckx joined the very exclusive same-year Giro-Tour club. The only other members at the time were Coppi and Anquetil.

**1971.** The layout of the 1971 Tour was a substantial departure from those of previous years. First of all it was shorter, much shorter. In fact it was the shortest Tour since 1905. At 3,585 kilometers it was much like current Tours which fluctuate between 3,300 and 3,600 kilometers. Given the 760-kilometer reduction in distance from the previous year it is no surprise that the 1971 Tour was raced at a then-record speed of 37.29 kilometers per hour, almost 2 kilometers per hour faster than 1970.

The Tour continued to push the limits of what the riders could tolerate when it crammed 3 stages into the first day of racing after the Prologue. There were 2 rest days but there were 3 long transfers, one of which was done by air for the first time. It was a weird, almost figure-eight route starting in Mulhouse and then zigzagging in and out of

France going to Switzerland, Germany, Belgium as it headed northwest. Then it struck due south for the Massif Central and Puy de Dôme, followed by the Alps, the Pyrenees and then Paris.

Merckx changed sponsors and now wore the famous brown Molteni jersey that most racing fans associate with him. The core of Belgians that he assembled was remarkable for their talent and power. Herman van Springel (who had just won the Giro), Joseph Bruyère, Julien Stevens, Victor van Schil and Rini Wagtmans were superb riders who had in past years or could now command leadership on other teams. Not surprisingly after the 1970 Tour, Italo Zilioli moved on to another team, Ferretti, and had 2 major race wins in 1971, Tirreno–Adriatico and the Trofeo Laigueglia.

Merckx had won 52 races the previous year, including his only Belgian Championship. His 1971 spring would have been a wonderful career for almost any other top pro. I'll list a few of the races he won before the Tour: Paris–Nice, Milan–San Remo, Het Volk, Liège–Bastogne–Liège, Dauphiné Libéré, Midi Libre. Over the entire 1971 season he disputed 124 races and won an astonishing 54 of them, culminating in winning the World Championships in Mendrisio. It is generally though that it was during this 1971 Tour that Merckx acquired the nickname "The Cannibal", although Merckx's biographer Vanwalleghem dates it somewhat earlier. The name came from the daughter of Christian Raymond, a rider on the Peugeot team, who thought that was how Merckx rode, devouring the competition. The world agreed and the name stuck.

Who was there to challenge the man who was winning almost half the races he entered, who had crushed the competition in 1969, and after gaining an insurmountable lead halfway through 1970 just stopped riding offensively and cruised to Paris? The one man who thought he could topple the great Belgian was Luis Ocaña. Champion of Spain his first year as a pro, he had enjoyed an excellent spring in 1970 (winning both the Dauphiné Libéré and the Vuelta) and was thought to be the man to give Merckx trouble that year, but bronchitis slowed the delicate Spaniard.

Ocaña's 1971 lead-in was quieter, with a second in the Dauphiné and thirds in Paris–Nice and the Vuelta. The Dauphiné foreshadowed what was to come. Merckx had held the lead from the starting team time trial to the final stage, an individual time trial. Ocaña had been able to drop Merckx in the mountains, on the Granier to be specific, but bad weather on the following mountain, the Forclaz, kept him from "finishing him off". As we will see, the past is prologue.

The other man with the physical strength to challenge Merckx, Dutchman Joop Zoetemelk, lacked the fire, drive and confidence to try seriously to attack and beat him.

There were other fine riders. Bernard Thévenet put his wonderful talent on display with his stage 18 solo win at La Mongie the year before, his first as a pro. In the Dauphiné he was third to Merckx and Ocaña, 1 minute, 43 seconds back. In a very short period of time he had come very far.

Lucien van Impe had moved up from twelfth in 1969, his first Tour, to sixth in 1970. His admiration and affection for Bahamontes, the great Spanish climber, shaped his ambitions. What van Impe cared most about was climbing. Given that he grew to be the finest climber of his age he always ended the Tour with a high placing. But men who have the King of the Mountains prize as their goal usually fall a bit short of claiming the overall win.

The Prologue of the 1971 Tour was an 11-kilometer team time trial, the first time the team format was used in a Prologue. Merckx and his squad of Italian-sponsored Belgians won it convincingly, beating second-place Ferretti by 1 minute, 48 seconds and Zoetemelk's Flandrias by 2 minutes, 16 seconds. The times didn't count towards the individual General Classification with only time bonifications in play for the top placing teams, but the results did make clear that the peloton could probably expect another caning from Merckx and his team.

With the Prologue victory, Merckx started the 1971 Tour in Yellow.

The next day was the grueling 3-split-stage ordeal. The first, 62 kilometers to Basel in Switzerland, ended with all 130 riders finishing together. Coming in twentieth, Wagtmans was the best-placed of Merckx's Molteni riders who were all sitting at the top of the classification standings after the team time trial and therefore got to wear the Yellow Jersey for a few hours. On the second leg of the day Merckx captured enough intermediate sprint time bonuses to regain the lead by 4 seconds over his teammate van Springel. The 3-stage schedule was so hectic that some riders hadn't finished the second stage of the day when the third was starting. During that final stage Merckx captured another bit of bonus time and extended his lead by another second.

Stage 2, 142 kilometers going from Mulhouse to Strasbourg had one climb, the Firstplan which began at kilometer 42. The pace up the mountain was fiercely fast with Zoetemelk cresting the top with a 10 second lead over Spanish climber José-Manuel Fuente. Another 10 seconds back a group of 20 had formed, containing most of the Tour hopefuls including Merckx, Thévenet, Ocaña, Roger de Vlaeminck and Gosta Petterson. On the descent they came together, less Fuente, who had 2 flats. The break of über-riders pushed their advantage home. By kilometer 107 their lead over the chasing peloton was 6 minutes, 30 seconds. At Strasbourg where the sprint was to be contested in the velodrome they were 9 minutes, 30 seconds ahead. Absolutely determined to make his mark early in the Tour and demoralize the opposition, Merckx took terrible chances on the track to gain the time bonuses in play. Especially desirous of beating Roger de Vlaeminck he had van Springel lead him out, and beat his Belgian rival by a few centimeters.

For all but the 15 riders who made it to Strasbourg with Merckx the Tour was over. There would be no possibility of gaining over 9 minutes on all the talent that had been in that break. Aimar missed the move and was made a domestique of van Impe by team manager Jean Stablinski. There were many other fine riders who were now either reduced to helping higher placed teammates or riding for stage wins or other minor competitions: Joaquim Agostinho, Cyrille Guimard, Ferdi Bracke, Franco Balmamion, José-Manuel Fuente and Rolf Wolfshohl.

As the Tour circled around northern France and headed towards the Massif Central Merckx rode aggressively and used his team hard in order to maintain his slim 37 second lead over third place de Vlaeminck (second-place van Springel was a Merckx teammate). While Merckx was riding each stage as if it were a 1-day classic, Ocaña was lying low. Jacques Anquetil had been advising the Spaniard and his counsel was predictable. Ocaña was not to waste any energy and was to wait for the mountains. Prudence and traditional stage race tactics said that there was no point in getting into a watt-burning contest with Merckx on the roads leading to the hills when the stakes were so low.

Before stage 8 and the ascent of the Puy de Dôme the General Classification was very tight:

1. Eddy Merckx
2. Herman van Springel @ 26 seconds
3. Roger de Vlaeminck @ 37 seconds
4. Gianni Motta @ 40 seconds
5. Gosta Petterson @ 42 seconds
6. Joop Zoetemelk @ 44 seconds

It was on stage 8, a 221-kilometer day that ended on top of the Puy de Dôme, where the first fireworks of the Tour were shot off. Merckx started the stage in his normal way, spending energy as if there were no Tour tomorrow. No careful calculations, no clever tactics, no subtlety. As usual Merckx just put the peloton under relentless pressure. There was nothing more than sheer power needed to crush the other riders Merckx-style. That entire day Merckx had been leading and attacking, hounding the field, chasing anything that tried to get away, trying to break the morale and the resolution of the peloton.

In the thick fog on the ride to the summit of the Puy, first Thévenet attacked. Then Luis Ocaña, riding in the select group that had been able to stay with Merckx, accelerated. He got a gap. Merckx could not go with him. The gap grew. Still Merckx was helpless. Unable to counter the move, he watched the Spaniard ride away.

Joop Zoetemelk and Joaquim Agostinho, sensing the Belgian's tiredness, also managed to escape. Ocaña crossed the finish line at the top of the old volcano alone. Zoetemelk followed 7 seconds later. Then Agostinho came in 13 seconds after Ocaña. Then Merckx, another 2 seconds later. This was a revelation. Perhaps Merckx did not have a bottomless well of energy. The effect of the day was to bring the real contenders to within striking distance of the Belgian.

The new standings:

1. Eddy Merckx
2. Joop Zoetemelk @ 36 seconds
3. Luis Ocaña @ 37 seconds
4. Gosta Petterson @ 1 minute 16 seconds
5. Bernard Thévenet @ 1 minute 58 seconds

On stage 10, the first day in the Alps, Merckx punctured descending the penultimate mountain, the Cucheron. His follow car was delayed and he was stuck waiting for help while Thévenet, Petterson, Ocaña and Zoetemelk rode away. He never caught them. Merckx came in 1 minute, 36 seconds behind the day's 4 leaders. Thévenet won the stage and Zoetemelk took the Yellow Jersey. Ocaña was now only 1 second behind Zoetemelk in General Classification. Merckx's stage 8 and 10 performances were like throwing chum into a tank full of sharks. They sensed the possibility that the great man might be vulnerable.

The next day, stage 11, had 2 important climbs: the Côte de Laffrey—with stretches of 13% gradient—and the ascent to Orcières-Merlette.

On the Laffrey, Ocaña, Zoetemelk and van Impe took off with the instigation of an attack by Agostinho. Merckx gave chase. Ocaña was aware that Merckx was having digestion problems that day and felt this was the time to attack.

On the final climb up to Orcières-Merlette, Ocaña was alone, having dropped his fellow breakaways many kilometers earlier.

Behind, Merckx begged the peloton to help him chase, but Merckx had spanked them all once too often. With the exception of his teammates, Merckx received virtually no help from a peloton that was enjoying his distress. Understanding the situation, Merckx hammered away. He caught Agostinho and Zoetemelk, but Ocaña was on fire. He flew up to the summit, increasing his lead with every pedal stroke. When the stage was over, van Impe had lost almost 6 minutes to Ocaña. Merckx came in third, 8 minutes, 42 seconds after the Spaniard. Both Merckx and Ocaña had put in magnificent performances. But it was Ocaña who carried the day, having been away alone for 60 kilometers.

The day was ridden so hard and so fast that if the Tour had enforced its rules for elimination cutoff times only 39 riders would have remained in the Tour. By relaxing the rule only 3 riders were booted, but one of them was the very excellent Belgian racer Walter Godefroot. Still, 20 riders quit during this stage.

While vowing to fight on, Merckx was gracious about Ocaña's victory, saying "Today Ocaña tamed us all." He called Ocaña's ride extraordinary and that even if he had been feeling well, the new Ocaña would have been the superior rider. Recognizing that Ocaña had reached the "peak of his physical powers" he very realistically conceded, "given the lead that Luis Ocaña has I don't see how, at the moment, the Tour de France could possibly slip through his fingers. It's virtually impossible for me to make up the deficit, unless I find new strength from somewhere or unless he performs very badly. But I don't want to think about that, I don't believe it will happen."

We asked Celestino Vercelli, riding the 1971 Tour on Franco Balmamion's SCIC team about the day and if Merckx intentionally let the other riders break away. He said, "No, no, Merckx never let anybody break away!! But that day...we don't know.... The start was on an upgrade and he wasn't that brilliant in the beginning. Maybe he was still warming up and his adversaries, Ocaña, Agostinho, Zoetemelk noticed that and decided to break away immediately...Maybe he didn't expect such a early breakaway from the others, or maybe he just wasn't prompt enough for that uphill start. Anyway it was a hard-fought stage, Merckx was behind and therefore the leading group never slowed down! I don't remember now how much Merckx lost at the end...He took it badly, but not because he wasn't helped...with those hills it wouldn't have changed things that much if the group had tried to help him. He did take it badly because it had never happened to him to be behind and lose so much time. Usually he was the one who was 9 minutes in front of the others!"

The General Classification after stage 11: one can understand Merckx's glum assessment. How could one hope to pull almost 10 minutes from the flying Spaniard?

1. Luis Ocaña
2. Joop Zoetemelk @ 8 minutes 43 seconds
3. Lucien van Impe @ 9 minutes 20 seconds
4. Gosta Petterson @ 9 minutes 26 seconds
5. Eddy Merckx @ 9 minutes 46 seconds
6. Bernard Thévenet @ 10 minutes 8 seconds

The twelfth stage was another strange chapter of this spectacular Tour. It was a transition stage after the Alps. From the gun Merckx's teammate Rini Wagtmans took off. Merckx, Aimar, Armani, Huysmans and 4 others joined him. For the next 250 kilometers, the lead group pounded away with all they had.

When the attack occurred Ocaña had been in the back, signing autographs. A chase was organized. Hour after hour the 2 groups relentlessly hammered away. Merckx was out to teach Ocaña a lesson and take back some serious time. Under the hot southern French sun the lead fluctuated between 1 and 2 minutes. Luciano Armani out-sprinted the others in the Merckx group after what was effectively a 5 hour, 25 minute super-intense team pursuit. Cyrille Guimard led in the Ocaña-Thévenet-Zoetemelk group only 1 minute, 56 seconds later.

Merckx had taken back 2 of the 9 minutes he needed to win the lead back from Ocaña. But at what a huge cost in effort! The racers had ridden so fast that they showed up in Marseille an hour earlier than the most optimistic projections for the stage. There was no one at the finish to greet the racers. It was the fastest stage to date in Tour history, 45.351 kilometers an hour. Marseille mayor, Gaston Deferre, was so upset that he vowed not to let the race visit his city again, a vow that was kept until 1989, 3 years after Deferre's death.

Celestino Vercelli remembers that day very well. "We arrived in Orcières-Merlette and then we had a rest day. The day after there was another incredible stage, the twelfth, from Orcières-Merlette, in the Alps, to Marseille. It was 300 kilometers long, with 20 kilometers of downhill and then 280 kilometers in the Reno Valley. Merckx was quite furious about the previous stage and so he decided to break away with 5 or 6 teammates right away, in the first 20 kilometers. Some other riders followed them and the group immediately gained several minutes. He needed to recover the 9 minutes he lost and he meant to do so by arriving in the valley with several minutes' lead with a good group of about 8 riders. This way it would have been very difficult for the rest of the peloton behind to catch them in the 280 kilometers of the valley. What happened instead is that during the descent they went so fast that when they braked for the turns the brake pads overheated the rims. The glue holding the tubular tires to the rims melted and their tubular tires came off the rims. This happened to 2 or 3 of Merckx's teammates and so they could not help him anymore in the valley. And by the way...this also happened to me!! Otherwise I would have been in the first 10 riders at the end of that stage. This happened much more often to the big riders like me, because we had to use the brakes more heavily. Because of this Merckx lost some riders along the way who would have been a fundamental help to the plan.

"In the 280 kilometers of flat road he personally pulled the group for 250 kilometers on his own! And of course the peloton behind him went very fast. There were all of Merckx's adversaries who were very motivated to catch him. They all worked together for that. It was basically Merckx alone against all the others. And despite that they never caught him. If he had not lost his teammates on the descent he would have been in Marseille at least 10 minutes before his adversaries and he would have recovered all the time from Ocaña.

"Another thing I remember about that day is the terrible heat. I remember the sound of the cicadas for all of the 300 kilometers. We went so fast that when we arrived in Marseille there was no television there to broadcast our arrival because we were so early! So the arrival was never filmed. At that time they usually showed only the last part of each stage on TV and we arrived before they could start doing that! In the 10 years I was a professional this never happened again."

The next day's 16.3-kilometer individual time trial did little for Merckx. He was able to slice off 11 seconds plus the time bonus from Ocaña's big lead. At this point Ocaña was still 7 minutes, 23 seconds ahead of Merckx in the General Classification.

This would be settled in the Pyrenees.

Stage 14, from Revel to Luchon, took in the Portet d'Aspet, the Col de Menté and the Portillon. Ocaña knew Merckx was tiring and planned to leave the Belgian and everyone else on the Portillon.

Near the summit of the Col de Menté, a powerful, violent rainstorm with blinding hail struck. The Menté's roads turned to dangerous, potholed mud. The riders could barely see their way. Merckx, knowing that he had few peers in a descent, took off down the dangerous, partially washed out road. Ocaña and Cyril Guimard, his companions over the crest of the mountain, were able to descend with him. Presciently, Ocaña's director Maurice De Muer warned Ocaña against descending with Merckx.

4 kilometers down the mountain, Merckx crashed, taking Ocaña with him. Merckx fixed his chain and was back riding in a flash.

Not so Ocaña. He needed a new wheel. Ocaña's team BIC service car parked to take care of him. Zoetemelk came careening down the mountain. He swerved to avoid the BIC service car and slammed into Ocaña instead. Then, Joaquim Agostinho came flying down the hill and also hit Ocaña.

Ocaña, in a coma, was taken away in an ambulance. Jose-Manuel Fuente won the stage. Merckx followed in $6^1/_2$ minutes later with van Impe, Aimar, Zoetemelk and Vicente Lopez-Carril.

Ocaña later fully recovered, but his Tour was over. Merckx was again in Yellow. In deference to the fallen Spaniard, Merckx refused to wear the Yellow Jersey until the day after.

The new standings:

1. Eddy Merckx
2. Joop Zoetemelk @ 2 minutes 21 seconds
3. Lucien van Impe @ 2 minutes 51 seconds
4. Bernard Thévenet @ 4 minutes 46 seconds

The next day, Tuesday July 13, was the shortest road stage in the history of the Tour. The terrible weather that had been the cause of Ocaña's misfortune continued to harass the riders during the 19.6-kilometer climb to Superbagnères. Fuente was one of that small group of riders that included Ocaña and Roger de Vlaeminck who never felt daunted or oppressed by Merckx's excellence. Their challenges to Merckx's reign make for some of the finest racing of the era. After a couple of hard attacks Fuente went clear of everyone 6 kilometers from the summit. Thévenet and van Impe were also able to break loose and finish a half minute after Fuente. Zoetemelk and Merckx were another 30 seconds adrift. Now van Impe was in second place, 2 minutes, 17 seconds behind. Even though Fuente had won 2 stunning solo back-to-back stage victories, he had lost too much time in stages 12 and 13, both times needing special dispensation from the judges to continue the race because he had finished outside the time limit.

The following day, Wednesday, the riders were asked to perform superhuman duty with a split stage day that started with a big ride in the Pyrenees. In the morning the riders had to climb the Peyresourde, the Aspin, the Tourmalet and the Aubisque. The major result of this last day of climbing was to end Thévenet's threat to the Overall when he lost almost 4 minutes to Merckx. Both Zoetemelk and van Impe, rather than gain time, lost a few seconds. Without Ocaña, Merckx was back in control. In the afternoon they had to ride another 57.5 kilometers. Van Springel won the short stage in a 2-man break. Merckx along with van Impe and Zoetemelk were part of a chasing group of 11 who were able to put another 13 seconds between themselves and the field. Merckx was now riding a race of redemption knowing that his performance was being viewed through the lens of Ocaña's absence.

Lucien van Impe in action in stage 15.

Before the start of stage 17 Merckx visited the now recuperating Ocaña. Horrible though the accident and his injuries had originally appeared, he ended up with only bad bruises and lacerations and was already recovering. The stage was a mostly flat course that ended in Bordeaux. Not content with owning the Yellow Jersey, Merckx wanted a firmer hold on the green Sprinter's Jersey. Merckx held a 5-point lead over Cyrille Guimard whom Merckx also remembered as one of the riders who helped Ocaña stay close to him in the lightning-fast stage into Marseille. Looking for an opportunity for a grand exploit when Raymond Riotte attacked with 65 kilometers to go, Merckx and 3 others joined him. Riding like, well, Merckx, Merckx drove the break to a lead of 2 minutes, 26 seconds over the first chasers. The main field with most of the former hopefuls finished 3 minutes behind. Merckx's winning that stage ended Guimard's hopes of Green; Merckx had the Points Competition locked up.

There was only the final day's individual time trial which Merckx easily won.

Final 1971 Tour de France General Classification:

1. Eddy Merckx (Molteni): 96 hours 45 minutes 14 seconds
2. Joop Zoetemelk (Mars-Flandria) @ 9 minutes 51 seconds
3. Lucien van Impe (Sonolor) @ 11 minutes 6 seconds
4. Bernard Thévenet (Peugeot) @ 14 minutes 50 seconds
5. Joaquim Agostinho (Hoover-De Gribaldy) @ 21 minutes

Climbers' Competition:

1. Lucien van Impe: 228 points
2. Joop Zoetemelk: 179 points
3. Eddy Merckx: 136 points

Points Competition:

1. Eddy Merckx: 202 points
2. Cyrille Guimard: 186 points
3. Gerben Karstens: 107 points

Yet, if that tragic moment hadn't occurred on the Col de Menté.... My personal feeling is that Ocaña was riding a superb, tactical race and showed that he had the power and endurance to beat Merckx. Only once did he let his ego get ahead of him, when he decided to follow Merckx down the mountain and that error cost him the race. Merckx himself has expressed his distress at Ocaña's unfortunate accident, "Whatever happens, I have lost the Tour. The doubt will always remain." But really, there is no doubt. The best man, the one with the lowest elapsed time in Paris, won. Fortune has always played an important part in the Tour.

**1972.** The 1971 Tour left everyone involved dissatisfied. Ocaña felt that he would have won the Tour if he hadn't crashed. Merckx was bothered by those who felt that his 1971 win was a gift of circumstance, not the result of a true athletic victory. Both set out to settle things. Publicly exchanged words between the 2 made the situation a bit warmer.

1972 had started out well for Merckx. He won Milan–San Remo, Liège–Bastogne–Liège and the Flèche Wallonne. His winning ways continued at the Giro that year, when he beat Gimondi by a resounding 7 minutes, 42 seconds. He also won the Giro's sprinters' and combine competitions, and his Molteni team had won the Team General Classification. In addition, he was the reigning World Pro Road Champion, entitled to wear the Rainbow Jersey.

Ocaña's win list was not nearly as impressive but he was concentrating on preparing for the Tour. He did however win the Dauphiné Libéré. This was still viewed as about the most important pre-Tour tune-up race. It often has many of the same climbs as the Tour. Both riders seemed to be ready for a rematch.

Each had a particular strategy to win. Ocaña planned to repeat his 1971 plan, lie low and attack in the mountains. He publicly said that he would be willing to give up a full minute by stage 6 at Bayonne. Merckx felt that Ocaña did not have the same reserves of energy and needed to recover after several hard days. The plan was simple, keep hammering the Spaniard until he ran out of gas.

One man must not be forgotten: the 36-year old evergreen Raymond Poulidor. His spring included victories in Paris–Nice, the Critérium National and the Catalonian Week as well as second in the Flèche Wallonne.

Felice Gimondi, Joop Zoetemelk and Bernard Thévenet were entered but it was assumed that the 1972 Tour would be between Ocaña and Merckx.

The route of this edition seemed like a throwback to the pre-1951 Tours, almost completely avoiding the interior roads of France. Starting in Angers in the Loire Valley, the route headed northwest to Brittany and made a great counter-clockwise semi-circle around the circumference of France until it reached the Vosges and then headed almost due west for Paris. At 3,846 kilometers it was almost 250 kilometers longer than 1971. It did have 4 split stages but none with 3 races in 1 day.

Merckx threw down the gauntlet in the Prologue 7.2-kilometer time trial, winning it and beating Poulidor by 12 seconds, Zoetemelk by 13 seconds and Ocaña by 15 seconds.

The first stage was won by a rapidly rising talent on Poulidor's Gan-Mercier squad, Cyrille Guimard. With the stage-win time bonus the talented racer from the city of Nantes was in the Yellow Jersey, ahead of Merckx by a slim 7 seconds.

Over the next 3 stages Guimard sprinted well, fighting for intermediate sprint time bonuses. Merckx raced with the same aggressivity, getting into breaks and not missing an opportunity to improve his position, no matter how small the bonification.

Stage 3b was a 16.2-kilometer team time trial which was won by Merckx's Molteni squad. The teams' times mattered only for the team classification and didn't count against the individual riders' General Classification except that the first 5 riders of the top 3 teams received a bonus of 20, 10 and 5 seconds respectively. Those 20 seconds put Merckx back in the lead. But Guimard was hot. The next day was raced in hard winds that split the field into echelons. Although Merckx tried to escape from the final lead group of 22, he was pulled back by Ocaña and Thévenet, and Guimard won. Guimard was again the overall leader, this time by 19 seconds over Merckx. Several riders missed that crucial break: Zoetemelk, van Impe and Poulidor. 3 minutes are a lot to give up on a flat stage before the climbing even starts in a Tour containing both Merckx and Ocaña.

Stage 5b was a 12.7-kilometer individual time trial. Merckx won it, beating Ocaña by 15 seconds and Guimard by 24. Because Guimard had been so vigilant in accruing bonus seconds and denying them whenever possible to a very hungry Merckx, he still had the lead, now by only 9 seconds.

At the end of stage 6 before the first Pyrenean stage Ocaña was where he expected to be, about a minute behind Merckx. The General Classification stood thus:

1. Cyrille Guimard
2. Eddy Merckx @ 11 seconds
3. Roger Swerts (Merckx's right hand man on the Molteni team) @ 30 seconds
4. Luis Ocaña @ 1 minute 2 seconds
5. Yves Hézard @ 1 minute 21 seconds
6. Bernard Thévenet @ 1 minute 25 seconds
7. Walter Godefroot @ 1 minute 36 seconds
8. Felice Gimondi @ 1 minute 42 seconds

The first day in the mountains with the Aubisque demonstrated that Ocaña could no longer use Merckx as a plaything. On the upper reaches of the summit these 2 riders were away, along with several others. From the group of remaining elite climbers Ocaña attacked and Merckx closed the gap, bringing most of the chasers with him but dropping van Impe. Ocaña went again and this time only Merckx could answer, and again without trouble. The 2 went over the mountain together and on the descent Ocaña punctured while Merckx continued. The next mountain was the Soulor. Ocaña descended the mountain in the rain and the fog, desperate to catch Merckx. Not possessing Merckx's skills, Ocaña crashed, this time bringing down Thévenet who was riding with him. Up front, Merckx was receiving generous help from Zoetemelk and Guimard. The result, under the circumstances, could have been far worse for Ocaña who lost only 1 minute, 49 seconds. He was now almost 3 minutes down on Guimard and Merckx. For Thévenet, it was a disaster. Roger Pingeon had helped the fallen Frenchman chase but his crash had been hard. He ended up losing 6 minutes, 32 seconds. Even though he had suffered a concussion and was taken to the hospital for examination, he started the next day's stage. Guimard had hung on and still had an 11 second lead on Merckx.

Tellingly about the man's character, Ocaña complained that Merckx had attacked him when he was having mechanical trouble and when he had crashed. Merckx pointed out that Ocaña had done the same thing to him the year before.

Hans Junkermann was assessed a 10 minute penalty after stage 7 for testing positive for dope. He withdrew after stage 13. Junkermann was one of the protagonists in the 1962 Tour's "Wiel's affair".

Stage 8 forced the riders to tackle the Tourmalet, the Aspin and the Peyresourde. Thick fog and streets wet with melting snow made high-speed descents dangerous. Using classic racing tactics the Molteni team sent Roger Swerts up ahead on a break to be there to help Merckx when he would inevitably arrive. Merckx, Poulidor, Thévenet and Ocaña went over the top of the Tourmalet about 4 minutes behind Swerts. Gimondi, Zoetemelk, and van Impe were several minutes behind but on the descent all the best riders came together. On the Aspin Thévenet lost contact but got help from teammate Raymond Delisle and clawed his way back. That left the final climb, the Peyresourde, where van Impe was able to get clear. When Merckx jumped after him Ocaña couldn't hold his wheel. Merckx caught van Impe on the descent and beat him in the sprint. Ocaña finished only 8 seconds behind, but this was a far different race than 1971. Since Guimard finished almost 3 minutes behind Merckx, Merckx was the new leader. Guimard was second at 2 minutes, 33 seconds and Ocaña was third at 2 minutes, 48 seconds. The situation wasn't hopeless for Ocaña and Guimard, if one thought the situation comparable to 1971. But Merckx wasn't riding like last year. He was more like his 1970 self, but more measured, more careful, not trying to win everything.

The third day in the Pyrenees, stage 9 with the Ares and Portet d'Aspet, didn't affect the standings. What was notable was the abandonment of Roger Pingeon. While he had been down in the classification it was hoped he would remain in the race to help his teammate, Bernard Thévenet. Despite pleas from his team, he was adamant about quitting. He returned to the Tour one more time in 1974 and came in eleventh.

The General Classification after the Pyrenees:

1. Eddy Merckx
2. Cyrille Guimard @ 2 minutes 37 seconds
3. Luis Ocaña @ 2 minutes 52 seconds
4. Felice Gimondi @ 4 minutes 19 seconds

In the stage between the Pyrenees and the stage 11 ascent of Mont Ventoux, Merckx crashed but suffered no lasting or serious harm. Stage 11 was ridden with a flat, slow lead-in to the climb, the riders wanting to save their energy for what they knew to be a tough fight once they reached Mont Ventoux. Sure enough, at the base of the mountain the Moltenis went to the front and started to push the pace so hard that good riders such as Gimondi were dropped. 13 kilometers from the summit the lead group had been cut down to the elite riders of the race: Merckx and his teammate Vandenbossche, Ocaña, van Impe, Poulidor, Zoetemelk, Thévenet, Agostinho and Mariano Martinez. Agostinho fell and took the unlucky Thévenet with him. Then Ocaña started a series of attacks, 4 in all. Merckx was able to respond to all of them, but the Ocaña-inflicted damage was profound. Only Poulidor was able to stay with Merckx and Ocaña. Poulidor then hammered the pair with several attempts of his own to break loose, all unsuccessful. At this point resignation set in and the pace slowed, allowing van Impe, Thévenet and Martinez to get back on. After sitting on the group for a few hundred meters Thévenet then attacked and broke clear. Pounding up the mountain for all he was worth with Merckx chasing so hard he dropped the others, Thévenet reached the top of the mountain a full 34 seconds ahead of Merckx. Ocaña had Merckx in sight, but he couldn't close the 5-second gap. It was a terrific performance by Thévenet who only days before had been in a hospital bed. Merckx was now leading with second-place Ocaña 3 minutes, 1 second behind.

Stage 13 from Orcières-Merlette to Briançon with the Vars and Izoard mountains was one that Merckx, having a good sense of the historical importance of the climbs and victories in Briançon, wanted to win badly. Thys, Bartali, Coppi, Bobet, Gaul and Gimondi had been first across the line in the Alpine city. A surprise: Merckx had never before ridden over the Izoard until this day. He marshaled his team at the base of the Vars. Soon there were only 16 riders in the front. Raymond Delisle went clear of this group and Merckx chased with Agostinho in tow. Again, Ocaña could not answer. Merckx caught and passed Delisle on the descent. Guimard, also a skilled descender, bridged the gap up to Merckx on the valley before the Izoard. On the ascent of the Izoard Merckx dropped Guimard. He didn't wait at the top but continued down the mountain and cruised into Briançon a minute and a half in front of his first 4 chasers, Gimondi, Guimard,

Poulidor and van Impe. Ocaña, who had done a lot of the work in the valley between the 2 passes, came in another 10 seconds after the Gimondi group.

The General Classification at this point didn't seem to hold out much hope for the others:

1. Eddy Merckx
2. Luis Ocaña @ 4 minutes 43 seconds
3. Cyrille Guimard @ 5 minutes 32 seconds
4. Felice Gimondi @ 7 minutes 13 seconds
5. Raymond Poulidor @ 8 minutes 20 seconds

The following day had stage 14 split into 2 pieces. The morning stage was only 59 kilometers that ended in Valloire after climbing the Lautaret and the Galibier. The afternoon climbing was more formidable, being a full 151 kilometers and going over the Télégraphe, the Grand Cucheron and the Granier. Of the 132 riders who started the Tour, 92 were left in the race. On the first half-stage Zoetemelk was first over the Galibier. Merckx was able to catch him on the descent and then out-sprint him in Valloire. Again Ocaña was unable to go with Merckx when the Cannibal chased a serious attacker.

The second half was hectic and full of aggression that started 5 kilometers from the top of the Granier and continued until the end of the stage in Aix les Bains. The 8 best riders of the Tour—Merckx, Guimard, Gimondi, Zoetemelk, van Impe, Agostinho, Poulidor and Martinez—ended the stage together with the real sprint between Merckx and Guimard. The photos gave the win to Guimard by a hair. Ocaña was the big loser of the day, coming in thirty-third, 5 minutes, 19 seconds behind Guimard.

Stage 15 was a short 28-kilometer ride up Mont Revard. In 1965 the Mont Revard stage had been an individual time trial that had ruined Poulidor's chances when it was stunningly won by Tour freshman Gimondi. This time Poulidor beat Gimondi. But further up front it was another fight between Guimard and Merckx. Again it was a Guimard victory but it was so close that Merckx took only one hand off the bars to signal victory. Guimard had such perfect, quick reflexes that seeing the opening, he threw his bike across the line and took the stage.

Ominously Guimard was suffering serious pain in his knee. He was getting pain killers injected each morning so that he could see his way to the end of each stage.

Ocaña's condition had been deteriorating as well. When he crashed in stage 7 he contracted a lung infection. It was finally too much for him and he withdrew from the Tour at the end of stage 14b.

The Alps were finished. Here were the standings:

1. Eddy Merckx
2. Cyrille Guimard @ 6 minutes 20 seconds
3. Raymond Poulidor @ 9 minutes 54 seconds
4. Felice Gimondi @ 10 minutes 1 second
5. Lucien van Impe @ 14 minutes 3 seconds
6. Joop Zoetemelk @ 15 minutes 45 seconds

The only climbing left was the stage 17 visit to the Vosges. Van Impe had boasted that he would be first to the top of the final climb, the Ballon d'Alsace. Thévenet was too strong that day for van Impe to make good on his braggadocio. But the real story was Guimard. Under constant medical attention, he struggled that day, coming off on the first 2 climbs and then getting back on. On the Ballon, suffering, he lost 2 minutes. The next day he suited up and quit after riding 10 kilometers.

The only thing standing in Merckx's way was the final time trial held on the penultimate stage. Going into the time trial Poulidor was in second place, leading Gimondi by a slim 4 seconds. That day Merckx was the fastest with Gimondi a fine second, 34 seconds behind, relegating Poulidor to third.

Merckx had done what only Anquetil had been able to accomplish, win 4 Tours in a row. He had equaled Coppi's 7 Grand Tours with only Anquetil ahead on that count with 8. Also, Merckx was only the second rider (after Coppi in 1949 and 1952) to twice win the Giro and the Tour in the same year.

At the final award ceremony Guimard was the presenter of the sprinter's Green Jersey. Merckx, the winner, gave the jersey back to a weeping Guimard telling him that it was really his.

Final 1972 Tour de France General Classification:

1. Eddy Merckx (Molteni): 108 hours 17 minutes 18 seconds
2. Felice Gimondi (Salvarani) @ 10 minutes 41 seconds
3. Raymond Poulidor (Gan-Mercier) @ 11 minutes 34 seconds
4. Lucien van Impe (Sonolor) @ 16 minutes 45 seconds
5. Joop Zoetemelk (Beaulieu-Flandria) @ 19 minutes 9 seconds

Climbers' Competition:

1.  Lucien van Impe: 229 points
2.  Eddy Merckx: 211 points
3.  Joaquim Agostinho: 163 points

Points Competition:

1.  Eddy Merckx: 196 points
2.  Rik van Linden: 135 points
3.  Joop Zoetemelk: 132 points

There were many more prizes. Coming up with new competitions that could then be sold to a sponsor seemed to be the real occupation of the Tour. Awards were given for elegance, teamwork, combativity, good humor, for the fastest stage of the Tour, for the first to the top of the highest point of the Tour, for the best team, for the most Hot Spot sprints as well as for General Classification, points, mountains and combine for best overall. It was starting to look a bit sordid as the awards ceremonies went on endlessly.

Goddet and Lévitan didn't see any other way to make the Tour work. Cycling and the Tour were going through a rough patch. It was rumored that during the mid-1970's the organization had to beg some of the good teams to come and ride the race. Today many teams consider the year a failure if they don't get a Tour invitation so that their sponsors can show their logos world-wide.

**1973.** The route of the 1973 Tour, the sixtieth since Desgrange inaugurated the Tour in 1903, was an inept design that was put together to extract the maximum amount of money possible out of the greatest number of cities that would pay to host a stage start or finish. There were 20 stages listed but 6 of them were split stages. There were 2 rest days but that didn't come close to compensating for the long days and short nights that were made worse by the transfers at the end of the stages to the next start town. Ocaña complained that he could barely get 6 hours of sleep, hardly the rest needed for recuperation in the most important of the Grand Tours. It showed in the numbers. With an average speed of 33.407 kilometers per hour the 1974 Tour was the slowest since Louison Bobet's 1954 win.

Like the 1954 Tour, the 1973 edition started in Holland, this time in the town of Scheveningen. It plowed through Belgium to Roubaix in France. From there until the Pyrenees it hugged the perimeter of France and then went to the Massif Central for a climb up the Puy de Dôme. The riders transferred to Bourges and then shot due north to Paris. Not only was the 1973 Tour logistically daunting; at 4,150 kilometers, it was also the longest since 1970.

Merckx decided not to ride the Tour de France in 1973 and he can hardly be blamed after his successful spring campaign. He won Paris–Roubaix, Liège–Bastogne–Liège, Het Volk, Ghent–Wevelgem, Amstel Gold and the other 2 Grand Tours, the Vuelta a España and the Giro d'Italia. In 1973 he entered 136 races and won 51 of them. That compares well with his other years at the top. In 1970 he won 52 times, in '71 he gained 54 victories and in '72, 50 wins.

Luis Ocaña had also had an excellent run-up to the Tour with wins in the Tour of the Basque Country, the Catalonian Week and the Dauphiné Libéré and a second to Merckx in the Vuelta.

Still, despite his good form and his stunning challenge to Merckx before crashing out of the Tour in 1971, Ocaña was not looked upon by all as a favorite to win the 1973 Tour. He was seen as fragile, brittle. In his 4 attempts at the Tour to date, he had failed to finish 3 times and had managed only a thirty-first in 1970. He had effectively crashed out of the 1969, 1971 and 1972 Tours. Like Poulidor he was plagued by enough consistent misfortune that one finally and regretfully concludes that it must be their characters and abilities that caused them so much trouble, not bad luck. Superior riders like Merckx, Hinault, De Vlaeminck and Armstrong rode intelligently and almost always avoided trouble.

The other competition? Certainly Bernard Thévenet, who finished ninth the year before, had to be considered a threat. His ninth was a fine result considering he finished stage 7 with a concussion and couldn't remember riding the final kilometers.

Joop Zoetemelk, always riding almost well enough to win, had the legs if not the zeal to emerge victorious. Zoetemelk, who had produced 2 successive second places in the Tour, changed teams. He had been on the Mars-Flandria team, managed by Brik Schotte. Zoetemelk was unhappy because Schotte, who was not convinced that Zoetemelk could win the Tour, devoted the team's resources to helping Roger and

Erik de Vlaeminck earn stage wins. In 1973 Zoetemelk moved to Gitane.

There was one other rider who could be considered a threat, but only if things truly went his way and went very wrong for the others. That rider was the small Spanish climber José-Manuel Fuente who turned pro for the 1970 season. The next year, although he struggled with the long, high-speed flat stages in the Tour, he was able to win 2 mountain stages. In the 1972 Giro he and Merckx had a legendary confrontation during the fourth stage climb to Blockhaus. Fuente donned the Pink Jersey but he was indiscreet and hinted to journalists that Merckx might test positive for dope (he didn't). Merckx retaliated by racing with increased intensity and within 2 stages had the lead back for good, with Fuente finishing a credible second. In the 1973 Giro Fuente was only able to muster an eighth place but then went on to signal his good condition by winning the Tour of Switzerland. Although both were spectacular climbers, Fuente was a less complete rider than Charly Gaul, who had been excellent against the clock.

Joop Zoetemelk won the 7.1-kilometer Prologue by less than a second, denying second-place Poulidor yet another chance to spend at least a half day in Yellow. To the joy of the bike-mad Dutch spectators Zoetemelk, the reigning Dutch Road Champion, had the privilege of winning this first stage in his home country. His glory was short-lived when Belgian Willy Teirlinck won the next morning's half-stage and became the new leader. Ocaña's luck continued to hold when 10 kilometers into the stage a dog ran in front of the peloton and took down Ocaña and Herman van Springel. Both were up and brought back to the field by their teammates.

It was clear that van Springel suffered no lasting damage. With 20 kilometers to go in the afternoon stage he bridged the gap up to one of Ocaña's domestiques, José Catieau, who had tried his hand at breaking away. Once powerhouse rider van Springel joined Catieau, Catieau stopped working, not wanting to help a man who was a serious threat to Ocaña's ultimate victory. Van Springel was an old pro and knew the game. He dragged the Spaniard to the finish line where Catieau jumped around him and took the stage win. Van Springel couldn't have been too angry since he was awarded the Yellow Jersey after beating the pack by over 2 minutes.

Stage 3 made it clear that Ocaña was not going to wait for the mountains to gain time if an appropriate opportunity presented itself on the flats. Run on a hot day between Roubaix and Reims over cobbles, it was a good chance for the *rouleurs* to drop the hammer on the smaller climbers like Fuente and drop it they did. At about kilometer 66 Guimard broke loose with a couple of other riders. They were quickly joined by some elite racers including Ocaña, Schleck, Mortensen and Catieau (all riders on Ocaña's BIC team) and Barry Hoban. Missing the move and massing for a chase were van Impe, van Springel, Zoetemelk, Godefroot, Thévenet and Poulidor. The pursuit was on and the Ocaña/Guimard group kept their lead while the chasing group lost Godefroot and a couple of others. Guimard, the best sprinter in the lead group, led the break into Reims 2 minutes, 34 seconds ahead of the Zoetemelk group. Catieau was back in Yellow and Ocaña had pulled out the iron gauntlet and smacked his rivals hard. Fuente lost 7 minutes, 17 seconds that day.

Zoetemelk took a few seconds back the next day but he was still down 2 minutes on a man who was determined to win and seemed to have the physical tools to do it.

Going into the mountains at the start of stage 7a, here was the General Classification:

1. José Catieau
2. Willy De Geest @ 1 minute 16 seconds
3. Leif Mortensen @ 1 minute 34 seconds
4. Herman van Springel @ 1 minute 48 seconds
5. Luis Ocaña @ 1 minute 59 seconds
6. Juan Zurano @ 2 minutes 27 seconds
7. Gustaaf van Roosbroeck @ 2 minutes 50 seconds
8. Joop Zoetemelk @ 4 minutes 4 seconds

It was to be a double stage day in the Alps. The first stage of the day was an 85-kilometer encounter with the 1,283-meter high Solève. Ocaña attacked and dropped everyone but Zoetemelk who stayed with him until a couple of kilometers from the summit and then he had to drop away as well. Ocaña took over the lead when he finished a minute ahead of the finest climbers in the world: Thévenet, van Impe, Fuente and Zoetemelk. The nearest real challenger, van Springel, was sitting in third place, 2 minutes, 20 seconds behind an Ocaña who seemed to be riding with the same panache that he had shown in 1971.

After Fuente had attacked over and over to no effect, Bernard Thévenet won the afternoon stage. Escaping in the rain and hail with a kilometer to go, he was only able to take 15 seconds out of Ocaña for the day's work, coming nowhere close to getting Ocaña to loosen his grip on the lead. After the first day in the mountains Ocaña was in control. The other riders hoping to wear Yellow had floated near the top. Guimard, suffering from a recurrence of his knee problems withdrew from the Tour.

Here was the new General Classification:

1. Luis Ocaña

2. Joop Zoetemelk @ 2 minutes 51 seconds

3. Herman van Springel @ 2 minutes 55 seconds

4. Bernard Thévenet @ 3 minutes 17 seconds

5. Lucien van Impe @ 3 minutes 19 seconds

Stage 8 was a big day. The riders had to ride 237.5 kilometers crossing the Madeleine, the Télégraphe, the Galibier, the Izoard and the climb to the finish at Les Orres.

On the Télégraphe, José-Manuel Fuente attacked, beating Ocaña to the top by 5 seconds. On the descent, the other main contenders joined the 2 climbers. Over the crest of the Galibier the positions were reversed and Ocaña preceded Fuente with the others more than a minute back down the mountain. Fuente kept attacking but this year Ocaña was not a racer to be dropped. The race was now between Ocaña and Fuente. Although they were fellow Spaniards, they did not like each other. As the pair ascended the Izoard, Fuente stopped working, content to sit on Ocaña's wheel. Ocaña was furious at having to do all the work and started swearing at the little Spaniard, calling him unprintable names. Then, to put salt in the wound, Fuente scooted by Ocaña over the crest of the Izoard to take the climber's points. Sometimes there is a cosmic justice. Fuente flatted. Ocaña accelerated and rode gloriously alone to the summit at Les Orres. Fuente came in about a minute later. Thévenet and Martinez, the best of the rest, followed in at 7 minutes. Zoetemelk, Agostinho, Poulidor and van Impe, superb riders all, struggled in more than 20 minutes after Ocaña.

Ocaña now had a 9-minute lead over Fuente in the General Classification. Zoetemelk was fifth, more than 23 minutes behind. Ocaña had utterly shattered the field with one of the most masterful rides in cycling history. 12 riders had to leave the Tour that day for failing to make the time cut. They had held onto team cars and when the time penalties for the towing infractions were added to their day's results they were over the limit.

But the peloton was growing exhausted and angry, not from the racing but from the bus rides and train trips that the transfers mandated as well as the long days and short nights. Writers started use terms like "capitulation" to characterize the combination of an intolerable racing schedule and an unrelenting, dominating Ocaña.

The next day Spaniard Vicente Lopez-Carril took off for a long solo excursion. The weary peloton let him go. They had had enough of the Alps and knew they would have to sign in for the start of the next day's stage at 7:30 in the morning.

Ocaña was creating a lead of Merckxian proportions. Here was the General Classification after stage 9:

1.  Luis Ocaña

2.  José-Manuel Fuente @ 9 minutes 8 seconds

3.  Bernard Thévenet @ 10 minutes 16 seconds

4.  Michel Périn @ 19 minutes 57 seconds

5.  Joop Zoetemelk @ 23 minutes 15 seconds

The third time trial, this time 28.3 relatively flat kilometers at the base of the Pyrenees over a road that rose only slightly, showed that Ocaña had enough raw horsepower to beat the entire field. Fuente, who started 2 minutes ahead of Ocaña barely missed the humiliation of being caught.

Ocaña's time trials carried a harbinger of the future. Starting in the latter stages of the Dauphiné he was riding titanium frames made by Speedwell Gearcase Company of Birmingham, England. In the Tour he used the titanium frame on some of the road stages and from what I can tell in the pictures, all of the time trials. It would be another 20 years before all the problems titanium presented could be solved to the satisfaction of the finest racers but it was indicative that if a superior bike could be developed, it would be used.

The afternoon's short half-stage was a 76-kilometer race to the Pyrenees 2000 ski station with its final steep 12 kilometers providing a real "bite". Fuente tried repeatedly to leave the pack behind but the others were having none of it. 2 kilometers from the top van Impe jumped off the front and made his escape stick. Ocaña finished with the other mountain goats resulting in no change to the standings. The exhausted racers got a rest day before 2 truly hard days of climbing.

Stage 13 had 4 big Pyrenean climbs: the Puymorens, Portet d'Aspet, Col de Menté and the Portillon. On the descent of the Portet d'Aspet Poulidor crashed and had to be helicoptered off the mountain. His Tour was finished. Fuente had managed to escape the field over the Col de Menté, but the others caught him at the bottom of the hill. Zoetemelk attacked and got clear before the final climb. Ocaña also broke loose and chased, catching and dropping the Dutchman on the final climb and winning a clear solo victory.

The second day in the Pyrenees with the Aspin, Tourmalet and Soulor opened with a hard, cold rain. A few racers who were out of contention tried their legs, but the peloton was not in a mood to take chances in the sometimes impenetrable fog on the descents. There was no real change to the top of the General Classification.

The General Classification after the Pyrenees:

1. Luis Ocaña
2. José-Manuel Fuente @ 14 minutes 56 seconds
3. Bernard Thévenet @ 15 minutes 32 seconds
4. Joop Zoetemelk @ 24 minutes 57 seconds

And so things stood as the Tour headed north to Bordeaux for the penultimate time trial. Along the flatter stages the riders showed their anger with the tough scheduling by riding slowly. While this may have made their days even longer, delaying their time on the massage and dinner tables, their rage was real. After stage 16 the racers were scheduled to ride a special train to the next city. Since the stage ended an hour later than the most pessimistic projected time, the train had departed and the riders had to travel in buses that had been cooking in the hot July sun.

Ocaña appeared to have taken it a bit easy on the time trial, coming in fourth to his fast moving teammate Joaquim Agostinho. Fuente seemed to be running out of gas as the Tour neared its completion. Over the 12.4 kilometers he lost enough time to let Thévenet take his second place on the podium.

There was one more chance for the climbers to assert themselves, stage 18, which ended at the top of Puy de Dôme. Fuente knew that with another time trial to come he had to take time out of Thévenet. He attacked but he brought a knife to a gunfight. Thévenet finished 14 seconds ahead of him. And up front Ocaña and van Impe were racing for all they were worth. Ocaña beat the Belgian by 4 seconds but the effort caused both of them to collapse at the finish line.

That Ocaña was in no way weakening even at the end of the Tour was evident when he won the final time trial at Versailles, beating Thévenet by 25 seconds over the 16-kilometer course. Fuente's fatigue became even more clear when Thévenet beat him by 54 seconds. Compare this to the Prologue where Fuente beat Thévenet by 2 seconds. Worse, in the final week Fuente slipped to second in the Mountains Competition to his countryman Pedro Torres.

Ocaña won 6 stages on his way to triumphing over a peloton that had more or less capitulated after the first week. And what if Merckx had been there? This hypothetical question is particularly hard to answer because Ocaña and Merckx avoided racing each other most of the year. They did meet in the Vuelta where Merckx won on a course that was tailor-made for him, beating Ocaña by 3 minutes, 46 seconds, who in turn beat Thévenet by 30 seconds. Ocaña lashed Merckx with his most savage attacks in the Vuelta's difficult sixteenth stage but Merckx was able to respond and close the gaps. One would be led to believe that in 1973 Merckx was the superior rider. The only qualification to this is that Ocaña was riding on a different level in July than he had been during early May when the Vuelta was held. I give the edge to Ocaña. And if the 2 had been in France in July the already smashed peloton would have suffered a mugging that would have probably eliminated half the riders.

Final General Classification of the 1973 Tour de France:

1. Luis Ocaña (BIC): 122 hours 25 minutes 34 seconds
2. Bernard Thévenet (Peugeot) @ 15 minutes 51 seconds
3. José-Manuel Fuente (KAS) @ 17 seconds 15 seconds
4. Joop Zoetemelk (Gitane) @ 26 minutes 22 seconds
5. Lucien van Impe (Sonolor) @ 30 minutes 20 seconds

Climbers' Competition:

1. Pedro Torres: 225 points
2. José-Manuel Fuente: 216 points
3. Luis Ocaña: 192 points

Points Competition:

1. Herman van Springel: 187 points
2. Joop Zoetemelk: 168 points
3. Luis Ocaña: 145 points

**1974.** Merckx came to the Tour with wins in both the Giro d'Italia and the Tour of Switzerland. He started the early season well, winning one of the first races on the European calendar, the Italian Trofeo Laigueglia. The rest of Merckx's spring was not up to his normal standards. For the first time since 1965, his first year as a pro, he didn't win any Spring Classics. It wasn't for lack of trying. In 1974 he entered 140 races but won only 38 of them, a sharp fall-off from his 51 victories the year before. Yet, with the exception of the Classics, his list of 1974 victories is stunning: Giro d'Italia, Swiss Tour, Tour de France and the World Road Championship. He produced second places in both the Catalonian Week and Ghent–Wevelgem, a third in Paris–Nice and was fourth in the Tour of Flanders, Paris–Roubaix and the 5 Days of Dunkirk. But the wins weren't generally coming with the same ease. He was starting to get a little ragged at the edges. If Merckx had been anything less than a Nietzscheian siege engine of will his career would surely have been longer but perhaps his win list shorter. Health problems got in the way. Writers described his difficulties differently. Some write about his having the flu. Merckx himself says he had a sore tailbone. Immediately after winning the Tour of Switzerland, Merckx had surgery on his perineum. The surgery was performed on June 22 with the Tour starting on June 27. As one might expect, the wound from the surgery never healed during the Tour and it gave him trouble the entire time. He would often end the stages with a bloody chamois.

Denying the world the rematch everyone wanted, neither Zoetemelk nor Ocaña entered the 1974 Tour. Zoetemelk crashed in the Midi-Libéré and ended up in the hospital with a life-threatening case of meningitis. Ocaña crashed while racing in a 4-day pre-Tour tune-up race, the Tour de L'Aude, and went home. From that point he failed to communicate with either his sponsor (BIC) or his *directeur sportif,* Maurice De Muer, and was fired.

The other great hope, Bernard Thévenet, even though he started the Tour, was hopelessly banged up from several crashes in the Vuelta.

The 1974 Tour remained about the same length as the year before, 4,098 kilometers. Counting split days as individual stages, the Tour organization crammed 27 stages and 2 rest days into the 3 weeks of racing. There were fewer of the onerous transfers that had reduced 1973's peloton into a surly, slow-moving group of exhausted riders but they were still a source of vigorous complaint. For the first time the Tour went to England for a stage. The 1974 Tour went clockwise, starting in Brittany, circling the perimeter of France before heading inland for Paris a couple of stages after the Pyrenees.

If there were any doubts about Merckx's form they were laid to rest with the 7 kilometers of the Prologue, which Merckx won. His very loyal teammate, Joseph Bruyère, was third at only 8 seconds behind. The next day in the first road stage, Bruyère got in the winning break with Herman van Springel (who did all the work) and Ercole Gualazzini (who won the sprint). Because of his excellent Prologue, Bruyère took over the lead in General Classification. It doesn't look as if this was the way Merckx wanted it to play out. From the very first intermediate sprint Merckx was out dueling with the sprint specialists, fighting for the bonus seconds in play. It looked as if Merckx was out to do what had not been done since Romain Maes in 1935, he wanted to take the Yellow at the start of the Tour and hold it all the way to Paris. Van Springel's ambition foiled the grand plan.

Bruyère is an interesting rider. His career was devoted to one thing: helping his good friend Eddy Merckx win races. He followed Merckx from team to team, always riding as hard as he could to help Merckx, never thinking of himself. Merckx said that Bruyère almost never realized how good he was, but when his morale was high, he had the power to pulverize the field.

The second stage was held in Plymouth, England. The entire Tour was ferried in a big, tiring transfer to race on a yet unopened highway. The riders were livid because British Immigration held them up as they tried to fly back to France. British racer Barry Hoban said that he

wasn't back in his hotel until 10 at night. The experiment was suffi-
ciently disliked that it was over 10 years before it was attempted again.

By virtue of the intermediate bonus sprints, Merckx regained the
Yellow Jersey from Bruyère after the fourth stage. It was a tenuous hold:
only 4 seconds separated Merckx from Bruyère. And it was actually
more tenuous than that. Gerben Karstens was second on that stage but
felt that he had been victimized by collusion between Merckx and Belgian super-sprinter Patrick Sercu. Even though they were on different
teams, Sercu and Merckx were lifelong friends and partners during the
winter track season. Karstens felt that Merckx was helping Sercu earn
the points leader's Green Jersey. Karstens was so furious over Merckx's
friendly help that he failed to report to dope control on time. For this
serious infraction, Karstens was penalized 10 minutes. Upset, the riders
threatened a strike over what they perceived as an overly hard punish-
ment. The next day he was reinstated and with the time bonus for his
second place, Gerben Karstens was in Yellow with 2-second lead on
Merckx.

As the Tour moved across northern France and into Belgium and
then back into France the sprinters (Merckx included) fought hard for
the dribs and drabs of seconds that were available. Because the lead was
so close it changed several times.

After unloading several hard attacks that were brought back by a
fast moving field, Merckx won a 55-man sprint for stage 7. With the
time bonuses he had accrued Merckx was now in Yellow. The rankings
stayed basically unchanged as the Tour brought the riders to the base of
the Alps. The General Classification at this point shows that things had
been staying very close and that sprinters Karstens and Hoban had been
doing very well:

1. Eddy Merckx
2. Gerben Karstens @ 13 seconds
3. Joseph Bruyère @ 50 seconds
4. Barry Hoban @ 1 minute 4 seconds
5. Michel Pollentier @ 1 minute 10 seconds

The first day in the Alps, stage 9, had 2 hard climbs. At the start
of the second and hardest ascent of the day, the Rousses, all the major
contenders were together. Spanish champion Vicente Lopez-Carril tried

to get away but with several kilometers of hard work Merckx was able to bring him back and in the process, dropped all but 11 others. The big surprise was 38-year old Raymond Poulidor's escape near the summit. He was caught on the descent but it was a shock to see the man who had first ridden the Tour in 1962 drop Merckx, Joaquim Agostinho and Italian climbing specialist Wladimiro Panizza. Merckx won the stage but it required grit to chase down the attacks. It appeared that even with several of the best stage racers sitting this Tour out, the others were in no mood to let Merckx have anything without a fight. On the other hand, Merckx was clearly willing to battle for every scrap on the table.

The next day was a variation on the same theme. There was 1 major climb, the 1,500 meter Mont du Chat. Lopez-Carril's teammate Gonzalo Aja took flight near the summit with Poulidor hot on his wheel. Poulidor caught Aja on the descent but they couldn't keep Merckx from joining them near the finish. Merckx, being by far the superior sprinter, took the stage.

The riders had a day of rest before tackling the hardest Alpine stage with the Couchette, Grand Cucheron, Télégraphe and Galibier on the day's schedule. The better riders arrived at the foot of the Télégraphe together. The Télégraphe really must be considered part of the Galibier because after the crest of the Télégraphe there is only a short descent and then the Galibier proper is ascended. As the peloton climbed the Télégraphe the best 13 riders of the Tour including Merckx, Poulidor and Lopez-Carril, broke loose. Thévenet was able to get into that group and then faded slowly back, eventually abandoning. Near the crest Lopez-Carril took off with Merckx chasing. The riders came together again and then Roger Pingeon attacked and took Lopez-Carril with him. Again Merckx had to chase but this time with Lopez-Carril's team-mates Aja and Galdos on his wheel. Again Merckx caught Lopez-Carril and again the Spaniard attacked and got a gap. This time he made it stick. Lopez-Carril must have taken terrible chances because he actually gained time on Merckx on the descent. Once off the mountain he raced the final 20 kilometers to the finish line in Serre Chevalier as if he were being chased by the hounds of hell. Cannibal, hounds of hell, it was probably all the same to Lopez-Carril. And he did it! After attacking Merckx over and over and finally getting free, Vicente Lopez-Carril arrived at the end of the stage with a 54-second lead on Merckx who had Galdos and Aja glued to his wheel. Merckx was in an impossible situation. If he were to slow down and avoid dragging Aja, Lopez-Carril would close in on Merckx in the General Classification. Continue chasing as hard as he could and he drags Aja along on a free ride and helps a dangerous rival. No good choices. Pingeon came in $2^1/_2$ minutes later. Poulidor had been dropped and although he had a good, high placing at tenth, he lost 6 minutes, 17 seconds.

The new General Classification:

1. Eddy Merckx
2. Gonzalo Aja @ 2 minutes 20 seconds
3. Vicente Lopez-Carril @ 2 minutes 34 seconds
4. Wladimiro Panizza @ 4 minutes 41 seconds
5. Joaquim Agostinho @ 5 minutes 16 seconds
6. Raymond Poulidor @ 7 minutes 32 seconds

The next day included Mont Ventoux, but not as a hill-top finish. The riders ascended the windy mountain in blistering heat and came together on the descent. A very complex set of time bonuses for the first riders over the summit gave Aja a couple of seconds over Merckx while Vicente-Carril lost a half-minute. The stage was won by Merckx domestique Jozef Spruyt in a small break that escaped on the final run-in.

Across Provence the sprinters fought for stage wins and Hot Spot sprints in stifling heat, racing that didn't change the General Classification.

Stage 15, the first Pyrenean stage, had only 1 major ascent, the Port d'Envalira, famous in Tour history as the scene of Anquetil's famous crisis in the 1964 Tour. Only about 15 riders were with Merckx at the crest of the climb but the real adventure was just a few kilometers from the finish. Right behind Merckx and the others in the front of the break, a crash took down Poulidor, van Springel, Galdos and several others. Galdos, who was sitting in sixth place, turned out to have a hairline fracture in his femur. He was an important part of the Spanish challenge and now Aja and Lopez-Carril would be without his valuable services.

When stages 15 and 16 took the Tour into Spain, Basque separatists bombed some of the team and press cars. Lopez-Carril, who was the Spanish Champion, wore the blue and green KAS colors those days rather than tempt fate by wearing the Champion's Jersey which sported the colors of the Spanish flag, thereby being a target for the Spanish-hating partisans. By the time the Tour returned to France no one had been hurt but it gave everyone a very justifiable scare.

Stage 16 was 209 kilometers from Seo de Urgel to St.-Lary-Soulan/Pla d'Adet. The riders would climb the Porto de Canto, the Porto de la Bonaigua, the Portillon, the Peyresourde and a final ascent to Pla d'Adet. The important riders arrived at the base of the final climb together.

On the lower slope of the climb to Pla d'Adet van Impe's teammate Willy van Neste took off with Spanish Miguel-Maria Lasa, a teammate of Lopez-Carril, rushing off the front to join him (Lasa later came off and finished over 7 minutes down). And then who emerged from the front of the peloton? Raymond Poulidor! Poulidor chased, caught and dropped van Neste and was off the front of the final climb, alone. Back in the front group Lopez-Carril attacked and dropped Merckx who was now looking haggard. Alain Santy, a member of Poulidor's Mercier squad took off as did Belgian rider Michel Pollentier. Merckx dug deeper, struggling to keep the fleeing attackers in sight as the gradient in the final meters approached 24 percent. Poulidor held his lead for a brilliant stage win, his first since 1965, with Lopez-Carril 41 seconds behind. Merckx finished an exhausted 1 minute, 49 seconds after Poulidor. He was still in Yellow but there were 2 more days of Pyrenean mountains to go.

1. Eddy Merckx
2. Vicente Lopez-Carril @ 2 minutes 24 seconds
3. Gonzalo Aja @ 4 minutes 20 seconds
4. Wladimiro Panizza @ 5 minutes 58 seconds
5. Raymond Poulidor @ 6 minutes

Stage 17 had 2 of the more fearsome climbs in the Tour's bandolier, the Aspin and a finish at the top of the Tourmalet. Peugeot rider Jean-Pierre Danguillaume broke clear near the top of the Aspin, which had been placed near the start of the stage. Because the stage was still young, Danguillaume's action elicited no reaction from the peloton. Undeterred by the long way to the finish, the Frenchman put his head down and descended the Aspin as if he had rails instead of wet asphalt under him. His move was wonderfully successful and he finished 2 minutes, 26 seconds ahead of...Raymond Poulidor! Poulidor had hammered the leaders on the final ascent and finished alone. Merckx was over 3 minutes back but Lopez-Carril, also tiring in the final stages of this super-aggressive Tour, could do no better. Poulidor was now in third place:

1. Eddy Merckx
2. Vicente Lopez-Carril @ 2 minutes 25 seconds
3. Raymond Poulidor @ 5 minutes 18 seconds

Stage 18 gave the real climbers a final chance to gain time. In this last mountain stage they would not only have to mount a serious attack that would crack Merckx, but also forge a gap that would withstand 2 more individual time trials totaling 50 kilometers. This was a tall order. After only a few kilometers into the stage the riders went over the Tourmalet. Lopez-Carril, showing some wear and tear, came off but clawed his way back to the leaders. On the final climb, the Soulor, Danguillaume got into a small group, none of whom posed any threat to the Overall. The group was allowed its freedom. For the descent and final ride into Pau, Danguillaume had his rear wheel changed, not because he had a flat tire, but because he wanted bigger gears in order to force the hot pace he needed to stay away. And stay away he did, getting his second consecutive stage win. Back in the peloton all the contenders stayed together, more or less conceding the Tour to Merckx.

The full extent of Lopez-Carril's exhaustion was clear after the stage 19b time trial. Only 12.4 kilometers long, the Spaniard lost almost a full minute to Merckx, who won the stage.

The final time trial contained a surprise. Michel Pollentier, a small rider on the Belgian Carpenter team won the 37.5-kilometer stage 21b individual time trial in Orléans, beating Merckx by 10 seconds. That was interesting but the bigger news was the gap between Poulidor and Lopez-Carril. Poulidor beat the Spanish Champion, described by cycling writer David Saunders as "looking positively ghastly" after his ride, by 2 minutes, 17 seconds. That lifted Poulidor to second place with the huge gap of a single second.

On the final stage to Paris Poulidor's Mercier team was able to help him gain a few more seconds of time in one of the intermediate sprints. Lopez-Carril's team was too tired to defend their leader. The race was Merckx's and Poulidor had another second place.

Merckx's 1974 Tour win allowed him to, first of all, equal Anquetil's 5 victories, but unlike Anquetil Merckx had so far won every Tour he had entered. By winning 8 stages in 1974 he now had 32 stage wins, finally passing the record of 25 owned by André Leducq. He is also the first and only man to have won the Italian, Swiss and French Tours in a single year. Clearly the Merckx of 1969 was long gone but the 1974 Merckx had shifted his tactics, scrambling for little time bonuses, conceding nothing, fighting for everything. This time, it was not in the spirit of tyrannical excess but out of necessity in order to fend off a peloton that no longer feared him.

Final 1974 Tour de France General Classification:

1. Eddy Merckx (Molteni): 116 hours 16 minutes 58 seconds
2. Raymond Poulidor (Gan-Mercier) @ 8 minutes 4 seconds
3. Vicente Lopez-Carril (KAS) @ 8 minutes 9 seconds
4. Wladimiro Panizza (Brooklyn) @ 10 minutes 59 seconds
5. Gonzalo Aja (KAS) @ 11 minutes 24 seconds

Climbers' Competition:

1. Domingo Perurena: 161 points
2. Eddy Merckx: 118 points
3. José-Luis Abilleira: 109 points

Points Competition:

1. Patrick Sercu: 283 points
2. Eddy Merckx: 270 points
3. Barry Hoban: 170 points

**1975.** Merckx was the reigning World Road Champion, having won the title decisively in Montreal the previous fall. While he didn't win any Classics in 1974, he was back to his winning ways in 1975. He won Milan–San Remo, Amstel Gold, the Tour of Flanders and Liège–Bastogne–Liège. He also won the Catalonian Week and the Tour of Sardinia. He was second in Paris–Nice (to Joop Zoetemelk), Paris–Roubaix (to Roger de Vlaeminck) and The Tour of Switzerland (losing to Roger de Vlaeminck by 55 seconds). Merckx wanted to surpass Anquetil's record of 5 Tour wins and there seemed no reason to think he couldn't do it.

Bernard Thévenet seemed to have everything needed to challenge Merckx except Merckx's good fortune. His spring was lower key than the relentless Merckx's but he did win the Dauphiné Libéré and was second to Merckx in Liège–Bastogne–Liège. The win in the Dauphiné was especially notable because he had contracted shingles earlier in the year while he was contesting the Vuelta and yet was able to recover in time to win an important stage race. This would be his sixth Tour. It took Louison Bobet 6 attempts before he could finally win the Tour. Miguel Indurain needed 7 tries before he finally won. Some riders are like bright shooting stars; others need time to grow and mature. Perhaps they might also need other dominating riders to grow old.

Poulidor (whose best major spring placing was fourth in Liège–Bastogne–Liège), Zoetemelk, Ocaña, Gimondi, van Impe and Agostinho came. But there was also a new generation of riders, Francesco Moser, Giovanni Battaglin and Hennie Kuiper among them, who would challenge the old order.

The 1975 Tour was 4,000 kilometers split into 25 stages counting the Prologue and the split days, of which there were only 2. To counter the mitigating effect of this reduction the Tour made sure there were lots of transfers, which the riders detested. Starting in Charleroi, Belgium, the 1975 edition was counter-clockwise (Pyrenees first) with a trip to the Massif Central and Puy de Dôme before encountering the Alps. There was no team time trial this year, the only year between 1962 and 1995 where this occurred.

The Tour shelved the Combine classification and invented a new one. The Best Young Rider would be awarded the White Jersey previously worn by the Combine leader.

1975 brought one innovation. If you will remember, Henri Desgrange did not begin recognizing the top climbers until the King of the Mountains classification was first calculated in 1933. Spaniard Vicente Trueba was the first winner. In 1934, it became an official category and the prize was awarded to France's Rene Vietto. It wasn't until 1975 that the now famous Polka-Dot Jersey was created and awarded. The Jersey's sponsor was chocolate maker Poulain, whose wrappers were polka dot; though another theory holds that Lévitan had seen a polka-dot jersey at a velodrome and it had appealed to him. Zoetemelk was the first to wear the Dots after earning it in the Prologue.

1975's Tour had 140 starters divided into 14 teams. Let's look at the size of the Tour's peloton over its first 72 years. The first Tour where Desgrange had to promise expense money to assemble his field had 60 starters. The trend since the end of the Second World War was a slowly growing Tour peloton.

1911: 80 starters
1920: 113
1930: 100
1939: 79
1950: 116
1960: 128
1970: 150
1975: 140
1986: 210
2005: 189

Young Francesco Moser showed his class by winning the Prologue, 6.25 kilometers over a technical, or more correctly treacherous course, nicking Merckx by 2 seconds.

Repeating his 1974 non-stop aggression, Merckx hammered the field in the 2 races run the first day. He split the pack on the first of them, putting Thévenet, Poulidor, Agostinho, Ocaña and Kuiper a minute down by the time the second day of racing was half over. He did it again in the afternoon but this time Thévenet and Poulidor were alert and made it into the break. Not so Galdos, Kuiper, Lopez-Carril and Ocaña. Moser went with both moves and retained his slim 2-second lead over Merckx. This tenuous situation remained unchanged over the next 3 stages which Merckx mercifully allowed to end in field sprints.

At the stage 6 Merlin-Plage 16-kilometer individual time trial Merckx took over the lead after a clean win. Moser finished 33 seconds behind and Thévenet, Ocaña and Poulidor all lost about a minute. This was looking like another Merckx Tour:

1. Eddy Merckx

2. Francesco Moser @ 31 seconds

3. Michel Pollentier @ 1 minute 9 seconds

4. Bernard Thévenet @ 2 minutes 7 seconds

Previous Tours had shown that once time was given up to Merckx, it was only in exceptional circumstances that it could be regained. Moser was a big man who could not climb with the best, so he presented no threat. Pollentier was a rising star but not of sufficient ability to topple Merckx. Thévenet had already been put on the defensive. The next day Moser won the stage, but in the big picture of a 3-week Tour with the mountains yet to be climbed, the win had no effect.

Before the Tour hit the Pyrenees the riders had their first substantial time trial, 37.4 kilometers over a more challenging, hillier course than the Prologue or the Merlin–Plage ride. Both Merckx and Moser suffered flat tires but Merckx was able to win, beating Thévenet by 9 seconds. Merckx acknowledged the quality of Thévenet's ride, making it clear that the Frenchman presented a real danger.

Stage 10 was the first climbing day with the Soulor and the smaller Esquillot. All of the good riders finished together (including Moser) 8 seconds behind Gimondi. The next day showed no repeat of that equipoise. With the Tourmalet, Aspin and the Pla d'Adet the race would be seriously engaged. Van Impe was first over the first 2 climbs, ambitious to win not only the Climbers' points but the stage itself. By the time the lead riders reached the base of the Pla d'Adet ascent there were only 8 left to contest the final assault. Thévenet, sensing that this was the moment, attacked. Merckx closed up to him only to have Zoetemelk take off. Thévenet raced after him, dropping Merckx in the process. Zoetemelk was well and truly gone and Thévenet couldn't close the gap, finishing 6 seconds behind the Dutchman. The pack had been tossed and gored. Merckx and van Impe finished about a minute down. Others had their Tour hopes shattered with the first hard day of climbing. Ocaña lost $2^1/_2$ minutes, Gimondi $5^1/_2$, Poulidor 6, Moser 11 and van Springel, who came so close to winning the 1968 Tour, lost 14 minutes.

Thévenet was indeed a dangerous man. This Tour was not turning out to be a Merckx walkover. The new General Classification with the Pyrenean climbing completed:

1. Eddy Merckx
2. Bernard Thévenet @ 1 minute 31 seconds
3. Joop Zoetemelk @ 3 minutes 53 seconds
4. Lucien van Impe @ 5 minutes 18 seconds
5. Luis Ocaña @ 6 minutes 43 seconds

The Tour moved to the Massif Central. The thirteenth stage with several second and third category climbs didn't affect the Merckx-Thévenet equation but most of the others were scattered back down the hillsides. Luis Ocaña and young Italian hope Giovanni Battaglin, both suffering with knee problems, abandoned.

Stage 14 with its finish at the top of Puy de Dôme completely changed the race, but its effect wouldn't become apparent for a couple of days. With 4 kilometers to go van Impe and Thévenet dropped Merckx. A couple of hundred meters from the summit a spectator standing in the crowd jumped out and punched the lone, chasing

Stage 14: Lucien van Impe and Thévenet have left Merckx about a minute back on Puy de Dôme.

Merckx hard in the gut (to be precise, Merckx says liver). Up ahead van Impe won the stage with Thévenet 15 seconds behind him. Astonishingly, Merckx was able to continue and finish only 49 seconds behind van Impe and therefore keep his Yellow Jersey. After crossing the line, in agony from the assault, Merckx vomited. He then rode down the hill and identified his assailant who, believe it or not, said it was an accident. Merckx still had a 58-second lead on Thévenet. To deaden the agony Merckx was forced to take painkillers. Worse, he was given blood thinners to counter the after-effects of the blow. The result of this to a man who was being put in continual difficulty by a capable Thévenet was, as we shall see, catastrophic.

July 13, 1975, stage 15 from Nice to Pra-Loup was historic. The previous day was a rest day, plenty of time to contemplate the 6 highly categorized mountains that would comprise the 5,266 meters of climbing the stage promised.

A warm, but not attacking tempo had been ridden all day until the fourth of the 6 climbs, the Col des Champs, where Thévenet initiated several brutal attacks but Merckx was able to come back each time. Because of the extreme difficulty of the constant, hard climbing, only the best riders of the age remained for the final kilometers up the penultimate climb, the Allos: Merckx, Thévenet, van Impe, Zoetemelk and Gimondi.

Merckx attacked 800 meters from the summit and no one could withstand his acceleration. The Belgian flew down alone over the primitive, partially washed out road. Gimondi followed. Trying to keep up with the flying Italian, the Bianchi team car flew off the side of the road, spewing its mechanic who ended up in a tree. The driver, Giancarlo Ferretti (most recently the boss of the Fassa Bortolo team) survived the crash when his car fell 150 meters down the hillside.

Back to the race.

Zoetemelk and van Impe came racing down the Allos, then 2 minutes after Merckx came Thévenet.

Merckx arrived at the beginning of the final ascent to Pra-Loup with a 90-second lead over Thévenet. He started to pound out the final kilometers, looking like the sure winner of the stage and the Tour. And then he cracked, completely out of energy. Merckx says that he went almost instantaneously from a state of well-being to "drunk". He was in a state of failure the French call a *défaillance*. He could barely turn the pedals. Merckx blames in part the medications he had to take after the Puy de Dôme assault. The first rider to come up to Merckx was Gimondi who could not believe what he was seeing. Gimondi went right on by.

Meanwhile Thévenet, who had suffered a flat earlier, was flying. He steamed past van Impe and Zoetemelk and then had Merckx in sight. On the 10% grade Thévenet was in the big ring. The big ring! Thévenet closed the gap and then wasn't sure about how to go about passing the great man. There was a strip of melted tar in the middle of the road. He didn't look at him as he went by, making sure that the strip of melted road was between them so that Merckx could not jump across and get on Thévenet's wheel. That would risk getting stuck in the tar. Meanwhile, in the follow car his director, Maurice De Muer, had no such scruples, screamed "Go on, pass him, he's cooked!"

After passing Merckx, Thévenet kept driving himself hard and passed Gimondi, finally crossing the finish line alone for one of the most epic and famous days in the history of cycling.

The day's results:

1. Bernard Thévenet
2. Felice Gimondi @ 23 seconds
3. Joop Zoetemelk @ 1 minute 12 seconds
4. Lucien van Impe @ 1 minute 42 seconds
5. Eddy Merckx @ 1 minute 56 seconds

Which yielded the following General Classification:

1. Bernard Thévenet
2. Eddy Merckx @ 58 seconds
3. Joop Zoetemelk @ 4 minutes 8 seconds
4. Lucien van Impe @ 5 minutes 14 seconds
5. Felice Gimondi @ 8 minutes 19 seconds

Stage 16 took in the Vars and Izoard climbs. The day after Thévenet's triumph at Pra-Loup Louison Bobet came by to visit the new Yellow Jersey. Bobet had always felt that the Izoard is the climb upon which legends are built. He told Thévenet that he must be first over the big mountain with the Yellow Jersey on his back. Meanwhile,

Merckx may have been down but he was not out and Thévenet knew it. He described his lead of 58 seconds over Merckx as a "puff of air". Having lost the Yellow Jersey, Merckx was demoted to wearing the Rainbow Jersey of the World Champion. On the descent of the Vars he escaped but the race came together on the Izoard where Thévenet left everyone behind, winning alone by 2 minutes, 22 seconds.

But Merckx would not give up even though he had told reporters that after stage 16 Thévenet had won the Tour. Stage 17 took in the Madeleine, the Aravis, the Colombière and finished with the Avoriaz. Early in the stage Merckx crashed. Bloody and in pain, slightly disoriented, he continued, attacking and fighting every kilometer along the way. He came in third, beating Zoetemelk and Thévenet by 2 seconds.

After the stage was over it was determined that Merckx's cheekbone and jaw were broken. He soldiered on, unwilling to give up. He could only take liquid food, his broken face bones making it impossible for him to chew solid food. In later years, Merckx said that he regretted not abandoning the 1975 Tour.

Stage 18 was a 40-kilometer mountain time trial. While van Impe won on his favorite turf, it is notable that Merckx was third, beating Thévenet by 15 seconds.

From then on it was just a few stages to Paris and the acclaim the French gave their hero, the first French winner since Pingeon in 1967. This was the first time the Tour ended on the Champs Elysées, ending the Tour's long history of finishing at velodromes. From 1903 until 1967 the Tour ended at the *Parc des Princes*. Then from 1968 to Merckx's 1974 victory it ended at the Municipal Velodrome, usually referred to as the "*Cipalé*".

To me, 1975 was Merckx's greatest Tour. Winning in 1969 when everything was perfect, when he had the finest, strongest, most powerful body in the world was impressive. After he crashed in Blois and he had to work harder to win, he might have been less of an athlete but he was a finer racer. In 1975, when everything went wrong, it was his character that was indomitable and admirable and showed that he was truly a great racer and a great man.

For all the bad luck, between assaults and broken bones, Merckx still ended up in second place in the overall General Classification of the 1975 Tour, only 2 minutes, 47 seconds behind Thévenet and over 2 minutes ahead of Lucien van Impe. This was the first and last Tour ride by Francesco Moser. Moser would go on to win the Giro, a host of classics, the World Championships and the World Hour Record. But the Tour didn't suit the Italian, just as it was a bad fit for Binda, Girardengo and so many other great Italian racers.

Had Merckx not been assaulted or crashed, in other words, had he raced healthy, would he have won the 1975 Tour de France? This is always a difficult question because stage racers usually expend only enough effort to win. They always try to keep some energy in reserve. Clearly the Merckx of the early 1970's was gone, but even dosed with painkillers and blood thinners and with a broken jaw, Thévenet could not take 3 minutes out of the wounded Belgian lion. The race goes to the strongest man who does not suffer catastrophic misfortune so there is no reason to minimize Thévenet's win, but I believe a healthy Merckx would have been the victor. As our history progresses we'll see that Thévenet's win was acquired at a terrible moral and physical cost. It was in the 1970s that the use of steroids gave the racers the ability to train harder, recover more quickly and ride faster. Like the use of amphetamines in the 1950s and 1960s it was a devil's bargain.

Final 1975 Tour de France General Classification:

1. Bernard Thévenet (Peugeot-BP): 114 hours 35 minutes 31 seconds
2. Eddy Merckx (Molteni) @ 2 minutes 47 seconds
3. Lucien van Impe (Gitane-Campagnolo) @ 5 minutes 1 second
4. Joop Zoetemelk (Gan-Mercier) @ 6 minutes 42 seconds
5. Vicente Lopez-Carril (KAS) @ 19 minutes 29 seconds
6. Felice Gimondi (Bianchi) @ 23 minutes 5 seconds
7. Francesco Moser (Filotex) @ 24 minutes 13 seconds

Climbers' Competition:

1. Lucien van Impe: 285 points
2. Eddy Merckx: 206 points
3. Joop Zoetemelk: 171 points

Points Competition:

1. Rik van Linden: 342 points
2. Eddy Merckx: 240 points
3. Francesco Moser: 199 points

The press caravan in 1975 had an American member for the first time—our friend Owen Mulholland.

# Chapter 3

## 1976–1982. Bernard Hinault is masterful in a Tour era deeply troubled by rampant doping and the Tour's declining financial position

**1976.** Eddy Merckx started 1976 by winning Milan–San Remo for a seventh time. He also won the Catalonian week. But that was it for Merckx in the win column for spring in 1976. He managed a second place in the Tirreno–Adriatico stage race, but only sixth place in Paris–Roubaix and Liège–Bastogne–Liège. In the Giro, he came in eighth. Not able to find his usual form and needing surgery for saddle-sores, he did not enter the 1976 Tour. There would be no rematch between Bernard Thévenet and Eddy Merckx that year.

There were plenty of other fine young cannibals, however. Bernard Thévenet went to the Tour fresh off a win in the Dauphiné Libéré. Luis Ocaña, looking for another shot at glory, had come in second in the Vuelta and fourth in Paris–Nice.

Joop Zoetemelk was the odds-on favorite. He won Flèche Wallonne and had high placings in the Dauphiné Libéré, Amstel Gold and the Tour of the Mediterranean. He had been second in the Tour in 1970 and 1971 and had never finished worse than fifth.

Every Tour is different. Each year the cast of players changes slightly as older racers retire and new young men with fresh ambitions arrive. The route changes each year as well and with differing emphasis on flat roads, time trials or mountains, different racers can find some years suit their talents more than others. The 1976 Tour was clockwise, starting on France's west coast, circling north up to Belgium before heading south for the Alps. There the 1976 Tour departed from tradition. Normally after one of the 2 major mountain ranges is ridden there are several transition stages before the hard climbing resumes. This year there were 5 days of climbing in the east, starting in the Vosges in stage 7 and ending in stage 11. Then there was a rest day before 3 very hard days in the Pyrenees. That was 8 days in a row of mountains. If that weren't enough, stage 20 finished at the top of the Puy de Dôme. Importantly, 5 of the mountain stages ended with hilltop finishes. This is a huge advantage to smaller riders who don't have the power to maintain a time advantage gained on a climb through a long descent and flat roll-in to a distant finish line. No wonder Lucien van Impe announced that he would be riding this Tour for the overall win, not his usual King of the Mountains title. Van Impe's changed circumstances involved more than just having a race itinerary that matched his talents. His previous manager was Jean Stablinski who is often credited with having one of the finer tactical minds in cycling. Stablinski was replaced with Cyrille Guimard who had mounted a real threat to Merckx in the 1972 Tour. Guimard was so recently retired that he was still the 1976 French Cyclocross Champion. In taking over the Gitane-Campagnolo team he remade the squad so that van Impe would have better support. As we'll see in unfolding years, Guimard not only knew how to ride and win his own race, he knew how to get others to ride and win for him.

There was a new comet in the heavens. Belgian racer Freddy Maertens turned professional in 1972. His fantastic sprinting, time trialing and overall strength let him win all but the steepest races. In 1976, the first year he rode the Tour, he won 54 races including the World Pro Road Championships and the Belgian Road Championships. His erratic career was at its peak in 1976 and 1977 before it fell off to almost nothing. Then, in an astonishing act of will, he rebuilt his career and won the 1981 World Championship.

Maertens did not disappoint Belgian fans who were unhappy with the absence of Merckx. From the gun he was on fire. He won the Prologue time trial thumping a monstrous 55 x 12 gear, and then the first stage. Then he won the stage 3 time trial, beating such accomplished chrono men as Ferdi Bracke by 2 minutes, 23 seconds, Raymond Poulidor by almost 3 minutes and Bernard Thévenet by

3 minutes, 32 seconds. When the Tour entered the Vosges mountains he won stage 7. In stage 8, he managed only second to Peugeot's ace sprinter Jacques Esclassan.

With the riders poised to begin their days in the Alps in stage 9, the General Classification stood thus:

1. Freddy Maertens
2. Michel Pollentier @ 2 minutes 4 seconds
3. Hennie Kuiper @ 3 minutes 16 seconds
4. Jean-Pierre Danguillaume @ 3 minutes 23 seconds
5. Raymond Poulidor @ 3 minutes 31 seconds

Van Impe, Zoetemelk and Thévenet were sitting at about 4 minutes behind Maertens.

Stage 9 was 258 kilometers that had the pack ascend the Luitel before finishing at the top of l'Alpe d'Huez, the first hilltop finish there since 1952. Even sprinter Freddy Maertens made it over the Luitel with the good climbers. But when Peugeot rider Raymond Delisle opened the hostilities on the Alpe, Maertens was tossed. From then on Zoetemelk and van Impe attacked and counter-attacked each other all the way to the top with Zoetemelk getting the win by 3 seconds. Poulidor, Thévenet, Baronchelli, Kuiper and the others were what a modern military man would call "collateral damage". They were incidental victims of a relentless shooting war between the 2 best climbers of the time. The result of the day's brawl was that van Impe was in Yellow with Zoetemelk trailing by only 8 seconds. Maertens was third, down about a minute.

The next day was another *mano-a-mano* climbing fight between the 2 leaders. After ascending the Lautaret, the Izoard, and the Montgenèvre, Zoetemelk was again only able to beat van Impe and Thévenet by 1 second. Zoetemelk now trailed van Impe by only 7 seconds in the Overall. The pace was so hard 7 riders were eliminated for failing to finish within the time limit.

The third mountain stage was one of those races in which the peloton just doesn't feel like racing. They let José-Luis Viejo ride away without being chased. His final margin of victory, 22 minutes, 50 seconds, was the Tour's largest postwar solo winning margin. The peloton was content to rest their tired legs. Indicative of the slower pace, sprinters Gerben Karstens and Freddy Maertens took second and third places.

With the Alpine stages completed, here was the General Classification:

1. Lucien van Impe

2. Joop Zoetemelk @ 7 seconds

3. Raymond Poulidor @ 1 minute 36 seconds

4. Bernard Thévenet @ 1 minute 48 seconds

The first stage in the Pyrenees, the fourth mountain stage, was another odd day. Van Impe and Zoetemelk were only worried about each other. They kept an eye on each other and let Raymond Delisle, an excellent but slightly aging racer, get away. Delisle was eighth in General Classification when the stage started. When it was over, Delisle was in Yellow and van Impe and Zoetemelk were almost 3 minutes behind.

The next stage didn't affect the standings. The big guns held their fire. The only notable event was that stage winner Regis Ovion failed his drug test and his name was stricken from the record of that stage. Willy Teirlinck was awarded the stage.

It was stage 14, the fifth of these mountain stages, that made history.

In previous Tours, van Impe had won 3 of his eventual 6 Polka-Dot Climber's Jerseys, in the same fashion as modern riders Laurent Jalabert or Richard Virenque have done it. They would go out early on a mountain stage and scoop up the points in all the early mountains, not always worrying about getting caught and dropped on the final climb by the men seeking overall victory. The Polka-Dot Jersey was generally van Impe's entire ambition. In later years he has said that he regrets those years in which he turned to trying for the overall victory. He thinks he might have had 10 Climbers' Jerseys instead of his 6.

There were 4 major climbs that day. On the second, the Portillon, Luis Ocaña attacked. Ocaña was no longer the dominating rider he had been in the early 1970s, but he was not to be ignored. Cyrille Guimard, van Impe's director, told van Impe to go after him. Van Impe was reluctant: Guimard and van Impe did not completely agree on tactics and goals that year. Guimard told van Impe that if he didn't go after Ocaña, he would run him off the road with his car.

Van Impe took off and caught Ocaña on the Peyresourde, the day's penultimate climb.

Zoetemelk didn't chase him. He may have thought van Impe was chasing some Climbers' points and not really going after the overall lead. And surely by now Ocaña was nothing more than a shell of his former self. Instead Zoetemelk sat on the wheel of the man whose Yellow Jersey was threatened by the attack, Raymond Delisle. Normally this would be an astute strategy, forcing the leader to defend his position. It would have been astute except that Delisle could not close the gap. In fact, Delisle was exhausted and eventually lost over 12 minutes that day. Up the road, van Impe and Ocaña were flying.

Ocaña did the hard work on the flat road leading to the final climb, towing van Impe. Ocaña remembered that Zoetemelk had never helped him in his struggles with Merckx. This was a tough bit of payback.

On the final climb, the Pla d'Adet up to St.-Lary-Soulan, van Impe jumped away from Ocaña and won the stage and the Yellow Jersey. Zoetemelk came flying up the hill, going faster than van Impe, but it wasn't good enough. He was 3 minutes, 12 seconds too late.

The Ocaña/van Impe/Zoetemelk attacks shattered the peloton. 45 of the remaining 93 riders finished outside the time limit. Peter Post, the manager of the Raleigh team asked on behalf of the riders that the Tour management waive the elimination rule for the stage. They did.

The new General Classification with van Impe back in Yellow:

1. Lucien van Impe
2. Joop Zoetemelk @ 3 minutes 18 seconds
3. Raymond Delisle @ 9 minutes 27 seconds
4. Walter Riccomi @ 10 minutes 22 seconds
5. Raymond Poulidor @ 11 minutes 42 seconds

The final day in the Pyrenees, even with the Aspin, Tourmalet and the Aubisque, didn't change the top of the standings. The lions had to digest their kill.

The stage 17 time trial showed that van Impe was a more rounded rider than one might expect. Ferdi Bracke won it but van Impe was able to beat Zoetemelk by more than a minute. That put Zoetemelk $4^1/_2$ minutes behind the Belgian climber with only one more chance to take the Tour leadership, the stage 20 climb to the top of Puy de Dôme. Zoetemelk won the stage, beating van Impe by an unimportant 12 seconds. Impressive, but to no real effect. That moment of careful, conservative calculation on the road to St.-Lary-Soulan cost him the Tour. Zoetemelk was the better climber that year, but van Impe had the tactical genius of Guimard to give him the needed push.

Thévenet had been losing time and at stage 19 he finally abandoned, weakened by hepatitis.

Lucien van Impe won the Tour, beating Zoetemelk by 4 minutes, 14 seconds. It was his only Tour victory and he remains the last Belgian to win the Tour. To this day, he is troubled by Guimard's remarks that van Impe would not have won the Tour without his encouragement and threats. Van Impe says that Guimard talked to him as if he were a child, and after the 1976 season, van Impe changed teams.

Freddy Maertens won 8 stages in the 1976 tour, equaling the record set by Charles Pélissier in 1930 and Merckx in 1970 and 1974.

And Raymond Poulidor? He finished third, 12 minutes, 8 seconds behind winner van Impe. This was the fourteenth and final Tour de France for the 40-year old Poulidor. He abandoned only twice and finished with 3 second and 5 third places. In all those years of riding the Tour from 1961 to 1976 he never spent a single day in Yellow, not one. Poulidor's 8 times on the podium is a record. Zoetemelk, Hinault, Ullrich and Armstrong each accumulated 7, and Anquetil, Merckx and Garrigou 6.

Celestino Vercelli, riding with G.B. Baronchelli, Walter Riccomi and Wladimiro Panizza on the SCIC-Fiat team, talked to us about the 1976 Tour: "This was the year the Cannibal Eddy Merckx stayed home. This Tour was won by van Impe. Every stage of this Tour was very, very hard. Just to get an idea of the difficulties we faced, in Bordeaux, in incredibly hot weather, we raced 3 stages the same day. In the evening in the hotel (hotel is a big word for the place we stayed), we slept in big rooms together. I was running a high temperature, I was very tired and hot. I don't have words for that day on the bike.

"When we were riding the Pyrenean stages, the asphalt melted. You can imagine the huge difficulties we faced riding in the mountains in the soft asphalt. In the descent the situation was better with the tires holding the soft road very well. The big problem was the difficulty in removing the asphalt from our legs in the evening."

Final 1976 Tour de France General Classification:

1. Lucien van Impe (Gitane-Campagnolo): 116 hours 22 minutes 23 seconds

2. Joop Zoetemelk (Gan-Mercier) @ 4 minutes 14 seconds

3. Raymond Poulidor (Gan-Mercier) @ 12 minutes 8 seconds

4. Raymond Delisle (Peugeot) @ 12 minutes 17 seconds

5. Walter Riccomi (SCIC) @ 12 minutes 39 seconds

Climbers' Competition:

1. Giancarlo Bellini: 170 points

2. Lucien van Impe: 169 points

3. Joop Zoetemelk: 119 points

Points Competition:

1. Freddy Maertens: 293 points

2. Pierino Gavazzi: 140 points

3. Jacques Esclassan: 128 points

**1977**. The Tour maintained its 4,000 kilometer length, this year 4,096 to be exact. There were 5 split stages and 7 transfers to sap the riders' strength. The Tour organizers are always tinkering with their Tour and in 1977 they decided to de-emphasize climbing after 1976's 8 back-to-back mountain stages. From a total of 5 the number of hilltop finishes was reduced to only 2. In addition, the individual time trial kilometers were increased from 89.8 to 105.2. An all-rounder with a powerful team to protect him on the flatter stages would find favor on this route. The rider who most completely fit that description was Bernard Thévenet with his black and white clad Peugeot team. Foreshadowing the disrepute that the 1977 Tour has, Thévenet was penalized for a positive dope test in the Paris–Nice stage race held in March.

The Tour's favorites were easy to ascertain. Thévenet, of course, was at the top of the list. Van Impe planned to try for a second win even though the course was less suited to his talents than the year before. Merckx was back for his last Tour. His 1977 spring added no major international victories to his palmares. The Miko-Mercier team had 2 contenders, Joop Zoetemelk and Raymond Delisle, who had moved from Peugeot. The TI-Raleigh team had Hennie Kuiper, 1975 World Road Champion and winner of the 1976 Tour of Switzerland.

Raleigh also had Dietrich "Didi" Thurau, who had turned professional late in 1974. He was part of the magnificent West German pursuit machine that dominated the sport at the time. He was hailed as a god by German cycling fans looking for a new Rudi Altig. He looked the part, handsome with broad shoulders. His first full year as a pro he won 5 races including his National Championship. In 1976 he won 7 races and again his National Championship. 1977 was his year: he won 25 races and had what turned out to be a stunning start to the Tour de France.

The Prologue 5-kilometer time trial in Fleurence just north of the Pyrenees was the perfect distance for one of the world's finest pursuiters. Thurau won it, beating his TI-Raleigh teammate Gerrie Knetemann by 4 seconds and Eddy Merckx by 8 seconds. Thurau's first day in his first Tour resulted in Yellow.

In the first road stage, 31 riders—a group that included Merckx, van Impe, Thévenet, Zoetemelk and Thurau—separated themselves from the rest of the pack. By finishing with this front group the young German preserved his small lead, 4 seconds on Knetemann and 7 seconds on Merckx.

While the 1977 Tour may not have been set up as a climber's Tour, climbing was there and unusually it started on stage 2. The day's 253 kilometers included the Aspin, the Tourmalet and the Aubisque. Thurau's ambitions were not unlike those of Rudi Altig back in 1964 when Altig wanted to be wearing Yellow when the Tour passed into Germany (Altig had to settle for Green that day). This year the Tour would head into Germany for stage 13 and Thurau deeply wanted to bring the Yellow Jersey to his home country. Stage 2 was a huge wall potentially ruining his chances.

On the Tourmalet, van Impe, Thévenet and Hennie Kuiper managed to get a 2-minute lead on a chasing group containing Merckx, Ocaña, Thurau and Michel Laurent. Merckx asked Thurau for help in pursuing the leaders. Merckx, being the superior descender, led down the Tourmalet and working together, they were able to regain contact with the trio on the Aubisque. The stage finished on the motor-raceway in Pau, not at the top of the Aubisque. This descent and ride into town allowed a bit of a regroupment. A lead bunch of 14 riders made it into

Pau together including all of the contenders except Ocaña: Thévenet, Thurau, Merckx, Zoetemelk, van Impe, Kuiper and Delisle. Thurau, a superb trackman, won the stage and dodged the bullet. He was still in Yellow, but Merckx was only 8 seconds back. No one could feel confident with the Cannibal that close.

The next 2 stages in the mountains maintained the status quo. So, instead of unleashing a rapid-fire series of attacks in the Pyrenees the climbers basically decided to wait for the Alps to contest the race.

Stage 5b was a 30.2-kilometer individual time trial at Bordeaux. Merckx, the master of the chrono was expected to deliver a devastating ride that would give him the lead. It did not turn out that way. Thurau took about a minute out of Merckx and Thévenet and almost 2 minutes out of Zoetemelk and van Impe. He now led Merckx by 58 seconds and Thévenet by 1 minute, 25 seconds.

As with many team time trials in the Tour's history, the short 4-kilometer stage 7b race didn't count in the individual riders' times. It was a race for team classification with the riders of the top 3 teams getting small bonifications. Merckx's Fiat-sponsored squad won with Thurau's Raleighs coming in third, costing Thurau 6 seconds of his slim lead.

At this point the overall standings were thus:

1.  Dietrich Thurau
2.  Eddy Merckx @ 51 seconds
3.  Michel Laurent @ 1 minute 22 seconds
4.  Bernard Thévenet @ same time
5.  Hennie Kuiper @ 1 minute 40 seconds

Before stopping in Germany, the Tour detoured to Belgium. Patrick Sercu, whom Merckx called the most gifted and perfect rider he had ever known, won the stage into Charleroi in a 170-kilometer solo break. The peloton came in 6½ minutes later. Not too bad for a sprinter! In case people might have thought that the long break dulled the edge of Sercu's jump, he won the next stage (after a rest day) into Germany in a mass sprint with all 95 riders in the Tour finishing together.

So Thurau did wear the Yellow Jersey into Germany, satisfying the delirious fans who surrounded his hotel, screaming their joy that one of their countrymen was in Yellow. Thurau managed to keep the lead for a little while longer, but the effort so far of holding off Merckx, Thévenet and the rest of the field was starting to show.

Before the stage 15b individual time trial up the Avoriaz, the top 6 riders were very close in time:

1. Dietrich Thurau

2. Eddy Merckx @ 51 seconds

3. Bernard Thévenet @ 1 minute 22 seconds

4. Hennie Kuiper @ 1 minute 40 seconds

5. Alain Meslet @ 2 minutes 9 seconds

6. Lucien van Impe @ 2 minutes 15 seconds

Zoetemelk had the fastest time up the 1,833-meter high mountain but it was only later revealed that he had failed the drug test. He was penalized 10 minutes and lost his placing, making van Impe the stage winner with Thévenet only 20 seconds behind him. Merckx came in at 1 minute, 13 seconds. The tired Thurau was fifteenth at 1 minute, 53 seconds. Bernard Thévenet was now in Yellow, Thurau second at 11 seconds, Merckx third at 25 seconds.

On the stage 16 climb up the Forclaz, Thurau was dropped. He fought his way back and managed to make contact on the last climb of the day, the Montets. Once again, not being a hill-top finish, Thurau was able to get control of the situation and win the sprint. Thévenet was in the same lead group and so stayed in Yellow.

It was on stage 17 that the Tour really sorted itself out. It was a 184.5-kilometer trek across the Madeleine, the Glandon and a final ascent up l'Alpe d'Huez. The Madeleine was a preliminary that had the effect of shelling Merckx who was suffering from dysentery.

Easily escaping, van Impe romped up the Glandon and headed for l'Alpe d'Huez with Thévenet's Yellow Jersey in mind. He was only 33 seconds behind in the General Classification and his Tour win last year had changed his ambitions. Even without Guimard to push and threaten him, he wanted a second Yellow Jersey and was willing to take chances to get it.

The wind was against van Impe as he rode in the valley to the Alpe. This is where he ran into the handicap of being a small man. Van Impe just didn't have the horsepower to drive his bike through the wind the way a larger, more powerful rider could. Determined, he kept on and managed to arrive at the base of l'Alpe d'Huez alone.

This is the ride that Thévenet says was the hardest in his career. He buckled down to work and started to chase the diminutive Belgian climber. For company he had Hennie Kuiper and Joop Zoetemelk. Kuiper was sitting in fourth place at 49 seconds and Zoetemelk was fifth at 1 minute, 13 seconds. At the time, no one yet knew that Zoetemelk would be penalized for his stage 15 positive dope test. The 2 of them sat on Thévenet's wheel and let the man with the Yellow Jersey do the hard work of defending his position. The strategy worked and the gap to van Impe got smaller, finally small enough that the follow vehicles behind van Impe had to pull out. As they did so van Impe was hit by one of the television cars. Knowing that the Tour was in play, van Impe immediately got back on his bike to resume the climb, only to have his rear wheel collapse.

A little bit further down the Alpe, sensing victory, Kuiper attacked and left Thévenet and Zoetemelk. While van Impe was getting a new wheel, Kuiper raced by and then Thévenet passed him. It must have been heartbreaking for van Impe to just watch his chances for Tour victory go up the mountain along with the speeding duo. With Kuiper almost a minute up the road, Thévenet's chase was a desperate fight to retain the lead.

Kuiper won the stage, slowing as he crossed the line, and Thévenet came in 41 seconds later. Thévenet was still in Yellow by the skin of his teeth. Van Impe's loss that day was terrible. He came in 2 minutes, 6 seconds after Kuiper. He surely would have been in Yellow if he had not been hit.

Thurau came in seventeenth, 12 minutes, 32 seconds later.

Thévenet was furious with Zoetemelk and Kuiper who were willing to just sit on his wheel and let him do all the work. He called them *petits coureurs*, little riders. About that day, Thévenet said, "I believe that I never went as deep as in 1977, against Hennie Kuiper on l'Alpe d'Huez. That's the only time in my life I reached my limit."

The devastation wrought on the peloton by the hard stage was made clear when 30 riders finished outside the time limit and were eliminated. Patrick Sercu and Ferdi Bracke were among the dispatched.

Here was the General Classification situation after the Alpe d'Huez stage:

1. Bernard Thévenet
2. Hennie Kuiper @ 8 seconds
3. Lucien van Impe @ 1 minute 58 seconds
4. Francisco Galdos @ 4 minutes 14 seconds
5. Joop Zoetemelk @ 5 minutes 12 seconds
6. Dietrich Thurau @ 12 minutes 2 seconds

Stage 18 showed that the doping problems were perhaps a bit deeper than the public realized. The first riders to cross the line, Agostinho and Antonio Menendez, were relegated after testing positive. Merckx, coming in third, was awarded the stage victory.

Thévenet won the stage 20 time trial, Kuiper's only real chance to take the lead. Instead of gaining time on the Frenchman, Kuiper now lost 28 seconds. Barring misfortune, this put the race out of the Dutchman's reach.

Thurau won the final day's time trial, showing the depth and the talent he had, but Thévenet was only 6 seconds slower. Kuiper lost another 12 seconds to the Frenchman who in 1975 had begun a renaissance of French Tour riding that would last a decade.

This was Merckx's last Tour de France. In 1978 he rode only 5 races, winning none of them. The great man had worn himself out after entering about 1,800 races and winning over 500 of them.

Final 1977 Tour de France General Classification:
1. Bernard Thévenet (Peugeot-Esso): 115 hours 38 minutes 30 seconds
2. Hennie Kuiper (TI-Raleigh) @ 48 seconds
3. Lucien van Impe (Lejeune) @ 3 minutes 32 seconds
4. Francisco Galdos (KAS) @ 7 minutes 45 seconds
5. Dietrich Thurau (TI-Raleigh) @ 12 minutes 24 seconds
6. Eddy Merckx (Fiat) @ 12 minutes 38 seconds

Climbers' Competition:
1. Lucien van Impe: 244 points
2. Hennie Kuiper: 174 points
3. Pedro Torres: 144 points

Points Competition:

1. Jacques Esclassan: 236 points
2. Giacinto Santambrogio: 140 points
3. Dietrich Thurau: 137 points

In the 1977 Tour, doping was really beginning to rear its ugly head. Or, it would be more correct to write, riders who doped were caught. Ocaña, Zoetemelk, Agostinho and Menendez failed dope tests during the Tour. As noted earlier, winner Bernard Thévenet had failed a drug test in Paris–Nice that spring. This was a strange time when it seemed that the drug rules were not enforced fairly. You will note that there were no Frenchmen in the above list of riders caught doping in the Tour. Mysterious rumors circulated about another 3 or 4 riders who had also failed their tests.

Thévenet would pay a very high price for his drug taking. That winter he checked himself into a hospital because his cortisone use had severely damaged his liver. He went public with his misdeeds and moreover, said that doping in the peloton was common. For this he was severely criticized by the press, by his fellow riders, and by his sponsor Peugeot.

This would probably be a good time to stop and look at the bikes of the era. I had the good fortune to get a Team Raleigh bike built in what I believe was the shop of Jan Legrand. I think it is indicative of the bikes of the time. I am going on memory here, so please forgive any errors.

The frame was Reynolds 531 steel. The bike, being Dutch, was heavier than the normal 21-pound racing bike of the era. It was lugged with a 25mm diameter top tube and a 28mm downtube. Tubing of that time for most uses was drawn to 0.6mm thickness in the center of the tubes and 0.9 at the butts. I assume my bike had slightly thicker tubing. The frame was fitted with short Campagnolo horizontal adjustable dropouts. It had no chrome.

The groupset was Campagnolo Super Record.

The wheels were 32-spoke laced on to Martano rims. Its tires were Clement Strada 66 cotton cold-treated tubulars.

Thévenet's bikes were not of the same class. The Peugeot team that he rode for were issued stock Peugeot bikes. The frames were of

531 like the Raleighs, but the workmanship was rather inferior. Merckx, who rode for Peugeot early in his career, said that the Peugeot bikes rode and handled like dogs. Like many champions, he had other builders supply him with bikes that were then painted and decaled with the sponsor's name. Instead of crisp Campagnolo side-pulls, they used Mafac centerpull brakes that had been updated only slightly since the 1950s.

The Simplex Super LJ derailleur set was certainly up to the standards of the time, superior in their shifting to the Campagnolo. The hubs, Maillard, were not that well made, their axles being prone to breaking.

The Stronglight crankset was pretty and shiny. But as anyone who rode one in competition could tell you, the spider was very flexible. It was easy to make the chain rub against the derailleur under even modest effort. The Maillard pedals were also inferior having poor bearings and fragile axles.

And with that machine, one that any weekend duffer today would shun with horror, Thévenet won 2 Tours de France. It's the legs.

**1978.** At 3,908 kilometers, the 1978 Tour was a little shorter than previous Tours of the 1970s. It had only 2 split stages and 2 rest days but it was loaded with transfers. Almost half the stages started in a different city than the previous day's finish. The delay in getting to the evening's hotel made life hard on the exhausted racers who wanted nothing more than to get a massage, dinner and a good night's sleep. Anger had been brewing for years. The 1977 Paris–Nice stage race had been marred by a rider's strike over abusive scheduling by the race promoter. The Tour was courting the same trouble with its 1978 route.

The Merckx-Thévenet era was over even though Thévenet would continue riding the Tour until 1981. 1978 marks the beginning of the Bernard Hinault regime. Hinault's nickname, *Le Blaireau* (The Badger) is apt. Hinault always seemed to be a man with a clenched jaw, fighting, full of aggression. Hinault said that his solution for those times when he didn't feel good in a race was to attack. Hinault was a complete rider, able to climb, sprint and time trial. He raced classics, stage races, national and world championships and won them all. He was the last of the breed.

Coming to the 1978 Tour, he was only 23 years old, yet his accomplishments to date were admirable. The year before, Hinault had won Liège–Bastogne–Liège, Ghent–Wevelgem and the Grand Prix des Nations. He also had the Dauphiné Libéré, the 1977 Vuelta a España and French Road Championship in his palmares. This was a list of wins that most professionals would call an excellent career and Hinault was just getting started. In addition to being the most gifted rider of his age, he had Cyrille Guimard, the most tactically astute man in the business, for his director.

Besides Hinault, the 1978 Tour was loaded with potential winners. Zoetemelk, the true "Eternal Second" (he came in second in the Tour 5 times) was again riding in the pink, purple and white of Miko-Mercier. Hennie Kuiper, who had forced Thévenet to dig so deeply on l'Alpe d'Huez the year before, had the strongest team behind him in the Peter Post-directed Raleigh squad. Van Impe moved over to C&A, the company that took over sponsorship of Merckx's team. Peugeot, with a weakened Thévenet, had no real alternative. Their Michel Laurent had been hailed as the great new hope of French riding, but he couldn't fulfill his nation's ambitions.

The 1978 Tour started in Leiden, Holland with the Prologue being held in a torrential rain storm. Not surprisingly, the top 4 places of the time trial were taken by Dutch riders: Jan Raas, Gerrie Knetemann, Zoetemelk and Kuiper. All but Zoetemelk rode for TI-Raleigh.

Because of the appalling weather conditions during the Prologue the directors of the teams held a meeting. They agreed to petition the Tour management to have the results of the Prologue not count towards the General Classification. All of the directors, that is, except the expected holdout, TI-Raleigh's Peter Post. His men had excelled in the tough conditions in their home country and had the most to lose. The Tour agreed to the directors' request. The results stood, but they would not be used in calculating the overall standings.

To make TI-Raleigh even unhappier, Jan Raas, winner of the Prologue, was denied the Yellow Jersey for the start of the first stage. With the change in the use of the Prologue times, it was planned to have last year's winner, Bernard Thévenet, don the Yellow Jersey for the first stage. Thévenet declined the privilege.

The Raleighs started the morning road stage full of anger. They hammered through the day's terrible weather. Jan Raas was able to get clear of the field and elude a speeding Freddy Maertens to win the stage and finally able to put on his Yellow Jersey with a tiny 1-second lead over Maertens. Raas said that if he never won another race, he was going to win this one.

The stage 4 team time trial was a long 153 kilometers. The Raleigh team, bursting with talent, buried themselves to win it and put their Klaus-Peter Thaler in Yellow. Because Thévenet had crashed and the team had missed their feed, Peugeot finished 13 minutes slower than Raleigh. As was the usual practice during that era, the Tour's rules that year did not apply the team time trial times to the individual riders' General Classification. Small time bonuses were awarded to the winning teams, minimizing the stage's damage.

Stage 8 was the first real test of the riders seeking overall victory, a 59.3-kilometer individual time trial. Young Bernard Hinault won the stage, beating Merckx's former right-hand man and good friend Joseph Bruyère by 34 seconds and Freddy Maertens by almost a minute. Bruyère of the C&A team was now in Yellow and Hinault had lifted himself to fourth place in the General Classification.

During the time trial Merckx rode in the C&A team car following his good friend Bruyère screaming "Allez, Joseph! Allez!" while beating on the side of the car door. How could anyone not do well with the great man yelling encouragement? Normally, in a time trial like this over rolling country with a pair of category-4 climbs, Bernard Thévenet would be in the top 5. His continuing health problems from doping were apparent with his twenty-second place in the stage at 4 minutes, 37 seconds.

At the end of stage 9, before the start of the climbing in the Pyrenees, the General Classification stood thus:

1. Joseph Bruyère
2. Jacques Bossis @ 2 minutes 7 seconds
3. Gerrie Knetemann @ 2 minutes 56 seconds
4. Bernard Hinault @ 3 minutes 32 seconds
5. Joop Zoetemelk @ 4 minutes 11 seconds

In the Pyrenees, Hinault gave confirmation that his climbing prowess was on the same level as his time-trialing. There was some skirmishing on the Marie Blanque during stage 10 but the real contenders all finished together. Stage 11 climbed the Tourmalet and the Aspin to St.-Lary-Soulan. Zoetemelk attacked on the final climb but that day he fell short. Hinault and Mariano Martinez were able to catch and drop the Dutchman. Martinez won the stage but Hinault was closing in on Bruyère. Bernard Thévenet, who had lost over 12 minutes in the previous stage and was dropped on the Tourmalet, the first major climb of the day, had to retire from the Tour.

The General Classification after stage 11:

1. Joseph Bruyère
2. Bernard Hinault @ 1 minute 5 seconds
3. Joop Zoetemelk @ 1 minute 58 seconds
4. Michel Pollentier @ 2 minutes 47 seconds

We've noted in earlier years that the Tour had become increasingly abusive of the riders. Trying to get every single sou possible, a day's racing might have as many as 3 stages scheduled. The racers were forced to get up early with insufficient sleep, endure short transfers and still race all-out. In general the conditions were appalling.

The day of stage 12 had 2 stages scheduled. The racers were required to get up at 5:00 AM after an exhausting, monumental stage the day before. Moreover, they had endured a transfer that didn't let them get to bed until midnight. The day's 2 half stages had the riders covering 254 kilometers. Goddet was apprised of a planned rider's strike. He tried to avert it by compromising and offering the day's total prize money to the peloton if they would at least race the final hour. The racers would have none of that. After riding so slowly that they were $1^1/_2$ hours behind the Tour's planned schedule, the riders stopped their bikes, dismounted and, led by Hinault, walked across the line in protest. The people of the little town of Valence d'Agen, where the stage finished, were furious that their 6 months of work preparing the city for the stage finish, as well as the fees paid to the Tour organization were wasted. The police had to protect the riders from the angry fans.

The public, incorrectly thinking that the professional racers were wealthy athletes who should endure a bit of hard work, generally failed to appreciate the striking riders' point.

The stage was annulled and the prize money was not awarded. Tour boss Jacques Goddet tried to blame the team managers for agreeing to the race conditions before the Tour started. Goddet showed no sympathy for the riders' complaints, noting that the race organization had consulted with the team managers several times before the route was unveiled. But it was the racers' point that while their employers had worked with the Tour, they, the riders themselves, had not taken part in the route discussions.

Bastille Day was a 52.5-kilometer individual time trial up Puy de Dôme. Perhaps 400,000 people were on the sides of the road to watch. With 6 kilometers to go, at the beginning of the climb proper, Zoetemelk changed bikes. Hinault's mechanic tried to do the same, but with the crowds pressing on all sides, he hit a spectator and ruined the front wheel of the spare lightweight bike. Zoetemelk won the stage with Pollentier just 46 seconds behind him. And most surprising, Bruyère was only 55 seconds behind. Hinault, after the bike fiasco, came in at 1 minute, 40 seconds.

Big Joseph Bruyère was still in Yellow. No one (Merckx excepted) expected him to do so well on the Puy de Dôme ascent.

Stage 16 was another big, hard mountain stage. The racers would tackle the Col De La République, the Grand Bois, the Luitel and finish at the top of l'Alpe d'Huez. Joseph Bruyère knew that it had been a miracle that he had been able to wear the Yellow Jersey this long. He knew his hours in the lead were numbered. It was on the Luitel that he cracked.

But up the road, little Michel Pollentier was scooting up the mountain. He went over the Luitel with a 13 second lead on Zoetemelk, Kuiper, Hinault and Agostinho. The chasers were slow to get organized. Pollentier kept pressing his advantage up the Romanche Valley leading to l'Alpe d'Huez.

He was able to hold his lead to the start of the hairpin turns of the Alpe. He had a gap of almost 2 minutes as Hinault, Kuiper and Zoetemelk closed in on him. Zoetemelk faltered in the final kilometers. Kuiper could see Pollentier up ahead as the tough Belgian crossed the line. Pollentier was first, Kuiper second, then Hinault and Zoetemelk.

This should have been Pollentier's triumph. He had won a stage so hard people would talk about it for all time and he was now wearing the Yellow Jersey. A bicycle racer could ask no more out of life.

Two hours after winning the stage Pollentier hadn't visited the doping control as every stage winner must do immediately after the race is over. He was finally found and brought to the van with 2 other racers selected for random tests. One of the 2, Antoine Gutierrez, seemed to have trouble producing a urine sample. The wary doctor, suspicious, pulled up his jersey and found a urine-filled bottle with a tube taped under his arm. Pollentier was found to have the same set-up. Pollentier's day in the sun was over. He was kicked out of the Tour.

Pollentier tried to explain that he had taken something for his breathing, but not knowing if it would trigger a positive test, he had tried to evade the controls. Later, it was found that he had taken amphetamines. Those do trigger a positive at a dope test.

This was a sad end of the Tour for a man who I am told by those who know him is a kind, gentle, friendly man who got caught doing wrong. Yes, he was a cheat. Yet, he was immensely talented rider with the worst pedaling style in the pro peloton. Look at any picture of him and he's got his head cocked to one side, at least one elbow out and knees flailing. But he could make his bike go like hell. In 1977 he won the Giro d'Italia, the Tour of Switzerland and the Belgian Road Championships. Before the Tour started in 1978 he had already won the Dauphiné Libéré and again his National Championship. He entered the Tour 3 more times after this, never finishing. Like Freddy Maertens, he trusted other people with his money and they lost it for him. He ended up selling tires out of his house.

To return to the race.

Zoetemelk was sitting in second place in the General Classification when Pollentier was disgraced. Zoetemelk, who over the years had his own difficulties with dope testing, became the Yellow Jersey. He already had 3 second places in the Tour. Was this to be his breakout win?

There was one more Alpine stage and with the crash of Hennie Kuiper (who broke a clavicle) there were now 2 remaining protagonists, Zoetemelk and Hinault, who finished together. After stage 17 and the climbing finished, Zoetemelk retained a fragile hold on his Yellow Jersey.

1. Joop Zoetemelk

2. Bernard Hinault @ 14 seconds

3. Joaquim Agostinho @ 6 minutes 13 seconds

4. Christian Seznec @ 8 minutes 25 seconds

5. Joseph Bruyère @ 10 minutes 25 seconds

He stayed in the lead until the inevitable meeting in the final time trial in stage 20, 72 kilometers of what Hinault did best. Hinault beat Zoetemelk by 4 minutes, 10 seconds and took over the lead. With only 1 more stage, the Tour was his, the result of a careful, measured, controlled effort. This was to be the first of 5 Hinault Tour de France victories.

Final 1978 Tour de France General Classification:

1. Bernard Hinault (Renault-Gitane): 108 hours 18 minutes
2. Joop Zoetemelk (Miko-Mercier) @ 3 minutes 56 seconds
3. Joaquim Agostinho (Velda-Flandria) @ 6 minutes 54 seconds
4. Joseph Bruyère (C&A) @ 9 minutes 4 seconds

Climbers' competition:

1. Mariano Martinez: 187 points
2. Bernard Hinault: 176 points
3. Joop Zoetemelk: 155 points

Points Competition:

1. Freddy Maertens: 242 points
2. Jacques Esclassan: 189 points
3. Bernard Hinault: 123 points

**1979**. The 1979 edition of the Tour had 5 individual time trials totaling 165.3 kilometers and 2 team time trials covering 176.8 kilometers. Previously team time trials had counted only towards the team classification. The stage winning and placing bonifications were all that affected the riders' General Classification. In this Tour the team's real time in the stage counted towards the individual riders' elapsed time. This was a huge benefit for riders on powerful, well-drilled teams like TI-Raleigh and Renault-Gitane. If any Tour might be accused of being designed for a particular rider, this is the one. While Bernard Hinault could race well in any of the disciplines, he was the master of the chrono. The many kilometers of time trialing in this Tour particularly suited Hinault and his very strong Renault team.

The route entailed many transfers. Drawn on a map it looks like little random lines drawn from one point to another, bearing no relationship to each other. Slightly shorter than the year before at 3,765 kilometers with 24 stages it was becoming very close to the present day Tour. While there were many transfers, there were no split stages. 1978's riders' strike had finally gotten through to the organizers. However, the Tour continued to have split stages occasionally until 1991. Since then the Tour has looked for other ways to find money rather than degrading the quality of the race.

There were really only 2 men entered who could be considered real contenders for the Yellow Jersey in Paris, the same 2 who had made the race the year before, Bernard Hinault and Joop Zoetemelk. This would be Zoetemelk's ninth Tour. There seemed to be no lessening of his powers having come second in his first attempt in 1970 against Merckx and second for a fourth time in 1978 when he came in 4 minutes behind Hinault.

The race started off in a predictable way with Raleigh's Gerrie Knetemann winning the 5-kilometer Prologue in Fleurence with Zoetemelk and Hinault tied at 4 seconds slower.

The 1979 Tour didn't have flat or transition stages to get the rider's legs used to the rhythm of mountain racing. There were no preparatory stages before the climbing. The first stage went directly from Fleurence, northeast of the Pyrenees into the mountains, crossing the Col de Menté and the Portillon. With the stage's bad weather making the race dangerous, a teammate of Joaquim Agostinho's, René Bittinger was allowed the stage win. The Tour's lions all watched each other and finished together 45 seconds after Bittinger.

Stage 2 was a time trial up to Superbagnères, a 23.9-kilometer affair climbing to the 1,800 meter high ski station. Winning it put Hinault in Yellow with Zoetemelk and Agostinho at 53 seconds. Hinault ripped up the mountain so fast 5 riders were eliminated from the Tour for failing to make the time cutoff. Sean Kelly's Splendor team was particularly hard hit, 2 of the *hors délais* riders were his domestiques.

Stage 3 went over the Peyresourde, the Aspin and the Soulor. Even with a puncture on the descent of the Aspin, Hinault won it from the 13 men in the lead group. Second place, at the same time, was Rudy Pevenage, who later became famous for being Jan Ullrich's personal coach.

With the Pyrenean climbing completed, the Tour had already sorted itself out:

1. Bernard Hinault
2. Joop Zoetemelk @ 53 seconds
3. Joaquim Agostinho @ same time
4. Hennie Kuiper @ 1 minute 49 seconds
5. Sven-Ake Nilsson @ 2 minutes 15 seconds
6. Giovanni Battaglin @ 2 minutes 19 seconds

Even with Hinault's team taking a surprising fifth place in the team time trial the following day—won by the big, strong Dutch horses of Raleigh—Hinault remained in the lead, but the gap was narrowed to just 12 seconds over Zoetemelk. Hennie Kuiper, riding for Peugeot, says that team director Maurice De Muer made a terrible mistake in selecting very fragile tires for the team's use. Suffering 5 punctures, Kuiper remains convinced that he lost a chance to wear the Yellow Jersey that day since Peugeot finished only 31 seconds behind Raleigh. Further, he wonders if that change to the dynamics of the race set him just far enough back to keep him from fighting Hinault on nearly equal terms.

Hinault kept the lead until stage 9, extending it slightly by taking Hot Spot intermediate sprints. The stage 8 team time trial allowed Hinault, with his powerful, Renault team, to add almost a minute to his lead which was now 1 minute, 18 seconds.

Stage 9, a ride over the "Hell of the North", the tough cobbles of Northern France with a finish in the famous Roubaix velodrome, showed the world what Hinault was made of. At about the 100-kilometer point in the stage Zoetemelk joined a dangerous group of escapees: Thurau, Ludo Delcroix, André Dierickx, Pollentier and Didier Vanoverschelde. Hinault missed the move and had to chase. He flatted. He chased again and was held up by strikers blocking the road. He got through and flatted again. Undeterred he continued the chase while Zoetemelk pressed home his advantage. Hinault came into the Roubaix velodrome in a group that included Kuiper, van Impe and Battaglin 3 minutes, 45 seconds after Zoetemelk's breakaway. Zoetemelk was in Yellow and Hinault was in tears.

Jacques Anquetil commented that by showing such strength in adversity, fighting to regain the escapees and limiting his deficit in the

General Classification to only 2 minutes, 8 seconds with his relentless chase, Hinault had won the Tour. Or rather, on the cobbles while facing terrible luck, that day Hinault did not lose the Tour.

The post-Roubaix General Classification:

1. Joop Zoetemelk
2. Bernard Hinault @ 2 minutes 8 seconds
3. Sven-Ake Nilsson @ 4 minutes 48 seconds
4. Ueli Sutter @ 4 minutes 49 seconds
5. André Dierickx @ 5 minutes 23 seconds
6. Hennie Kuiper @ 6 minutes 38 seconds

Stage 11, in Brussels, was a 33.4-kilometer individual time trial. Hinault turned in an outstanding ride, beating Zoetemelk by 36 seconds. The gap between them on the overall was now 1 minute, 32 seconds with Zoetemelk still the leader.

From Belgium the Tour headed south into the Vosges. Hinault and Zoetemelk didn't start shooting just yet. The only real news was that Italian hope Giovanni Battaglin was found positive for dope and received a 10-minute penalty, properly ruining his chances for a high placing.

The Tour then moved to the Alps where the Tour would be settled. Stage 15 was a 55-kilometer hill-climb time trial from Evian up to Morzine-Avoriaz. Hinault won the stage, crushing Zoetemelk who rode 2 minutes, 37 seconds slower. The difference wasn't necessarily because Hinault was the stronger rider. Zoetemelk's hill-climb was a mechanical nightmare requiring 2 bike changes. All in all, it was probably a fair thing, balancing the karmic books after Hinault's Roubaix stage problems. Hinault was now in Yellow for good. Zoetemelk was 1 minute, 48 seconds behind him in the General Classification. Lest the reader think that Zoetemelk was a hopeless second-rater, the third place in the General Classification was Hennie Kuiper who was behind 11 minutes, 47 seconds. Hinault and Zoetemelk were the class of the pack with Hinault the uniquely gifted racer of his generation.

The next day had 3 major passes, and Hinault was able to extend his lead by almost a minute. While Hinault was taking big pieces of time out of the Dutchman, he was also riding like the older Merckx, snagging little time bonifications in the intermediate sprints. For

Zoetemelk, it was the Merckx nightmare all over again, chasing a relentless, aggressive competitor who would concede nothing.

Stage 17, with the Madeleine, Télégraphe, Galibier and hilltop finish at l'Alpe d'Huez compacted into 166 kilometers ended in a draw for the 2 leaders.

On stage 18, Zoetemelk finally managed to beat Hinault, but only by 47 seconds. Stage 18 had originally been planned to be a trip over the Izoard but road construction had required a last-minute change. The stage started at the top of l'Alpe d'Huez, where the previous stage had ended, went over the Morte and then climbed back up the Alpe.

With the mountains finished, Hinault appeared to have earned his second Tour. Zoetemelk and Hinault had opened up an astonishing gap on the rest of the field:

1. Bernard Hinault

2. Joop Zoetemelk @ 1 minute 58 seconds

3. Hennie Kuiper @ 21 minutes 23 seconds

4. Joaquim Agostinho @ 21 minutes 58 seconds

5. Jean-René Bernaudeau @ 23 minutes 40 seconds

Zoetemelk lost another minute in the final time trial. That was it. Or was it? On the final ride on the Champs Elysées Zoetemelk attacked and got away. Hinault himself went after him, bridging alone up to the fleeing Dutchman. Together they managed to extract a gap of 2 minutes, 18 seconds on the field. In the end, Hinault won the final sprint between the 2 and won the Tour. Paul Sherwen, who today does the Tour commentary on Versus, finished third in the field sprint.

There is a sad epilogue to this stage. Joop Zoetemelk failed the drug test (it was for Nandrolone) on this final stage and was penalized 10 minutes. Even with the 10-minute penalty, Zoetemelk still finished second, so far ahead of the rest of the field were he and Hinault.

Hinault was only 24 years old and had already won 2 Tours. At the other end, third-place Joaquim Agostinho was 37, at the far limit of how old a successful stage racer can be. Hinault's Renault team was far and away the best in the Tour. Hinault won not only the General Classification, he also won the sprinters' Points Classification. His domestique Jean-René Bernaudeau was the best young rider and Renault won the team classification.

Final 1979 Tour de France General Classification:

1. Bernard Hinault (Renault-Gitane): 103 hours 6 minutes 50 seconds
2. Joop Zoetemelk (Miko-Mercier) @ 13 minutes 7 seconds
3. Joaquim Agostinho (Flandria) @ 26 minutes 53 seconds
4. Hennie Kuiper (Peugeot-Esso) @ 28 minutes 2 seconds
5. Jean-René Bernaudeau (Renault-Gitane) @ 32 minutes 43 seconds

Climbers' Competition:

1. Giovanni Battaglin: 239 points
2. Bernard Hinault: 196 points
3. Mariano Martinez: 158 points

Points Competition:

1. Bernard Hinault: 253 points
2. Dietrich Thurau: 157 points
3. Joop Zoetemelk: 109 points

Zoetemelk and Nilsson of the Miko team sported 7-speed rear clusters this year when the norm was 6 cogs. This cost Zoetemelk in 1 wheel change as the mechanic had trouble finding a working replacement. Interestingly, the podium was the same 3 men as the year before.

**1980.** In the last couple of years there had been some important realignments in the team rosters. Hennie Kuiper, second in the 1977 Tour and fourth in 1979, changed teams a couple of times. He had been with the very powerful TI-Raleigh team but Kuiper and team boss Peter Post's relentless, driving management style weren't a good mix. He moved to the DAF Trucks team and then in 1979, he switched to Peugeot. Peugeot team boss De Muer's successful management of Thévenet made Kuiper think that De Muer could turn him into a Tour winner as well.

Meanwhile, Joop Zoetemelk left his old team of Miko and moved to TI-Raleigh. Zoetemelk now had the strongest team and perhaps the most driven and demanding director in Peter Post to help him win the Tour. This was the 33-year old Zoetemelk's tenth attempt to win. He had 4 second places starting with his first entry in 1970 when he was runner up to Merckx. Zoetemelk had also come in fourth twice and fifth once. Like Poulidor and Gimondi, Zoetemelk was an excellent racer who had to contend with giants. His racing started with Merckx, continued with Thévenet and went through the Hinault era. Even though the 1980 route wasn't as mountainous as other editions, Post was pleased. This might seem counter-intuitive given that Zoetemelk was an excellent climber. Post figured that with his team of mostly big, strong Dutchmen, they could protect Zoetemelk for more of the race and he would spend less time isolated in the high mountains. Post takes credit for motivating Zoetemelk, convincing him that his record of high Tour placings and prestigious race wins meant he could actually win the Tour de France.

Bernard Hinault was planning on winning 3 Tours in a row, making him, at the young age of 25, the equal of Louison Bobet. That spring he had already won the Giro with a solid margin of 5 minutes, 43 seconds over Vladimiro Panizza. In addition to 3 sequential Tour wins he was hoping to add the rare Giro-Tour double and join Coppi, Anquetil and Merckx. This would be fine company indeed.

The weather during the first half of the Tour was terrible: cold, wet and rainy. This would have consequences for the peloton in a few short days.

The 1980 Tour started in Frankfurt, Germany. For the first time in his short Tour career, Hinault won the Prologue. He kept the lead until stage 1b, a 45.8-kilometer team time trial. The Raleighs almost always did well in this discipline and they delivered the goods this day, putting their Gerrie Knetemann at the top of the standings. Knetemann didn't get a chance to get too comfortable in his Yellow Jersey because in stage 2, Rudy Pevenage led in the winning 3-man break that included Yvon Bertin and Pierre Bazzo. The trio had extracted a 10-minute gap from the pack, giving the lead to Bertin, one of Hinault's domestiques, second place to Pevenage with Pierre Bazzo in third place. The next day Bertin finished in a small group of stragglers, 15 minutes down. Pevenage was now the Yellow Jersey.

Hinault won stage 4, the first individual time trial. It wasn't enough for Yellow, given the big advantage the stage 2 breakaways still had, but he could surely smell it.

Hinault riding to victory in the stage 4 time trial.

The General Classification after the time trial stood thus:

1. Rudi Pevenage
2. Pierre Bazzo @ 1 minute 4 seconds
3. Bernard Hinault @ 5 minutes 41 seconds

4. Gerrie Knetemann @ 6 minutes 58 seconds

5. Henk Lubberding @ 7 minutes 6 seconds

6. Joop Zoetemelk @ 7 minutes 11 seconds

The next day was ridden over the tough pavé of Northern France in terrible weather. It was 250 kilometers of what Hinault called "those swinish cobbles". Hinault hated this kind of racing even though his power and personal drive allowed him to excel in terrible conditions. He and Hennie Kuiper finished 2 minutes ahead of the field, putting him a bit closer to the lead, 3¹/₂ minutes behind Pevenage.

As the peloton continued to ride hard in the cold, wet weather, tendinitis started to appear in the peloton. It was said that over 50 riders were riding the race in real pain. Cynics thought the eruption of peloton-wide connective-tissue problems indicative of widespread steroid use. High steroid intake weakens tendons because it suppresses the body's ability to repair damaged tissues.

The next day, Hinault himself started to show the first symptoms of tendon problems in his knee (this in no way specifically impugns Hinault, who never failed a drug test). Stage 7a was a 65-kilometer team time trial. Raleigh won again. Ominously, Hinault could not take his pulls in the Renault pace line.

From here on, Hinault spent a lot of the time riding at the back of the peloton talking with the Tour doctor or with his team director, Cyrille Guimard. The press wrote reams about Hinault's knee, all done, in the words of Les Woodland, with the gravity normally reserved for dying kings.

Hinault took the Yellow Jersey from Pevenage in the stage 11 time trial. It was clear that Hinault was not riding at his best. Zoetemelk won the stage with Hinault coming in fifth, a rare show of weakness for the Badger. The day's top finishers:

1. Joop Zoetemelk

2. Hennie Kuiper @ 46 seconds

3. Joaquim Agostinho @ 1 minute 9 seconds

4. Bert Oosterbosch @ 1 minute 12 seconds

5. Bernard Hinault @ 1 minute 39 seconds

That yielded the following General Classification:

1. Bernard Hinault
2. Joop Zoetemelk @ 21 seconds
3. Rudy Pevenage @ 1 minute 29 seconds
4. Hennie Kuiper @ 1 minute 31 seconds
5. Pierre Bazzo @ 2 minutes 40 seconds

Zoetemelk says that at the time he was not aware of the very dire state of Hinault's knee. Later he recalled, "My Tour started badly. I was never really well. But everything hinged on the second week, after Bordeaux, where I won the time trial. Bernard Hinault had an off-day. Normally he was much stronger than me, but he had knee problems. I didn't know he was going to abandon.... I said to myself, if I won the time trial, why can I not win in the mountains? Now I had my chance!"

The next day, the Tour stood poised at the foot of the Pyrenees with Hinault leading Zoetemelk by 21 seconds. Hinault said he would never quit the Tour in Yellow.

Yet, the pain was too much even for Hinault. At 10:30 PM on the evening before stage 13 Guimard interrupted the Tour directors' dinner to inform them that Hinault had to withdraw from the Tour. Hinault and Guimard knew that the next day's menu of the Aubisque, Tourmalet, Aspin and Peyresourde would be far too much for a limping man who was struggling on the flat stages. It was ironic that this was Guimard's duty. Guimard had to be lifted from his bicycle in tears in the 1972 Tour while in second place and holding the Green Jersey.

The lead was now the possession of Joop Zoetemelk. The first and only big Pyrenean day made it clear that Zoetemelk was not going to change his basic tactics. He continued to race not to win; instead he was riding not to lose. This negative, conservative approach had cost him dearly in years past. Now that he was in the lead and probably the strongest man with the strongest team in the Tour to ride for him, the Anquetil approach made sense. He let Miko rider Raymond Martin scamper away for a solo win (Martin was first over the 3 final climbs), but made sure dangerman Kuiper was kept close at hand. He came out of stage 13 with a 1 minute, 10 second lead over Kuiper. Zoetemelk, like Merckx before when he had inherited the lead from Ocaña, refused to wear the Yellow Jersey the first day he was in the lead.

After stage 13, the General Classification:

1. Joop Zoetemelk
2. Hennie Kuiper @ 1 minute 10 seconds
3. Raymond Martin @ 4 minutes 37 seconds
4. Johan De Muynck @ 6 minutes 53 seconds
5. Pierre Bazzo @ 7 minutes 10 seconds

Three days later the Tour moved to the Alps. Zoetemelk chose not to display his sparkling climbing skills, letting Belgian non-contender Jos Deschoenmaecker win stage 16 to Pra-Loup. His concern wasn't winning stages, it was not losing the Tour. 3 kilometers from the top of the Pra-Loup climb one of Zoetemelk's domestiques, Johan Vandevelde, had his gears slip, causing him to swerve and crash Zoetemelk. Cut on both his thigh and arm, Zoetemelk remounted and continued racing up the mountain. He did more than limit the damage, distancing himself from Kuiper by another 16 seconds, increasing his lead to 1 minute, 34 seconds.

The next day, with the Galibier, Madeleine and Joux-Plane, Zoetemelk showed the effects of the previous day's crash, coming off early in the stage. He was protected and paced by his fellow Raleigh-riding Dutchmen who kept him in contention all day. Other riders who didn't have a chance for Yellow in Paris flew up the hills. Zoetemelk was content to finish thirteenth, but a half-minute ahead of Kuiper. By riding carefully and conservatively, he was slowly building his lead.

On the third Alpine day he again let non-contenders fly, but he showed that he had plenty of strength, finishing with Lucien van Impe. Kuiper was clearly weakening, finishing fourteenth, $2^1/_2$ minutes behind Zoetemelk.

With the major climbing finished, Zoetemelk was in control:

1. Joop Zoetemelk
2. Raymond Martin @ 5 minutes 22 seconds
3. Hennie Kuiper @ 5 minutes 35 seconds
4. Johan De Muynck @ 8 minutes 27 seconds

That left the stage 20 individual time trial as the only serious obstacle to Zoetemelk's victory. Held in St. Etienne, the center of what was then a thriving French cycle industry, Zoetemelk won his second time trial of the 1980 Tour, giving him a near bullet-proof lead with only 2 stages to go. Kuiper's fourth place that day was good enough to put him back in second overall.

By the end of the Tour, Zoetemelk had hammered out a commanding lead, one for which there should be no apologies.

Final General Classification of the 1980 Tour de France:

1. Joop Zoetemelk (TI-Raleigh): 109 hours 19 minutes 14 seconds
2. Hennie Kuiper (Peugeot) @ 6 minutes 55 seconds
3. Raymond Martin (Miko-Mercier) @ 7 minutes 56 seconds
4. Johan De Muynck (Splendor) @ 12 minutes 24 seconds
5. Joaquim Agostinho (Puch) @ 15 minutes 37 seconds

Climbers' Competition:

1. Raymond Martin: 223 points
2. Ludo Loos: 162 points
3. Ludo Peeters: 147 points

Points Competition:

1. Rudy Pevenage: 194 points
2. Sean Kelly: 153 points
3. Ludo Peeters: 148 points

Much has been made of the fact the Zoetemelk was an excellent racer, but not a *patron*, a leader, an alpha male. He did not have the commanding authority of Merckx, Hinault, or even his own teammate, Jan Raas. In that moment of inattention in stage 16 when Vandevelde caused Zoetemelk to crash, Zoetemelk was very nice and friendly about the whole episode and told Vandevelde not to worry, that these things happen. Marguerite Lazzell speculated that had Vandevelde crashed Hinault, the same generous sentiments would not have been expressed. Even after Zoetemelk took over the Tour lead, teammates Knetemann and Raas were the team's leaders, giving the riders their directions.

Zoetemelk has suffered a lot of criticism over his victory, saying that it was a gift because of Hinault's departure. Zoetemelk said it just about the best, "Surely winning the Tour is a question of health and robustness? If Hinault does not have that health and robustness and I have, that makes me a valid winner."

Hinault agreed, "There is no need for him to say that he won because I abandoned. That would take away from his victory. My problems were of my own making. It is always the absent rider who is at fault. I was absent and he took my place." Ah, the supreme, generous confidence of a born winner.

The Zoetemelk of 1980, like the post-Blois-crash Merckx, was not a racer at the peak of his powers. Jean-Paul Ollivier thinks Zoetemelk was at his best in 1974, before his Midi Libre crash and meningitis. His 1980 win at age 33 is a tribute to both his determination to return to the highest levels of competitive cycling and his persistence. He rode the Tour a total of 14 times, finishing every time. He ended up winning the Dutch and World Championships, the Vuelta, Paris–Nice, the Tour de France (and was second 6 times), the Tour of Romandie, Amstel Gold and a host of other important races. He was one of the finest racers to have ever turned a pedal.

Hinault recovered from his tendinitis soon enough to regain his form and win the World Road Championships that fall.

**1981.** The 1981 Tour still had 2 split stages, the second 2-race day coming after a long 246-kilometer stage to Roubaix. There were a total of 25 stages, counting the Prologue, and at 3,758 kilometers it was slightly longer than current Tours.

Hinault had a superb spring. Wearing the Rainbow Jersey of the World Champion, he won Paris–Roubaix, Amstel Gold, the Critérium International and the Dauphiné Libéré. He didn't try the Giro this year, being content to reassert his dominance of the Tour de France. Perhaps last year's tendon problems concentrated his attention and let him know that he wasn't bulletproof.

Who was there to challenge him? Zoetemelk was now 34 years old. Van Impe and Agostinho, the other well known Grand Tour men were really holdovers from the Merckx-Thévenet era. That duo had never displayed the ability to take on the Badger when he was on form.

The 1981 Tour started the same way the '80 Tour did. Hinault won the Prologue time trial and aggressively hammered the field in stage 1. He might have gained several minutes if Guimard had not told him to let up and not take chances in the rain. He kept the Yellow

Jersey until the first team time trial in stage 1b. Raleigh won it and the stage 4 team time trial as well. That meant that Raleigh had won 7 in a row of these tests of team power and precision. Also following the 1980 pattern, Gerrie Knetemann was the Raleigh man in Yellow. The 1981 team time trial rules were generous in the extreme to the teams that did well, giving the Raleigh team members a 2-minute time bonus.

Stage 5 was the first day in the Pyrenees, 117.5 kilometers from St. Gaudens to St.-Lary-Soulan. Ever the commander, Hinault led over the Peyresourde. On the Pla d'Adet, Lucien van Impe took charge, leading the remaining riders in the front group: Hinault, the Spanish rider Alberto Fernandez and a revelation, Australia's Phil Anderson. Van Impe won the stage by 27 seconds, but Anderson was able to match Hinault and Fernandez stroke for stroke. Anderson, riding for Peugeot, became the first Australian to wear the Yellow Jersey.

Anderson's glory was short-lived. He had a fragile 17-second lead over Hinault and faced a 26.7-kilometer individual time trial the next day. As expected, Hinault won the stage and reclaimed the lead. Gerrie Knetemann was second in the time trial, only 3 seconds behind Hinault. Anderson acquitted himself very well, coming in third, only 30 seconds slower than the Badger. Hinault, with the time bonus, now had a lead of 13 seconds in the General Classification over Anderson. The time trial was at Pau where year ago Hinault was forced to abandon the Tour. He reclaimed his lead in the same city a year later, making a single garment with a seam in the center out of the 2 Tours.

Over the next several days the race made its way through northern France and Belgium. Anderson lost little pieces of time here and there as Hinault took the occasional bonus sprint and padded his lead. By the time the race reached Mulhouse for the stage 16 individual time trial, the tenacious Anderson was still in second place, but now 57 seconds behind the aggressive Frenchman. The story of Bernard Hinault is always about time trials and this was no exception. Hinault won it, putting another 2 minutes between himself and Anderson.

Before the Alps began with stage 16, the General Classification stood thus:

1. Bernard Hinault
2. Phil Anderson @ 2 minutes 58 seconds
3. Gilbert Duclos-Lasalle @ 6 minutes 37 seconds

4. Jean-François Rodriguez @ 8 minutes 35 seconds

5. Gery Verlinden @ 8 minutes 56 seconds

6. Lucien van Impe @ 9 minutes 38 seconds

Anderson's undoing started in stage 16 with 4 major climbs including the Ramaz and the Joux-Plane. Both Anderson and Kuiper lost $4^1/_2$ minutes. Hinault finished with the god-like climbers van Impe and Zoetemelk. Anderson was still in second, but he was now 7 minutes, 39 seconds behind Hinault. Van Impe had moved up to third, 2 minutes behind Anderson.

Stage 17 was where the dream ended completely. It covered the Madeleine, the Glandon and ended at the top of l'Alpe d'Huez. Blowing up on the Glandon, Anderson lost 17 minutes. Hinault and van Impe finished seconds behind stage winner Peter Winnen. Hinault had hammered out a $9^1/_2$-minute lead over the new second place, van Impe.

Stage 18, the final day in the Alps, was a series of first and second category climbs, 4 in all. Hinault stamped his seal of authority on the entire Tour by riding away on the last climb. As he led the lucky few remaining riders up the first category Pleynet, he made a strong backward look—or perhaps glare would be a better word—at his followers, and with a couple of accelerations rode away. New French hope Jean-René Bernaudeau tried to stay with him, but Hinault was not to be contained that day.

With the heavy climbing finished, the standings had taken this form:

1. Bernard Hinault

2. Lucien van Impe @ 12 minutes 12 seconds

3. Robert Alban @ 13 minutes 22 seconds

4. Joop Zoetemelk @ 15 minutes 9 seconds

5. Johan De Muynck @ 15 minutes 53 seconds

There was still one more time trial, 46.6 kilometers that presented Hinault with another opportunity to further crush a field that could do nothing with the flying Frenchman. Hinault won and took another 2 minutes out of van Impe.

Greg LeMond is often given credit for the revolution in racer pay. He deserves the credit but in fact his influence predates his famous contract with La Vie Clare in 1985. Phil Anderson was and is a natural entrepreneur. Rather than accept the 100-franc pay for holding up a bottle of Perrier at the end of the stage, Anderson contacted Coca-Cola and got them to pay him to hold up a Coke, upsetting the Tour organizers, of course. Since back then riders had to buy their own socks, gloves, and headbands, he contacted Qantas Airlines and had them make some imprinted articles to use. Peugeot figured out that they could do the same thing, so that bit of income was cut off. After the 1980 season Peugeot offered him an increase of $690.00 a month to the munificent total of $1,400 a month. Even accounting for 25 years of inflation, it wasn't much. Anderson was friends with the LeMond family. Greg's father advised Anderson to hire a lawyer to negotiate for him. That created a stink but Anderson's lawyer had a point; Anderson was being offered less than the lawyer's secretary. With professional help Anderson was able to get a fair deal. And, he didn't have to buy his own racing socks any more.

The final 1981 Tour de France General Classification:
1. Bernard Hinault (Renault): 96 hours 19 minutes 38 seconds.
2. Lucien van Impe (Boston) @ 14 minutes 34 seconds
3. Robert Alban (La Redoute) @ 17 minutes 4 seconds
4. Joop Zoetemelk (TI-Raleigh) @ 18 minutes 21 seconds
5. Peter Winnen (Capri-Sonne) @ 20 minutes 26 seconds

Climbers' Competition:
1. Lucien van Impe: 284 points
2. Bernard Hinault: 222 points
3. Jean-René Bernaudeau: 168 points

Points Competition:
1. Freddy Maertens: 428 points
2. William Tackaert: 222 points
3. Bernard Hinault: 184 points

One has to go back to 1973 and Luis Ocaña's nearly 16-minute victory over Bernard Thévenet before a larger winning margin appears. The entire 1981 Tour was a masterful, controlling ride—a then-record pace of 38.173 kilometers per hour—performed by a Bernard Hinault who could do everything. That made 3 Tour victories for the Badger.

Freddy Maertens, who had been so good in the mid 1970s, winning as many as 54 races in a single year, had suffered an inexplicable collapse. He won only 2 races in 1979 and 1 in 1980. Then, in 1981 he came back. He won his third Tour de France points title (the Green Jersey), winning 5 stages to do it, and later that year the World Road Championship. In the remaining 6 years of his racing career he won only 2 more races. Like René Vietto and Michel Pollentier, Maertens trusted others with his money and ended up financially ruined.

Another note about the 1981 Tour. This was the first time in Tour history that an American entered. Jonathan Boyer had been racing in Europe for the top Parisian amateur squad ACBB. He turned pro in 1977. Guimard signed him to ride the 1981 Tour in support of Hinault. Boyer finished a very credible thirty-second in his first Tour. Boyer was very good. He rode 4 more Tours, managing twelfth in 1983. I remember the rare television stories about the Tour in those days, centering on the lone competing American. Boyer would give whiny interviews complaining that it was all so hard. My racing friends would yell back at the TV, "Of course it's hard, it's the goddamn Tour de France." Back then we had no idea how hard it really was.

**1982.** Hinault didn't have his usual long list of spring wins this year. He had only 1 major victory, but it was a big one, the Giro d'Italia, with 5 stage wins (if you count the Prologue team time trial). Hinault still wanted to go where the air was thin and join Coppi, Anquetil and Merckx in the Giro-Tour Double Club. The last time he tried to become one of the immortals, in 1980, his knee couldn't sustain the effort of the 2 Grand Tours and had to retire mid-way through the Tour de France.

For the first time since 1968, the Tour started without Lucien van Impe. His Metauro team was not thought strong enough to ride both the Giro, which it had just finished, and the Tour. Van Impe tried to get a 1-month contract with a team that would ride the Tour, but his efforts were fruitless. Andre Darrigade and van Impe co-held the record with 13 successive Tour starts and completions. Van Impe was not able to take the number to 14 and make the record his own.

The 1982 Tour started in Basel, Switzerland. Hinault won the Prologue and started the Tour in Yellow.

The ever-surprising Phil Anderson won stage 2 from Basel to Nancy, France. He was part of a 6-man break from which he escaped with about 8 kilometers to go, coming across the line a full 4 seconds clear. He got another chance to don and fight to keep the Yellow Jersey. As the Tour headed northwest back into France Anderson kept his lead. Meanwhile, Hinault kept banging away, fighting with Sean Kelly for the little intermediate sprint time bonuses.

Stage 5 was scheduled to be a team time trial, but the stage had to be cancelled after several teams were already on the road. Striking steel workers, who had learned that 1,000 of their fellow employees were about to be fired, blocked the road. Undeterred, the Tour organizers fit the time trial into the morning of stage 9. There, Raleigh showed that it had lost none of its ability to dominate Tour team time trials, winning its eighth in a row. Hinault's Renault squad came in second and Anderson's Peugeots were fifth. Because the times were adjusted according to a system of bonuses rather than applying the real elapsed times, Anderson was still in Yellow. Hinault was stalking him at only 28 seconds back.

Stage 8 presented an interesting question that went unanswered. French Road Champion Regis Clère went away early and acquired a lead of almost 13 minutes. The stage was to end with 15 6-kilometer laps on a circuit at Chateaulin. It was Clère's audacious plan to arrive at the circuit, do a lap and then sit in on the field when it arrived to do its laps. Unfortunately for Clère, he got a flat tire just before arriving at the circuit and had to get his rear wheel changed. The change was done incompetently and his tire rubbed. It took 2 more stops before his bike was right. Too much time had been lost to put his plan into action and he was absorbed by the pack. Would drafting the lapped field have been legal? We'll never know. Frank Hoste, the Belgian champion, won the stage.

The appointment with destiny could not be postponed. Stage 11 was a 57.3-kilometer individual time trial. Gerrie Knetemann, who had so often come within seconds of matching Hinault in time trials, beat him by 18 seconds this time. Anderson came in twelfth, 3 minutes, 5 seconds behind Knetemann.

Stage 14 time trial in Martiques. Zoetemelk loses 55 seconds to Hinault.

The General Classification stood thus:

1. Bernard Hinault
2. Gerrie Knetemann @ 14 seconds
3. Phil Anderson @ 2 minutes 3 seconds

Before the race had ever hit the high mountains, Hinault was clearly in control. The Pyrenees came first. Hinault didn't win or even make the podium of the 2 Pyrenean stages. He just rode as hard as necessary to keep in sight the men who could threaten him in the General Classification. Kelly won the first day in the Pyrenees. The final climb of the second of the 2 stages demonstrates the care Hinault could show in conserving his resources. There were 8 riders left in the front group on the road to St.-Lary-Soulan. Swiss rider Beat Breu took off, but being almost 10 minutes down in the General Classification, Hinault ignored him. The other riders with Hinault, including Zoetemelk, Robert Alban and Bernard Vallet, refused to go to the front, forcing Hinault to lead. With 2 kilometers to go to the summit the attacks started. Hinault just rode at his speed, staying with Zoetemelk, knowing that Zoetemelk had decided he could not win and was riding for second place. And so Hinault played it, generating press speculation that Hinault was weakening. I guess they needed some sort of interesting story to write.

After the Pyrenees was another time trial. This one he won, and with that victory he fattened his already comfortable lead. Here was the overall after stage 14, and the Alps ahead:

1. Bernard Hinault
2. Phil Anderson @ 5 minutes 17 seconds
3. Joop Zoetemelk @ 5 minutes 26 seconds

In the Alps, Hinault again didn't bother doing anything more than making sure his opposition was in sight. So far, he hadn't won any road stages.

Stage 19 was the final time trial and again Hinault won it with Knetemann only 9 seconds slower. Hinault was going so fast at the end of his ride that he covered the last kilometer in exactly 1 minute. That's 60 kilometers an hour!

Normally in the modern Tour de France, the final stage is a promenade into Paris with a furious finale as the race blasts up and down the Champs Elysées. By this time the Tour's winner has almost always been decided. On this day of celebration and spectacle the Yellow Jersey is careful and usually tries to stay out of trouble. But in 1979, Zoetemelk and Hinault had defied that tradition when Zoetemelk refused to lay down his arms in the final stage. He broke away and Hinault personally came after him and beat him in the sprint for the stage win.

In the final stage of the 1980 Tour Zoetemelk was terrified that with the bad weather that year, he might crash on the wet roads of the final stage and lose his best-ever chance to win the Tour. At the close of the 2004 Tour Lance Armstrong finished 19 seconds behind the leaders in the last stage, not wanting to get caught in a stupid crash just before the end of the race.

This year, 1982, Hinault joined the specialty sprinters in their elbow-banging, bike-thrashing rush over the cobbles of the Champs Elysées to the final finish line, beating them all. He had his road stage win, the most spectacular and prestigious of them all.

Tour writers have characterized Hinault's 1982 win as his most effortless. His form was so fine and his opposition so far below him that he seemed almost ordained the winner before it even started. He had at last joined Coppi, Anquetil and Merckx in the elite group of riders who had won the Giro and the Tour the same year. That made 4 Tour wins for Hinault. Only Anquetil and Merckx had more.

Sean Kelly claimed the first of his 4 Green Jerseys. Dutchmen ended in second through fourth place in the General Classification.

The final 1982 Tour de France General Classification:

1. Bernard Hinault (Renault): 92 hours 8 minutes 46 seconds
2. Joop Zoetemelk (Coop-Mercier) @ 6 minutes 21 seconds
3. Johan Vandevelde (Ti-Raleigh) @ 8 minutes 59 seconds
4. Peter Winnen (Capri-Sonne) @ 9 minutes 24 seconds
5. Phil Anderson (Peugeot) @ 12 minutes 16 seconds

Climbers' Competition:

1. Bernard Vallet: 278 points
2. Jean-René Bernaudeau: 237 points
3. Beat Breu: 205 points

Points Competition:
1. Sean Kelly: 429 points
2. Bernard Hinault: 152 points
3. Phil Anderson: 149 points

# Chapter 4

## 1983–1990. A new generation of riders takes over, including the first Tour winner from the New World

**1983.** Who could beat Hinault in the Tour? After his flawless victory in 1982 there seemed to be no one who could topple the mighty Breton. It wasn't who would stop Hinault. It was "what". That spring he won the Vuelta and the Flèche Wallonne. During the Vuelta his tendinitis flared up again. It was the same right knee that caused him to abandon the Tour in 1980. On the eve of the start of the Tour, Hinault announced that he could not start. He had to quit racing and let his body heal or risk irreparable damage. That left his Renault team without a captain. At first they thought they would go for stage wins and perhaps their Marc Madiot or Laurent Fignon could earn the Best Young Rider category. As events will show, they really didn't know what they had on their team.

The Tour was again wide open with a new crop of young riders looking to contest the race. Colombia's national team was invited, bringing in several superb climbers although only the most optimistic believed that any of them were real General Classification hopes. Merckx said that the individualistic racing style in Colombia with its solo breakaways in the mountains made them poor contenders for a high placing. The high-speed early stages over bad roads would sap their reserves and weaken them for the mountains.

Forcing the smaller climbers to drain themselves while trying to maintain a hot pace throughout the pre-climbing stages of a Tour had been a Merckx stage-racing tactic.

Peugeot's Phil Anderson would require watching, having come in tenth in the 1981 Tour, his first. In 1982 he was fifth, wore Yellow for 10 days and won the second stage. In the spring of 1983 he had already won Amstel Gold, the Tour de l'Aude and the Tour of America as well as a second place in the Tour of Romandie. He had 2 weaknesses. The first was his suspect climbing abilities. The second was the crucial problem of team support. While he was Peugeot's number 1 protected rider, being a man from the English-speaking world he couldn't count on the absolute commitment of his team to support him. Those were different days.

It is interesting to note that no one really had the slightest clue as to who would win the Tour. Pierre Martin gathered the prognostications of 8 of the Tour's leading experts including the great writers Philippe Brunel and Pierre Chany. The eventual winner was not on anyone's top-8 lists. The 1983 Tour was truly a cipher to all.

After the 1982 Tour had tired the riders with too many transfers, the organizers promised that the 1983 Tour would have no transfers. The promise was easy to make and difficult to keep. There were several including a long one by high-speed train before the final stage in Paris.

Belgian Eric Vanderaerden won the Prologue and kept the lead until the stage 2 team time trial, a 100-kilometer brute. The Coop-Mercier team won giving the Yellow Jersey to Jean-Louis Gauthier. When his teammate Kim Andersen got into a break the next day and beat the field by 2 minutes, the lead migrated to the Dane, the first man of his country to ever wear Yellow. Meanwhile, Joop Zoetemelk's constant losing battle with the mass spectrograph continued. He turned up positive for dope again and was penalized his usual 10 minutes.

This was to be a Tour in which misfortune played a large part, starting with Hinault's tendinitis. A new super climber, Scotsman Robert Millar, crashed in stage 3 and lost almost 17 minutes. Any hope of a high General Classification for him ended right there. A crash caused by Vanderaerden in the Roubaix velodrome took down Phil Anderson and French champion Marc Gomez. Gomez had to retire. Because it happened in the last kilometer, even though he had to walk his bike across the finish line, Anderson lost no time.

As the racers made their way across Northern France they had to endure stages long enough to remind one of the early days of the Tour. Stage 4 was 300 kilometers, stage 5 was 257 kilometers. Through all of this, Kim Andersen kept the Yellow Jersey. Meanwhile, Sean Kelly had been chasing intermediate sprint bonuses and moving up the leader board. On stage 9 he managed to get the lead, but only barely. Before the stage 10 trip into the Pyrenees, here was the General Classification:

1. Sean Kelly
2. Kim Andersen @ 1 second
3. Phil Anderson @ 39 seconds
4. Joop Zoetemelk @ 1 minute 24 seconds

The first day in the mountains and the only Pyrenean stage was 201 kilometers from Pau to Bagnères de Luchon. The riders would face the Aubisque, the Tourmalet, the Aspin and the Peyresourde. The first 2 were rated as *hors catégorie* and the second 2 were first category climbs. Van Impe led over the Aubisque but it was Robert Millar who won the stage in front of Pedro Delgado. Pascal Simon was third at 1 minute, 13 seconds and became the new Yellow Jersey. Seventh in the stage was one of Hinault's young lieutenants Laurent Fignon, who had decided to go with Simon that day, 4 minutes, 23 seconds behind Millar.

And Phil Anderson? He crashed on the Aubisque and had his shoe come off. He had to undo the double knots (cycling shoes used laces back then) before he could get the shoe back on. Meantime, none of his teammates waited for him to pace him back up to the peloton. He did make contact with the leaders before the summit of the Tourmalet, the second climb, but the effort cost him dearly. Since Kim Andersen, who was the Yellow Jersey, had not been able to follow the leaders, Phil Anderson was the virtual Yellow Jersey. And here's where the suspect support of the Peugeot team comes in to play. Even though Anderson was the virtual Tour leader, his teammate Pascal Simon attacked him. As writer John Wilcockson noted, Simon could do this simply because he was French and Anderson wasn't. With the crash and tiring chase efforts, Anderson finished twenty-fifth, 12 minutes, 41 seconds after the stage winner Millar.

Phil Anderson was demoted to being a domestique for Simon.

In the General Classification Fignon had lifted himself up to second place, 4 minutes, 22 seconds behind Simon.

The General Classification after the big Pyrenean stage:

1. Pascal Simon
2. Laurent Fignon @ 4 minutes 22 seconds
3. Jean-René Bernaudeau @ 5 minutes 34 seconds
4. Sean Kelly @ 6 minutes 13 seconds
5. Joop Zoetemelk @ 6 minutes 21 seconds (his penalty for doping wasn't announced until the end of stage 11)

Earlier I wrote that misfortune would be writ large on the 1983 Tour. Early in stage 11 Joaquim Agostinho took off. Pascal Simon's Peugeot teammate Gilbert Duclos-Lassalle went with him. The Peugeot team, concerned that such an accomplished rider as Agostinho was away, started pulling him back. Agostinho's SEM teammate, Jonathan Boyer, went up front to be with the Peugeot chasers. Not wanting him there interfering with the pursuit, they tried to push him back, out of the way. In the resultant crash, 2 Peugeot riders went down, Bernard Bourreau and Pascal Simon. In his first day of riding in the Yellow Jersey, Simon had crashed and broken his shoulder blade. Simon remounted and with help from his team, finished the stage in sixty-first place, in the same group as Kelly, van Impe and Fignon.

The next 6 stages were an agony for Simon as he kept the Yellow Jersey as long as he could. He really did very well as the Tour went through the Massif Central, losing only a little time to Fignon. He was aided by a perception in the peloton that it would be gauche to attack the wounded man. There was a feeling that eventually he would be forced to abandon.

It was in the stage 15 time trial up Puy de Dôme that having only 1 working shoulder really began to tell. Fignon closed to within 52 seconds of Simon. Simon's performance was remarkable because he had to climb the extremely steep final kilometer of the dead volcano sitting down. Phil Anderson, despite his domestique duties, had so far managed to stay in the top 10 in the General Classification. That day on the steep slopes Anderson lost another 4 minutes, ruining his chances for a place on the podium in Paris.

The new General Classification:

1. Pascal Simon
2. Laurent Fignon @ 52 seconds

3. Sean Kelly @ 1 minute 29 seconds

4. Pedro Delgado @ 1 minute 45 seconds

The sense of entitlement that colors the professional peloton's attitude towards drugs was made very clear during stage 13. Patrick Clerc of the SEM team had been riding under a suspended sentence for refusing (along with Bernard Hinault) to give a urine sample after a criterium the previous year. It was announced that Clerc was the fourth rider of the 1983 Tour to fail a drug test. With this failure his sentence should have been imposed automatically. To protest this potential penalty the riders did a go-slow ride and it's said that Duclos-Lassalle rode up to Colombian rider Patrocinio Jimenez, who was off on a breakaway, and got him to join the slowdown. After trying and failing to talk the riders out of their plans to ruin the stage and desperate to avoid a riders' strike, Tour boss Lévitan capitulated and announced that the sentence had been abrogated and Clerc could continue to ride.

The Pascal Simon drama had to end, and on stage 17 it did. He had earned the love and respect of the fans, but his broken shoulder kept him from participating in the final ceremony of the day where the Tour leader puts on his Yellow Jersey. Facing 6 major climbs covering 223 kilometers and ending at the top of l'Alpe d'Huez, Simon's keeping the Yellow Jersey was out of the question. Simon abandoned after 95 kilometers and 2 climbs and Fignon, who took fifth in the stage, became the Yellow Jersey.

The General Classification now stood thus:

1. Laurent Fignon

2. Pedro Delgado @ 1 minute 8 seconds

3. Jean-René Bernaudeau @ 2 minutes 33 seconds

4. Peter Winnen @ 3 minutes 31 seconds

5. Sean Kelly @ 4 minutes 20 seconds

Because Fignon had already helped Hinault win the Vuelta, Renault boss Cyrille Guimard had originally planned not to bring his 22-year old rider to the Tour. Troubled that Fignon already had 1 Grand Tour under his belt this year, Guimard was hesitant to have him ride another 3-week competition. He didn't want to run the risk of over-racing his wonderful new young talent. With Hinault out of the Tour, Guimard decided that he needed Fignon's help. He put Fignon in the

Renault roster but planned to pull him the minute he looked tired. In 1984 Guimard again had Fignon ride 2 Grand Tours, this time the Giro and the Tour. Fignon had a wonderful 1984 Tour, but could not ride the Tour in 1985, nor could he compete effectively again for years. Perhaps Guimard's original instincts were correct.

There were 2 more Alpine stages, one a time trial. Fignon did not cover himself with glory but he rode well enough to keep Peter Winnen in second place. Under Guimard's direction, Fignon was riding economically and carefully.

By stage 21, the penultimate day of the 1983 Tour, Fignon had a solid lead but had failed to win a stage. A win in the 50-kilometer individual time trial at Dijon let Fignon silence his critics and show that he was a deserving winner. Phil Anderson finished ninth, the best-placed rider on his team.

At 22, Fignon was one of the youngest winners of the Tour. He also joined another exclusive club, those who had won the Tour in their first attempt. The other freshman postwar winners were Coppi, Koblet, Anquetil, Merckx, Gimondi and Hinault.

The final 1983 Tour de France General Classification:

1. Laurent Fignon (Renault): 105 hours 7 minutes 52 seconds
2. Angel Arroyo (Reynolds) @ 4 minutes 4 seconds
3. Peter Winnen (Ti-Raleigh) @ 4 minutes 9 seconds
4. Lucien van Impe (Metauromobili) @ 4 minutes 16 seconds
5. Robert Alban (La Redoute) @ 7minutes 53 seconds

Climbers' Competition:

1. Lucien van Impe: 272 points
2. Patrocinio Jimenez: 195 points
3. Robert Millar: 157 points

Points Competition:

1. Sean Kelly: 360 points
2. Frits Pirard: 144 points
3. Laurent Fignon: 126 points

**1984.** Sports are cruel. *L'Équipe* describes the 1984 Tour as an intergenerational conflict. Fignon at 23 represented the new guard and Hinault, at the ripe old age of 29 was of an older demographic cohort, close to being ready for the ash heap.

Fignon is an interesting character. He was nicknamed "The Professor" because of his scholarly appearance with his oval wire-framed glasses and his time in college. When interviewed in later years about his cycling accomplishments, he is strangely diffident, saying that what he did wasn't terribly important. He's rather like Marlon Brando in this way. In an interview, Brando talked about acting and asked why there was so much fuss about such an unimportant pursuit. Both men had striven for years to become the best in the world at their craft, yet both were often oddly dismissive of the entire source of their reputations and fame. A pose? In Fignon's case, I think not. Fignon is an intelligent, thoughtful man who always had a prickly edge to his personality.

But for a couple of years, god, could he ride a bike, his own oblique, non-denial of drug use in later years notwithstanding.

Coming to the Tour, he was sporting the tricolor jersey of the Champion of France. He came in second in the Giro, losing the leader's Pink Jersey to Francesco Moser on the final day, a time trial. The Giro was clearly stolen from Fignon. The highest mountain stage was cancelled in order to keep Moser from losing gobs of time to Fignon, the superior climber. The Giro organizers claimed that snow was blocking the pass, but pictures were produced showing clear roads. Then in the time trial, Fignon was the victim of another outrage. The television helicopter flew low and in front of Fignon, creating a headwind, while Moser was followed by the helicopter, creating a tailwind. The numerous pushes Moser received from the fans when he was climbing in the high mountains were also ignored by the officials.

And that, in a nutshell, explains why the Giro is only an important regional race and the Tour de France is the Holy Grail of cycling.

Hinault switched teams. He left Cyrille Guimard and Renault and went to a new team, La Vie Claire, which sported very distinctive Mondrian-inspired jerseys. After his knee operation Hinault had told Renault to choose between himself and the team manager Cyrille Guimard. With Guimard's stunning record as a manager, they intelligently made the long-term decision to stick with Guimard. Hinault said that a major reason for the change was the desire to have a greater say in team management. Given the strong-willed Breton's temperament, this is not hard to believe. Further, either Hinault or Fignon had to change teams. It would be impossible for 2 of the finest racers in France to be on the same team, competing for the same victory. That never works, as we will see in a couple of years.

Hinault's spring racing seemed to say that he had not returned with his old punch. The time out of competition while his knee was repaired was not without cost. Returning to the highest levels of sporting fitness takes time. He did win the 4 Days of Dunkirk, but he came in second in the Dauphiné Libéré and third in Paris–Nice. His Classics placings weren't inspiring either.

Round 1: Hinault. Hinault won the Prologue for the fourth time, beating his former teammate Fignon by 3 seconds. Jacques Anquetil said that if he were Hinault, he would not have tipped his hand and let the others know that he was in such fine form by winning something as unimportant as a Prologue. For Hinault, I don't think there was ever an unimportant Tour win.

But wait, who's this at ninth with the same time as Zoetemelk and Stephen Roche? American racer Greg LeMond finished only 12 seconds behind the finest living time trialist and beat one of the only men to ever best Hinault in a time trial when he was at the top, Gerrie Knetemann. LeMond was riding his first Tour this year and was on Guimard's Renault team with Laurent Fignon. Showing signs of first-Tour jitters, LeMond had forgotten the mandatory sign-in and was still tightening his toe straps when the starter finished his countdown.

LeMond had entered his time of glory. The year before he won the Dauphiné Libéré in the spring, and in the fall became World Champion. His victory in the Worlds was a stunning solo win after more than 7 hours of racing. He showed both extraordinary strength and endurance and the ability to read a race. LeMond often displayed a superb understanding of the psychology of the peloton. He could also be caught strangely unaware and flat-footed, a defect that would cost him dearly later in his career.

Round 2: Renault and Fignon. Renault won the stage 3 team time trial. Hinault's La Vie Claire team was a distant seventh at 55 seconds. The stage victory wasn't enough to give a Renault rider the Yellow Jersey, but it put Renault riders Fignon, Madiot and LeMond well up in the General Classification. The Colombian team, inexperienced in the highly technical and precise event, was last in the 51-kilometer stage. Their manager joked that the Colombian team fell apart in the final 50 kilometers.

The General Classification after the team time trial stood thus:

1. Jacques Hanegraaf
2. Adri van der Poel @ 1 second
3. Marc Madiot @ 4 seconds
4. Ludo Peeters @ 9 seconds
5. Greg LeMond @ 10 seconds
6. Laurent Fignon @ 13 seconds

Stage 5 had one of those dopey early breaks that no one expects to succeed, unless success is defined as time on the world's televisions. 3 riders took off in search of TV time: Paolo Ferreira, Maurice Le Guilloux and Vincent Barteau. Ferreira was a member of the unimportant (to this story, at least) Sporting Lisboa team. But Le Guilloux was a member of Hinault's La Vie Claire squad and Barteau was a Renault. The 2 most important teams in the Tour were neutralized because they would not chase down their own team members. Moreover, the politics of Northern European racing had created an intense rivalry between the Raleigh-Panasonic team and Kwantum. This intensity paralyzed them and strangely prevented their chasing the break because neither had a rider up the road and they often, as in this case, only worried about each other. The break's lead grew. At the end of the stage they were 17 minutes, 42 seconds ahead of the listless peloton. It was thought that Barteau would easily win the sprint but Ferreira stunned everyone by crossing the line first.

This gave the crafty Guimard another card to play. His Vincent Barteau was now the Yellow Jersey. Le Guilloux was 1 minute, 33 seconds behind Barteau. Round 3 to Guimard.

Stage 6 was a sprinter's stage but it did have a lasting effect. Sean Kelly threw an elbow at Gilbert Glaus in the sprint and was relegated to one-hundred-fortieth place. The loss of the second-place points in the Green Jersey competition cost him dearly. At the end of the Tour, Frank Hoste ended up beating Kelly by only 4 points for the Green Jersey. With a cleaner sprint in stage 6 Kelly would have had the 1984 Green Jersey in his collection.

The first real contest to see who was ready to race was the 67-kilometer individual time trial of stage 7. Riding better than he had dared hope, Fignon beat Hinault where he lived, winning the stage and putting Hinault another 49 seconds back. The General Classification was already starting to sort itself out.

1. Vincent Barteau

2. Maurice Le Guilloux @ 3 minutes 7 seconds, already faltering

3. Paolo Ferreira @ 9 minutes 57 seconds

4. Laurent Fignon @ 12 minutes 54 seconds

6. Bernard Hinault @ 14 minutes 23 seconds

8. Greg LeMond @ 15 minutes 3 seconds

Hinault's third place in the time trial (Sean Kelly also finished ahead of him) brought about a change to Hinault's attitude and tactics. He understood that this Tour would be tough to win. He started to fight hard for the intermediate sprint bonus seconds. In stage 9, Hinault and Kelly had dueled for the third of the intermediate sprints. After Hinault had won the sprint they looked back at the peloton and saw that they had created a sizable gap. They put their heads down and pressed on with several other riders who had also detached themselves in the sprint. Caught napping because they expected the sprinters to slow and rejoin the peloton were LeMond, Fignon, Zoetemelk and Stephen Roche. A chase was organized and the 2 groups hammered down the road to Bordeaux at 60 kilometers an hour. Finally, facing a headwind and realizing that the gain would be too small for the effort, the Hinault/Kelly group sat up. But Hinault had once again shown that he was always willing to attack any time and any place. And Guimard, with his young team, had also proven that he could respond to the Badger's best efforts.

No one expected Barteau or his breakaway companions to come out of the mountains with their lead intact. But Barteau had some steel in his spine.

There was only 1 Pyrenean stage, 226 kilometers that went over the Portet d'Aspet, the Core, Latrape and a first category ascent to Guzet-Neige. Robert Millar was the angel with wings, winning stage 11 and leaving his closest follower, the Colombian Luis Herrera, 41 seconds behind. LeMond, getting over a cold that had been bothering him, had trouble and got dropped on the first climb. Being a superb descender he regained contact and through sheer determination, managed to finish sixteenth, not far behind Hinault. Fignon, sensing weakness in Hinault, wanted to attack well before the finish. Guimard, wary of the Badger, told Fignon to hold his fire until 3 kilometers from the summit, thus making it unlikely that Hinault would be able to regroup and respond. It worked perfectly and Fignon took almost a minute out of Hinault. Barteau surprised almost everyone by finishing only a little behind LeMond. He was still in Yellow.

Stage 11 results:

1. Robert Millar

7. Laurent Fignon @ 2 minutes 13 seconds

13. Bernard Hinault @ 3 minutes 5 seconds

16. Greg LeMond @ 3 minutes 42 seconds

19. Vincent Barteau @ 4 minutes 10 seconds

That left the General Classification thus:

1. Vincent Barteau

2. Maurice Le Guilloux @ 7 minutes 37 seconds

3. Laurent Fignon @ 10 minutes 33 seconds

5. Bernard Hinault @ 12 minutes 38 seconds

9. Greg LeMond @ 14 minutes 35 seconds

Round 4 to Renault.

Barteau was proving to be rather strongly attached to the Yellow Jersey. He survived the Pyrenees with a loss of only 2 minutes. With their teammate in Yellow, Fignon and LeMond could sit on. If someone wanted to take the Yellow from Barteau, he would have to attack and get past Fignon, who was riding as he normally did, coolly, with no unneeded expenditure of energy.

Hinault now seemed unworried about such plebian concerns as conserving his strength for the best possible, most efficient moment to take back the needed time and went on the offensive. We noted that his normal way was to attack if he felt weak or at a loss. It's a noble sentiment, but sometimes, nobility on those terms can be suicidal. As Tour founder Henri Desgrange said, it's *la tête et les jambes* (head and legs). It didn't seem that Hinault had the legs and he damn sure wasn't using his head.

Stage 14 went through the rolling countryside of the Massif Central. Faded Belgian hope Fons de Wolf, in an extraordinary exploit, went on a long solo break. At one point he had put 25 minutes between himself and the peloton. By the time the stage was over he still had 17 minutes, 40 seconds and had temporarily lifted himself to fourth place in the General Classification. The next day he paid for his effort and finished 23 minutes behind the stage winner Frédéric Vichot.

While Hinault may have been riding with a touch of an air of desperation, Fignon had also changed. He seemed to be getting stronger and was obviously growing more confident. On the day that de Wolf won, Hinault had attacked hard for second place in the stage. Fignon easily sped by the Badger causing Raymond Poulidor to pronounce himself astonished at Fignon. The next day Fignon won the field sprint.

The coming days held a 22-kilometer time trial and the Alpine stages. Even though he was riding in a state of grace, Fignon said that with only a 2-minute lead over Hinault, the slightest weakness would cost him dearly.

Stage 16 was an individual time trial with a tough 800-meter climb in the final half. Seeming to fly up the final kilometers of the mountain, Fignon beat Hinault, this time by 33 seconds.

Stage 17 was when things really got sorted out. It was a trip to the top of l'Alpe d'Huez passing over 3 other highly rated climbs on the way. Hinault had hoped that he could wear down his young rival. This seemed like an empty hope as Fignon was demonstrating a mastery that was Hinault's only a few years ago.

Hinault attacked 5 times on the penultimate climb, the Laffrey. Each time Fignon rode back to him. After the fifth assault Fignon was without teammates and the front group had been reduced to the climbing elite of the Tour. Then it was Fignon's turn. Fignon and Luis Herrera separated themselves from the others. They did this without specifically attacking. They just rode faster than any other rider could. Over the top and on the descent Hinault chased like a madman. Riding through the valley leading up to the steep hairpins of l'Alpe d'Huez Hinault caught the duo. Like a shark with the smell of blood in the water, the furious Hinault attacked and put some distance between himself and the Fignon/Herrera pair.

Looking back, Fignon said that the attack in no way concerned him. He said he thought Hinault's effort laughable. Herrera set a blistering pace up the mountain with Fignon, Millar and Arroyo on his wheel and caught Hinault. As Herrera raced for the summit, Fignon was the last man dropped by the flying Colombian. Looking at the stage results below, one can see that Robert Millar was over 3 minutes behind Herrera. Fignon's superiority to a specialist climber like Millar on what should be his ideal terrain gives an idea of the magnificent form Fignon enjoyed in 1984.

Round 5 and the fight to Fignon. Herrera's stage win was the first by a Colombian, non-European, and amateur.

Stage 17 results:

1. Luis Herrera

2. Laurent Fignon @ 49 seconds

3. Angel Arroyo @ 2 minutes 27 seconds

4. Robert Millar @ 3 minutes 5 seconds

5. Rafael Acevedo (another Colombian) @ 3 minutes 9 seconds

6. Greg LeMond @ 3 minutes 30 seconds

7. Bernard Hinault @ 3 minutes 44 seconds

The consequences of the stage were immense.

Barteau's dream was over. He had to give up the Yellow Jersey to Laurent Fignon.

Herrera was having a fabulous year with a near win in the Red Zinger Classic. After his Alpe d'Huez stage victory the president of Colombia called him. Since then, Herrera's life in today's war-ravaged Colombia has been tough. He's been kidnapped twice and has to pay protection money regularly just to be left alone.

The angry, raging Hinault had lost 3 minutes to Fignon, but he was in no way subdued. He was looking for another opportunity to try to savage his competitors. Fignon, on the other hand, seemed to enjoy tormenting Hinault in press interviews. Samuel Abt put Fignon's attitude nicely, "If you couldn't kick a man when he was down, when could you kick him?"

The General Classification after stage 17:

1. Laurent Fignon
2. Vincent Barteau @ 4 minutes 22 seconds
3. Bernard Hinault @ 5 minutes 41 seconds
4. Robert Millar @ 8 minutes 25 seconds
5. Greg LeMond @ 8 minutes 45 seconds

The next stage was challenging. It included the Galibier, the Madeleine and a finish at La Plagne. All 3 were *hors catégorie* climbs. Hinault was soon dropped by the leaders and chased back on. By this point Hinault was so reduced in circumstances that he, the *Patron* of the peloton, attacked in the feed zone. He was soon brought up short for that move by Fignon and LeMond's Renault team. He was again dropped on the Madeleine and chased back on the descent.

Ever the patient man, Fignon assumed command on the final climb to La Plagne, dropping everyone, even the Colombians. This was the last element Fignon needed both to put the icing on the cake of this Tour and to silence those critics who carped that Fignon had not yet won a high mountain stage. He did this time, completely dominating his competitors. Hinault finished the stage in tenth place, almost 3 minutes behind Fignon. LeMond finished third in the stage, lifting him from fifth to third place in the Overall, only 1 minute, 13 seconds behind second place Hinault. Hinault trailed the flying Fignon in the General Classification by a giant 8 minutes, 39 seconds.

Two days later Fignon did it again, winning stage 20 alone on the hilltop finish at Crans-Montana.

Stage 22, the Tour's penultimate stage was a 51-kilometer individual time trial. Fignon won again, although Sean Kelly, when the times were rounded to the nearest second, finished with the same time. Hinault lost another 36 seconds.

The final General Classification of the 1984 Tour de France:

1. Laurent Fignon (Renault-ELF): 112 hours 3 minutes 40 seconds
2. Bernard Hinault (La Vie Claire) @ 10 minutes 32 seconds
3. Greg LeMond (Renault-ELF) @ 11 minutes 46 seconds

4. Robert Millar (Peugeot) @ 14 minutes 42 seconds

5. Sean Kelly (Skil) @ 16 minutes 35 seconds

Climbers' Competition:

1. Robert Millar: 284 points

2. Laurent Fignon: 212 points

3. Angel Arroyo: 140 points

Points Competition:

1. Frank Hoste: 322 points

2. Sean Kelly: 318 points

3. Eric Vanderaerden: 247 points

Bernard Hinault earned the admiration of cycling fans for his refusal to give up. Every day he went out looking for some chink in Fignon's armor, some way to break his young rival. It wasn't to be. In 1984 Laurent Fignon was vastly superior to any other rider and was never seriously challenged. With complete command of the race, he could and did ride patiently, opening up time on his rivals when it suited him.

**1985.** Fignon could not return to defend his title. An inflamed Achilles tendon required surgery, forcing Fignon to sit this one out. So who was there to fill the vacuum? Hinault, of course. He could never be written off in any race he entered. To many, last year's Tour de France third-place Greg LeMond had matured and was the other choice as a possible winner.

The politics of this Tour were as complicated as any and they would have repercussions for both Hinault and LeMond for more than just this Tour. Hinault's La Vie Claire team hired the talent-filled LeMond from Renault. Cynics say that this was to neutralize LeMond, the greatest single threat to an attempt on a fifth Tour win by Hinault.

But why would LeMond go to La Vie Claire, centered around the single most driven racer in the world? What room would there be for LeMond? My understanding is that LeMond took a thoughtful approach to switching teams. He is said to have liked Koechli, the director of La Vie Claire, better than Renault's Guimard. His good friend

Steve Bauer was on La Vie Claire, begging LeMond to come on over. And, not knowing that Fignon would drop out of competition in 1985, Hinault seemed to be preferable to the difficult Fignon. In addition, Bernard Tapie, the owner of La Vie Claire, had scads of money and was using it to promote his various companies. LeMond made no secret of his belief that racers were underpaid for the value they brought to their sponsors and deserved a substantial increase in pay. In no small way, over time, LeMond's financial demands elevated the pay of good racers on the other teams as well. The contract with La Vie Claire was said to be for 3 years and worth a million dollars (actually it was $225,000 the first year, $260,000 the second year and $300,000 the third year). This was big money in those days.

Moreover, LeMond was very unhappy with the way the Renault team and its sponsors had handled the use of his name. Manufacturers who had supplied the Renault team with its racing equipment had used LeMond's name and picture, claiming an endorsement of these products by LeMond. As was the usual practice of the time, they had done this without securing LeMond's explicit permission. LeMond sued several of the suppliers.

Guimard, negotiating with LeMond, believed he was in the driver's seat and told LeMond "You need me. I don't need you...if you don't stay with me you'll never win the Tour," and refused to give in to LeMond's demand to increase his then $125,000 salary. He wasn't asking Guimard to match Tapie's big bag of cash. He says he would have been happy with $150,000. As we shall see, it probably would have been better for both of them to reach an accommodation. For starters, in this Tour with Fignon out, Guimard didn't have a General Classification contender.

I have long held that the single most talented bicycle racer to have ever turned a pedal in the post-Merckx era and probably since Coppi is Greg LeMond. As a junior he won everything and he did it with the natural ease of a born winner. That is not to say he didn't work hard. Lots of racers work hard. The ones who float to the top are the talented winners.

As a junior he went over to Belgium to race. Back in the '70s and '80s many Americans traveled to Belgium to try to make it in the tough, high speed, ultra-competitive arena of the world's most bike-mad country. Almost all faltered or failed, going home broke, tired, sick and miserable. LeMond didn't falter. He thrived. For the week he was there he won or placed second in every single race he entered. Then he won the Junior World Championships. It was always one natural step after another. Winning the World Pro Road Championships in Switzerland at the ripe old age of 22 surprised no one. He was signed by the finest team in the world with the most respected director in the world, Renault and Cyrille Guimard. His freshman Tour yielded a third place amid the blistering war being fought by Hinault and Fignon.

I was in a race with LeMond only once (I can't say I raced him). It was a criterium in the little tourist town of Solvang, California, my last race as a Category 1 racer before I retired. From the gun the race was red hot. Lap after lap had the peloton strung out in one long line that extended halfway around the town. I was in the middle of the pack saying my prayers, hoping that I would not be the one who let the string break. Then the pace eased. I knew that probably whatever break had been dangling off the front was either caught or was out of sight. A few laps later a slender rider went right by me, bumping me gently. It was LeMond. He had lapped a field with another rider and was headed to the front for more. He was still a damn junior!

To resume. It was announced that the La Vie Claire riders would ride for whichever of the 2 showed the best and most likely Tour-winning form. LeMond had helped Hinault win the Giro in the spring. This Tour Hinault was going for his second Giro-Tour double.

Let's follow this Tour in detail because it is fascinating. Hinault used every tool at his disposal to keep LeMond, a man he knew to be at least his equal and possibly his superior, in a subordinate position.

Hinault showed his stuff by winning the Prologue with LeMond suffering a mechanical near the end, coming in fifth, 21 seconds back.

The first 2 stages were long eastward treks across northwestern France. By virtue of his excellent sprinting ability, Eric Vanderaerden was able to take over the lead. He still had it after the La Vie Claire victory in the stage 3 team time trial. I remember seeing the end of that time trial on TV. Bernard Hinault's delirious fans ran out to greet their champion who took terrible fright at the rushing, swarming crowd. He screamed at them to get away and started swinging his fists.

The relative position between Hinault and LeMond (still 21 seconds behind Hinault) had not changed much by the end of the 3 stages. The La Vie Claire team time trial win did put 8 of their riders in the top 10 in the General Classification.

Stage 4 saw La Vie Claire rider Kim Andersen get in a 7-man break that beat the pack to the finish by 46 seconds, thereby earning him the Yellow Jersey. Stage 6 reminded the world that LeMond was a complete rider when, apparently on a lark, he sprinted with the kamikazes into Reims. Kelly and Vanderaerden won the sprint that was far from clean. Vanderaerden, moving up through holes in the peloton that weren't there, came even with Kelly and started to force him into the barriers. Kelly pushed back. Vanderaerden put his arm out against Kelly. The sprint went to Vanderaerden but the 2 carried their argument all the way to the awards podium where Vanderaerden was given the Yellow Jersey. The judges decided to relegate both of them. LeMond, who had crossed the line fourth was moved up to second in the stage and bagged the 20-second time bonus. He was now in third place in the General Classification, 2 seconds ahead of Hinault. This situation was only to last until stage 8.

75 kilometers long, the stage 8 individual time trial through the Vosges started to sort things out. Hinault was by far the best man at the discipline that he had almost made his own. No one came within 2 minutes of him that day. There had been some speculation as to why Hinault had not been chasing time bonuses this Tour as in some years past. Perhaps he had been saving his energy so that he could deliver a smashing time trial and unquestionably demonstrate his superiority. He did indeed establish that superiority. Hinault caught his 2-minute man Sean Kelly, and then, despite's Kelly's efforts to remain close to the Frenchman, Hinault went on to take almost another minute out of him. German rider Didi Thurau was penalized for drafting Charly Mottet. When he assaulted a racing official at the start of the next day's stage Thurau was thrown out of the Tour.

The time trial's results:

1.  Bernard Hinault
2.  Stephen Roche @ 2 minutes 20 seconds
3.  Charly Mottet @ 2 minutes 26 seconds
4.  Greg LeMond @ 2 minutes 34 seconds

With only a couple of stages before the Alps, Hinault was back in his familiar Yellow Jersey. La Vie Claire was putting on an impressive display of force with their Hinault, LeMond and Bauer in the top 4.

The General Classification now stood thus:

1. Bernard Hinault
2. Greg LeMond @ 2 minutes 32 seconds
3. Sean Kelly @ 2 minutes 54 seconds
4. Steve Bauer @ 3 minutes 21 seconds
5. Phil Anderson @ 3 minutes 44 seconds
6. Stephen Roche @ same time

The next 2 stages took the Tour south through the Vosges and the Jura. Again, no change in the relative positions of the contenders for the overall lead.

Stage 11 was the first day of heavy climbing, going 195 kilometers from Pontarlier up to Morzine/Avoriaz. The race would climb the first-category Pas de Morgins, the second-category Le Corbier and finally the first-category finish up the Avoriaz to Morzine. It was a classic Hinault performance. He went away early with Luis Herrera, who was too far down in the General Classification to be a threat to Hinault. Hinault made the usual deal, letting Herrera take the summits and the Climbers' points and the stage win while Hinault got the improvement to his overall time. Hinault wasn't interested in anything except gaining that time and doing it in such a way as to leave no doubt who was the leader of the team and the *Patron* of the Tour. Herrera won the stage with Hinault 7 seconds back. LeMond was blocked. He couldn't chase his teammate but he eventually attached himself to Pedro Delgado and Fabio Parra, another of the Colombians, and finished fifth, losing 1 minute, 41 seconds. He was now 4 minutes behind Hinault. Stephen Roche was 5 minutes, 52 seconds adrift.

The twelfth stage didn't change anything even though it had 3 first and 4 second category climbs. The General Classification at the top was unchanged.

It was clear that the effort was telling on Hinault. The stage 13 time trial was won by Eric Vanderaerden with Hinault about 1 minute slower over the 31.8 kilometers. LeMond, hit yet again with mechanical trouble, lost another minute and a half to Hinault, being 2 minutes, 30 seconds slower than Vanderaerden.

The General Classification now stood thus:

1. Bernard Hinault
2. Greg LeMond @ 5 minutes 23 seconds
3. Stephen Roche @ 6 minutes 8 seconds
4. Sean Kelly @ 6 minutes 35 seconds
5. Steve Bauer @ 8 minutes 23 seconds

The Tour, before it had made it to the Pyrenees, looked to be about wrapped up.

Stage 14 changed everything. It was a little detour through the Massif Central of France with a single first category climb. Again Herrera took off early. LeMond joined Delgado, Millar and 5 others in a hard chase. Back in the peloton Hinault marked Roche and the others, hoping that LeMond would get away and solidify his hold on second place. The strategy worked and the Hinault group came in to the finish 2 minutes behind winner Luis Herrera (who had crashed earlier that day and remounted) and 1 minute behind the LeMond group. With less than a kilometer to go Hinault, Phil Anderson and 4 others crashed badly. The riders were beginning their sprint and touched wheels. Hinault lay there for some minutes being checked over by the Tour's doctor. He climbed back on his bike and rode across the line, his face and particularly his nose a bloody mangle of flesh. That's a scene that gets played over and over again when TV shows want to show something dramatic about the Tour: Hinault determined to finish, blood dripping from his face.

When a rider crashes inside the final kilometer as Hinault did, Tour rules say that a rider gets the same time as the group he was in. He lost time on LeMond, but was still well in control of the lead. But more importantly, his nose was broken. Hinault found it difficult to breathe. In addition, his hard work in the Alps had left him showing signs of fatigue.

LeMond was now 3 minutes, 32 seconds behind Hinault with Roche still 6 minutes, 14 seconds off Hinault's pace.

Stage 17 is the stage everyone still talks about. It was a very tough Pyrenean stage from Toulouse to Luz-Ardiden totaling 209.5 kilometers. They had to climb the second-category Aspin followed by the 2 *hors catégorie* mountains, the Tourmalet and Luz-Ardiden.

On the Tourmalet Hinault's trouble became crystal-clear when he couldn't stay with the leaders. First LeMond, Roche and Delgado dropped him. Then, struggling with bronchitis in the moist air as well as having breathing trouble caused by his broken nose, Hinault also lost contact with his group which contained Herrera, Millar, Kelly, Anderson and several others. On the descent Hinault caught Kelly's group.

Up ahead Delgado was away. Stephen Roche, with LeMond (who had been told to mark Roche), was chasing and feeling good. Roche wanted the stage win. At the base of the road up to Luz-Ardiden a television crew told LeMond that the Hinault group was several minutes back. Roche and LeMond pulled away from those chasing them on the final climb to Luz-Ardiden. LeMond could see that he was the stronger of the 2 as Roche lifted the duo further and further away from the chasers.

La Vie Claire Team assistant director Maurice Le Guilloux drove up next to LeMond. LeMond asked for permission to attack Roche and take the stage win. Le Guilloux forwarded the orders of team director Koechli. Koechli, afraid that LeMond would take the lead and the Yellow Jersey, told LeMond to wait for Hinault. LeMond pressed him for the exact time gap. Le Guilloux, a former devoted domestique of Hinault's, was evasive. LeMond pressed him harder and was told that Hinault was only 40 seconds behind. The momentum was coming out of the break as LeMond and Le Guilloux argued. Herrera caught and passed them. LeMond waited some more. Anderson and Kelly arrived but without Hinault.

Hinault was still several minutes back down the mountain. LeMond had acquired a decisive lead that was now melting away. The Tour could have been his right there. No doubt. None whatsoever. LeMond was getting stronger with every passing day of the Tour as Hinault was weakening.

LeMond relates, "Koechli said to me, 'How dare you attack Hinault when he's in difficulty?'" Koechli denies saying this, only that LeMond was not yet strong enough to take on the responsibilities of the leadership of the Tour. The real story was that La Vie Claire, a French company, was not yet ready for their young American to be the leader of the Tour and put their beloved Hinault in the shadow. A French La Vie Claire winner served the best commercial interests of the company. Also, international professional racing had not become as cosmopolitan as it is now. English speaking riders often faced resentment and hostility from the teams that hired them and sometimes sabotaged them when they did too well.

*VeloNews* editorial director John Wilcockson talked to Koechli about this in 2005. Koechli denies making LeMond wait, saying that he authorized LeMond to make one attack and that he had to drop Roche. Roche was riding well and was too dangerous to play with. So, did Le Guilloux make up the orders? Someone made the order for LeMond to wait; someone made the decision to lie to him.

Robert Millar noted that when Hinault saw he was in trouble, Hinault remained a calm professional and rode in his 25-tooth sprocket at his normal cadence rather than dropping to a bigger gear and ruining his legs for the next day in the mountains.

So there you have it.

The stage results:

1. Pedro Delgado
2. Luis Herrera @ 25 seconds
3. Fabio Parra @ 1 minutes 29 seconds
4. Sean Kelly @ 2 minutes 52 seconds
5. Greg LeMond @ same time
12. Stephen Roche @ same time
18. Bernard Hinault @ 4 minutes 5 seconds

The General Classification after stage 17:

1. Bernard Hinault
2. Greg LeMond @ 2 minutes 25 seconds
3. Stephen Roche @ 5 minutes

William Faulkner once wrote that at least once in his life every Southern boy imagines that it's a hot day in July, referring to Gettysburg and particularly Pickett's Charge. How would he have reacted if he were being misused by General Lee that day and ordered into that inferno? I think the same is true of every cyclist of the right age. We all imagined ourselves on the mountain, climbing to Luz-Ardiden. In our imagination, awaiting us at the top of the mountain is a stage win in the Tour de France and the real possibility of cycling immortality by cinching ownership of the Yellow Jersey. How would we react if Paul Koechli demanded that we slacken our pace for a wounded teammate? When we found that we had been lied to and Hinault was much further down the hill, would we continue to wait? None of us could answer that question. I still can't 20 years later. I do know that one of the greatest injustices in the history of sport was done to LeMond that day.

At the finish of the stage LeMond was in tears, frustrated with rage. Hinault, knowing that he had been handed his fifth Tour on a platter because LeMond had been willing to wait, promised to help him win the Tour next year. Greg had said that his real goal was a stage win and the Yellow Jersey for a few days. He felt that these were legitimate goals which he had the right to expect in this situation.

Regarding Hinault's promise to help LeMond, we'll see in 1986 how much that was worth.

The next stage went over the Soulor and the Aubisque. Roche got his stage win and LeMond, understanding that La Vie Claire had decreed that Hinault was to win the Tour, took only 15 seconds out of Hinault. It should be noted that Roche was flying and if he had taken a lot of time out of Hinault in stage 17 he would have been extremely dangerous in the stage 18 double stage in the mountains. Koechli's concern about Roche was quite rational.

There was the formality of the final time trial. LeMond won it, his first Tour stage win, beating Hinault by only 5 seconds but confirming his ability as a natural stage racer, one who grew stronger during a 3-week race.

The final General Classification of the 1985 Tour de France:

1. Bernard Hinault (La Vie Claire): 113 hours 24 minutes 23 seconds
2. Greg LeMond (La Vie Claire) @ 1 minute 42 seconds
3. Stephen Roche (La Redoute) @ 4 minutes 29 seconds
4. Sean Kelly (Skil) @ 6 minutes 26 seconds
5. Phil Anderson (Panasonic) @ 7 minutes 44 seconds

Climbers' Competition:

1. Luis Herrera: 440 points
2. Pedro Delgado: 274 points
3. Robert Millar: 270 points

Points Competition:

1. Sean Kelly: 434 points
2. Greg LeMond: 332 points
3. Stephen Roche: 279 points

Hinault claimed his fifth Tour joining Anquetil and Merckx in the record books. He also did his second Giro-Tour double. But the win was cheap and could never be held on the same level as those of his 2 predecessors.

Epilogue to 1985: In the 1987 Giro d'Italia Stephen Roche rode with Roberto Visentini on the Italian Carrera team. Roche had lost the lead to Visentini in a time trial. In the mountains Roche flew while Visentini could not keep up with the leaders. Like Koechli to LeMond in the 1985 Tour, Roche's director told Roche to wait for his faltering leader. Roche told him no, and hammered up the mountain and re-took the lead. Visentini came in many minutes later, completely out of contention for the lead. Roche won the Giro while Visentini later abandoned.

Jacques Goddet, who had taken over management of the Tour when Tour father Henri Desgrange took ill in 1936, retired from active direction of his share of the Tour. Félix Lévitan was left the sole manager of the enterprise. Goddet was responsible for restarting the Tour after World War Two. He oversaw the Tour while the nature of bike racing changed, from the use of 1-speed bikes ridden on long stages that emphasized endurance to the quicker, speedier sport we know today. Goddet worked to preserve Desgrange's original intent of making the Tour "inhuman" in its difficulty. This caused Goddet to be insensitive to the rider's demands that split stages be ended. Yet, he bent when he had to. His legacy to us is the Tour. All sports fans should be grateful for his determination to preserve the Tour's culture and to continue the race we all love the most.

Indicative of the increasing influence of Americans in the Tour, Coca-Cola signed a 12 year deal with the Tour to replace Perrier as the race's official drink.

**1986.** Hinault had said to LeMond, "In '86 the Tour will be for you. I'll be there to help you." So easy to say in the heat of a moment when a teammate had made the sacrifice of a lifetime to let him win the

1985 Tour. Now, would Hinault have the character to fulfill his promise when he can taste immortality with 6 Tour wins? This year saw not only the entry of American Greg LeMond with his ace climbing friend Andy Hampsten and Canadian Steve Bauer but also the entry of the first American team. 7-Eleven-Hoonved was entered with Bob Roll, 1984 Olympic gold medalist Alexei Grewal, Chris Carmichael, Eric Heiden, Alex Stieda, Jeff Pierce, Raul Alcala, Davis Phinney, Doug Shapiro (who had ridden on Joop Zoetemelk's Kwantum-Decosol Tour team in 1985) and Ron Kieffel. After the riders on La Vie Claire, they were the cream of the North American crop. I'll spoil one bit of the story right here. Bob Roll, who does analysis of bike racing on the Versus television network, was the highest placed 7-Eleven rider in Paris (sixty-third overall), despite getting sick mid-way though the 1986 Tour. Bob Roll was a very good rider.

If the politics and complicated jockeying amidst the tension of the La Vie Claire intra-team rivalry were tough in 1985, 1986 was even more difficult.

LeMond's spring had been good, but not spectacular: second in Milan–San Remo, third in Paris–Nice, fourth in the Giro d'Italia (a crash had cost him important time), and third in the Tour of Switzerland.

LeMond's La Vie Claire teammate Andy Hampsten established his *bona fides* as a racer of the first rank when he won the Tour of Switzerland only a few short weeks before the start of the Tour. Hinault used that win as fodder for his psychological war against LeMond when he announced that Hampsten's Swiss victory made Hampsten, not LeMond, his real heir. How charming.

Hinault's spring was rather quiet with no top placings in important races.

Laurent Fignon, riding the colors of his team's new sponsor Systeme U, was working on his comeback after surgery on his Achilles tendon. He must have found some rather good form because he won the Flèche Wallonne in the spring.

Thierry Marie began the first of his 3 Prologue victories at the kickoff of the 1986 Tour. Hinault was third at 2 seconds, Fignon and LeMond were seventh and eighth at 4 seconds.

Stage 1, a short 85-kilometer race run in the outskirts of Paris saw 7-Eleven rider Alex Stieda take off at the 40-kilometer mark. He was eventually joined by 5 other riders, but not until Stieda had collected the intermediate sprint bonuses. The group of 6 managed to stay away from the charging field by only meters when they crossed the line. With the time bonuses Stieda had collected on his early solo effort, he was now the shock owner of the Yellow Jersey, the first North American (Canadian) to wear Yellow.

That same Saturday afternoon the teams lined up for a 56-kilometer team time trial. The 7-Eleven team was game to try to keep the Yellow Jersey but its efforts came apart when Eric Heiden crashed. Several other 7-Eleven riders scraped the curb to avoid following Heiden to the ground. That weakened the casings of their tires, causing several flat tires. Stieda, exhausted from his morning effort, ran out of gas. Carmichael and Pierce had to drop back and bring Stieda home making sure they got him there in time to avoid having him eliminated by missing the time cutoff. Stieda made it to the finish in time, but his tenure in Yellow was over.

Fignon's Systeme U squad won the stage. La Vie Claire had a bad day, losing almost 2 minutes. Thierry Marie, being a Systeme U rider, was back in Yellow with his teammates occupying the top 7 places in the General Classification.

Stage 3, in the northern roads of France, ended near the Belgian border. And there the freshman 7-Eleven team had another major success. Davis Phinney won the sprint by inches even after having been in a break for a lot of that day, making him the first American to win a road stage. As far as the real General Classification contenders were concerned, this was just another day to stay out of trouble.

It stayed that way until stage 9, a 61.5-kilometer individual time trial at Nantes. Now the Tour de France started in earnest. The stage results:

1. Bernard Hinault

2. Greg LeMond @ 44 seconds

3. Stephen Roche @ 1 minute 1 second

32. Laurent Fignon @ 3 minutes 42 seconds

LeMond's performance was far better than his time showed. He flatted and it is estimated he lost almost a minute. It was clear that Fignon hadn't found his 1985 form yet.

General Classification:

1. Jorgen Pedersen
2. Stephen Roche @ 1 minute 5 seconds
3. Bernard Hinault @ 1 minute 10 seconds
8. Greg LeMond @ 1 minute 59 seconds

Stage 12 was the first day in the Pyrenees with 4 highly rated climbs. The final climb was the first category Col de Marie-Blanque, followed by 45 kilometers of descent and flat before the finish at Pau.

The first major climb was the first category Burdincurutcheta at kilometer 80. Several groups of riders detached themselves. Notably, Hinault with Luis Herrera and Claude Criquielion were moving up from the second group to the leaders. Over the second climb, the Bargargui, Eduardo Chozas broke away on the descent. Hinault with teammates LeMond, Hampsten and Jean-François Bernard along with several other riders gave chase. After Chozas was caught, Hinault and Bernard attacked and got away. Pedro Delgado bridged up to them. They eventually spit out Chozas as the now 3 riders worked hard to put real distance on the racers behind them. LeMond was stuck. He could not chase his 2 teammates (Hinault and Bernard) up the road. Hinault and Delgado tore up the road, gaining scads of time on him as LeMond sat in the chasing group. Finally LeMond was able to extricate himself, taking along only Herrera. Hinault let Delgado have the stage, he had enough booty when LeMond came in 4 minutes, 37 seconds later. This was helping LeMond win the Tour? Hinault knew that if he were on the attack and in the lead, he would neutralize LeMond.

The General Classification at this point:

1. Bernard Hinault
2. Greg LeMond @ 5 minutes 25 seconds
3. Urs Zimmermann @ 6 minutes and 22 seconds
4. Pedro Delgado @ 6 minutes 57 seconds
15. Laurent Fignon @ 12 minutes 43 seconds

The stage was so tough and the pace so hot, 17 riders abandoned. The next morning 2 more quit, including Fignon.

Stage 13 only got harder with 4 major climbs: the Tourmalet, the Aspin, the Peyresourde and the final *hors catégorie* climb to

Superbagnères. On the descent of the Tourmalet Hinault attacked and got away. At the bottom he had a lead of 1 minute, 43 seconds. Again LeMond was stuck, unable to race. He had to let the others do the chasing. By the bottom of the Aspin, the gap between Hinault and about 30 chasers was 2 minutes, 54 seconds.

On the Peyresourde, Hinault started to show signs of fatigue. A much reduced chase group of Zimmermann, LeMond, Hampsten, Millar and Herrera had cut the lead to 25 seconds. On the descent of the Peyresourde, Hinault was caught.

The final climb to the ski station of Superbagnères is 16 kilometers of *hors catégorie* work. Hinault rode with the group that had caught him, totaling 9 riders. On the climb he attacked again and got away. Now it was just Hampsten, LeMond, Zimmermann, Millar and Herrera chasing and with 10 kilometers to go, Hinault was caught.

With 7 kilometers to go Hampsten attacked and took LeMond with him. Hampsten pounded up the mountain for all he was worth, while LeMond still hesitated, sitting on Hampsten's wheel. Then, as Hampsten could no longer keep up the infernal pace, he yelled at LeMond to take off and win the stage. LeMond finally shed his hesitancy and raced up the mountain for a great stage win as Hinault was being passed by rider after rider further down the mountain. LeMond's gain on Hinault that day was 4 minutes, 39 seconds, almost the same amount of time he lost the day before. Hinault was in Yellow but LeMond had shown that he had the ability to win the Tour, sitting only 40 seconds behind the fading leader.

The stages after the Pyrenees that went across southern France heading towards the Alps changed nothing in the General Classification.

Stage 17, the first Alpine stage, was the scene of the denouement of this story, with crossings of the Col de Vars, Col d'Izoard and a hilltop finish at the top of the Col de Granon. The first climb was rated first category and the final 2 were *hors catégorie*.

Various groups attacked and riders were scattered all over the mountains. The story that matters to us is on the descent of the Izoard. Zimmermann, sitting in third place in the General Classification, got a gap. LeMond, acting as an attentive domestique, latched onto his wheel. Hinault was about 90 seconds behind them. On the Granon, LeMond, ever dutiful, sat on Zimmermann as the Swiss rider poured on the gas. Hinault, now aware of the situation attacked hard but Zimmermann with LeMond in tow was gaining time with every pedal stroke. Eduardo Chozas, never in contention for the overall, had been off the front and won the stage, but that didn't matter to LeMond. He was in Yellow.

Stage 17: Zimmermann with an attentive LeMond on his wheel.

The next day was no easier with the Galibier and its little brother the Télégraphe, followed by the Croix de Fer and a hilltop finish at l'Alpe d'Huez.

On the descent of the Galibier Hinault attacked with Bauer on his wheel. LeMond, Zimmermann and Pello Ruiz-Cabestany caught him as they continued the descent. On the short ascent up the Télégraphe Hinault made another attempt to get away, this time making it stick for 15 kilometers. LeMond, Bauer and Ruiz-Cabestany managed to hook up with Hinault without bringing Zimmermann, who was sitting ahead of Hinault in the General Classification. The quartet put down their collective heads and started to work. The pace was too hot for Bauer and Ruiz-Cabestany and on the first category Croix de Fer it was just Hinault and LeMond.

This was the day Zimmermann saw his chances for winning the Tour disappear. 7 kilometers from the top of the Croix de Fer Zimmermann was in a group that included Hampsten, Pascal Simon and Joop Zoetemelk. They were 3 minutes, 10 seconds behind LeMond and Hinault. Zimmerman dug deep and attacked, trying to get up to the duo. He closed the gap a little, being 2 minutes, 50 seconds behind at the top.

On the descent Hinault and LeMond flew. Both were superb bike handlers. Years ago former 7-Eleven rider Jeff Pierce and I were talking about this stage and I remember the one thing Pierce wanted to make sure that I understood: LeMond could descend and descend extremely fast. At the beginning of the Alpe, in Bourg d'Oisans, LeMond and Hinault were 4 minutes, 50 seconds ahead of Zimmermann. LeMond and Hinault continued to throw high heat on the mountain until Hinault conceded and asked LeMond to back off, his words being, "Stay with me". Generously LeMond joined hands with his tormentor and pushed Hinault ahead a bit so that he could take the stage victory. LeMond had survived another test from his little French helper. Hinault had buried Zimmermann and had claimed second place in the General Classification. The gift of the stage win was nice of LeMond, but I'd have completely dropped Hinault and left him for dead as far down the mountain as possible to make sure he couldn't try something later. Hinault never gave up, and would take any advantage that opportunity or his own talents presented. To prove my point, in a post-stage interview Hinault said, "The race isn't over." You can imagine LeMond's dismay.

The General Classification after l'Alpe d'Huez:

1. Greg LeMond

2. Bernard Hinault @ 2 minutes 45 seconds

3. Urs Zimmermann @ 7 minutes 41 seconds

4. Andy Hampsten @ 16 minutes 46 seconds

Owen Mulholland sent me these comments regarding stage 17: "As you note, Hinault attacked on the short 2-kilometer climb out of Valloire that serves as the southern slope of the Col de Télégraphe. I'm not sure why Greg was caught napping so often by these surprise attacks. It's impossible to imagine, say, Merckx, missing such moves time after time. Anyway, once again Hinault was gone and Greg was stuck. However the descent of the Télégraphe is extremely sinuous and was made for Greg's fabulous descending skills. I remember his talking (laughing) to Hinault later about how he'd gotten rid of Zimmermann on that descent. It seems Zimmermann skidded across a corner trying to hang onto Greg's wheel and that's the last anyone up front ever saw of the poor Swiss that day! I believe (but am not absolutely certain) Bauer was already away, but in any event he was in the front, so when Greg and Bernard hooked up with him and a few others in the flat valley of the Maurienne, Steve lowered his head and motored to the foot of the Croix de Fer. Poor Zimmermann never stood a chance."

Stage 20 was the next real test, a 58-kilometer individual time trial at St. Etienne. LeMond's normal luck continued when he crashed at kilometer 37. He remounted and found his brake rubbing the rim. He had to change bikes, costing him still more time. Hinault rode his time trial perfectly and won the stage, beating the crash-starred LeMond by 25 seconds. Zimmermann was unable to present any challenge and finished almost 3 minutes behind Hinault. While the race tightened a little, there was no real change in the overall standings.

There was 1 last day in the mountains of this really tough Tour. Stage 21 went into the Massif Central with several highly rated climbs culminating in a hilltop finish at the famous Puy de Dôme. The contenders had more or less accepted their positions while riders seeking individual glory in the closing days of the race sought their day in the sun. The only real action that could affect things was on the final ascent. LeMond pulled away from Zimmermann who distanced himself slightly from Hinault. LeMond was now 3 minutes, 10 seconds ahead of Hinault and had only 2 more stages to negotiate.

LeMond's luck stuck to him like a bad rumor. Shortly before entering Paris on the final day's stage, LeMond crashed badly enough to need a new bike. Hinault and his La Vie Claire teammates waited for him and motored him safely back into the field. Hinault, ever the tough competitor joined the final field sprint on the Champs Elysées and nailed fourth place. Big Guido Bontempi was the winner.

Paul Kimmage, who rode for the RMO squad, wrote about the final stage in this Tour in his book *Rough Ride*. Many of the riders were on their last legs by the time the final day in Paris arrived. In 1986, of the 210 riders who started, only 131 finished. The veterans told Kimmage about the blistering speeds of the final kilometers on the Champs Elysées. Fearful of getting dropped while the whole world watched, more than a few took amphetamines to get them over the Tour's final cobblestones. Kimmage asked the others if they weren't afraid of getting caught in the dope controls. No, he was told, only the winner and top finishers are tested after the final stage. They knew they were free to stick the needles in their arms.

The race was finally over and Greg LeMond had fulfilled his promise. When he was 17 he had written down his goal of winning the Tour de France.

Here's the final 1986 Tour de France General Classification:

1. Greg LeMond (La Vie Claire): 110 hours 35 minutes 19 seconds
2. Bernard Hinault (La Vie Claire) @ 3 minutes 10 seconds
3. Urs Zimmermann (Carrera) @ 10 minutes 54 seconds
4. Andy Hampsten (La Vie Claire) @ 18 minutes 44 seconds.
5. Claude Criquielion (Hitachi) @ 24 minutes 36 seconds

Climbers' Competition:

1. Bernard Hinault: 351 points
2. Luis Herrera: 270 points
3. Greg LeMond: 265 points

Points Competition:

1. Eric Vanderaerden: 277 points
2. Josef Lieckens: 232 points
3. Bernard Hinault: 210 points

Hinault won the Polka-Dot Climber's Jersey and Hampsten earned the white Young Rider's Jersey. In addition, La Vie Claire won the team General Classification. This was a dominating performance in a Tour in which the only real question was which of the La Vie Claire riders would actually win.

Over the years the debate about this Tour has grown ever more heated.

Hinault has defended his actions repeatedly, saying that he was really helping LeMond by challenging him and forcing him to earn the Tour. Hinault's answer to his critics, "I'd given my word to Greg LeMond that I'd help him win and that's what I did. A promise is a promise. I tried to wear out rivals to help him but I never attacked him personally…It wasn't my fault that he didn't understand this. When I think of some of the things he has said since the race ended, I wonder whether I was right not to attack him…I've worked for colleagues all my life without having the problems I had with Greg LeMond."

Here's Owen Mulholland's view from his *Uphill Battle*, discussing Hinault's repeated attacks in the Pyrenees:

"[Hinault] once told me he liked to 'play' with cycling, and doing something this outrageous 2 days in a row may have been his idea of play. No one will ever know because when he explained himself, Hinault played with words. And when credibility disappears so does reliability. Was this a gamble to win in a super-dominant manner? Was he trying to tire out the opposition so LeMond could go easily into the lead? Was this a bold gesture for the hell of it, a 'playful' gesture? Who can tell because Hinault's actions could be interpreted in myriad ways, and his words, intentionally deceptive, meant nothing. On such a 'solid' basis LeMond had to make decisions."

Of course, Hinault reneged on his promise. His words, that he was trying to toughen LeMond or get him to earn his Tour, are obvious nonsense. Hinault should be as ashamed of uttering such silliness as he should be of failing to honor his promise in a clear-cut, transparent way. Life really isn't all that complicated.

**1987**. On March 17, Félix Lévitan found his office locked. The problem was said to be the finances involved with a proposed American race. Émilion Amaury, owner of *L'Équipe* and the Tour, had turned the management of his organization to his son Philippe. Lévitan could no longer call upon the friendship of Émilion Amaury to protect him. Lévitan was sacked and replaced by an interim manager Jean-François Naquet-Radiguet, who lasted only a year.

LeMond was turkey hunting and was accidentally shot by his brother-in-law. That April 20, 40 shotgun pellets tore into his body. He lost $^3/_4$ of his blood and his right lung collapsed. 30 of the pellets could not be removed because of their location, including pellets in his heart lining, liver, small intestine and diaphragm. The short-term consequences of the accident were that LeMond could not return in 1987 to contest the Tour. The long-term effects on LeMond were even greater. The lead in his body left him damaged goods. Even though we will see him return in later years for wonderful victories, he was never the same and eventually had to retire with mitochondrial myopathy. This disorder interferes with the cell's basic ability to produce energy.

Hinault, seeing that he could no longer ride at the top, retired. He rode his last race in November of 1986.

So who was there? Laurent Fignon was still working on finding his old form. That spring he did rather well with a third in both Paris–Nice and the Vuelta a España and several other top-10 placings.

Jean-François Bernard, out from under the shadow of LeMond and Hinault, was expected to do very well. His team, Toshiba-La Vie Claire was a superb formation with Steve Bauer, Kim Andersen and Niki Ruttimann there to back him up.

Pedro Delgado had been showing promise in previous Tours. His team, PDM, was one of the finest in the world. He would have such sterling riders as Gerrie Knetemann, Gert-Jan Theunisse and Steven Rooks helping him. Delgado's spring was an easy, low-key lead-in to the Tour with no notable wins.

Andy Hampsten, with a fourth in the 1986 Tour under his belt and now riding for 7-Eleven, should have been licking his chops at the mountainous 1987 Tour.

Stephen Roche, who played such a large, but perhaps unintentional part in LeMond's 1985 famous ride to Luz-Ardiden, was having a wonderful year. Roche's racing had been up and down. A crash in the Paris Six-Day started the series of never-ending knee problems and attempts to surgically correct them. In 1987 his knee was holding together. Coming to the 1987 Tour he had already won the Tour of Romandie and the Giro d'Italia. He took second in Liège–Bastogne–Liège (he says that if he had been more tactically astute, he would have won it: "I rode like an amateur that day.") and fourth in Paris–Nice.

The 1987 Tour was designed to be tough. It was, in Roche's words, "one of the most mountainous since the war," with a record 26 stages, counting the Prologue. The Prologue was held in West Berlin. Europe was still divided between East and West and would remain so until the autumn of 1989. Dutchman Jelle Nijdam won the Prologue, but several of the Tour contenders, showing their form, were hot on his heels.

1. Jelle Nijdam: 7 minutes 6 seconds
3. Stephen Roche @ 7 seconds
7. Jean-François Bernard @ 9 seconds
8. Miguel Indurain @ 10 seconds
23. Pedro Delgado @ 19 seconds
26. Andy Hampsten @ 20 seconds

The Tour slowly made its way across Germany and moved into France when stage 5 ended in Strasbourg. The Yellow Jersey had already changed hands a few times as the sprinters enjoyed their stint in the Tour. The high speeds caused the large (209 starters) and nervous peloton to suffer repeated crashes. The Europeans blamed a lot of the crashes on the Colombians, whom they considered poor bike handlers. At one point in stage 10, after a Belgian hit a Colombian in the head with a water bottle, a couple of other Colombians went after him and started a fight.

By the time of the 87.5-kilometer stage 10 individual time trial from Saumur to Futuroscope, the first real test of the Tour, the only rider in the top 15 with any real hope for a high General Classification was Systeme U's Charly Mottet. The others had been riding quietly in the pack, trying to stay out of trouble while the big rouleurs and sprinters gained time bonuses that moved them up to the front of the leader's list. The time trial sorted things out. Roche won it with Mottet second at 42 seconds. That put Mottet in Yellow.

The General Classification at this point:

1. Charly Mottet
6. Stephen Roche @ 3 minutes 23 seconds
8. Jean-François Bernard @ 5 minutes 31 seconds
15. Pedro Delgado @ 6 minutes 41 seconds

Stage 13 was the first day in the Pyrenees. The contenders stayed together all the way to Pau even with 4 highly rated climbs. The day was so hot the tar on the road melted. Worse, there was an attack on the descent of the second category Bargargui. The high speeds and hard braking in the corners melted the glue holding the tires to the rims. Some riders rolled the tires off their rims, others had their tires explode from the heat build-up, causing several crashes. The stage removed the non-climbers from the top of the roster of the General Classification:

1. Charly Mottet
2. Jean-François Bernard @ 1 minute 52 seconds
3. Stephen Roche @ 3 minutes 23 seconds
6. Pedro Delgado @ 6 minutes 24 seconds
14. Andy Hampsten @ 11 minutes 24 seconds

Stage 14 with the Aubisque, the Marie-Blanque and a finish at Luz-Ardiden, caused no real change to the General Classification.

The Tour headed towards the Massif Central. Stage 18's individual time trial up Mont Ventoux promised to shake things up and it did not disappoint. Jean-François Bernard rode the ride of his life. Never before had he risen to such heights and never again would he perform at such an extraordinary level. Bernard won the stage and the Yellow Jersey. Look at some of the times of his competition to get an idea of how well the Frenchman rode the 36.9-kilometer time trial:

1. Jean-François Bernard: 1 hour 19 minutes 44 seconds
2. Luis Herrera @ 1 minute 39 seconds
3. Pedro Delgado @ 1 minute 51 seconds
5. Stephen Roche @ 2 minutes 19 seconds
9. Charly Mottet @ 3 minutes 58 seconds
25. Andy Hampsten @ 6 minutes 12 seconds

The General Classification situation:

1. Jean-François Bernard
2. Stephen Roche @ 2 minutes 34 seconds
3. Charly Mottet @ 2 minutes 47 seconds
4. Pedro Delgado @ 3 minutes 56 seconds

It seemed so beautiful for Bernard, the chosen heir of Hinault and the great hope of French cycling. He had a good lead and was climbing and time trialing well. He turned out to be a far better rider than his opposition had supposed. He should have been able to keep the Yellow all the way to Paris. But fate knocked on the door. The next day was a mountainous stage and with the Tour a Wild West wide-open shootout, he was not going to be allowed to keep the lead without mounting a serious defense.

Near the top of the first real climb, Bernard flatted and was unable to get his bike serviced before the other racers had disappeared up the mountains.

Bernard's luck didn't get any better. Mottet and his Systeme U teammates had hatched a plan to attack Bernard in that day's feed zone. They packed extra food to carry them through the long day. For insurance, Mottet told Roche about the plan to make sure there would be enough horsepower to keep Bernard and his tough La Vie Claire team at bay. Mottet knew the area and saw that the feed zone was just after a very narrow bridge, which would really slow the peloton. Things happened exactly as Mottet predicted. Bernard, who had been chasing to get back on terms with the leaders after his flat tire was forced to a stop at one point when the peloton slowed upon reaching the bridge. Mottet, Delgado and Roche were already up the road and putting real time between themselves and the furiously chasing Bernard.

Bernard was never able to rejoin the leaders and came in 4 minutes, 16 seconds after Delgado and Roche. Roche was now in Yellow with Mottet only 41 seconds behind and Delgado stalking him at 1 minute, 19 seconds. Delgado and Roche had dropped Mottet, who had planned the day's skullduggery in the first place.

But wait, this gets better.

Stage 20 was another tough alpine stage that finished with the first category Côte de Laffrey and the *hors catégorie* Alpe d'Huez. The final climb up the Alpe had the riders coming in one at a time. Federico Echave won the stage. The first real General Classification rider to finish was Laurent Fignon who was finally starting to get his legs. Fignon rolled in sixth, 3 minutes, 25 seconds after Echave. Delgado was next, 19 seconds later. Roche was fifteenth that day at 5 minutes, 28 seconds. Delgado now took the Yellow and Roche was 25 seconds behind. Spain was so transfixed with the excitement of Delgado's struggle with Roche for the lead that the Spanish parliament suspended its deliberations so that the members could watch the stage.

The next day was finer still. The giant mountains kept coming at the riders like mosquitoes on a hot Louisiana night. Stage 21 went from Bourg d'Oisans up to La Plagne, 185.5 kilometers of pure effort. Along the way were the Galibier, the Madeleine and the final climb to La Plagne, all *hors catégorie* climbs. Now Roche wasn't a climber, as he has said over and over in many interviews. He was like so many truly fine racers, capable of putting out so much power that he not only had absolute power to time-trial and ride the flats well, he possessed superb relative power, or as we usually say, a good strength to weight ratio. That ratio allowed him to handle the mountains well. Yet he knew the specialist climbers like Delgado could give him trouble on their own turf.

Fignon launched a hard attack and won the stage. But the real drama was Roche's story. In the November, 2003 *Cycle Sport* magazine he gave an interview about that fateful day:

"I had the Jersey at Villard-de-Lans [stage 19, won by Delgado]. But Delgado took it back from me the next day at the summit of l'Alpe d'Huez [stage 20, related just above]. I was not a climber like him. Between the descent of the Galibier and the foot of the Madeleine [stage 21, the stage we are discussing] I attacked because he was isolated. I passed him and rejoined the group ahead. Afterwards I climbed the Madeleine alone. Delgado and his teammates caught me again at the foot of La Plagne. I said to myself, 'What am I going to do? If I stay with him he'll kill me. I'll never get to the top.' I let him go and conceded 1'10", 1'15".

"But he didn't trust himself. And 4 kilometers from the line, I attacked at top speed. I gave it everything I had. And I got to within a few seconds of him. Psychologically, that was my most beautiful victory."

After his titanic effort to bring Delgado back, Roche collapsed at the finish and needed oxygen. He was taken to a hospital but was found to be perfectly fine.

The General Classification now, after Roche was penalized 10 seconds for taking an illegal feed:

1. Pedro Delgado

2. Stephen Roche @ 39 seconds

3. Charly Mottet @ 3 minutes 12 seconds

The next day, the last one in the Alps finishing at Morzine, Roche was able to take another 18 seconds out of Delgado. The Spaniard was tiring. They were now only 21 seconds apart. Roche felt confident that his superior time-trialing abilities would give him the Yellow in the final time trial.

So it came down to the penultimate stage, a 38-kilometer time trial, the "race of truth" at Dijon. Bernard's results let us know that this would have been an even more interesting race, if that were even possible, if he had not had that unfortunate flat.

The stage results:

1. Jean-François Bernard: 48 minutes 17 seconds

2. Stephen Roche @ 1 minute 44 seconds

7. Pedro Delgado @ 2 minutes 45 seconds

The Yellow Jersey was Roche's. And with only the final stage into Paris left, it was his to keep.

That last stage into Paris had a big surprise in store for the 7-Eleven team. Jeff Pierce won the stage in a solo victory with Steve Bauer only 1 second behind him.

In that same interview in *Cycle Sport*, Roche said some kind words that reflected well on both Roche and Delgado.

"The memory of the Tour de France that will stay with me all my life is when I retook the jersey in Dijon. I went through the ceremony and then on the Jacques Chancel TV program Delgado was already in the middle of doing his interview. I arrived on the set and Delgado got up. He embraced me. Chancel said to him 'Less than an hour ago he took the Yellow Jersey from you and now you embrace him?' Delgado replied, 'I have had 4,500 kilometers in which to win the jersey, and I couldn't do it.' It was beautiful when he said that."

This was a fantastic Tour with 8 different men wearing the Yellow Jersey, equaling the 1958 record.

The final 1987 Tour de France General Classification:

1. Stephen Roche (Carrera): 115 hours 27 minutes 42 seconds

2. Pedro Delgado (PDM) @ 40 seconds

3. Jean-François Bernard (Toshiba) @ 2 minutes 13 seconds

4. Charly Mottet (Systeme U) @ 6 minutes 40 seconds

5. Luis "Lucho" Herrera (Café de Colombia) @ 9 minutes 32 seconds

Climbers' Competition:

1. Luis Herrera: 452 points

2. Anselmo Fuerte: 314 points

3. Raul Alcala: 277 points

Points Competition:

1. Jean-Paul van Poppel: 263 points

2. Stephen Roche: 247 points

3. Pedro Delgado: 228 points

That year Roche won the Giro, the Tour and went on to win the World Championship. Only one other rider in the history of the sport, Eddy Merckx, has been able to win all 3 in a single year.
*Erin Go Bragh.*

**1988**. Jean-François Naquet-Radiguet was replaced by his brother-in-law Xavier Louy as the Tour Director. Naquet-Radiguet was thought to be a bit too independent and made too many important decisions on his own that seemed to reflect poor judgment, including a planned Montreal, Canada start for the 1992 Tour.

Roche had 2 knee operations between his World Championship win and the start of the new season. He was quite unable to race the Tour. I remember seeing him on TV in 1988 undergoing therapy for his knee as he voiced his terrible frustration at not being able to race in his rainbow jersey.

LeMond had recovered from his hunting accident and signed with the PDM squad. He injured his right knee in a Belgian *kermesse* in late March and was troubled all spring with the injury. He attempted the Giro, but quit after 5 stages. He was forced to return to the United States for surgery and recuperation.

As far as major Tour General Classification contenders, that left Pedro Delgado, second the previous year, as the man to beat. He lost the 1987 Tour by only 40 seconds. At no time had Roche, the winner, significantly outclassed him.

Andy Hampsten and the American 7-Eleven team were entered. But Hampsten had just won the Giro a few weeks before and the team had buried itself to keep him in the lead when he took the Pink Jersey after a remarkable ascent—and a frightening descent—over a freezing Gavia Pass. Would they recover enough to vie for the Tour?

Luis Herrera won the Dauphiné in early June by bounding up the Col de Porte on the final stage, taking the lead from Acacio Da Silva. Charly Mottet had led in the early stages but had tired. Herrera showed superb form, but winning the Dauphiné is tough, draining work and often leaves its winner flat for the Tour. It would turn out to be true for Herrera in the 1988 Tour.

The 1988 Tour was the shortest since Henri Desgrange recast the race in 1906. At only 3,286 kilometers, it was even shorter than almost all of the Tours of the past decade. With 22 stages, the average stage length was only 149 kilometers. This held out the promise of a super-fast race.

The Tour was scheduled to open with a 6-kilometer Prologue. To comply with UCI rules, it was shortened to a "Prelude" that was run according to some rather odd rules. The teams rode a team time trial and let a single rider go with a flying start to ride the final kilometer, the only part that counted toward the General Classification. Guido Bontempi won with a time of 1 minute, 14 seconds. Bontempi's hold on the Yellow Jersey was almost as short as his Prelude. Canadian Steve Bauer managed to beat the pack home on the first stage by 8 seconds. It was enough to put him in Yellow.

Then it was Bauer's turn to give up the lead the next day. The heir and sponsors of the old TI-Raleigh squad, Panasonic, narrowly beat Bauer's Weinmann team, earning the Yellow Jersey for Teun van Vliet. None of this mattered much to the overall lead. Even the stage 6, 52-kilometer individual time trial didn't really smoke out the leaders. What the time trial did do was eliminate several riders from probable contention. Fignon and Kelly, each losing about 2 minutes, displayed lackluster form. Sprinter Jelle Nijdam held the lead.

In stage 8, the ever-attentive Steve Bauer got into a 16-man break initiated by Herrera that beat the pack by 23 seconds, giving Bauer the Yellow Jersey. The Tour remained a simmering cauldron of hot competitors. The race was turning out to be a fast one, setting a new record so far for average speed.

It was in stage 11, from Besançon to Morzine that the Tour boiled over. Stage 11 had 2 highly rated climbs, the first category Pas de Morgins and the category 2 Le Corbier. On the Morgins, French hopes Laurent Fignon and Jean-François Bernard lost contact with the leaders after Urs Zimmermann opened the day's hostilities. Steve Bauer was able to maintain contact with the front group and stayed with them for the rest of the stage, preserving his lead. The real contenders finished together with the exception of Colombia's Fabio Parra who soloed in 20 seconds ahead of the others. Fignon's Tour hopes were dashed when he lost 19 minutes.

Stage 12 was 227 kilometers, going from Morzine to l'Alpe d'Huez, crossing along the way the Pont d'Arbon, the Madeleine, and the Glandon before finishing at the top of l'Alpe d'Huez. Bauer had kept his Yellow Jersey after the hilly stage 11. Stage 12 would be a tougher test for the Canadian. Fignon abandoned the Tour that morning before even starting the stage.

Delgado signaled his determination to shake things up when he attacked 2 kilometers from the summit of the Glandon, and only Steven Rooks could stay with him. On the descent they were caught by Fabio Parra and Gert-Jan Theunisse but the chasing pack couldn't close the gap.

Things exploded on the final run up the 21 hairpin turns of the Alpe. Fabio Parra repeatedly tried to get away, but he couldn't get through the crowds that blocked the leading motorcycles. Dutchman Steven Rooks managed to escape, closely followed by Delgado and Rooks' good friend Theunisse. Parra was 6 seconds behind Delgado. The rest of the field, including all of the erstwhile contenders, were scattered down the mountain. Luis Herrera was only 1 minute, 6 seconds behind, but Hampsten was tenth, 4 minutes, 21 seconds back. Pedro Delgado had established himself as the clear leader of the Tour as he donned the Yellow Jersey. Theunisse, in one of his many run-ins with doping controls during his career, was found positive. He had 10 minutes added to his time. Bauer finished 2 minutes, 34 seconds behind Rooks and had to cede his Yellow Jersey to Delgado.

The General Classification now stood thus:

1. Pedro Delgado
2. Steve Bauer @ 25 seconds
3. Fabio Parra @ 1 minute 20 seconds
4. Steven Rooks @ 1 minute 38 seconds
5. Luis Herrera @ 2 minutes 25 seconds

The next day (stage 13), Delgado nailed the box shut with his victory in the 38-kilometer uphill individual time trial. Bernard was second at 44 seconds and Rooks was third at 1 minute, 9 seconds. Steve Bauer lost his second place in the Overall to Steven Rooks, who was now 2 minutes, 47 seconds behind the Spaniard.

Now came a rest day that was also a transfer day to the Pyrenees.

Delgado rode carefully, yet masterfully in the Pyrenees. Stage 14, with several tough climbs at the end, wasn't contested by the men seeking Yellow. It did show that even the Tour de France could have organizational snafus. A kilometer from the end the follow cars were supposed to go straight and the riders were to bear left. In the confusion, the day's likely winner, Philippe Bouvatier, went with the cars. The stage winner, Massimo Ghirotto, recognizing Bouvatier's probable victory, offered Bouvatier the stage prize, a new Peugeot car. The Tour organization came up with a second car so that Ghirotto could keep his prize. In those days, a domestique's income was very poor and this was a tremendous act of generosity on Ghirotto's part.

Stage 15 was the 1988 Tour's Queen Stage, with some of the great cols of the Tour: Portet d'Aspet, the Col de Menté, the Peyresourde, the Aspin, the Tourmalet and Luz-Ardiden. Delgado had let Laudelino Cubino and Gilbert Duclos-Lassalle, non-contenders, get away. In the final rush to the finish Delgado bolted, leaving such vaunted climbers as Parra, Theunisse and Rooks to do what they could to limit the damage. Generously, he eased before the line to let Duclos-Lassalle take second place in the stage, Cubino having finished 6 minutes before. With the Pyrenees finished, Delgado had a 4 minute, 6 second lead on second place Rooks. With a stage up to Puy de Dôme, where he should do well, and a 46-kilometer individual time trial looming as the only obstacles, he should have been able to feel that the Tour was his.

The standings after the Pyrenees:

1. Pedro Delgado
2. Steven Rooks @ 4 minutes 6 seconds
3. Fabio Parra @ 5 minutes 50 seconds
4. Steve Bauer @ 7 minutes 25 seconds
5. Gert-Jan Theunisse @ 7 minutes 54 seconds

After the finish of stage 15 to Bordeaux a rumor started that ended up on television that evening: Delgado had tested positive for a banned drug. The journalists knew about the positive before Delgado did. The next day Tour officials confirmed that Delgado had tested positive for Probenecid. We'll stop here for just a second. Probenecid turns up every so often in dope tests. It is unusual that a healthy person would ever need Probenecid since it is rarely dispensed even to sick people. It acts as a diuretic and helps some people with gout. It can also increase the potency of antibiotics. Victims of drug-resistant gonorrhea are given Probenecid to increase the efficacy of their regimen of antibiotics. It is also called for in some AIDS cases. But Probenecid was found to have another effect. It drastically slows the urinary excretion of the metabolites of steroids. When an athlete pees into a bottle for a drug test, the testing scientist is often not looking for the drug itself. He is looking for the by-products that the body produces as it metabolizes the drug. This is how steroids are detected, by looking for the chemicals the body produces in eliminating the drug.

Probenecid keeps these telltale chemicals from being present in urine, thus circumventing the drug test; the Probenecid itself, however, is present.

Here's where it gets interesting. Probenecid was on the Olympic Committee's list of banned drugs. The UCI (the governing body ruling cycling) was going to ban the drug after the Tour. It was not on the list of banned drugs during the 1988 Tour. Technically, Delgado had committed no offense in using Probenecid as it was not yet a banned drug. 2 days after the positive test, the second sample (there is always an "A" and "B" sample tested independently for the protection of the racer) was tested and confirmed the positive for the drug. The Spanish government sent sports ministers and lawyers to France to argue Delgado's case. They were not going to surrender a third Spanish Tour winner (after Bahamontes and Ocaña) without a fight. Because there was no actual offense Delgado could continue the Tour without penalty. The day of the announcement that Delgado was clear was also the day Theunisse received his 10-minute penalty for his doping positive. Ironically, it was steroids that showed up in Theunisse's test sample, the same class of chemicals that Delgado was thought to be hiding with Probenecid.

To this day, Delgado maintains his innocence and acts as if his continuing the Tour under the drug cloud was an act of heroism. He said he took the Probenecid to take care of problems with his legs. He later said that he was given a drink by a spectator on the route. Merckx thought the conflicting stories reflected poorly on the man, calling the defense Delgado offered "rubbish". If he was innocent, then he competed under very tough emotional conditions. He was tested over and over again during the Tour and came up positive only once. But barring evidence to the contrary, I tend to believe that mass spectrographs are more reliable than the words of racers caught with a positive sample. Delgado is a genuinely nice man. The racers and the fans liked him. Because of this geniality, Delgado was able to elicit a great deal of sympathy from the fans. The riders staged a 10-minute strike the next day in sympathy for Delgado and against the inept handling of his case. It should also be noted that Delgado had been tested at least 10 times during the 1988 Tour and only this one time had he turned up positive for Probenecid.

On the stage 19 ascent up Puy de Dôme Johnny Weltz and Rolf Golz had a substantial lead, 15 minutes with 50 kilometers to go. But then things stirred in the peloton. On the climb Delgado demonstrated his complete mastery by easily dropping all the others and finishing third, $5^{1}/_{2}$ minutes behind Weltz. Delgado was now almost 5 minutes ahead of second-place Rooks.

Delgado wanted to win the 46-kilometer individual time trial to make a clean win of it all. Held on rolling terrain near Dijon, Delgado was able to come close to winning the stage. He was ahead at every checkpoint but the finish line. The wind had become strong during the day and finally it was too much for Delgado to overcome. His fourth place at 11 seconds to the winner Juan Martinez-Oliver was still the best time of any of the top men. Rooks finished twentieth, 2 minutes, 26 seconds behind.

Hampsten and his team were indeed shot after the Giro. The Giro winner never was able to display his normal brilliance in the high mountains. The 7-Eleven team was dogged by misfortune that started even before the race had started. Bob Roll crashed before the "Prelude" and had to be replaced at the last minute. During the second stage team time trial Dag-Otto Lauritzen crashed. Roy Knickman failed to make the time cutoff on the eighteenth stage to Limoges, and that same day Jeff Pierce, who had been struggling, was also eliminated.

Final 1988 Tour de France General Classification:

1. Pedro Delgado (Reynolds): 84 hours 27minutes 53 seconds
2. Steven Rooks (PDM) @ 7 minutes 13 seconds
3. Fabio Parra (Kelme) @ 9 minutes 58 seconds
4. Steve Bauer (Weinmann-La Suisse) @ 12 minutes 15 seconds
5. Eric Boyer (Systeme U) @ 14 minutes 4 seconds
15. Andy Hampsten (7-Eleven) @ 26 minutes

Climbers' Competition:

1. Steven Rooks: 326 points
2. Gert-Jan Theunisse: 248 points
3. Pedro Delgado: 223 points

Points Competition:

1. Eddy Planckaert: 278 points
2. Davis Phinney: 193 points
3. Sean Kelly: 183 points

The 1988 Tour did live up to its expectation as a fast race. The average speed was 38.909 kilometers per hour, the fastest Tour so far. And it was a strange Tour for Belgium. For the first time since 1910, not 1 rider from the bike-mad country won a stage.

Epilogue to the 1988 Tour. In 2000 Steven Rooks admitted to taking amphetamines and testosterone during his racing career. He just didn't get caught.

**1989**. The Tour organization again changed Tour directors. The appointment of Jean-Marie Leblanc was one of the most important events in the history of the Tour de France. In its desperate search for income the Tour had multiplied the various prizes and classifications, each one having a sponsor and most being unimportant to all but the most dedicated racing fan. Wanting to bring clarity and therefore credibility to the Tour, Leblanc slashed the list of competitions and then raised the cost of sponsoring the remaining, now more visible ones. Under Leblanc the Tour underwent a renaissance, becoming wildly popular and financially sound. Leblanc's tenure coincided with the beginning of the trend of many of the finest Tour contenders making the Tour de France their only real goal for the season. With ever larger corporate money entering racing, the need for gigantic results to justify the big investments in teams drove more and more attention to the Tour. Leblanc's skill in running the Tour only served to magnify this tendency.

Leblanc, like all Tour directors before him except Naquet-Radiguet, had been a journalist. He was the chief cycling correspondent of *L'Équipe* before becoming Tour boss. Moreover, Leblanc had been a pro rider with Tour racing experience, having entered and finished both the 1968 and the 1970 Tours.

Both Greg LeMond and Laurent Fignon were back racing with dedication. They were in good form and finally achieving good results.

LeMond's recovery from his shooting accident and knee surgery was long and hard. In the early season races he had done reasonably well. He was fourth in the Critérium International and sixth in the Tirreno–Adriatico. LeMond had not won a race since his 1986 Tour de France victory.

In the Giro he suffered like a dog finishing a lackluster thirty-ninth, almost an hour behind. It seemed that he just could not find that old magic. His wife, Kathy, flew to Italy to give him moral support. He stuck to it, refusing to give up. In the final stage, a 53.8-kilometer time trial, LeMond came in second. He was able to beat the overall Giro winner, Fignon, by over a minute on that stage. The strength was returning. LeMond's team however, was not a Grand Tour Team. His ADR Belgians (including Johan Museeuw) would not be able to give him the help he would need in the high mountains. He would have to race with his head all the time.

Fignon, who had been unable to truly contend for a major stage race since he had surgery on his Achilles tendon in 1984, had finally found the way to win. In 1989 he had already won Milan–San Remo and the Giro d'Italia. Fignon had an outstanding team in Super U, including future Tour winner Bjarne Riis.

With Pedro Delgado also in good shape and seeking redemption after his tainted 1988 victory, this would indeed be an interesting Tour.

And that's just how it started out, interesting. At the Prologue, where every rider is assigned a specific start time, Delgado signed in 20 minutes early then went off to warm up. Somehow, he lost track of the time. He showed up at the start house 2 minutes, 40 seconds late. The clock had been ticking off the seconds since his start time. The clock for a rider's time trial starts with or without the rider, it is quite indifferent. Delgado roared off and did a very credible time trial, his actual time on the road being only 14 seconds slower than winner Erik Breukink. But because of his delayed start, he was now hamstrung with a deficit of almost 3 minutes at the opening of the Tour de France. Fignon and LeMond both finished at the same time, 6 seconds off Breukink's time. The shootout between the 2 had started at the first possible opportunity.

The second stage team time trial highlighted the differences in the teams. Fignon's Super U squad won the stage, with the team finishing intact, not losing any men on the road. LeMond's ADR team came in a respectable fifth, a minute slower over the 46-kilometer course, losing 3 men along the way. Delgado's Reynolds-Banesto team finished dead last. Demoralized after his botched start to the Tour, Delgado couldn't keep up with his team. His teammates had to wait for him and nurse him to the finish. After only 2 stages Delgado was almost 10 minutes down in the overall. This was a spectacular reversal of fortune after his previous year's dominance.

LeMond wins the stage 5 time trial.

The next real test was the first individual time trial in stage 5. At a long 73 kilometers, it would really make a difference. Whatever emotional or morale problem Delgado may have been having in the first couple of stages, he was clearly over them now. LeMond was also coming on form. His suffering in the Giro was starting to pay off. LeMond used the new triathlon bars that narrowed the rider's frontal profile. This is standard equipment for any time trial bike today, but back then this was revolutionary stuff. Fignon should have been paying attention.

1. Greg LeMond: 1 hour 38 minutes 12 seconds
2. Pedro Delgado @ 24 seconds
3. Laurent Fignon @ 56 seconds
4. Thierry Marie @ 1 minute 51 seconds
5. Sean Yates @ 2 minutes 6 seconds

The General Classification after the stage 5 time trial:

1. Greg LeMond
2. Laurent Fignon @ 5 seconds
3. Thierry Marie @ 20 seconds
4. Erik Breukink @ 1 minute 51 seconds
5. Sean Yates @ 2 minutes 18 seconds

Stage 9 was the first day in the Pyrenees, going from Pau to Cauterets, crossing the Marie-Blanque, the Aubisque, the Bordères and the Cambasque. Delgado's teammate, Miguel Indurain, was first over the final 3 big climbs and won the stage. Delgado was really back in action, completely revived and fighting, finishing about a minute and a half behind Indurain. LeMond and Fignon finished together, another 30 seconds back. No change to the General Classification except that Delgado continued to move up.

Stage 10 with the Tourmalet, Aspin, Peyresourde and Superbagnères made a little difference to the standings. On the final climb LeMond, feeling ever more confident, attacked. Fignon caught him and countered. LeMond tried to answer, but couldn't. Fignon managed to put 12 seconds between himself and LeMond. Fignon now had the lead by a margin of 7 seconds. Stephen Roche's knee, which had given him so much trouble over his career, flamed up again. He struggled in terrible pain over the mountains, refusing to abandon during the stage. But

that was it, Roche's Tour was over. Paul Kimmage says that during that
very evening while Roche was in misery in his hotel room, the management of his team was already in talks with LeMond to see if he would
come over to the Fagor squad the following year. This bike racing is a
hard business.

    This tense, tight situation with Fignon's 7-second lead remained
until the 39-kilometer individual time trial of stage 15, with 2 first category climbs. Steven Rooks won the stage, Delgado was fourth at 49
seconds, LeMond right behind him at 57 seconds. Fignon was tenth at

LeMond takes stage 19 at Aix les Bains just in front of Fignon. Delgado
and Theunisse also got the same time that day.

1 minute, 44 seconds. LeMond took the Yellow Jersey back with a 40-second lead over Fignon.

In the next day's stage with the Izoard, LeMond was able to gain another precious 13 seconds. They say baseball is a game of inches. The 1989 Tour was a game of seconds. Each second was a pearl beyond price as the 2 athletes battled with unabated intensity.

Stage 17, with the Galibier, the Croix de Fer and a finish up l'Alpe d'Huez scrambled the eggs again. On the final ascent Fignon attacked and took Delgado with him. LeMond could not go with the Frenchman. LeMond gave up 1 minute, 19 seconds and the Yellow Jersey to Fignon. Fignon now had a 26-second lead over LeMond. Delgado had clawed his way to third place after being down almost 10 minutes.

Fignon was finding the Alpine air to his liking. He took another 24-second chunk out of LeMond's side when he won stage 18. The gap was now 50 seconds. While publicly optimistic, LeMond is said to have privately conceded the race at this point.

These men were so close, the degree of equipoise so perfect, this has to be one of the great races of history. Stage 19, with the Porte, Cucheron and Granier climbs proved it. LeMond won this stage with Fignon right with him getting the same time. Neither was giving up a single second if it could be helped.

So, here was the General Classification going into the final stage, a 24.5-kilometer time trial from Versailles to Paris. This must be the most famous and talked about race against the clock in the history of the sport.

1. Laurent Fignon

2. Greg LeMond @ 50 seconds

3. Pedro Delgado @ 2 minutes 28 seconds

4. Gert-Jan Theunisse @ 5 minutes 36 seconds

LeMond had done wind-tunnel testing and had perfected his riding position. For the time trial he had an aerodynamic helmet and the aero bars which he had used to good effect in stage 5. The run-in to Paris was slightly downhill. LeMond decided that he didn't want to get time splits. He said that he would just go as fast as he humanly could, hoping he wouldn't blow up before the end. The idea that he could take almost a minute out of an in-form Fignon in such a short distance was not preposterous, but it was unlikely. Being in second place, LeMond went before Fignon. LeMond thumped a monster 54 x 12 gear driving it a steaming 54.545 kilometers an hour. This was the fastest time trial ever ridden in the Tour de France and remained the record for years to come.

Fignon had other troubles besides LeMond. He had acquired a nasty saddle sore in stage 19. It was so bad he couldn't pedal properly. He was in real pain and unable to sleep the night before the time trial. As he had done on every other occasion going back to his second place in the 1984 Giro, Fignon shunned the niceties of aerodynamics. He didn't use tri bars or an aero helmet. He even wore a wind-dragging ponytail. His saddle sore prevented his getting a good warm-up before he started his ride.

As the race leader, Fignon had the privilege of going last. With each pedal stroke he lost time. Yet, when he came on to the Champs Elysées he still had the overall lead by 2 seconds. It was in those final meters that he lost those next, oh-so-precious 10 seconds. LeMond had to watch and wait in agony to see if his roll of the dice had succeeded.

The Tour was LeMond's. Fignon had lost the closest Tour in History. When Fignon learned that he had lost, he fell to ground with a moan, in tears. LeMond yelped with joy. If there is to be a winner, there must also be a loser.

Here's how the time trial went:

1. Greg LeMond: 26 minutes 57 seconds
2. Thierry Marie @ 33 seconds
3. Laurent Fignon @ 58 seconds


The Final 1989 Tour de France General Classification:

1. Greg LeMond (ADR-Agrigel): 87 hours 38 minutes 35 seconds
2. Laurent Fignon (Super U) @ 8 seconds
3. Pedro Delgado (Reynolds) @ 3 minutes 34 seconds
4. Gert-Jan Theunisse (PDM) @ 7 minutes 30 seconds
5. Marino Lejarreta (Paternina) @ 9 minutes 39 seconds

Climbers' Competition:

1. Gert-Jan Theunisse: 441 points
2. Pedro Delgado: 311 points
3. Steven Rooks: 257 points

Points Competition:

1. Sean Kelly: 277 points
2. Etienne De Wilde: 194 points
3. Steven Rooks: 163 points

An aerodynamicist once calculated that if Fignon had just cut off his ponytail to reduce his drag, he would have been able to go fast enough to have won the Tour. The gents at memoire-du-cyclisme.net figured that at the speeds LeMond and Fignon were traveling in the final time trial, the 8 seconds in the final Overall amounted to 82 meters, less than a football field after 3,257 kilometers.

LeMond went on that fall to cap his season with his second World Road Championship.

**1990**. At the start of the 1990 season LeMond was noticeably overweight. The situation was not improved when he had a bout of mononucleosis (Brits call it "glandular fever"). On the plus side, for the first time in his career, LeMond had a strong team that was dedicated to him. There were no split loyalties of the sort both he and Stephen Roche had been forced to deal with in earlier years. And unlike his 1989 ADR team, his new team, sponsored by a children's clothing company "Z", had riders who could assist him during the entire Tour. His "Z" helpers included climber Robert Millar, all-around strongmen Gilbert Duclos-Lassalle (a future 2-time Paris–Roubaix winner) and Ronan Pensec. These were good men to have on one's side.

While there may have been justifiable worries about LeMond's fitness to contest the Tour de France, these fears were almost immediately put to rest with the Prologue time trial. Thierry Marie, who made a habit of winning these mini-time trials, won this one. LeMond was second at only 4 seconds. Raul Alcala scored third with just about the same time. Fignon was fifteenth at 19 seconds.

The first stage was another of those dopey stages in which a break of riders, generally thought to be General Classification non-threats, was allowed to get away. The pack must have had a day of *non compos mentis* because this was a group of good racers.

Claudio Chiappucci, who never had any regard for conservative tactics, took off when the first stage was only 6 kilometers old. Steve Bauer, Ronan Pensec and Frans Maassen quickly joined him. For the first 30 kilometers the quartet was only able to squeeze out a 30-second lead. Then, as is often the case, the peloton relented in its chase, perhaps slowed by a crash that took Pedro Delgado down. The lead increased and by the end of the stage the pack was 10 minutes, 35 seconds behind the 4 speedy adventurers. All of these riders except Chiappucci were well known quantities. Bauer was fourth in the 1988 Tour. Pensec had a sixth and a seventh in his past Tours. They were tough riders who would probably surrender their time in the high mountains only after a tough fight. But Chiappucci?

So far, Chiappucci had shown himself to be a competent but unspectacular racer. The previous year he was forty-sixth in the Giro and eighty-first in the Tour. He did manage to win the Giro del Piemonte and score a second in the hilly Giro del Trentino. This year he had improved, with a seventh in Paris–Nice and a commendable twelfth in the Giro. This did not seem to be the stuff of a Tour contender on the level of Fignon or Delgado. But wait, Chiappucci was King of the Mountains in this year's Giro. Hmmm…

Bauer was in Yellow yet again. The General Classification now stood thus:

1. Steve Bauer
2. Frans Maassen @ 2 seconds
3. Claudio Chiappucci @ 9 seconds
4. Ronan Pensec @ 21 seconds
5. John Carlsen @ 9 minutes 3 seconds
6. Guido Winterberg @ 9 minutes 44 seconds
7. Thierry Marie @ 10 minutes 24 seconds
8. Greg LeMond @ 10 minutes 28 seconds

As the Tour went clockwise across northern France and then headed south for the Alps, the general situation remained unchanged, with the stage 1 breakaway quartet sitting on top of the leader board and Bauer in Yellow. A crash in stage 4 cost Robert Millar over 9 minutes and effectively eliminated the winner of the 1990 Dauphiné from contention.

Raul Alcala blistered the stage 7 time trial with Miguel Indurain second to him at a distant 1 minute, 24 seconds. LeMond picked up some time on the 4 breakaways, he was now 10 minutes, 9 seconds behind Bauer. Fignon, again unable to ride well, abandoned. The important news of the time trial was that the 4 stage-1 breakaways had ridden credible time trials. The closest rider to the top 4 was Raul Alcala and he was still over 7 minutes behind Bauer.

Stage 10, with its finish at the Le Bettex ski station, saw the first casualty of the Gang of 4. Bauer finished fiftieth, 4 minutes, 7 seconds behind stage winner Thierry Claveyrolet who had taken off early in search of Hot Spot sprint points and then stayed away to the finish. Behind, on the final climb an aggressive Delgado blew up the chasing group but wasn't able to gain more than 19 seconds on the other contenders. More importantly for the moment, Bauer had come in behind Pensec and Chiappucci. The pair finished in the LeMond group which included Rooks, Alcala, Gianni Bugno, Miguel Indurain and Andy Hampsten. The Yellow Jersey was now the property of LeMond's teammate Ronan Pensec.

LeMond continued to chew away at the deficit in little bites. Stage 11 crossed the Glandon, the Madeleine and finished atop l'Alpe d'Huez. Gianni Bugno and LeMond finished with the same time, with Erik Breukink just off their wheels. Pensec lost 48 seconds and Chiappucci lost 1 minute, 48 seconds. Pensec was still in Yellow with an increased lead over Chiappucci.

The standings after the major Alpine climbing was finished:

1. Ronan Pensec
2. Claudio Chiappucci @ 1 minute 28 seconds
3. Greg LeMond @ 9 minutes 4 seconds

Stage 12 is where it starts to get really interesting. The 33.5-kilometer individual time trial included a second category climb and ended Ronan Pensec's hopes of taking the Yellow Jersey to Paris. Erik Breukink continued to display his fine form by winning the stage with Delgado only 30 seconds back. LeMond was fifth at 56 seconds. Chiappucci showed he was made of stern stuff with an eighth place, 1 minute, 5 seconds behind Breukink and only 9 seconds slower then LeMond. Pensec was forty-ninth at 3 minutes, 50 seconds.

The General Classification at this point:

1. Claudio Chiappucci
2. Ronan Pensec @ 1 minute 17 seconds
3. Erik Breukink @ 6 minutes 55 seconds
4. Greg LeMond @ 7 minutes 27 seconds
5. Pedro Delgado @ 9 minutes 2 seconds

Chiappucci had the Yellow Jersey and the Tour had a day of rest. Keeping the Yellow Jersey would be a real challenge as Breukink, Delgado, LeMond, Hampsten and the others with high General Classification ambitions continued their bellicosity when the race resumed. The very next day into the Massif Central, stage 13, Chiappucci missed the crucial break that included LeMond, Breukink, and Delgado, and lost almost 5 minutes. Doing a lot of the chasing himself, Chiappucci had at one point closed to within 33 seconds. But getting almost no help from the other teams, making contact with the talented riders ahead of him was an almost impossible task. Well, he was the Yellow Jersey and it wasn't the job of the other teams to defend it for him.

Breukink, who was having the Tour of his life, had pulled within 2 minutes, 2 seconds of Chiappucci, and LeMond was just a tad further back at 2 minutes, 34 seconds. If LeMond wanted the win, he had to get by both Chiappucci and a beautifully riding Erik Breukink.

In stage 14 Breukink and LeMond took a small bite out of Chiappucci, about 10 seconds. If they could keep up the pressure, the small Italian would just bleed little dabs of time all over France. Would Chiappucci run out of Tour before he ran out of time?

Stage 16 to Luz Ardiden with the Aspin and the Tourmalet in the middle decided the Tour and showed that both LeMond and Chiappucci were athletes worthy of admiration.

Chiappucci decided on a gigantic roll of the dice. He couldn't let LeMond and Breukink continue to ride their race, forcing him to give up time each stage. He attacked as soon as the race hit the first major climb, the Aspin, taking 6 others with him. Again Chiappucci was forced to do all the work. He took off and was first over the summit, 34 seconds ahead of the first group. Chiappucci pressed on and by the time he was halfway up the Tourmalet he had extended his lead to 3 minutes, 20 seconds. LeMond grew alarmed. If Chiappucci held this much lead by the end of the day he would probably be able to withstand any assault LeMond could mount with only 1 mountain stage and 1 time trial left.

LeMond dropped all but Delgado and Indurain as he attacked to get back on terms with the small, tough Italian. By distancing himself from Breukink at this point, he potentially eliminated his only other real threat.

LeMond did a kamikaze descent, making up a whole minute, and closed the gap to Chiappucci. LeMond and Chiappucci were now part of a small group in the lead that included Indurain, Fabio Parra and Marino Lejarreta. On the final climb to Luz-Ardiden, after riding hard at the front as long as he could, Chiappucci had to surrender when Fabio Parra attacked. LeMond and Indurain were among the small group who went with Parra. Near the finish Indurain attacked and LeMond had to let him go.

Indurain won the stage with LeMond only 6 seconds back. Chiappucci came in fourteenth, 2 minutes, 25 seconds behind Indurain. That left Chiappucci with only a 5-second lead, a very slim hold on the Yellow Jersey with a time trial coming up.

The last stage in the mountains with the Aubisque and the Marie-Blanque changed nothing at the top of the standings. Breukink, LeMond and Chiappucci finished with the same time. LeMond had a scare, however. On the Marie-Blanque Chiappucci and Delgado attacked. Seconds later LeMond flatted. He got a slow wheel change and then had to change his bike. With the 2 challengers up the road, LeMond chased with a surprising fury. His descent down the mountain was frighteningly fast. LeMond was a truly skilled descender and this time he put those abilities to use. The race marshal on the motor bike said that he had never seen a descent like LeMond's that day. Up ahead Chiappucci had 4 Carrera teammates helping him while further back the 4 "Z" riders who were with LeMond could mostly just hang on while the World Champion blasted down the road. Eventually contact was made and LeMond made known his displeasure with their forcing an attack while he was getting a repair. Later LeMond said that at that moment he truly feared that the race was lost.

With some good fortune and some smart riding, LeMond had things where he wanted them. He was to face a man with a 5-second lead who had never shown any special flair for riding against the clock.

The stage 20 45.5-kilometer individual time trial played out exactly as LeMond had hoped and Chiappucci had dreaded.

1. Eric Breukink: 1 hour 2 minutes 40 seconds

2. Raul Alcala @ 28 seconds

3. Marino Lejarreta @ 38 seconds

4. Miguel Indurain @ 40 seconds

5. Greg LeMond @ 57 seconds

17. Claudio Chiappucci @ 3 minutes 18 seconds

LeMond had won his third Tour, this time without ever winning a stage.

The final 1990 Tour de France General Classification:

1. Greg LeMond (Z): 90 hours 43 minutes 20 seconds

2. Claudio Chiappucci (Carrera) @ 2 minutes 16 seconds

3. Erik Breukink (PDM) @ 2 minutes 29 seconds

4. Pedro Delgado (Banesto) @ 5 minutes 1 second

5. Marino Lejarreta (ONCE) @ 5 minutes 5 seconds

Climbers' Competition:

1. Thierry Claveyrolet: 321 points

2. Claudio Chiappucci: 179 points

3. Roberto Conti: 160 points

Points Competition:

1. Olaf Ludwig: 256 points

2. Johan Museeuw: 221 points

3. Erik Breukink: 118 points

There was an interesting addition to this Tour. A team of Soviet riders sponsored by Alfa-Lum came to the Tour and did very well. Dmitri Konyshev won stage 17. Team members Piotr Ugrumov and Djamolidine Abdoujaparov would make a serious impression on the European pro circuit over time. East German Olaf Ludwig, riding for Panasonic, won the Green Jersey. Times were changing.

More than 1 writer at the time speculated that if Miguel Indurain had ridden for himself instead of for Delgado, he probably would have won the Tour. Who knows?

# Chapter 5

## 1991–1995. Miguel Indurain wins
## 5 sequential Tours

**1991.** Of course, after his 1989 and 1990 Tour victories, LeMond was expected to be the man to beat in the 1991 edition. His spring was less auspicious than ever. He abandoned the Giro and finished twelfth in the Tour of Switzerland. But a less than sparkling spring was never a sign that LeMond should be counted out of the Tour de France.

Thierry Marie started the 1991 Tour the same way he had the year before, by winning the Prologue time trial.

The real racing started with the first stage. A break of serious Tour men got away: LeMond, Erik Breukink, Sean Kelly and Rolf Sorensen among them. With the time bonuses and his good Prologue, LeMond was back in Yellow. This was a 2-stage day. The afternoon was a team time trial: Sorensen's Ariostea squad won the stage and put him in the Yellow Jersey, which he kept until stage 5. He hit a traffic island 4 kilometers from the finish of that stage and broke his clavicle. His Tour was over.

Prologue specialist Thierry Marie showed that he could do more than just a few kilometers at speed. He won the sixth stage with an astounding 234-kilometer solo break, the third-longest post-war escape by a single rider (Albert Bourlon's 253-kilometer ride in 1947 remains the postwar record). At the end of the stage the pack was breathing down his neck, but he had 1 minute, 54 seconds to spare. That was enough to put him back in Yellow for a couple of days.

Stage 8's long 73-kilometer individual time trial brought out the real Tour riders. Miguel Indurain won the stage.

Here are the times of the top finishers:

1. Miguel Indurain: 1 hour 35 minutes 44 seconds
2. Greg LeMond @ 8 seconds
3. Jean-François Bernard @ 53 seconds
4. Erik Breukink @ 1 minute 14 seconds
5. Gianni Bugno @ 1 minute 31 seconds

That put LeMond back in Yellow. In the Overall, Breukink was 1 minute, 13 seconds back and Indurain was at 2 minutes, 17 seconds.

A couple of days later, things got messy. Before the start of stage 10, 2 riders on the PDM team quit the Tour. Along the road to Quimper where the stage finished, a couple of other PDMs retired. That evening it was revealed that several PDM riders including Erik Breukink, Sean Kelly and Raul Alcala were very ill. Only the riders and none of the support staff of the team were sick, which ruled out food poisoning. Eventually Jonathan Boyer, spokesman for the team, said that it might have been a bad glucose drip (perfectly legal) that infected the riders. The team withdrew from the Tour amid speculation that a doping program gone wrong was involved. Nothing was ever proven to that effect and the PDM team always denied using banned substances.

The real action of the Tour began with the first Pyrenean stage, from Pau to Jaca with 2 first category climbs. A break got away on the first climb, the Soudet. By the second climb, the second category Ichère, the break was established and contained 3 riders of real class: Luc Leblanc, Pascal Richard and Charly Mottet. LeMond was unable to either get up to the break or enlist help from the other teams. By the end of the day, with a winning margin of almost 7 minutes over the LeMond group, Leblanc had gained the lead with LeMond 2 minutes, 35 seconds down.

It was the next stage, unlucky (for LeMond) number 13 that changed the face of the Tour and set the tone for the next 4 years as well. It was a 232-kilometer stage that crossed the Pourtalet (category 1), the Aubisque (*hors catégorie*), the Tourmalet (*hors catégorie*), the Aspin (category 2) and the final ascent to Val Louron (category 1). Only the well-prepared and truly competitive would survive the stage with their high classifications intact.

It was on the Tourmalet that fortunes were reversed. LeMond broke away near the bottom of the mountain. Indurain chased, bringing with him Leblanc, Hampsten, Chiappucci, Gianni Bugno, Charly Mottet and Gérard Rué. Near the top, with just 500 meters to go, LeMond slid off the back. He could do nothing as he watched the others slowly distance themselves from him. At the top of the Tourmalet LeMond, as he fought with every ounce of energy he could command to keep them in sight, was only 17 seconds behind the leading group. Never one to give up, LeMond descended with that terrific ability that had saved him so many times before. He rejoined the leaders, but Indurain had taken off. In a giant gear, LeMond bolted from the leading group, fully understanding the importance of what was happening. This was the Tour's pivotal moment. At the foot of the Aspin, he could see Indurain. Once the climbing began anew, LeMond lost ground again, unable to keep pace with the soaring Spaniard.

Meanwhile, Claudio Chiappucci had extracted himself from the leaders and was chasing Indurain. Getting word from his director that the Italian was on his way, Indurain slowed to allow Chiappucci to join him. The 2 then relayed each other to the finish with Chiappucci taking the stage and Indurain taking the overall lead. LeMond finished 7 minutes, 18 seconds later. The Yellow Jersey, Luc Leblanc, fared worse. As LeMond fought to get back on terms with Indurain and Chiappucci, Leblanc was jettisoned from the chasers. He came in sixteenth, 12 minutes, 36 seconds after Chiappucci.

Here is the General Classification after Indurain made his Tour abilities very clear:

1. Miguel Indurain
2. Charly Mottet @ 3 minutes
3. Gianni Bugno @ 3 minutes 10 seconds
4. Claudio Chiappucci @ 4 minutes 6 seconds
5. Greg LeMond @ 5 minutes 8 seconds
6. Laurent Fignon @ 5 minutes 52 seconds
7. Andy Hampsten @ 7 minutes 25 seconds
8. Luc Leblanc @ 7 minutes 51 seconds

Stage 16 showed that LeMond had absolutely no intention of giving up. He had been down this much time before and had managed to win the Tour. On a day with no highly rated climbs, he fought to get into breaks and when caught, went again. He got second in the stage and pulled back 26 seconds. This was a hard but successful day's work.

There was no avoiding the fate that awaited him the next day with its finish at the top of l'Alpe d'Huez after the Bayard and Ornon, both second category climbs. Gianni Bugno took the stage with Indurain and Leblanc right on his wheel. Chiappucci and Rooks were 43 seconds back. LeMond, Theunisse and Hampsten were about 2 minutes behind.

The final Alpine stage was the cruelest of all, 255 kilometers covering the Aravis, the Colombière (both first category) and then the Joux-Plane (*hors catégorie*). Thierry Claveyrolet won the stage with most of the contenders, including Indurain, about 30 seconds behind. LeMond was fifty-ninth at 7 minutes, 52 seconds, accompanied to the finish by his teammate Robert Millar.

LeMond broke away again on stage 17 and snatched back a minute and a half. Because LeMond was no longer a threat to Indurain, Indurain was content to finish in the middle of the pack.

The twenty-first and penultimate stage was a 57-kilometer time trial. Indurain won it, Bugno was second and LeMond was third. The Tour was sealed.

On the final day with the criterium up and down the Champs Elysées Djamolidine Abdoujaparov, nicknamed the "Tashkent Express", was involved in a spectacular crash. With less than a kilometer to go, Abdoujaparov, the wearer of the Green Jersey, ran into a barrier and went flying. It took a quarter of an hour before he could get up and cross the line. Because it was in the last kilometer, Tour rules mandated that he get the same time as the pack and he was allowed to keep his Green Jersey.

The final 1991 Tour de France General Classification:

1. Miguel Indurain (Banesto): 101 hours 1 minute 20 seconds
2. Gianni Bugno (Gatorade-Chateau D'Ax) @ 3 minutes 36 seconds
3. Claudio Chiappucci (Carrera) @ 5 minutes 56 seconds

4. Charly Mottet (RMO) @ 7 minutes 37 seconds

5. Luc Leblanc (Castorama) @ 10 minutes 10 seconds

6. Laurent Fignon (Castorama) @ 11 minutes 27 seconds

7. Greg LeMond (Z) @ 13 minutes 13 seconds

8. Andy Hampsten (Motorola) @ 13 minutes 40 seconds

9. Pedro Delgado (Banesto) @ 20 minutes 10 seconds

10. Gérard Rué (Helvetia) @ 20 minutes 13 seconds

Climbers' Competition:

1. Claudio Chiappucci: 312 points

2. Thierry Claveyrolet: 277 points

3. Luc Leblanc: 164 points

Points Competition:

1. Djamolidine Abdoujaparov: 316 points

2. Laurent Jalabert: 263 points

3. Olaf Ludwig: 175 points

Miguel Indurain raced with the economical style of Jacques Anquetil. He did nothing more than necessary in the mountains. Only if an obvious or extraordinary opportunity presented itself did he attack. He was content to let his time trialing and watchful riding do the rest. It makes for a less exciting job for this chronicler of the Tour, especially after the tumultuous years of Hinault, Fignon, Delgado and LeMond. A look at the final General Classification shows a real generational shift. Delgado, LeMond and Fignon, who had been so dominant, were now well down in time while younger riders surfaced.

A sad coda to this and the previous Tour should be mentioned. In 2004, in an interview in the French newspaper *Le Monde*, Greg LeMond said, "In 1990 I won the Tour and my team [Z] won the top-team classification. One year later, not one of us could follow the pace in the pack. There had been a radical change." He went on to note that when he was winning, his $VO_2$ Max—maximum oxygen consumption, the basic measurement of an athlete's aerobic capacity—was tops among professional racers. Today, LeMond said, his energy output numbers would put him in the fifty-first percentile. In other words, the Greg

LeMond of 1990 who won the Tour de France would be sent back for water bottles today.

Commenting on this interview in an open letter, Andy Hampsten wrote "Like Greg, I, too, saw what I believe were the effects of EPO when it entered pro cycling in the early '90s. In the first years it grew from a few individuals reaping obscene wins from exploiting its 'benefits', to entire teams relying on it, essentially forcing all but the most gifted racers to either use EPO to keep their place in cycling, quit, or become just another obscure rider in the group."

These athletes spoke out honestly with a real concern for the direction of the sport. They received almost nothing but opprobrium for their trouble. Their words are the results of experience and have wisdom in them.

**1992.** It was clear from Indurain's spring racing results that he had maintained his masterful 1991 form. He won the 1992 Giro d'Italia the same way he won the 1991 Tour de France—a la Anquetil. He contained his rivals in the mountains and won both time trials. He also won the Spanish Road Championships and the Tour of Catalonia. He was ready to join Coppi, Anquetil, Merckx, Hinault and Roche by going for the Giro-Tour double.

Gianni Bugno, who was second to Indurain in the previous year's Tour, was gunning for a Tour victory. Looking back, we can see that 1990 and 1991 were really Bugno's best years. He came to the Tour as the reigning World Champion. His spring was quiet but a third in the Dauphiné Libéré and a second in the Tour of Switzerland showed that his condition was coming on at just the right time. Chiappucci's second in the Giro (to Indurain) signaled that he too was ready to race.

The 1992 edition flitted all around western Europe. To commemorate the signing of the Maastricht treaty and its promise of an integrated European Union with a single market, the Tour schedule called for visits to Spain, France, Germany, Holland, Belgium, Italy and Luxembourg.

The action started with a Prologue in San Sebastian, Spain. Indurain nailed it and set the tone of the race. In second place was a new revelation, Swiss rider Alex Zülle. Riding for the Spanish ONCE team, he was only 2 seconds slower than Indurain. The next day, by getting his hands on an intermediate time bonus, Zülle was able to land the Yellow Jersey.

Miguel Indurain, in an interview in *Cycle Sport Magazine*, said:
"If by magic I were going to ride the Tour in 2003, what would interest
me most would be the Prologue. It's the most emotive moment, where
the tension accumulated during a year of work is released like a gun-
shot."

Zülle's ownership of the precious garment was short-lived. While
the 1992 Tour mostly avoided the Pyrenees, it did make sure that the
riders got a taste of the lash with a trip up the Marie-Blanque. That
brought out another new face, Richard Virenque. Virenque was not
originally included in his team's lineup for the Tour and was a last-
minute addition. He won the stage and took the lead from Zülle, who
finished 12$^1/_2$ minutes behind the flying Frenchman.

Virenque's possession of the lead would be just as short as Zülle's.
Stage 3 saw a break get a big 7-minute lead. Pascal Lino, a teammate of
Virenque's on the RMO squad, was in the group of escapees and took
over the lead with 2 minutes over Virenque and 6$^1/_2$ minutes on third-
place Indurain.

Virenque and Lino's RMO squad faced the 63.5-kilometer team
time trial in stage 4 knowing that they would lose time. Some teams
practice and become very skilled at team time trials. They ride with ability, close together, driving each other just hard enough so as not to tear
the team apart. They usually have riders who can put out the brute
horsepower needed to propel the team at high speed on the flats. Others teams are terrible and can lose tremendous amounts of time. For a
team with General Classification ambitions, Indurain's 1992 Banesto
squad was slightly weak in this discipline. The Panasonic team won.
Chiappucci's Carreras were only 7 seconds behind and Bugno's
Gatorade team was third at 21 seconds. The Motorola team, riding for
Andy Hampsten came in sixth, losing 48 seconds to Panasonic but
coming in 2 seconds faster than Banesto.

1992 was the first Tour appearance of one of the iron men of
American cycling, Frankie Andreu. This was the first of the 9 consecutive Tours Andreu completed, a superb record.

Here is the General Classification after the stage 4 team time
trial:

1. Pascal Lino

2. Richard Virenque @ 1 minute 54 seconds

3. Gianni Bugno @ 5 minutes 6 seconds

4. Claudio Chiappucci @ 5 minutes 20 seconds

5. Stephen Roche @ 5 minutes 28 seconds

6. Miguel Indurain @ 5 minutes 33 seconds

10. Laurent Fignon @ 5 minutes 49 seconds

12. Greg LeMond @ 5 minutes 55 seconds

For a race that was supposed to be dominated by the cool, unflappable, dare I say it, dull Miguel Indurain, the surprises kept coming. Stage 6 was a rough, hard northern European classic-type stage with tough, short hills, bad weather and cobbles. The race broke up into small pieces under the stress of a powerful breakaway that included some of the finest racers alive. Laurent Jalabert, Greg LeMond, Claudio Chiappucci and Brian Holm pounded away from the field with Jalabert getting his first Tour stage win. Indurain was in the first chase group, 1 minute, 22 seconds back. Lino, with a healthy time cushion, kept the lead. This put Chiappucci in third (at 3 minutes, 34 seconds) and LeMond in fifth (at 4 minutes, 29 seconds). This was good, aggressive tactical riding, not letting Indurain set all the terms of when and how the Tour would be contested.

As the Tour wound through the small countries of northern Europe, time bonuses moved around the relative positions of the riders a bit. There was no real effect on the General Classification of the Tour contenders until the stage 9 65-kilometer individual time trial in Luxembourg. Indurain delivered a hard lesson in the art of the chrono. Indurain overtook Laurent Fignon, who had started 6 minutes earlier. In less than 80 minutes Miguel Indurain had changed the complexion of the Tour. Here are the times of the stage:

1. Miguel Indurain: 1 hour 19 minutes 31 seconds

2. Armand de las Cuevas @ 3 minutes

3. Gianni Bugno @ 3 minutes 41 seconds

4. Zenon Jaskula @ 3 minutes 47 seconds

5. Greg LeMond @ 4 minutes 4 seconds

6. Pascal Lino @ 4 minutes 6 seconds

7. Stephen Roche @ 4 minutes 10 seconds

The resulting General Classification:

1. Pascal Lino
2. Miguel Indurain @ 1 minute 27 seconds
3. Jesper Skibby @ 3 minutes 47 seconds
4. Stephen Roche @ 4 minutes 15 seconds
5. Greg LeMond @ 4 minutes 27 seconds
6. Gianni Bugno @ 4 minutes 39 seconds
7. Jens Heppner @ 4 minutes 52 seconds
8. Claudio Chiappucci @ 4 minutes 54 seconds

Through the French Jura, even though there were rated climbs with attacking by riders who were not in contention for the Yellow Jersey, the real Tour men held their fire, keeping their powder dry for the first big Alpine day.

That day came on the thirteenth stage, 254.5 kilometers from St. Gervais to Sestriere in Italy. The climbing was substantial. The riders faced the Saisies (category 2), the Cormet de Roselend (category 1), the Iseran (*hors catégorie*), Mont-Cenis (category 1) and the first category climb to the finish at Sestriere.

Claudio Chiappucci was what Miguel Indurain wasn't. Where Indurain was cold, calculating, riding only to win and no more, knowing that whatever gaps he had allowed could be closed with a display of brute horsepower in the time trials, Chiappucci was the opposite. The Italian was willing to gamble, to take magnificent chances to gain time. He had to run these big risks knowing how vulnerable he was in the time trials. Indurain said that he had to have eyes on the back of his head when he raced Chiappucci.

Americans often express contempt for Chiappucci and his wild excursions and attempts to break away, failing to understand that his flamboyant style served him very well. His Grand Tour accomplishments are notable. Tour de France: twice second, a third and King of the Mountains. For the Giro: twice second plus a third, a fourth, a fifth along with 2 King of the Mountains and 1 Points Jersey. This is consistent riding at the very highest level.

As he had done in the 1990 stage to Luz-Ardiden, Chiappucci gambled and gambled big. The first major climb of the day was the Saisies. Chiappucci escaped with some other riders, but not with his main challengers, Bugno and Indurain. As far as they were concerned, this was far too early in such a monstrous stage to be taking off. By the time Chiappucci reached the top of the Iseran he was alone. Back in the leading group, the Banesto squad had at last recognized the threat. They assembled at the front and started working to bring the fleeing Italian back.

Bugno was riding the Tour to win. He knew that this was the Tour's moment, yet he was trapped with Indurain. He was stifled. Chiappucci was riding away with the race. He didn't want to escape and chase Chiappucci knowing he would be taking Indurain along. He finally decided that it was better to take his chances with Indurain rather than accept the sure loss of Chiappucci's riding to a mountain top win. Bugno knew that the solo Chiappucci would be finishing in Italy where the fanatical *tifosi* would lift him up the mountain with their thrilled and thrilling cheers.

When Bugno attacked, as expected, he took along Indurain as well as Andy Hampsten and Franco Vona. The great chase was on. I still remember how exciting it was on TV. I think nearly everyone watching was wishing the lone, brave Chiappucci up the mountains while surely, the inexorable, machine-like Indurain would run him down before the end of the stage.

Indurain couldn't catch his man. Chiappucci, after riding alone for 125 kilometers, celebrated a brilliant victory. Vona was only 1 minute, 34 seconds behind. Indurain, who ran out of gas on the final kilometers of the final climb, was third, 11 seconds behind Vona. Bugno and Hampsten were next behind him, another minute and a half down.

Chiappucci's big gamble didn't yield him the Yellow Jersey. Indurain had ridden well enough to put himself solidly in the lead. The General Classification after Sestriere:

1. Miguel Indurain
2. Claudio Chiappucci @ 1 minute 42 seconds
3. Gianni Bugno @ 4 minutes 20 seconds
4. Pascal Lino @ 7 minutes 21 seconds
5. Pedro Delgado @ 8 minutes 47 seconds
6. Stephen Roche @ 9 minutes 13 seconds
7. Laurent Fignon @ 10 minutes 11 seconds
8. Andy Hampsten @ 11 minutes 16 seconds

The next stage was another Alpine stage with the Galibier, the Croix de Fer and a finish on l'Alpe d'Huez. All 3 were *hors catégorie* climbs. Andy Hampsten was riding beautifully this year and this stage was the perfect showcase for his wonderful climbing abilities. He had been in the big break with Indurain on the big stage the day before and acquitted himself magnificently. Could he recover overnight from 5

Stage 14: Hampsten wins big on l'Alpe d'Huez.

major climbs and over 250 kilometers of racing and be able to take on the next day's monsters?

On the Croix de Fer, the penultimate climb, a couple of riders went clear of the highly reduced, Banesto-led peloton. Hampsten joined them with a couple of others. In the group of 5, importantly, was dangerman Franco Vona, who had come in second the day before. Well clear of the pack, they went over the crest of the Croix de Fer together. In the valley leading to l'Alpe d'Huez the group worked well together and continued to increase their advantage. They started up the Alpe with a lead of nearly 4 minutes. Hampsten started the climb at a good tempo and slowly wound it up, going from his 39-23 to the 21 and finally dropping to the 18! It's hard to explain to someone who has not ridden a climb of this severity (*hors catégorie*) how completely beyond the normal human experience ascending a mountain this steep this fast after a day's racing really is. Only a few people in the world can do it.

With about 7 kilometers to go Hampsten was alone, riding to victory in the most prestigious of mountain stages. This was his seventh Tour and his first Tour stage victory. If you're going to win, you might as well win big.

Back down the hill, although Hampsten wasn't a General Classification threat to them, Indurain and Chiappucci pulled back almost a half-minute on the final climb, coming in together at 3 minutes, 15 seconds. Earlier in the stage, Gianni Bugno had cracked badly. He came in twenty-sixth, 9 minutes, 4 seconds after Hampsten. Greg LeMond, tortured with saddle sores, could take no more and abandoned. Hampsten catapulted himself onto the podium with his stage win. Here is the Overall after l'Alpe d'Huez:

1. Miguel Indurain
2. Claudio Chiappucci @ 1 minute 42 seconds
3. Andy Hampsten @ 8 minutes 1 second
4. Pascal Lino @ 9 minutes 16 seconds
5. Gianni Bugno @ 10 minutes 9 seconds

The Tour then went over the Massif Central, but nothing happened to change the general order of the Overall. The only stage left that could affect the General Classification was the nineteenth, a 64-kilometer individual time trial. Again, Indurain put real distance between himself and his competitors. Bugno was only 40 seconds behind on that stage, lifting himself back onto the podium after losing his place with his disastrous l'Alpe d'Huez stage. Chiappucci was about 3 minutes slower. Andy Hampsten was the real loser that day being 5 minutes, 33 seconds behind the mighty Spaniard and being pushed down to fourth place in the General Classification.

With only 2 stages left, the competition to win the Tour was over.

The final 1992 Tour de France General Classification:

1. Miguel Indurain (Banesto): 100 hours 49 minutes 30 seconds
2. Claudio Chiappucci (Carrera) @ 4 minutes 35 seconds
3. Gianni Bugno (Gatorade-Chateau D'Ax) @ 10 minutes 49 seconds
4. Andy Hampsten (Motorola) @ 13 minutes 40 seconds
5. Pascal Lino (RMO) @ 14 minutes 37 seconds
6. Pedro Delgado (Banesto) @ 15 minutes 16 seconds.

Climbers' Competition:

1. Claudio Chiappucci: 410 points
2. Richard Virenque: 245 points
3. Franco Chioccioli: 209 points

Points Competition:

1. Laurent Jalabert: 293 points
2. Johan Museeuw: 262 points
3. Claudio Chiappucci: 202 points

Indurain had his second Tour and his first Giro-Tour double. Chiappucci not only came in second, he was King of the Mountains. It should be noted that Chiappucci had ridden so consistently that he was third in the race for the points leadership. After an exhausting battle with Belgian classics specialist Johan Museeuw, Laurent Jalabert won the Green Points jersey.

The 1992 Tour was the fastest to date with an average speed of 39.504 kilometers an hour.

**1993.** The start of the 1993 Tour was much like the start of the 1992 edition. Again Indurain had won the Giro and done it the same way as before. He won the 2 major time trials and let no one who was a danger run away from him in the mountains.

Claudio Chiappucci, one of the expected challengers to the mighty Spaniard's hegemony, was third in the Giro. His ability to beat Indurain was certainly questionable since he was so vulnerable in the time trials. As in the 1992 Tour de France, he finished more than 4 minutes behind Indurain in the Italian tour.

The 1993 Tour was run clockwise, starting near the western coast and working its way across the north of France. At 3,714 kilometers it was over 250 kilometers shorter than the year before, but right in the range of current Tours.

The Tour's Prologue certainly had a familiar sound with Indurain winning and Alex Zülle second to him, this time at 8 seconds. Bugno was third at 11 seconds.

Stage 1 saw Mario Cipollini victorious in the first of what would eventually be 12 Tour stage victories. In his 8 Tour starts Cipollini would never finish a single Tour de France.

The second stage was won by Wilfried Nelissen who started a 6-stage sprinter's grab fest as the jersey was shunted from sprinter to sprinter. There was one notable new face in that stage 2 sprint: 22-year-old Lance Armstrong, riding for Motorola, was seventh.

Stage 4, an 81-kilometer team time trial, was the first day that really affected the Tour. Cipollini's GB-MG team won it with the Spanish ONCE squad only 5 seconds behind. This was the start of ONCE's cultivation of the team time trial. They worked to perfect their ability in this event until in later years they almost came to own it with a dominance that was nearly as complete as the TI-Raleigh team of the 1970s. Motorola had also taken team time trials very seriously and had clearly been working on this discipline. They came in third, much better than the previous year's sixth. Indurain's Banesto squad was seventh, 1 minute, 22 seconds behind the GB team.

This stage later turned out to have an important effect upon the Tour. The CLAS team was rather slow, being about 2 minutes behind GB-MG. Because the riders had given each other pushes along the way and because of a too-long tow from the team car while CLAS team leader Tony Rominger had a loose water bottle cage fixed, the entire team was penalized another minute. That meant that Rominger and the CLAS team lost a total of 3 minutes, 6 seconds in this early stage.

Stage 6 was the fastest Tour road stage to date at 49.417 kilometers per hour. Winner Johan Bruyneel went on, of course, to greater fame as the *directeur sportif* of US Postal and Discovery. Other names promising future fame won the next 2 stages. Bjarne Riis won stage 7. In 3 years he would win the Tour outright.

Stage 8 was Lance Armstrong's first Tour de France stage victory. He worked with Raul Alcala and Ronan Pensec to bridge the gap up to 3 riders (including Stephen Roche) off the front. Armstrong let the others lead it out and won the 6-up sprint. Alex Zülle crashed when trash got caught in his wheel and lost over 2 minutes. As we'll see in future Tours, bad luck hung on Zülle like a cheap suit his entire career.

Indurain was forced to wait until stage 9 for the first individual time trial. Again he showed that when it came to riding against the clock, he had no peer. The stage results for the 59-kilometer stage:

1. Miguel Indurain: 1 hour 12 minutes 50 seconds
2. Gianni Bugno @ 2 minutes 11 seconds
3. Erik Breukink @ 2 minutes 22 seconds
4. Tony Rominger @ 2 minutes 42 seconds
5. Alex Zülle @ 3 minutes 18 seconds

The resulting top 5 in the general Classification:

1. Miguel Indurain
2. Erik Breukink @ 1 minute 35 seconds
3. Johan Bruyneel @ 2 minutes 30 seconds
4. Gianni Bugno @ 2 minutes 32 seconds
5. Bjarne Riis @ 2 minutes 34 seconds

In the stages leading up to the time trial Indurain had stayed completely out of trouble and had carefully avoided any serious time loss. With just 59 kilometers of time trialing he was in command and able to ride his defensive style for the remainder of the race.

Following the time trial came a rest day and then the first day in the Alps, going over the Glandon, the Télégraphe and finishing on the Galibier. Rominger set out to push the pace and win the stage. Yet, for all of his efforts, he could not dislodge Indurain. After 5½ hours of hard work he and Indurain finished together along with Motorola rider Alvaro Mejia. Hampsten was fourth at a little over a minute behind. Chiappucci clearly had suffered a bad day, finishing twenty-ninth, 8 minutes, 49 seconds behind. This time could never be made up on a rider of Indurain's class.

Rominger (left) and Indurain finish together at the top of Isola 2000.

The next day was another Alpine stage with Louison Bobet's favorite climb, the Izoard, followed by the Vars, both first category climbs. The stage finished with 2 *hors catégorie* climbs, La Bonnette and the finish at Isola 2000.

Again Rominger won the stage with Indurain right with him. Indurain was perfectly content to let Rominger take the stage win, being interested only in the Overall. Chiappucci, a bit resuscitated, was third at only 13 seconds back. Alvaro Mejia was again in the mix, finishing only 2 seconds behind Chiappucci. Hampsten was ninth, over 3 minutes slower than Rominger.

The Alpine stages seemed rather uneventful with the colorless Indurain marking the aggressive Rominger. Yet the 2 days had left carnage in their wake. Before the 2 Alpine stages started there were 171 riders in the Tour. 151 riders remained after the Alps. Indurain may have ridden in a conservative manner, not expending any unnecessary energy, but the rest of the peloton was getting thrashed as Rominger tried to drop the unflappable Spaniard.

The General Classification after the Alps:

1. Miguel Indurain
2. Alvaro Mejia @ 3 minutes 23 seconds
3. Zenon Jaskula @ 4 minutes 31 seconds
4. Tony Rominger @ 5 minutes 44 seconds
5. Bjarne Riis @ 10 minutes 26 seconds
6. Andy Hampsten @ 11 minutes 12 seconds
7. Claudio Chiappucci @ 14 minutes 9 seconds

The stages in southern France leading to the Pyrenees didn't change the General Classification.

The first Pyrenean stage, number 15, was huge with 7 major rated climbs. Colombian Oliviero Rincon set off for personal glory, getting away early with several other riders. Eventually he dumped them and soloed to victory. Back in the peloton, Rominger was still at it, refusing to accept Indurain as the given winner. And again Indurain finished right with Rominger along with Mejia, Riis and Jaskula.

Stage 16 was more of the same with the Peyresourde and the climb to Pla d'Adet. At the end of the day's racing the General Classification remained static. Jaskula won the day with Rominger right with him and Indurain 3 seconds behind them. There was 1 more stage in the Pyrenees, but it changed nothing. There was only 1 stage left that could affect the outcome, the 48-kilometer time trial of stage 19.

Going into the time trial, here was the General Classification:

1. Miguel Indurain
2. Alvaro Mejia @ 4 minutes 28 seconds
3. Zenon Jaskula @ 4 minutes 42 seconds
4. Tony Rominger @ 5 minutes 41seconds

It looked as if Motorola had finally made the podium with Mejia sitting in second place.

The time trial results:

1. Tony Rominger: 57 minutes 2 seconds
2. Miguel Indurain @ 42 seconds
3. Zenon Jaskula @ 1 minute 48 seconds
4. Johan Bruyneel @ 2 minutes 16 seconds
5. Gianni Bugno @ 3 minutes
9. Claudio Chiappucci @ 3 minutes 41 seconds
10.Alvaro Mejia @ 3 minutes 43 seconds

Rominger and Jaskula blasted Mejia right off the podium with only 1 more stage to go. Again Motorola had a pure climber on the podium who couldn't mash the big gears in the time trials. As with Andy Hampsten the previous year, the inevitable result was the loss of the podium place.

For Rominger, his victory in the time trial meant that Indurain had tired and was vulnerable. Rominger felt that if he had worked on a General Classification victory from the very first stage, avoiding the big time loss that hobbled him, he could have worn Indurain down and won the Tour. It's hard to know because Indurain, like Anquetil, never expended more energy than necessary. James Staart notes that Indurain was so exhausted from the 1993 Tour that he skipped many of the lucrative post-Tour criteriums. Indurain had pulled off a Giro-Tour double in 2 consecutive years, the first racer to have ever done so. But it was clearly at a real cost to his reserves. This made 3 Tours in a row for Indurain.

Indicative of the state of French stage racing, the highest placed Frenchman was Jean-Philippe Dojwa, fifteenth and more than a half-hour behind Indurain. Pascal Lino's stage 14 win was the only stage win in the 1993 Tour by a French racer.

The final 1993 Tour de France General Classification:

1. Miguel Indurain (Banesto): 95 hours 57 minutes 9 seconds
2. Tony Rominger (CLAS) @ 4 minutes 59 seconds
3. Zenon Jaskula (GB-MG) @ 5 minutes 48 seconds
4. Alvaro Mejia (Motorola) @ 7 minutes 29 seconds
5. Bjarne Riis (Ariostea) @ 16 minutes 26 seconds
6. Claudio Chiappucci (Carrera) @ 17 minutes 18 seconds
7. Johan Bruyneel (ONCE) @ 18 minutes 4 seconds
8. Andy Hampsten (Motorola) @ 20 minutes 14 seconds

Climbers' Competition:

1. Tony Rominger: 449 points
2. Claudio Chiappucci: 301 points
3. Oliviero Rincon: 286 points

Points Competition:

1. Djamolidine Abdoujaparov: 298 points
2. Johan Museeuw: 157 points
3. Maximilian Sciandri: 153 points

**1994.** In the 1994 Giro d'Italia, cracks in the impenetrable wall of Indurain's invulnerability started to show. Or at least seemed to. Indurain failed to win any of the Giro's 3 time trials. In the stage 1b 7-kilometer individual time trial, eventual Giro winner Evgeni Berzin beat Indurain by 3 seconds. Stage 8 was a fairer contest at 44 kilometers. This time Berzin beat the Spaniard by 2 minutes, 34 seconds. In the final time trial, stage 18, Berzin was 20 seconds faster over the 35 kilometers. Counting the final time trial in the 1993 Tour de France, this made 4 successive time trial losses for Indurain.

Moreover, Marco Pantani, a true pure climber, was able to get away on 2 consecutive days and gain enough time on Indurain to finish ahead of him in the General Classification. This put a dagger in the heart of the Indurain strategy: contain the climbers in the hills, letting them gain only insignificant amounts of time. Then, as Frankie Andreu said, kill them in the time trial. In the 1994 Giro, he could do neither.

The final podium for the 1994 Giro:

1. Evgeni Berzin
2. Marco Pantani @ 2 minutes 51 seconds
3. Miguel Indurain @ 3 minutes 23 seconds

Was this a portent for the Tour or just a careful training ride crafted so that Indurain would not be too tired to contest the final days of the Tour? In the 1993 Tour he ran out of gas. He was not the "extraterrestrial" he had been called. He was instead, just a gifted athlete at the top of his game.

Owen Mulholland has noted that this Tour had a particularly large crop of good climbers. Given Indurain's past inability to ride in the mountains with the very best mountain goats, riders such as Richard Virenque, Marco Pantani and Piotr Ugrumov were eagerly looking forward to contesting the Tour.

The Tour's 7.2-kilometer Prologue in Lille was Chris Boardman's first day in his first Tour de France. What a spectacular result for him when he won the Prologue, beating Indurain by 15 seconds and Rominger by 19. He was now the Yellow Jersey, the first Englishman to own it since Tom Simpson, 32 years before. Simpson's last day in Yellow was 4 years before Boardman was born.

The next day, a 234-kilometer sprinter's stage from Lille to Armentieres, saw one of the most spectacular crashes in Tour history. A policeman leaned out into the road to take a picture of the final sprint. Wilfried Nelissen slammed into him, breaking his collarbone and taking down Laurent Jalabert. Jalabert, who had won 7 stages and the points competition in the Vuelta earlier that year, was looking forward to repeating the process in his home country. Instead, after receiving terrible wounds to his face, he was taken to the hospital. Jalabert said that the crash changed his way of riding. Apparently under pressure from his devoted wife, Sylvie, for the remainder of his career he no longer sought out the dangerous bunch sprints. Marguerite Lazell says that although

Nelissen returned to racing, he was never again the racer he was before that crash.

Boardman was able to keep his Yellow Jersey until the stage 3 team time trial, 66.5 kilometers contested at Calais. GB-MG won the stage with Motorola just missing the win by 6 seconds. That must have deeply pained the team's manager Jim Ochowicz, who had dreamed of winning this event for years.

The GB-MG win gave Johan Museeuw the lead. Boardman, desperate to get the Yellow Jersey back for the next day's stage in England had hammered his team. Being a fairly inexperienced professional with extraordinary power (he had only turned pro in August 1993), he, as Armstrong did in his early team time trials, took such hard pulls that his teammates struggled to stay with him. I remember watching this stage on TV, yelling at Boardman on the television screen to take slower, longer pulls. Didn't do any good.

The Tour made another crossing of the English Channel, the first time since that less than successful journey in 1974. Back in 1974, the crowds were sparse and the racing was uninteresting, being held on an unopened expressway. This time, with 2 stages in England, the crowds were huge and the racers rode as if it were the Tour de France. Boardman did manage a fourth place in 1 of the stages, but he had lost too much time (1 minute, 17 seconds) in the team time trial to get back in Yellow. Ironically, Sean Yates, also a British rider, donned the Yellow Jersey on the Tour's first day back in France.

The Tour really started on stage 9, a 64-kilometer individual time trial. Was Indurain faltering? Was his Giro performance a guide to his Tour? Look at the times.

1. Miguel Indurain: 1 hour 15 minutes 58 seconds

2. Tony Rominger @ 2 minutes

3. Armand de las Cuevas @ 4 minutes 22 seconds

4. Thierry Marie @ 4 minutes 45 seconds

5. Chris Boardman @ 5 minutes 27 seconds

With the exception of Rominger, Indurain had humiliated the field. Boardman was the reigning Olympic Pursuit Champion and would go on that year to become the World Time Trial Champion. For all of his ability, he was over 5 minutes slower than Indurain. Almost half the field finished over 12 minutes behind than the Spaniard. The General Classification after the time trial:

1. Miguel Indurain
2. Tony Rominger @ 2 minutes 28 seconds
3. Armand de las Cuevas @ 4 minutes 40 seconds
4. Gianluca Bortolami @ 5 minutes 47 seconds
5. Thierry Marie @ 5 minutes 51 seconds

The time gaps were already beyond what could ever be recaptured from an in-form Indurain unless misfortune took him down.

Stage 11 would reveal all with its new climb up the Hautacam to Lourdes, a 17.3-kilometer *hors catégorie* climb with 1,170 meters of elevation gain and an average gradient of 6.8%. This is what the small, specialist climbers live for with their high power-to-weight ratio. Indurain may kill them in the time trials, but this was a chance to take the time back.

The first to take off up the mountain was Marco Pantani, second in the Giro earlier this year. Jean-François Bernard, who a few years earlier had been expected to inherit the mantle of Bernard Hinault as France's and the world's next great stage racer, was riding as a domestique for Indurain. Maybe he wasn't Hinault, but Bernard set a fiery pace up the Hautacam that shed most of the peloton. Halfway up the mountain, exhausted, he pulled off to let Indurain and the others take over. In past years Indurain would not let his climbing domestiques go all out in the high mountains because he couldn't match their pace. This year he could take what they could dish out and still be ready to hand out heaping helpings of suffering to those still on his wheel.

Indurain took over from Bernard and rode in his steady, smooth style with a high cadence that was so surprising in such a large man. He was finally left with only 2 riders, both Frenchmen. Luc Leblanc and Richard Virenque were the only men who could match Indurain that day. Then, after another couple of kilometers even Virenque couldn't take it. It was down to Leblanc and Indurain. The duo caught and passed Pantani. Leblanc tried to shed Indurain but could only gain a temporary gap that Indurain, with extreme effort, was able to close. At the summit Leblanc sprinted ahead for a close win.

This was a new Indurain. In the past, the mountains posed a threat, a manageable threat, but a danger to him nonetheless. Now Indurain could attack the field in the mountains and beat the best climbers at their own game. Look at the times for the stage:

1. Luc Leblanc
2. Miguel Indurain @ 2 seconds
3. Marco Pantani @ 18 seconds
4. Richard Virenque @ 56 seconds
5. Armand de las Cuevas @ 58 seconds
6. Pavel Tonkov @ 1 minute 26 seconds
7. Piotr Ugrumov @ same time
16. Tony Rominger @ 2 minutes 21 seconds

Suffering from stomach problems:

168. Claudio Chiappucci @ 23 minutes 57 seconds

The General Classification:

1. Miguel Indurain
2. Tony Rominger @ 4 minutes 47 seconds
3. Armand de las Cuevas @ 5 minutes 36 seconds
4. Piotr Ugrumov @ 8 minutes 32 seconds
5. Luc Leblanc @ 8 minutes 35 seconds

The peloton was in tatters after the first real climb of the Tour.

The next day was another Pyrenean stage with the Peyresourde, the Aspin, Tourmalet and the final climb to Luz-Ardiden. With the field put in its place, Indurain let a group of non-contenders get away. Richard Virenque led over the last 3 climbs and won the stage with a lead of over $4^1/_2$ minutes on Marco Pantani. Rominger, not well, withdrew from the Tour.

The Tour headed towards the Alps. On the way, there was stage 15, 231 kilometers from Montpellier to Carpentras with Mont Ventoux in the way. Early in the day the biggest man in the peloton, Eros Poli, took off. I clearly remember seeing this stage on TV. Back then, the weekend network coverage was spotty, spending infuriating amounts of time explaining the basics of bicycle racing and other needless garbage. But this stage and this adventure they covered.

The big man pedaled away from a completely indifferent peloton. Before he reached Mont Ventoux he had a lead of nearly half an hour. He couldn't get that big a lead without drawing down his stores of energy. The climb up Mont Ventoux seemed to be almost beyond him. Exhausted, he could barely turn over the cranks, looking terribly overgeared. He cleared the summit with several minutes in hand and sped down the other side. His big mass may have slowed him to a near standstill going up the hill, but going down, being big came in good stead. He won the stage 3 minutes, 39 seconds ahead of the first chasers. The contenders, Indurain, Pantani, Ugrumov, Virenque, and others came in together 4 minutes later. While Poli's ride was epic, nothing changed in the General Classification.

The first day in the Alps with the climb up l'Alpe d'Huez didn't change much either. Riders with no General Classification hopes were allowed to escape while Indurain stayed close enough to Leblanc and Virenque to keep them from becoming dangerous.

Stage 17 with its ascents of the Glandon, the Madeleine and an *hors catégorie* finish at Val Thorens was the day Piotr Ugrumov finally came out and tried for a real shot at glory. On a long break he dragged Colombian Nelson Rodriguez to the finish where the Colombian sprinted ahead of Ugrumov for the win. Ugrumov was now up to sixth in the General Classification at a little over 11 minutes behind Indurain. Note that the interesting story of this Tour is the race for the minor placings. No one believed that the 1994 Indurain could be shaken from his place at the top of the standings.

The next day with the Saisies, Croix-Fry and the Colombière, all tough climbs, Ugrumov again escaped and this time achieved his solo victory. Indurain, unworried, came in second, 2 minutes, 39 seconds later. Ugrumov's solo adventure allowed him to leap past Pantani and others to make it to the podium. Now he was sitting third at 8 minutes, 55 seconds, with Virenque in second place at 7 minutes, 22 seconds in the Overall.

Stage 19 was the clincher for the 1994 Tour. It was a 47.5-kilometer individual time trial that climbed the second category Les Gets and the first category Avoriaz. Ugrumov turned in a stunning performance. Here are the stage results:

1. Piotr Ugrumov
2. Marco Pantani @ 1 minute 38 seconds
3. Miguel Indurain @ 3 minutes 16 seconds
4. Luc Leblanc @ 3 minutes 50 seconds
5. Charly Mottet @ 4 minutes 12 seconds

Virenque came in eighteenth at 6 minutes, 4 seconds. With that collapse, he lost his place on the podium. Ugrumov moved up to second place and Marco Pantani regained third.

The final stage on the Champs Elysées was a fantastic, exciting race with Eddy Seigneur riding like a man possessed to take a solo win. Frankie Andreu was right on his heels, second at only 3 seconds.

The final 1994 Tour de France General Classification:

1. Miguel Indurain (Banesto): 103 hours 38 minutes 38 seconds
2. Piotr Ugrumov (Gewiss-Ballan) @ 5 minutes 39 seconds
3. Marco Pantani (Carrera) @ 7 minutes 19 seconds
4. Luc Leblanc (Festina) @ 10 minutes 3 seconds
5. Richard Virenque (Festina) @ 10 minutes 10 seconds

Climbers' Competition:

1. Richard Virenque: 392 points
2. Marco Pantani: 243 points
3. Piotr Ugrumov: 219 points

Points Competition:

1. Djamolidine Abdoujaparov: 322 points
2. Silvio Martinello: 273 points
3. Jan Svorada: 230 points

That made 4 sequential Tours for Miguel Indurain. Clearly, he was better than ever.

**1995.** Indurain skipped the 1995 Giro. Tony Rominger, the only man to have been able to mount a serious challenge to the Spaniard's reign, did ride the Giro and won it by winning all 3 time trials. Rominger held the leader's Pink Jersey from the second stage until the finish. In 1993 when Indurain had successfully ridden the Giro to victory, he was vulnerable to attack in the final week of the Tour. The Giro had grown too hard to be used as a mere steppingstone to the Tour, as we shall see.

Indurain's early spring was quiet as he concentrated on preparing for the Tour. Indurain did make his pre-Tour form abundantly clear with wins in the important stage races leading up to the Tour, including the Dauphiné Libéré, the Midi-Libre and the Vuelta a Rioja. Miguel Indurain was ready to roll.

The 1995 Tour was clockwise, starting in Brittany with a 7.3-kilometer Prologue time trial held in the twilight of the early evening. The first riders had dry roads. As the stage progressed, it started to rain. The last riders off had wet, slippery streets. Last year's Prologue winner, Chris Boardman, crashed heavily and was nearly hit by his own follow car. With both a broken ankle and wrist, Boardman's Tour was over almost before it began.

The Prologue winner was Jacky Durand, who had the good fortune to ride before the rain started. The favorites, seeded to ride later in the rain, seemed to be willing to give up a few seconds and remain safe. Indurain was thirty-fifth at 31 seconds, Rominger thirtieth at 26 seconds and Zülle twenty-sixth at 23 seconds. You have to finish the race to win it.

During stage 2 Laurent Jalabert won an intermediate sprint and acquired enough bonus time to take the Yellow Jersey from Durand. He kept it until stage 4 when he lost almost a minute in a crash near the finish.

The Tour's first real drama wasn't in the mountains and it wasn't in a time trial. Indurain chose to lay down the law during stage 7. Going from Charleroi to Liège over the lumpy Ardennes countryside, Indurain shot off the front. Only Johan Bruyneel, already up the road, was able to latch on to his wheel. As Lance Armstrong explained, the rest of the peloton could only watch him ride away. Bruyneel sat on Indurain as he carved a 50 second lead for the 2 of them. Bruyneel sprinted away from Indurain for the stage win and took the Yellow Jersey. But Indurain had shown how deep his stores of power went. Given what was to come next, it was a powerful act of intimidation.

Bruyneel's ownership of the lead was very short lived. The next day was the first individual time trial, 54 kilometers that took the Tour out of Belgium and back into France. This is what was especially extraordinary about Indurain's breakaway the day before. The core of Indurain's dominance was his time trialing ability. He felt so confident that he was willing to spend precious energy attacking on a road stage whose final result could never be certain, instead of conserving his strength for the coming time trial. Indurain won the time trial and the Yellow Jersey.

The stage results for the stage 8 time trial, from Huy to Seraing:

1. Miguel Indurain: 1 hour 4 minutes 16 seconds
2. Bjarne Riis @ 12 seconds
3. Tony Rominger @ 58 seconds
4. Evgeni Berzin @ 1 minute 38 seconds
5. Melchior Mauri @ 2 minutes 16 seconds
6. Laurent Jalabert @ 2 minutes 36 seconds

The General Classification after the time trial and just before the Tour's first day in the Alps:

1. Miguel Indurain
2. Bjarne Riis @ 23 seconds
3. Evgeni Berzin @ 2 minutes 20 seconds
4. Johan Bruyneel @ 2 minutes 30 seconds
5. Tony Rominger @ 2 minutes 32 seconds
6. Laurent Jalabert @ 2 minutes 47 seconds
7. Melchior Mauri @ 2 minutes 48 seconds
8. Ivan Gotti @ 4 minutes 19 seconds
9. Alex Zülle @ 4 minutes 29 seconds
10. Erik Breukink @ 5 minutes 11 seconds

The ninth stage took in 4 highly rated climbs ending in an ascent to La Plagne. Alex Zülle took off alone on a ride that gave him the stage win and second place in the Overall. Indurain, calmly chasing Zülle during most of the latter part of the stage decided to rocket up the climb to La Plagne. None of his companions could stay with him, just as in the stage to Hautacam the year before. Indurain closed to within 2 minutes of Zülle. Tonkov, Pantani, Gotti, Virenque and the rest were scattered 4 minutes and more behind.

The new General Classification:

1. Miguel Indurain
2. Alex Zülle @ 2 minutes 27 seconds

3. Bjarne Riis @ 5 minutes 58 seconds

4. Tony Rominger @ 6 minutes 35 seconds

5. Ivan Gotti @ 6 minutes 54 seconds

6. Laurent Jalabert @ 8 minutes 14 seconds

The next day with the Madeleine, the Croix de Fer and l'Alpe d'Huez, Pantani scooted away while Zülle and Indurain finished together. Riis was only 2 seconds behind the duo.

Bastille Day, stage 12, should have been an uneventful stage through the Massif Central as the Tour headed towards the Pyrenees. Should have been, but wasn't. Just 23 kilometers into the 222.5-kilometer stage, Laurent Jalabert and the Italian Dario Bottaro attacked. They were later joined by 2 members of Jalabert's ONCE team, Neil Stephens and Melchior Mauri. Mauri was sitting eighth in the General Classification. The escapees carved a huge 10 minute, 40 second lead. This made Jalabert the virtual leader and Mauri the virtual third place. With 3 ONCE riders in the break, it had cohesion and power. Eventually both Indurain's Banesto team and Bjarne Riis' Gewiss team started to work to bring them back. Too late. The chickens had flown the coop. All that could be done was to limit the damage. By the time the breakaway riders made it to the final climb their lead was still over 7 minutes.

After being led up the hill by his teammate Mauri, Jalabert took off for the solo win. He had been away for 198 kilometers.

Back in the field, Pantani jetted up the mountain but eased to let Indurain and Riis join him. He sprinted ahead to beat them at the end. Indurain had again contained any menace and was still safely in Yellow. Jalabert had moved up to third place in the Overall, 3 minutes, 35 seconds behind Indurain.

The first day in the Pyrenees didn't change anything. Marco Pantani escaped and Indurain controlled things, riding with second place Zülle and third-place Riis to the finish. This was the elite of this year's Tour and they kept a close eye on each other whenever possible.

Stage 15 was the Queen stage of the 1995 Tour de France, taking in the Portet d'Aspet, the Col de Menté, the Peyresourde, the Aspin, the Tourmalet and the final ascent to Cauterets/Crêtes-du-Lys. Except for the second category Aspet, these were all category 1 or *hors catégorie* climbs. This was a monumental day stuffed into 206 kilometers. Richard Virenque attacked and was first over every one of the passes. As the Frenchman was riding to a magnificent, glorious solo victory, there was something terrible happening back in the peloton that should have been receiving more television attention than the nonstop, and in retrospect, unseemly celebration of Virenque's adventure.

While Virenque was riding away from a demoralized peloton, on the descent of the Portet d'Aspet, several riders crashed. Among them was Fabio Casartelli, the 1992 Barcelona Olympic Road Race Champion who was riding for Motorola. The other riders were able to remount and continue. Casartelli had hit his head at high speed (estimated by some at over 90 kilometers an hour) against the concrete barrier on the side of the road. Shortly thereafter he died in the hospital of his head injuries, leaving his wife a widow and a young son fatherless. Arguments continue to this day regarding his lack of helmet and whether wearing one would have saved his life.

What is amazing is that Casartelli was only the third racer to die while riding in the Tour de France. If we eliminate Tom Simpson because his death was the result of a drug overdose (Anquetil argued that he died because he didn't take enough dope!), the only crash deaths in a century of the Tour de France have been Casartelli and Francesco Cepeda in 1935. It is an astonishingly safe enterprise given the terrible chances the riders take day after day. Immediately following Casartelli's death there was the usual discussion and hand-wringing as to whether the Tour should continue. Of course it did.

The next day's stage 16 was ridden as a neutralized procession with the results annulled, having no effect upon the standings. Just at the end of the stage the Motorola team rode together across the line.

On stage 18, a small break got away. Lance Armstrong, dropping his breakaway companions, came in alone to Limoges. Pointing the index fingers of both hands to the sky he dedicated the win to his lost comrade.

The only unfinished business left for the 1995 Tour was the final 46.5-kilometer time trial. Indurain made a clean win of it, beating second place Riis by almost a minute.

Indurain made it 5 sequential Tour wins, an unprecedented accomplishment. His 1995 Tour win came without his winning a single road stage. The only stage wins were time trials. I am sure that it wasn't because he couldn't. It was because the stage wins were unimportant to him and represented needless wastes of energy. Only owning the Yellow Jersey in Paris mattered and nothing could distract him from that goal.

The final 1995 Tour de France General Classification:
1. Miguel Indurain (Banesto): 92 hours 44 minutes 59 seconds
2. Alex Zülle (ONCE) @ 4 minutes 35 seconds
3. Bjarne Riis (Gewiss-Ballan) @ 6 minutes 47 seconds
4. Laurent Jalabert (ONCE) @ 8 minutes 24 seconds
5. Ivan Gotti (Mapei) @ 11 minutes 33 seconds
6. Melchior Mauri (Mapei) @ 15 minutes 20 seconds
7. Fernando Escartin (Mapei) @ 15 minutes 49 seconds
8. Tony Rominger (Kelme) @ 16 minutes 46 seconds
9. Richard Virenque (Carrera) @ 17 minutes 31 seconds
10. Hernan Buenahora (Castorama) @ 18 minutes 50 seconds

Climbers' Competition:
1. Richard Virenque: 438 points
2. Claudio Chiappucci: 214 points
3. Alex Zülle: 205 points

Points Competition:
1. Laurent Jalabert: 333 points
2. Djamolidine Abdoujaparov: 271 points
3. Miguel Indurain: 180 points

# Chapter 6

## 1996–1998. A new generation of powerful drugs, lax enforcement and a rider belief in entitlement to doping explodes into the Tour's greatest crisis

**1996.** Why shouldn't Miguel Indurain be considered a shoo-in for a record-breaking sixth Tour win? He was the reigning World Time Trial Champion. In June he won the Dauphiné Libéré against most of the riders he would face in July, winning 2 of the 8 stages along the way. Tony Rominger was second to the Spaniard in that race and Richard Virenque was third. Fernando Escartin and Luc Leblanc were excellent racers but they came in far behind Indurain. Indurain's other major threat, Telekom's Bjarne Riis, didn't finish the Dauphiné. 1994 Giro winner Evgeni Berzin could not be ignored, but having come in tenth in the 1996 Giro, over 14 minutes behind winner Pavel Tonkov, he seemed like an unlikely man to topple Indurain.

Alex Zülle, who came closest to Indurain in 1995, didn't ride the Dauphiné. Riding for the Spanish ONCE outfit his efforts were centered on Iberian races, of which he won 2.

Riis, like Indurain, had been slow to mature. He rode his first Tour de France in 1989 and came in an undistinguished ninety-fifth. He didn't finish the next year and in 1991 he was one-hundred-seventh. 1993 was his breakout year with a stage win and fifth overall in the Tour. The next year he slid to fourteenth but still captured a stage win. 1995 was even better with a very fine third place and a day in Yellow. In the winter, tired of friction with Evgeni Berzin, he moved from Gewiss to the well-financed and organized German Telekom team, managed since 1992 by Belgian tough-guy Walter Godefroot. As a racer Godefroot had been an entirely self-motivated champion with 150 pro victories to his name. He expected his riders to be filled with the same discipline that drove him to win Paris–Roubaix, the Tour of Flanders, Liège–Bastogne–Liège and 10 Tour stages. He was not the right manager for men of a gentler mentality and as the years progress we'll see him squander some of the finest talent in the world. But for now Riis, also a man of drive and self-confidence, was the man Godefroot was looking for. His team was lacking a first-class Grand Tour man, someone who could unseat Indurain. Riis' leaving the Gewiss team was the answer to Godefroot's prayers.

The 1996 Tour started with a Prologue in 'S Hertogenbosch in Holland, headed south to the Alps, then into the Massif Central, followed by the Pyrenees. After the mountains the Tour headed north through Aquitaine on the southwest coast of France. From there, the riders would endure a transfer for the final stage into Paris. This was one of those rare Tours that didn't go through either Normandy or Brittany. While there were 103.4 kilometers of individual time trialing, there were no team time trials.

Zülle showed that he was one of the finest riders in the world when racing against the clock (he became World Time Trial Champion that fall) when he won the Prologue on wet, rainy, slippery roads, beating time trial specialist Chris Boardman by 2 seconds. Riis and Indurain were almost tied, being 11 and 12 seconds slower, respectively. Indurain said that he rode carefully, wanting to avoid an accident.

The first 5 stages, with the exception of stage 4, were the playground of the sprinters. Frédéric Moncassin, Mario Cipollini and Erik Zabel, the fastest men in the world, each won stages. Only in stage 4 were they unable to control events when a 5-man break won with a $4^1/_2$ minute lead. GAN team member Stéphane Heulot was the highest placed of the escapees and therefore took the lead, which he held until stage 7 when the Tour hit the Alps.

Stage 6 had one notable and famous abandon. In miserably wet and cold conditions Lance Armstrong climbed off his bike, feeling poorly, thinking he had bronchitis. Full of optimism, he said he would concentrate on preparing for the Olympics in Atlanta. His Olympic performances in the fall were well below what a man soaring to the top of cycling's best should have done. Indicative of the expectations others had for him, the professional team Cofidis signed him for a $2.5-million, 2-year contract. It was during that fall that he was diagnosed with testicular cancer that had metastasized all over his body. We'll pick up his story in 1999.

Before the climbing started, the General Classification after stage 6 looked like this:

1. Stéphane Heulot
2. Mariano Piccoli @ 20 seconds
3. Alex Zülle @ 4 minutes 5 seconds
4. Laurent Jalabert @ 4 minutes 6 seconds
5. Evgeni Berzin @ 4 minutes 8 seconds
6. Abraham Olano @ 4 minutes 12 seconds
7. Bjarne Riis @ 4 minutes 16 seconds
8. Miguel Indurain @ 4 minutes 17 seconds

The major contenders were all clustered at or near 4 minutes. Heulot and Piccoli would surely be dispatched on stage 7—200 kilometers with the *hors catégorie* Madeleine, the first category Cormet de Roselend and a first category climb up to Les Arcs. The stage started taking its toll almost from the start. Jalabert was dropped about 8 kilometers from the summit of the Madeleine, which was enveloped in a thick, wet mist. The top contenders were together over the top with Riis willing to descend a bit faster than the others on the slippery roads. With no company and lots of climbing left he slowed and waited for the others. Heulot was able to go with the leaders on the Madeleine but could not keep up on the Roselend and abandoned, suffering horribly from tendinitis pain in his right knee. Descending the Roselend, Zülle crashed twice but refused to give up and managed to rejoin the leaders with help from his teammate Aitor Garmendia. On the climb to Les Arcs, Luc Leblanc, who was well back on the General Classification because of a stage 6 crash, attacked and but did not draw a response from the group with Virenque, Riis, Indurain, Olano and Rominger. Indurain himself looked good on the first 2 major climbs of the day, surely signaling to the others that they were competing for second place.

Then, just near the end of the climb, with about 3 kilometers to go to the finish, the unbelievable happened. Indurain was in trouble! He came off the back of the Riis group and probably for the first time in anyone's memory looked to be truly suffering. He signaled for a feed by wiggling a phantom bottle. He had ran out of food and had the "bonk". Other riders took pity on him and gave him food but it was a shock to all that such an error could be committed by an otherwise faultless rider. Indurain struggled in over 4 minutes behind the stage winner Leblanc. Zülle, paying the price of his earlier crashes, finished only 50 seconds ahead of Indurain. Both of them had given up so much time in the first hard day in the mountains that the other challengers felt that for the first time in years, the Tour was really in play. Berzin became the first Russian in Tour history to wear the Yellow Jersey.

The General Classification after stage 7:

1. Evgeni Berzin
2. Abraham Olano @ same time
3. Tony Rominger @ 7 seconds
4. Bjarne Riis @ 8 seconds
5. Jan Ullrich @ 30 seconds
6. Richard Virenque @ 31 seconds
11. Alex Zülle @ 2 minutes 30 seconds
14. Miguel Indurain @ 3 minutes 32 seconds

That was Saturday. Sunday, July 7 was a 30.5-kilometer uphill individual time trial to Val d'Isère. Berzin showed that his ownership of the Yellow Jersey was not a fluke. Indurain, a time trialist who could usually climb very well lost more ground to Riis and Berzin.

Results of the Val d'Isère time trial:

1. Evgeni Berzin: 51 minutes 53 seconds
2. Bjarne Riis @ 35 seconds
3. Abraham Olano @ 45 seconds
4. Tony Rominger @ 1 minute 1 second
5. Miguel Indurain @ same time
6. Jan Ullrich @ 1 minute 7 seconds

Indurain was now sitting in eleventh place, 4 minutes, 53 seconds behind the Russian.

Monday was expected to be the big day that would really sort things out with the Iseran, Galibier, Montgenèvre and a climb to Sestriere on the menu. The weather didn't cooperate. Winds clocked at over 100 kilometers an hour blew at the summits of the Iseran and the Galibier. The Tour organization shortened the stage to just 46 kilometers leaving the riders to contest the Montgenèvre and the final ascent to Sestriere. Almost from the start Riis started shooting. 3 times he attacked and was brought back. The fourth attack Riis unleashed was too much for the others and up the Montgenèvre he flew. He crested the top 20 seconds ahead of the about 15 riders left in the front chase group. On the final climb Riis extended his lead while Berzin couldn't take the pace set by Leblanc, Indurain and the others. When the smoke had cleared, Riis was the new leader. Riis rode over the 2 mountains at an incredible average speed of 39.019 kilometers an hour.

Here are the results of the stage:

1. Bjarne Riis
2. Luc Leblanc @ 24 seconds
3. Richard Virenque @ 26 seconds
4. Tony Rominger @ 28 seconds
5. Miguel Indurain @ same time
14. Evgeni Berzin @ 1 minute 23 seconds

The stage yielded a new General Classification, with Riis' young teammate Jan Ullrich looking awfully good. Indurain was in a deep hole that, given his normal Anquetil-type defensive tactics, looked hard to overcome:

1. Bjarne Riis
2. Evgeni Berzin @ 40 seconds
3. Tony Rominger @ 53 seconds
4. Abraham Olano @ 56 seconds
5. Jan Ullrich @ 1 minute 38 seconds
6. Peter Luttenberger @ 2 minutes 38 seconds
7. Richard Virenque @ 3 minutes 39 seconds
8. Miguel Indurain @ 4 minutes 38 seconds

The hardest Alpine climbing was completed and now the riders had to face the Massif Central. The French had hoped that Laurent Jalabert, the current world number-1 ranked rider, would be the man to wear Yellow in Paris but he had to abandon during stage 10 with gastroenteritis. While stage 10 had the Montgenèvre (again), it came too early in the stage for the climbers to stay away. In the end Telekom's Erik Zabel won the stage and secured the Green Sprinter's Jersey. Telekom now had both the Green and the Yellow. During the next couple of stages Riis' Telekom squad controlled the race, letting breaks of non-contenders get away but carefully policing the real threats. On the hard thirteenth stage Riis' men set a tough pace that caused both Rominger and Berzin to lose more time. Indurain was able to stay with the leaders until he flatted. Then, showing that he had both good form and courage, he made his way back to the Riis group.

That left things to be settled in the Pyrenees, which started with the stage 16 ride and its single major climb, the final ascent to Lourdes/Hautacam. This stage ended up being one of the most astonishing stages in racing history. I saw it on television and its defining moment is still clear in my mind. It was a 200-kilometer stage that had the best riders together at the start of the final climb, with Laurent Roux—who had been away for 160 kilometers—still slightly off the front. As soon as the climb began in earnest Zülle took off like a rocket and steamed right past Roux. Virenque dragged the elite climbers up to him and lost Rominger in the process. With 9 kilometers to go Riis tested the others with a probing attack and Indurain was able to stay with him. Riis turned the power down a bit. He went again and this time only 4 riders could stay with him. Now he did what I've never seen before or since. He eased a bit at first as if he were in trouble and rode next to the others, looking carefully at each of them. Convinced that they were all riding at their limits he went again and rocketed up the hill, leaving the others to their only option, limiting their losses to the super-strong Dane. He came in alone, almost a minute ahead of Virenque, 2 minutes, 28 seconds ahead of Indurain and almost 3 minutes ahead of Berzin. Riis gave what can only be called an unusual performance, giving up position and momentum on a steep mountain surrounded by the finest climbers in the world. Only the most profound confidence could have allowed him to do what he did. And Indurain, who was hoping to celebrate his thirty-second birthday with something more than another time loss to the Dane was clearly not the man he had been the year before.

If there were to be any chance of breaking Riis' grip on the lead it would have to come on stage 17 with its 7 climbs, of which 5 were second category or better: the Soulor, the Aubisque, the Marie-Blanque, the Soudet and the steepest, the Port de Larrau. On the Soudet Riis kept the pace high and there the first real selection occurred with 11 of the best riders surviving. The Festina team's Virenque and Laurent Dufaux hammered the remaining riders, putting Indurain out the back door. In the final run-in to Pamplona Dufaux and Riis escaped with Dufaux outsprinting the almost invulnerable Dane. With the finish in Pamplona, Spain, Indurain's fans were out in force, hoping for a miracle. The day's route even took the riders past Indurain's childhood home. Both the public and Riis paid tribute to the man who had hoped for better that year.

In interviews that afternoon Riis said that in addition to being directed by Godefroot, he was getting tactical advice from Laurent Fignon. It was Fignon who spotted the young Riis' talents and talked him into changing teams and riding for the Frenchman. With his 1989 narrow loss to LeMond still burned into his memory, Fignon told Riis to beware of playing with fate by being content with a 1-minute lead. Knowing that such a small margin can evaporate, Fignon advised Riis to continue being aggressive and to increase his margin over his competitors. But, after stage 17, look who was sitting in second place, his young domestique from the East German sports machine:

1. Bjarne Riis
2. Jan Ullrich @ 3 minutes 59 seconds
3. Richard Virenque @ 4 minutes 25 seconds
4. Laurent Dufaux @ 5 minutes 52 seconds
11. Miguel Indurain @ 15 minutes 36 seconds

Telekom now had the first 2 places on the podium, the Green Jersey, and in Jan Ullrich, the Best Young Rider.

The only way Riis could miss winning the Tour now was to stumble during the penultimate stage, a 63.5-kilometer individual time trial. Riis didn't stumble but he faltered. Looking tired after 3 hard weeks, he turned in a time that was sufficient to allow him to keep the lead. The real surprise was Ullrich who stormed the course at 50.452 kilometers per hour beating second place Indurain by 56 seconds and his team leader by 2 minutes, 18 seconds. Ullrich's performance showed that he was one of those rare, titanically talented men, like Greg LeMond, who grow stronger during even the hardest Tour. Indurain praised him with words that, as we'll see in the Armstrong years, had a touch of prophecy, "He is as strong as an ox and his performances in the mountains and in the time-trials makes him a definite winner, as long as he stays fit."

It took Riis 11 years as a pro to attain this level. It was a performance that the 32-year old would not repeat. Since that Tour victory, Riis has been dogged by accusations of EPO use, accusations that Riis steadfastly denied until 2007. Riis' confession was an important part of the dramatic events that rocked the 2007 Tour. We'll save the details of that episode for later. His young charge, Ullrich, became the first German since Kurt Stoepel in 1932 to make the Tour's podium.

The final 1996 Tour de France General Classification:

1. Bjarne Riis (Telekom): 95 hours 57 minutes 16 seconds
2. Jan Ullrich (Telekom) @ 1 minute 41 seconds
3. Richard Virenque (Festina) @ 4 minutes 37 seconds
4. Laurent Dufaux (Festina) @ 5 minutes 53 seconds
5. Peter Luttenberger (Carrera) @ 7 minutes 7 seconds

Climbers' Competition:

1. Richard Virenque: 383 points
2. Bjarne Riis: 274 points
3. Laurent Dufaux: 176 points

Points Competition:

1. Erik Zabel: 335 points
2. Frédéric Moncassin: 284 points
3. Fabio Baldato: 255 points

**1997**. Bjarne Riis set about the job of winning a second successive Tour. He would be over 33 years old but so were Scieur, Lambot,

Zoetemelk, Buysse, Bartali and Pélissier when they won. Of that group only Zoetemelk had won in the last 40 years. But Riis' domination had been complete and it was rational to believe that he could do it again. Although he had abandoned the Tour of Switzerland, he had good results in the spring including a win in the Amstel Gold Race that seemed to confirm his optimism. Moreover, he had a superb team. The Telekom squad was brimming with good, dedicated talent, including the previous Tour's second place, young Jan Ullrich.

There was a bit of a problem. Ullrich, while riding as a domestique for Riis, still ended up a close second to the Dane. As the 1996 Tour was drawing to a close and Riis was struggling with exhaustion, Ullrich was stronger than ever, winning the final time trial. I remember the dueling TV interviews early in the summer of 1997 with Riis asserting that Ullrich would ride for him, since Riis was the designated captain of the team. Ullrich seemed to demur on that point a bit. Anyone watching could see that the chains of servitude were not as strongly forged as Riis wanted to think they were. After the 1996 Tour and his terrific second place Ullrich declared that the Tour would be the centerpiece of his career.

Ullrich had turned pro for Telekom late in the 1994 season. He was a shoo-in to ride for Germany in the 1996 Atlanta Olympic Games but chose instead to ride the Tour to help Riis. Ullrich had no notable victories in the spring of 1997 but came to the Tour looking very good.

There was no rematch with Miguel Indurain. He retired at the end of the 1996 season, becoming the Olympic Time Trial Champion in August and starting but abandoning the Vuelta a España that September. The mantle of leadership of the Banesto team fell to Abraham Olano who had finished a credible ninth in the 1996 Tour, 3 minutes, 14 seconds ahead of Indurain.

Other men who could wear Yellow in Paris included last year's third place Richard Virenque, Alex Zülle, the fading Tony Rominger, Evgeni Berzin and a rising Italian star. Marco Pantani was a cycling type whose equal had not been seen since Charly Gaul. He was what the Italians call a *scattista*, a man who can explode on a steep climb when the other good climbers are already at their limit. This type of pure climber is the bane of men like Indurain, Ullrich and Hinault who find a rhythm on an ascent and can climb at a very high rate, but don't react well to changes of speed. Pantani in 1994, his second year as a pro, scored a second in the Giro and a third place in the Tour. In 1995 it looked as if his career was over after he suffered a terrible accident that shattered his femur. He doggedly set out to prove how very wrong the doctors were to doubt that the small climber would ever walk again. By early 1997 he was fully competitive. He abandoned the Giro but earlier had come in fourth in the Critérium International. Like Gaul, Pantani was a bomb who could go off any time the road went up.

The 1997 Tour was counter-clockwise (Pyrenees first) and set up to give the riders a relentless pounding in the mountains. The hard climbing started in stage 9 and continued without stop through the Massif Central and the Alps. After the Alps were concluded in stage 16, the riders would get a dose of the Vosges in stage 18. Not since the 1976 Tour stacked up all the climbing in 9 sequential stages had the mountains been all run up against each other. 1976 had yielded Lucien van Impe, the finest climber of his age as the winner. Might the 1997 Tour be as kind to Richard Virenque or Marco Pantani?

Chris Boardman did the job he was paid to do, winning the Tour's 7.3-kilometer Prologue time trial. Win it he did but Jan Ullrich was only 2 seconds slower and Zülle was only 5 seconds off the winner's pace. So strong were they that these men who would contend for Yellow were almost able to beat the Prologue specialist at his own game.

The first 4 stages run through Brittany and Normandy were dominated by the pure sprinters with Italian Mario Cipollini winning the first 2. Then Ullrich's teammate Erik Zabel won stage 3 and Nicola Minali bagged stage 4. Since the end of stage 1 Cipollini had been wearing the Yellow Jersey.

It was rumored that tension between Riis and Ullrich started with the first stage when Riis was caught in a massive crash and delayed. Ullrich didn't wait for the 1996 Tour winner to help him get back up to the field. The fast-moving early stages claimed 2 victims: Zülle suffered several crashes and finally gave up after the fourth stage and Tony Rominger had to withdraw with a broken collarbone.

The fifth stage saw the Tour's first real exploit when Cédric Vasseur went on a 147-kilometer break and won the stage by $2^1/_2$ minutes, 27 years after his father Alain had won a Tour stage. But unlike the father's win, Cédric's earned him the Yellow Jersey.

As the Tour headed for the Pyrenees the sprinters continued to own the race with Zabel winning 3 of the stages so far. His job was made easier because the ranks of the speedsters were considerably thinned. Belgian Tom Steels was thrown out of the Tour for throwing a water bottle at Frédéric Moncassin, Djamolidine Abdoujaparov was tossed from the Tour for a positive dope test, and Mario Cipollini quit with an injured knee.

After stage 8 and before the climbing began the General Classification stood thus:

1. Cédric Vasseur
2. Erik Zabel @ 1 minute 21 seconds
3. Chris Boardman @ 2 minutes 54 seconds
4. Jan Ullrich @ 2 minutes 56 seconds
5. Stuart O'Grady @ 2 minutes 59 seconds

Stage 9, held on Bastille Day, July 14, took the race from Pau to Loudenvielle by going over the Soulor, the Tourmalet, the Aspin, up to Val Louron-Azet before descending to Loudenvielle. Virenque was aggressive the entire day while Ullrich stayed with Riis who was having a tough start in the mountains. When Virenque attacked on the final climb Ullrich easily went with him, leaving his leader behind. Pantani and Laurent Brochard formed a lead group over the top. Brochard took off on the descent but Ullrich was uninterested in Brochard and kept his eye on Virenque. While Ullrich had no trouble marking Virenque, he initiated no attacks of his own, perhaps because Godefroot had not yet decided to give his young rider complete freedom to seek the big win. Vasseur was able to hang on to the lead for another day. The new General Classification showed that even though the Tour was still young, things had already begun to sort themselves out.

1. Cédric Vasseur
2. Jan Ullrich @ 13 seconds
3. Abraham Olano @ 1 minute 14 seconds
4. Bjarne Riis @ 1 minute 43 seconds
5. Richard Virenque @ same time

Riis continued to tell the press that he was still the team leader. In fact, he was doing very well and had a good position in the standings but Ullrich was clearly the stronger rider.

The next day was even harder, 252 kilometers that went over the Portet d'Aspet, the Port, the Port d'Envalira, the Ordino and a final 32-kilometer ascent to Andorra/Arcalis. Now Godefroot moved to backing Ullrich as his man. On the big last climb with 10 kilometers to go, Ullrich accelerated twice, and with the second acceleration, even the finest pure climbers in the world, Pantani and Virenque, were helpless before the his demonstration of power. Ullrich smoothly rolled up the mountain and into the Yellow Jersey.

The stage's results:

1. Jan Ullrich
2. Marco Pantani @ 1 minute 8 seconds
3. Richard Virenque @ same time
4. Francesco Casagrande @ 2 minutes 1 second
5. Bjarne Riis @ 3 minutes 23 seconds

Which yielded a new General Classification:

1. Jan Ullrich
2. Richard Virenque @ 2 minutes 58 seconds
3. Abraham Olano @ 4 minutes 46 seconds
4. Bjarne Riis @ 4 minutes 53 seconds
5. Marco Pantani @ 5 minutes 29 seconds
10. Cédric Vasseur @ 7 minutes 31 seconds

The post-stage comments indicated a new appreciation of Ullrich's extraordinary physical talents. Bernard Hinault thought he would be able to dominate the Tour for another 7 or 8 years. Virenque hoped Ullrich wouldn't go on a 5-Tour winning streak. Ullrich had clearly concentrated everyone's attention. After a rest day, a hilly 55.5-kilometer individual time trial was scheduled. Virenque had voiced his optimistic hope that he would only lose a couple of minutes in what was presumed to be Ullrich's specialty. His director didn't think a loss of 4 or more minutes would be a surprise. Virenque was the penultimate starter with Ullrich his 3-minute man. Just near the end Ullrich caught Virenque and increased his lead to 5 minutes, 42 seconds. Virenque had no intentions of giving up. With the Alps coming he said he would now be on the roads that would play to his advantage.

Stage 13 presented an opportunity to take a chunk of time out of Ullrich if it were indeed possible. It was an easterly run in from St. Etienne over flattish country with an ascent to the top of l'Alpe d'Huez. The steep slopes of the Alpe might give the pure climbers a chance to shake Ullrich and set a new tone for the Alpine stages. Ullrich was dropped but only by Marco Pantani and not until the riders were well into the climb. Making his way through hundreds of thousands of fans who formed a narrow defile, Pantani was able to beat Ullrich to the top by 47 seconds. Jean-Paul Ollivier says that Ullrich intentionally eased to let Pantani have the win, being careful not to let the diminutive climber gain too much time. Virenque's hope to start his challenge to Ullrich on the fabled Alpe turned out to be an empty one. He lost another 40 seconds to the German. Ullrich voiced the thought that Virenque had lost too much time to be considered a true threat to the Tour leadership. Pantani had moved into third place but so far Ullrich didn't seem to show any signs of weakness.

Two real climbing stages were left. Stage 14 started at Bourg d'Oisans, near the bottom of l'Alpe d'Huez, and went over the Glandon and Madeleine before the first category ascent to Courchevel. The evening after the Alpe d'Huez stage Virenque had been told that Ullrich was suffering from food poisoning. Virenque's Festina team decided that the next day (stage 14) would be the perfect time to deploy a set-piece assault on the supposedly ailing German. Once on the Glandon the Festina team, which had some good climbers, went all-out. By the time the front group crested the Glandon there were about 20 riders in the main lead group and Ullrich was isolated without teammates. In addition to being a fine climber, Virenque was a first rate descender. I talked to one of the professional drivers of the race officials' cars in important races and asked him who the best descenders were in the late 1990's. Richard Virenque's name was the first one he mentioned. Pantani was also high on his list.

Virenque decided to descend the Glandon aggressively with Ullrich close on his tail. Ullrich had a super light climbing bike that was a poor-handling, unstable affair that caused him to come close to grief more than once on the treacherous descent. At the bottom of the hill Ullrich slowed for some teammates but Virenque kept on alone. Riis put himself at Ullrich's service and got him back to Virenque in time for the final climb. There, Ullrich stayed with Virenque no matter how hard the Frenchman tried to get away. Virenque got the stage win but now he was down to just 1 climbing stage to take back 6 minutes, 22 seconds. The day had been a hard one. Frank Vandenbroucke led in 93 riders who finished 36 minutes, 56 seconds after Virenque. This was beyond the Tour time elimination cutoff, and special dispensation was made by the officials to keep the peloton from being reduced to 62 riders at one stroke.

The major protagonists of the 1997 Tour in the mountains. Pantani leads Virenque and Ullrich.

If there might be a stage where Virenque could recover some time, it was the fifteenth with the Forclaz, Croix Fry, Colombière and the Joux-Plane. It turned out to be a stage without high drama. Pantani had been complaining of a sore throat and breathing trouble since the Alpe d'Huez stage and had threatened to abandon. Yet he broke away on the final climb and also being a gifted descender, rode off for the stage win while Ullrich marked Virenque and finished with his nemesis.

With the Alpine stages finished, the General Classification stood thus:

1. Jan Ullrich
2. Richard Virenque @ 6 minutes 22 seconds
3. Marco Pantani @ 10 minutes 13 seconds
4. Bjarne Riis @ 11 minutes 55 seconds
5. Fernando Escartin @ 16 minutes 5 seconds

A chink in the German's armor showed in stage 18, the Vosges stage. On the penultimate major climb of the stage Ullrich had to let Virenque go. Showing grit, Ullrich was able to regain contact and finished with Virenque in the main group. Now there was only the final time trial the day before the stage into Paris. Ullrich didn't win it, but after defending his lead since the tenth stage he could be allowed a second place to Olano, one of the finest time trialists in the world. Virenque lost almost another 3 minutes to Ullrich over the 63 kilometers. He was tired as well. And also tired, having been unwell in the Alps, and perhaps a bit cranky was Riis. His final time trial was terrible. After damaging his bike in a fall, he suffered a series of mishaps as his mechanics couldn't get his wheel in correctly. Riis must have been furious at how the entire Tour turned out after he had prepared so carefully for what he was sure would be a repeat win. He finally threw his bike to the ground in fury, a move that was caught on worldwide television.

While Ullrich voiced worry that something could go wrong on the final stage, nothing did and he won what everyone thought would be the first in a series of Tour victories.

Final 1997 Tour de France General Classification:

1. Jan Ullrich (Telekom): 100 hours 30 minutes 35 seconds
2. Richard Virenque (Festina) @ 9 minutes 9 seconds
3. Marco Pantani (Mercatone Uno) @ 14 minutes 3 seconds
4. Abraham Olano (Banesto) @ 15 minutes 55 seconds
5. Fernando Escartin (Kelme) @ 20 minutes 32 seconds

Climbers' Competition:

1. Richard Virenque: 579 points
2. Jan Ullrich: 328 points
3. Francesco Casagrande: 309 points

Points Competition:

1. Erik Zabel: 350 points
2. Frédéric Moncassin: 223 points
3. Mario Traversoni: 198 points

**1998.** Always looking to make the Tour interesting as well as profitable for its owners, the 1998 edition started in Dublin, Ireland. The Prologue and the first 2 stages were to be held on the Emerald Isle. Then, without a rest day, the riders were to be transferred to Roscoff on the northern coast of Brittany. Then the Tour headed inland for a couple of stages before turning directly south for the Pyrenees, then the Alps and Paris. This wasn't a race loaded with hilltop finishes but it did have 115.6 kilometers of individual time trial including 52 in the penultimate stage. This should have been a piece of cake for Ullrich. He not only won the Tour de France in 1997, he won the HEW Cyclassics and the Championship of Zurich.

Ullrich was a well-rounded rider who could do anything and who truly deserved his Number 2 world ranking. But the demands of his fame were more than he could handle. His autobiography *Ganz oder Ganz Nicht* (All or Nothing at All) is disarmingly frank and honest about his troubles. After the 1997 Tour he signed contracts for endorsements that gave him enormous sums of money. He would never have to worry about a paycheck again. Over the winter his weight had ballooned and his form was suspect. In his words, he had begun 1998 with a new personal best, he weighed more than he had ever weighed in his entire life. In the post-Tour celebrations, he let himself go. He said that after winning the Tour, training was the furthest thing from his mind. He then fell into a vicious cycle. He couldn't find good form and good health. He would lie in bed frustrated, and shovel down chocolate. He would then go out and train too hard for his lapsed form and then get sick again.

He rationalized things. "I can't just train all year long. My life consists of more than cycling," he told himself. Meanwhile, his trainer Peter Becker ground his teeth in frustration seeing his prodigiously talented client riding fewer than 50 kilometers a day.

The results of his winter excess were obvious. He attained no notable successes in the spring, but in the new era of Tour specialization this wasn't necessarily a sign that things were going wrong. Yet in Ullrich's case there were few signs that things were going right. In March he pulled out of the Tirreno–Adriatico only 30 kilometers into the first stage.

Ullrich had a new foe in the 1998 Tour. Marco Pantani had been a Charly Gaul-type racer who would detonate on a climb and bring himself to a high placing in a single stage. In May he proved that he could do more than just climb when he won the Giro d'Italia. The signal that Pantani was riding on a new level was the penultimate stage, a 34-kilometer time trial. He lost only 30 seconds to one of the masters of the discipline, Sergey Gonchar. As we noted in 1997, Pantani had suffered a horrific racing accident in 1995 that shattered his femur. He became determined to return to his former high level and through assiduous training he exceeded his former level. There was a telling flag that wasn't made known until later. Technologists checking Pantani's blood after the accident in Turin found that his hematocrit was over 60 percent.

Hematocrit is the measurement of the percentage of blood volume that is occupied by red blood cells, the tools the body uses to feed oxygen to the muscles. Normal men of European descent have a hematocrit percentage in the low to mid 40s. It declines slightly as a response to the effects of training. It would not be expected to increase during a stage race, as some racers have asserted. Exceptional people may exceed that by a significant amount. Damiano Cunego, winner of the 2004 Giro, through a fortunate twist of genetic fate has a natural hematocrit of about 53. To improve sports performances endurance athletes took to using synthetic EPO or erythropoietin, a drug that raises the user's hematocrit. This is not without danger because as the hematocrit rises, so does the blood's viscosity. By the late 1990s athletes were dying in their sleep as their lower sleeping heart rates couldn't shove the red sludge through their blood vessels. Until 2004 there was no way to test for EPO so the only thing limiting how much EPO an athlete would use was his willingness to tempt death. A friend of mine traveled with a famous Spanish professional racing team in the 1990s and was horrified to see the riders sleeping with heart monitors hooked up to alarms. If the athlete's sleeping heart rate should fall below a certain number, he was awakened, given a saline injection, and put on a trainer. In January of 1997 the UCI implemented the 50% rule. If a rider were found to have a hematocrit exceeding 50% he would be suspended for 2 weeks. Since there was no test at the time to determine if a rider had synthetic EPO in his system, the 2-week suspension wasn't considered a positive for dope, only a suspension so that the rider could "regain his health". There were ways for cagey riders to get around the 50% limit, but that story is for 1999.

So let's get one thing straight and understood. Doping was and is part of the sport. As we proceed through the sordid story of 1998, the actions of the riders to protect themselves and their doping speak for themselves. Without a positive test no single rider may be accused but as a group they are guilty. As individuals, unless proven otherwise, the riders are all innocent. As Miguel Indurain asked after he was accused of doping long after he had retired, "How do I prove my innocence?" He's right. It's almost impossible to prove a negative, that is, that a rider didn't do something.

Yet, complicating matters is that a rational, knowledgeable person knows that just because a rider has never tested positive for dope doesn't mean that he has been riding clean. Many riders who never failed a drug test have later been found to be cheaters, as in the case of World Time Trial Champion David Millar. But again, we must be fair. In the absence of a positive test in which the chain of custody of the samples is guaranteed and a fair appeals process is in place to protect the rider's interests, I grit my teeth and consider a rider innocent.

The Prologue for the 1998 Tour was on July 11 but the story of the Tour starts in March when a car belonging to the Dutch team TVM was found to have a large cache of drugs. Fast forward to July 8. Team Festina *soigneur* Willy Voet was searched at a customs stop as he was on his way from Belgium to Calais and then on to the Tour's start in Dublin. What the customs people found in his car set the cycling world on fire. Among the items Voet was transporting were 234 doses of EPO, testosterone, amphetamines and other drugs that could only have 1 purpose, to improve the performance of the riders on the Festina team. For now we'll leave Voet in the hands of the police who took him to Lille for further searching and questioning.

In Dublin Chris Boardman won the 5.6-kilometer Prologue with a scorching speed of 54.2 kilometers an hour. Ullrich momentarily silenced his critics when he came in sixth, only 5 seconds slower. Tour Boss Jean-Marie Leblanc said that the Voet problem didn't concern him or the Tour, and that the authorities would sort things out. Bruno Roussel, the director of the Festina team expressed surprise over Voet's arrest.

The first stage was run under wet and windy conditions with Tom Steels, who had been tossed from the previous year's Tour for throwing a water bottle at another rider, winning the sprint. But the cold rain didn't cool down the Festina scandal. Police raided the team warehouse and found more drugs, including bottles labeled with specific rider's names. Roussel expressed yet more mystification at the events and said he would hire a lawyer to deal with all of the defamatory things that had been written about the team. The next day Erik Zabel was able to win the Yellow Jersey by accruing intermediate sprint time bonifications.

When the Tour returned to France on July 14 the minor news was that Casino rider Bo Hamburger was the new Tour leader. The big news was that Voet had started to really talk to the police and told them that he was acting on instructions from Festina team management. Roussel said he was "shocked". The next day things got still worse for Festina. Roussel and team doctor Eric Rijckaert were taken by the police for questioning. Leblanc continued to insist that the Tour was not involved with the messy Festina events and if no offenses occurred during the Tour, there would be no action taken to expel Festina.

While the race continued on its way to the Pyrenees with Stuart O'Grady now the leader, the first Australian in Yellow since Phil Anderson and the second ever, the Festina affair continued to draw all of the attention. The world governing body of cycling, the UCI, suspended Roussel. Both the Andorra-based Festina watch company and Leblanc continued to voice support for the team's continued presence in the race.

Stage 6, on July 15, turned the entire cycling world upside-down. Roussel admitted that the Festina team had systematized its doping. The excuse was that since the riders were doping themselves, often with terribly dangerous substances like perfluorocarbon (synthetic hemoglobin), it was safer to have the doping performed under the supervision of the team's staff. Leblanc reacted by expelling the team from the Tour. Then several Festina riders including Richard Virenque and Laurent Dufaux called a news conference, asserted their innocence and vowed to continue riding in the Tour.

There was still a race going on amid all of the Festina doings and the first real sorting came with the 58-kilometer time trial of stage 7. Ullrich again showed that against the clock he is an astounding rider. American Tyler Hamilton came in second and was only able to come within 1 minute, 10 seconds of the speedy German. Another American rider, Bobby Julich of the Cofidis team turned in a surprising third place, only 8 seconds slower than Hamilton. So now the General Classification with 2 more stages to go before the mountains:

1. Jan Ullrich

2. Bo Hamburger @ 1 minute 18 seconds

3. Bobby Julich @ same time

4. Laurent Jalabert @ 1 minute 24 seconds

5. Tyler Hamilton @ 1 minute 30 seconds

Virenque announced that the Festina riders would not try to ride the Tour after their expulsion. That took Alex Zülle, World Champion Laurent Brochard, Laurent Dufaux and Christophe Moreau, among others, out of the action. The reaction from the Tour management, the team doctors and the fans was indicative of the blinders all parties were wearing. The Tour subjected 55 riders to blood tests and found no one with banned substances in his system. The Tour then declared that this meant that the doping was confined to a few bad apples. What it really meant was that for decades the riders and their doctors had learned how to dope so the drugs didn't show up in the tests. And, in 1998 there was no test for EPO. The team doctors protested that the Festina affair was bringing disrepute upon the other teams and their profession. The fans hated to see their beloved riders singled out and thought that Festina was getting unfair treatment. Officials, reflecting upon the easy ride TVM had received in March when their drug-laden car was found, reopened that case.

Stage 10, the long anticipated showdown between Ullrich and Pantani, had finally arrived. It was a Pyrenean stage, going from Pau to

Luchon with the Aubisque, the Tourmalet, the Aspin and the Peyre-sourde. With no new developments in the drug scandals, the attention could finally be focused on the sport of bicycle racing. It was cold and wet in the mountains, which saps the energy of the riders as much as or more than a hot day. It was on the Peyresourde that the action finally started. Casino rider Rodolfo Massi was already off the front. Ullrich got itchy feet and attacked the dozen or so riders still with him. Pantani responded with his own attack and was gone. Pantani closed to within 36 seconds of Massi after extending his lead on the descent of the Peyre-sourde. Ullrich and 9 others including Julich came in a half-minute after Pantani. After losing the lead in stage 8 when a break of non-con-tenders was allowed to go, Ullrich was back in Yellow. Pantani was sit-ting in eleventh place, 4 minutes, 41 second back.

Stage 11, July 22, had 5 climbs rated second category or better with a hilltop finish at Plateau de Beille, an *hors catégorie* climb new to the Tour. As usual, the best riders held their fire until the final climb. Ullrich flatted just before the road began to bite but was able to rejoin the leaders before things broke up. And break up they did when Pantani took off and no one could hold his wheel. Ullrich was left to chase with little help as he worked to limit his loss. At the top Pantani was first with the Ullrich group a minute and a half back. While Pantani said he was too tired from the Giro to consider winning the Tour, he was slowly closing the gap.

After the Pyrenees and with a rest day next, the General Classifi-cation stood thus:

1. Jan Ullrich

2. Bobby Julich @ 1 minute 11 seconds

3. Laurent Jalabert @ 3 minutes 1 second

4. Marco Pantani @ same time

Festina director Roussel, still in custody, issued a public state-ment accepting responsibility for the systematic doping within the team.

On July 24, the day of stage 12, the heat in the doping scandal was raised a bit more, if that were possible. 3 more Festina team officials including the 2 assistant directors were arrested. A Belgian judge per-forming a parallel investigation found computer records of the Festina doping program on Erik Rijckaert's computer. Rijckaert said that the

Festina riders all contributed to a fund to purchase drugs for the team. 6 Festina riders were rounded up and questioned by the Lyon police: Zülle, Dufaux, Brochard, Virenque, Pascal Herve and Didier Rous. The scandal grew larger. TVM manager Cees Priem, the TVM team doctor and mechanic were arrested. A French TV reporter said that he had found dope paraphernalia in the hotel room of the Asics team.

So how did the riders handle this growing stink? Much as they did when they were caught up in the Wiel's affair in 1962. They became indignant. They were furious that the Festina riders had been forced to strip in the French jail and fuming that so much attention was focused on the ever-widening doping scandal instead of the race. In 1962 Jean Bobet talked the riders out of making themselves ridiculous by striking over being caught red-handed. There was no such voice of sanity in 1998. The riders initiated a slow-down, refusing to race for the first 16 kilometers.

On July 25 several Festina riders confessed to using EPO, including Armin Meier, Laurent Brochard and Christophe Moreau. The extent of the concern over the drug scandal was made clear when the French newspaper *Le Monde* editorialized that the 1998 Tour should be cancelled. It's important to note that what should have been outrage from the riders of the peloton, when confronted with the undeniable fact that they were racing against cheaters, was never voiced. Instead, the peloton defended the cheaters. When pro racers start screaming that they were robbed by the dopers then we may start to think that there has been some reform in the peloton. Until then, the pack is guilty.

As the Tour moved haltingly towards the Alps the top echelons of the General Classification remained unchanged. Alex Zülle issued a statement of regret admitting his use of EPO, saying what any rational observer should have assumed, that Festina was not the only team doping.

On Monday, July 27 the Tour reached the hard alpine stages. Stage 15 started in Grenoble and went over the Croix de Fer, the Télégraphe, and the Galibier to a hilltop finish at Les Deux Alpes. It was generally surmised that if Ullrich could stay with Pantani until the final climb he would be safe because the climb to Les Deux Alpes averages 6.2% with an early section of a little over 10% gradient. Ullrich's big-gear momentum style of climbing would be well suited to this climb.

Pantani didn't wait for the last climb. On the Galibier he exploded and quickly disappeared up the mountain. At the top he had

$2^1/_2$ minutes on Ullrich. On the descent Pantani used his superb descending skills to increase his lead on the now isolated Ullrich. By the start of the final ascent Pantani had a lead of more than 4 minutes. On the climb to Les Deux Alpes Ullrich's lack of deep, hard conditioning made itself manifest. He was in trouble and needed teammates Riis and Udo Bölts to pace him up the mountain. At the top of the mountain the catastrophe (as far as Telekom was concerned) was complete. Pantani was in Yellow, having taken almost 9 minutes out of the German who came in twenty-fifth that day. The new General Classification shows how dire Ullrich's position was:

1. Marco Pantani
2. Bobby Julich @ 3 minutes 53 seconds
3. Fernando Escartin @ 4 minutes 14 seconds
4. Jan Ullrich @ 5 minutes 56 seconds

Stage 16 was the last day of truly serious climbing with the Porte, Cucheron, Granier, Gran Cucheron and the Madeleine. On the final climb Ullrich showed that he was doing much better than the day before when he attacked and only Pantani could go with him. Since Pantani was the leader and had the luxury of riding defensively, he let Ullrich do all the work. If Ullrich couldn't drop Pantani, he could at least put some distance between himself and Julich and Escartin, which he did. Pantani and Ullrich came in together with Ullrich taking the stage victory in Albertville. Julich and Escartin followed the duo by 1 minute, 49 seconds. Ullrich was back on the General Classification Podium:

1. Marco Pantani
2. Bobby Julich @ 5 minutes 42 seconds
3. Jan Ullrich @ 5 minutes 56 seconds
4. Fernando Escartin @ 6 minutes 3 seconds

On Wednesday July 29, stage 17, the riders staged a strike. They started by riding very slowly and at the site of the first intermediate sprint they sat down. After talking with race officials they took off their numbers and rode slowly to the finish in Aix-les-Bains with several TVM riders in the front holding hands to show the solidarity of the peloton. If the reader thinks that the other members of the peloton did not know that the TVM team was doping I have ocean-front land in Arkansas for him to buy. Along the way the Banesto, ONCE and Risso Scotti teams abandoned the Tour. The Tour organization voided the stage allowing those riders who were members of teams that had not officially abandoned to start on Thursday.

Why all this anger now? First of all, the day before drugs were said to have been found in a truck belonging to the Big Mat Auber 93 team. The next day this turned out to be untrue. Then the entire TVM squad was taken into custody and the team's cars and trucks were seized. They, like the Festina team, were handled roughly by the police, sparking outrage from the riders not yet in jail.

Thursday, July 30, stage 18: Kelme and Vitalicio Seguros quit the Tour. That made all 4 Spanish teams out. Rodolfo Massi, winner of stage 10 was taken into custody, though a French court would clear him of all charges 2 years later. At the start of the stage there were now only 103 riders left in the peloton, down from 189 starters.

Friday, July 31, stage 19. TVM abandoned the Tour. It turned out that ONCE's team doctor Nicolas Terrados was also put under arrest after a police search found drugs on their bus that later turned out to be legal.

So now it was Ullrich's last chance to take the Tour with the 52-kilometer stage 20 individual time trial. Pantani was too good, losing only 2 minutes and 35 seconds to Ullrich. That sealed the Tour for Pantani. Ullrich acknowledged that he had not taken his preparation for the Tour seriously and paid a very high price for his lack of discipline. Sounding a note that will become a metaphor for the balance of his career, he promised to work harder in the future and not repeat his mistakes.

Of 189 starters in this Tour, 96 finished.

Final 1998 Tour de France General Classification:

1. Marco Pantani (Mercatone Uno): 92 hours 49 minutes 46 seconds

2. Jan Ullrich (Telekom) @ 3 minutes 21 seconds

3. Bobby Julich (Cofidis) @ 4 minutes 8 seconds

4. Christophe Rinero (Cofidis) @ 9 minutes 16 seconds

5. Michael Boogerd (Rabobank) @ 11 minutes 26 seconds

Climbers' Competition:

1. Christophe Rinero: 200 points
2. Marco Pantani: 175 points
3. Alberto Elli: 165 points

Points Competition:

1. Erik Zabel: 327 points
2. Stuart O'Grady: 230 points
3. Tom Steels: 221 points

Pantani became the first Italian to win the Tour since Felice Gimondi in 1965. He became the seventh man to do the Giro-Tour double, joining Coppi, Anquetil, Merckx, Hinault, Roche and Indurain.

The drug busts of 1998 did little to alter rider and team behavior. There would be more drug raids and more outraged screams from the riders. But the police knew what they were dealing with. The riders had formed a conspiracy to cheat and to break the law. Their code of silence was nothing more than a culture of intimidation to allow the riders to do what they had done for more than 100 years, take drugs to relieve their pain, allow them to sleep and improve their performance. Their anger at the treatment they received from the police is indicative of their sense of entitlement, their feeling that this was something that they could and sometimes had to do. On the other hand cops like to catch bad guys and when they do, they aren't always gentle.

Now, there is one other question that needs to be asked. Voet, who had chosen a lightly-traveled road on his way to Calais, was expecting the customs station at the French frontier to be abandoned. It wasn't and he was stopped and searched by border agents who seemed to be waiting for him. Roussel believes that when Tour Boss Jean-Marie Leblanc, who is conservative politically, talked Roussel into letting Bernadette Chirac, wife of conservative French President Jacques Chirac, do a bit of self-promotion when she visited the Tour for stage 7, the Tour became a target in the war between France's Right and the Left. The left-center coalition government had given the Ministry for Sports and Youth to the left-leaning Marie-George Buffet. Roussel hypothesized that Festina, Leblanc and the Tour were sacrificed to give

Buffet a victory against the Right and incidentally, against doping. Certainly it was clear after the 1998 Tour that systematized doping was part of the professional cycling scene and had been that way for some time. Roussel asks why did this festering problem erupt into scandal at this point? A deeper exploration of the subject is beyond the intended scope of this book. If the reader is interested, I recommend Les Woodland's *The Crooked Path to Victory* where the complex subject of sport, politics, dope and the 1998 Tour is dissected.

# Chapter 7

## 1999–2005. The Armstrong years. Lance Armstrong focuses on winning the Tour and dominates it as no other rider in its history

**1999**. Over the winter more allegations of drug use surfaced. Some could not be confirmed, others were obvious on their face. The only conclusion possible after one digested the accumulation of horrible information was that the situation was probably worse than the 1998 Tour led one to believe. And then it managed to deteriorate. After stage 5 in the 1999 Giro, the Italian National Sports Council (CONI) subjected 16 riders from 3 different teams to a new comprehensive blood and urine test. 2 of the riders tested positive for dope but no sanctions were applied. The riders, as they have always been since the start of testing, were incensed. Marco Pantani, Oscar Camenzind, Laurent Jalabert and Mario Cipollini held a press conference and declared that if the national sports organization intruded any further upon the testing regimen, which had heretofore been the responsibility of the UCI, they would stop racing. Of that group of 4, Pantani was not the only rider who would have drug problems. In 2004 Camenzind retired after receiving a 2-year suspension for EPO.

Before the start of the penultimate stage of the 1999 Giro, Marco Pantani was awakened so that a blood test could be administered. His hematocrit of 52 percent resulted in his being ejected from the Giro after he had won 4 stages and was leading in the General Classification. The cycling world was stunned. Pantani's *squalificato* seemed to affect many racing fans far more deeply than the Festina scandal, probably because of Pantani's powerfully heroic image. He had triumphed over a horrible accident and saved the Tour during its great crisis. Partisans of Pantani made accusations of a conspiracy. In fact, the riders have long known how to foil the hematocrit test. When they knew they would be subjected to a test they would take saline injections and aspirin and in no time hematocrit was within the legal limit. Some teams even provided the riders with small centrifuges so that they could "manage" their red blood cell concentration. By waking Pantani up to take the test he wasn't able to take measures to bring his hematocrit down. He was a goner. Pantani was too devastated by the disqualification to consider riding the Tour.

In mid-June the Tour announced that the TVM team along with several individuals including ONCE team manager Manolo Saiz and rider Richard Virenque would not be allowed to participate in the Tour. Missing from the list of banned riders were the Festina and Mercatone Uno teams and Marco Pantani. Later, the UCI overruled the Tour organization and insisted that the Tour allow Virenque and Saiz to participate. And the doping in pro racing continued with 4 riders tossed from the Tour of Switzerland for high hematocrits.

In June Ullrich announced that he had injured his knee in the Tour of Germany and would not be able to compete in the Tour. With Pantani and Ullrich out, the press cast about for a favorite. At the top of a lot of lists were Pavel Tonkov (1996 Giro winner), Alex Zülle, Fernando Escartin and Ivan Gotti (1997 and 1999 Giro winner).

And there was another rider to consider. He had withdrawn from the 1996 Tour and could not ride the 1997 and 1998 editions as he endured surgery and chemotherapy to cure what should have been a life-ending case of testicular cancer. In the fall of 1997 he announced the resumption of his professional cycling career. That return was bumpy with intermittent successes and withdrawals. But by mid 1998 he had clearly returned to the top ranks of professional cycling with a win in the Tour of Luxembourg, fourth in the Vuelta and fourth in the World Time Trial Championships. In 1999 he won the Prologue of the Dauphiné Libéré, and narrowly lost a 2-up sprint to Michael Boogerd in the Amstel Gold Race. Lance Armstrong had returned. But he returned a different athlete. He now trained and raced with a deliberate focus that turned out to be his most powerful weapon against his usual challenger, Jan Ullrich.

When Armstrong was diagnosed with cancer he had just inked a $2.5-million, 2-year contract with the French team Cofidis. Cofidis publicly promised to support Armstrong even if Armstrong couldn't fulfill the contract. Later, saying that he did not hear much from Armstrong (who was busy trying to keep from dying), Cofidis boss François Migraine sent Alain Bondue to the U.S. to find out exactly what was happening and to renegotiate the contract.

Armstrong said he expected Cofidis to demand that the contract be re-written. It is Bondue's renegotiating of the contract while Armstrong was in the hospital undergoing his third cycle of chemotherapy that infuriated the rider.

Migraine says that Cofidis did end up paying Armstrong approximately $600,000.

Cofidis then invited Armstrong's agent to travel all the way to France so they could inform him that they were terminating Armstrong's contract. Later they offered Armstrong a new contract for 1998 with a vastly reduced salary of $180,000 plus performance incentives. Migraine thought that he had a deal with Armstrong at this point.

Feeling he had only an offer from Cofidis, Armstrong made a hard search for a new team that would offer better terms. Armstrong signed with the American US Postal squad and it was in their blue outfit that he was riding the Tour. While Armstrong was not on many possible Tour winner lists, Miguel Indurain had said that he thought Armstrong had a serious chance of winning the Tour.

With Pantani, Ullrich and Riis not starting the Tour, 1999 was one of those rare years in which there were no former Tour winners. The 1999 Tour started in the Loire Valley town of Le-Puy-de-Fou and went clockwise (Alps first) up to northeastern France and then a big transfer to begin the Alps on stage 9. After the Alps came the Massif Central, the Pyrenees and then the final time trial on the penultimate stage.

Armstrong showed that he had mastered the first component of a successful Tour rider, time trialing, winning the 6.8-kilometer Prologue and beating Zülle by 7 seconds. Armstrong said that this day was doubly sweet, that he got more than the pleasure of the Yellow Jersey. After completing his ride and learning that he was the winner, he went by the Cofidis team who were there with the team managers. These were the managers who had come to his hospital bed when he was in the worst throes of chemotherapy and told him that they needed to re-do his contract. "That was for you," he told them.

The Tour was upended on the second stage. Starting at Challans, southeast of Nantes, the riders were sent to the island of Noirmoutier before returning to the mainland and a finish in St. Nazaire. The riders had to negotiate the Passage du Gois, a narrow 4-kilometer long road that is submerged except at low tide. Even when exposed, it is a dangerous, slippery road. Worse, there was a hard crosswind. Making the situation even more dire, the entire peloton reached the constricted road intact. Armstrong, Olano, Escartin, Tonkov, Virenque and Julich were in the front of the pack when it made the treacherous crossing and emerged unscathed. But behind them was chaos. A crash took down Zülle, Gotti and Michael Boogerd who were then badly delayed in the mess. The teams that had managed to get clear of the passage without damage went to the front of the lead group and pulled hard in order to derive the maximum benefit. The Zülle group eventually came in 6 minutes, 3 seconds after Tom Steels led in the front lucky 70 riders. At one terrible, early blow, Zülle, a wonderfully talented but accident-prone rider, was out of contention. With the time bonuses the sprinters were earning, Estonian sprinter Jaan Kirsipuu was now the leader with Armstrong only 14 seconds back in second place.

Stage 4 was notable because tailwinds allowed the riders to set a new record for the fastest road stage, 50.356 kilometers per hour, beating the 1993 record held by Johan Bruyneel.

While there were several fine sprinters in the 1999 Tour, the finest, far and away, was Tuscan Mario Cipollini. By the end of stage 7 he had done what no postwar rider had done, win 4 stages in a row. One had to go back to the 1930 Tour when Charles Pélissier was the reigning speed demon to find the last 4-time consecutive stage winner. As they raced over the flatter roads of Northern France, the fast finishers enjoyed the time in the Tour when they could strut their stuff. The next day, in Metz, was a 56.5-kilometer individual time trial. Then the mountains had to be conquered. The General Classification men would come out of hiding after a period where their primary job had been to avoid trouble.

During the time trial, misfortune struck 2 important riders. Bobby Julich crashed and had to abandon. Abraham Olano crashed and lost enough time that the man who started after him, Armstrong, caught and passed him. Armstrong's victory in the stage was substantial. Zülle, who came in second, could only come within 57 seconds of him.

The new General Classification with a rest day to be followed by the first Alpine stage:

1. Lance Armstrong
2. Christophe Moreau @ 2 minutes 20 seconds
3. Abraham Olano @ 2 minutes 33 seconds
4. Stuart O'Grady @ 3 minutes 25 seconds

The remaining big question was whether Armstrong could climb with men like Zülle, Escartin and Virenque. Before he came down with cancer, he couldn't. The ninth stage would certainly settle the question with the Tamié, Télégraphe, Galibier, Montgenèvre and a hilltop finish at Sestriere on the day's menu. It was a cold, wet day with hail on the descent of the Montgenèvre. Virenque got away on the Galibier and was the first over the Montgenèvre but couldn't hold his lead. On the descent of the Montgenèvre Escartin and Gotti took wild chances and managed to create a gap of about 30 seconds. On the final climb a small group of 5 of the best including Armstrong and Zülle were together. With less than 7 kilometers to go Armstrong jumped away. He caught and passed Escartin and then went right on by a dumbfounded Gotti. With the encouragement of Bruyneel coming over his earphone Armstrong rode ever harder and further from his chasers. The only credible threat coming up the road was from Zülle, but he couldn't close the gap. Armstrong crossed the line alone, 31 seconds ahead of Zülle and $2^1/_2$ minutes ahead of Virenque.

The new General Classification:

1. Lance Armstrong
2. Abraham Olano @ 6 minutes 3 seconds
3. Christophe Moreau @ 7 minutes 44 seconds
4. Alex Zülle @ 7 minutes 47 seconds

Armstrong was now in the ideal position. He had a healthy lead, one so large that he could ride economically, just keeping his danger-men in check. He didn't have to waste energy on offensive exploits. In fact, he had been in control since the crash in stage 2 but insecurity about Olano's climbing abilities had prevented US Postal from relaxing. Armstrong adopted exactly that conservative strategy for the next day's stage to the top of l'Alpe d'Huez. With over 6 minutes in hand he planned to avoid disaster and let the others try to take the race from him. At the base of the Alpe the fast pace caused Olano to drop off. Part way up the climb Italian Giuseppe Guerini took flight with Tonkov hot on his tail. Tonkov couldn't catch Guerini but he was just dangerous enough that Armstrong went after him. Near the top a photographer got right in Guerini's way and the 2 went down together. Guerini jumped back on his bike and was able to regain his momentum and stayed away for a terrific victory with Tonkov only 21 seconds back. The Armstrong/Zülle group came within 4 seconds of Tonkov at the end. The net result for the day with Olano's 2-minute time loss was that Armstrong now had a lead of 7 minutes, 42 seconds over the still second placed Spaniard. Zülle was now third, 5 seconds behind Olano.

Now the Tour went across the Massif Central. While this terrain didn't have the dramatic climbs of the Alps and the Pyrenees, the sawtooth stage profiles were demanding. An escape could do damage if the leaders' teams weren't alert and willing to work hard. Stage 12 was a classic stage of this sort with 6 climbs rated category 2 and 3; stage 13 had 7 rated climbs. While these days were characterized by constant attacks and high temperatures, the top of the standings didn't change.

Before the start of the 2 Pyrenean stages the Tour took its second rest day. There were now 3 stages left that could affect the Tour's outcome: the 2 remaining days in the mountains and the 57-kilometer time trial. If the pure climbers wanted to take back time from Armstrong, time was running out.

Stage 15 had 6 big mountains: the Ares, Menté, Portillon, Peyresourde, Val Louron, and a hilltop finish at Piau-Engaly. From the first climb the non-stop attacks started. Virenque, Laurent Brochard and others shattered the peloton. In the now-reduced pack, US Postal kept a high but not hot pace since most of the breakaways were not threats to the leadership. But when Fernando Escartin took off on the Portillon, Armstrong himself went after him. Escartin went again on the Peyresourde and began to hook up with riders who had escaped earlier. Escartin dropped all the other riders and soloed in for the win. Virenque and Zülle, who had been able to withstand Armstrong's attempts to drop them, managed to beat the Yellow Jersey to the finish by 9 seconds. For Armstrong and his team those final kilometers of that stage represented a rare episode of support failure. Armstrong bonked. He ran out of food and couldn't keep up with the others. Again Olano had been the main casualty, this day coming in 7 minutes after Escartin and losing his second place in the standings.

That afternoon rumors of a possible Armstrong dope positive became more solid when the French paper *Le Monde* announced that a drug test had shown Armstrong to be using a corticosteroid. The cycling press could not believe that Armstrong could emerge from cancer and be the extraordinary stage racer he had become, and fanned the rumors. It turned out to be the skin cream Armstrong had been using to fight saddle sores. It contained minute traces of cortisone, but Armstrong had been cleared by the Tour authorities to use the medicine.

Stage 16 would be tough with the Aspin, Tourmalet, Soulor and the Aubisque. With a descent into Pau after the final climb, this stage would not give the pure climbers the chance to get real time if Armstrong should falter. While there was action off the front, Armstrong stayed focused on his rivals. On the Tourmalet, a hard acceleration by Postal rider Kevin Livingston caused Virenque to lose contact. The main worries were Escartin and Zülle who were both indefatigable and strong. At the top of the Tourmalet Escartin attacked and took Zülle and Armstrong with him. Escartin tried again on the Soulor and again Armstrong stayed with him. In the final drive to Pau Armstrong let the others go, not needing to fight for a stage win or further tire himself. After the Pyrenees the General Classification stood thus:

1. Lance Armstrong
2. Fernando Escartin @ 6 minutes 15 seconds
3. Alex Zülle @ 7 minutes 28 seconds
4. Laurent Dufaux @ 10 minutes 30 seconds
5. Richard Virenque @ 11 minutes 40 seconds

Armstrong chose to ride the stage 19 time trial to win, rather than playing it safe and riding carefully. But he beat Zülle by only 9 seconds. The main loser of the day was Escartin, who not unexpectedly, lost gobs of time and his second place. The Tour was now Armstrong's. Like the 1971 Tour (when Ocaña crashed out while in Yellow), this is a Tour that invites speculation. What if Zülle had not crashed in the Passage du Gois and lost 6 minutes? Now I understand that all the riders had to ride the same roads, it was the same for everyone and Armstrong was the heads-up savvy rider who made sure he was in the front of the peloton on that dangerous road. But if Zülle, who did crash a lot, had not lost that time, then perhaps Armstrong would not have had the luxury of a defensive ride. It would surely have been a closer Tour that might have gone another way.

Armstrong joined an elite group (Merckx, Hinault and Indurain) when he won all of the 1999 Tour's time trials. That French cycling was still at a low ebb was made clear. The highest placed Frenchman was Virenque at eighth place, 17 minutes, 28 seconds behind Armstrong. For the first time since 1926, in the era of Belgian Tour hegemony, no Frenchman had won a stage. In 1926 the highest placed French rider came in eighth as well.

Final 1999 Tour de France General Classification:

1. Lance Armstrong (US Postal): 91 hours 32 minutes 16 seconds
2. Alex Zülle (Banesto) @ 7 minutes 37 seconds
3. Fernando Escartin (Kelme) @ 10 minutes 26 seconds
4. Laurent Dufaux (Saeco) @ 14 minutes 43 seconds
5. Angel Casero (Vitalicio Seguros) @ 15 minutes 11 seconds
6. Abraham Olano (ONCE) @ 16 minutes 47 seconds

Climbers' Competition:

1. Richard Virenque: 279 points
2. Alberto Elli: 226 points
3. Mariano Piccoli: 205 points

Points Competition:

1. Erik Zabel: 323 points
2. Stuart O'Grady: 275 points
3. Christophe Capelle: 196 points

**2000**. The lead-in to the expected rematch between the 3 active tour winners began to take on the appearance of a soap opera. While Armstrong studiously trained and reconnoitered the important roads of the 2000 Tour, Ullrich and Pantani both had a problematic winter and spring. In January Pantani announced that both the Giro and the Tour would be the centerpieces of his 2000 season. He spent part of the winter training in the Canary Islands. Ullrich escaped the cold of his native Germany by training in Mallorca. As the early season races drew nigh Pantani postponed his racing start, feeling that things were not "tranquil". He was dealing with the stress of returning to racing after more than just a short absence from racing. In fact, he hadn't been riding at all. After his 1999 Giro expulsion, Pantani had basically hung up his bike. Moreover, Pantani was harassed by a judicial investigation into his 1999 Giro disqualification. In Italy there is a crime called "sporting fraud" and Pantani was potentially culpable. Later an inquiry would also be opened into the circumstances of his 1995 Turin crash and the extremely high hematocrit hospital technicians found him to have.

In March Armstrong pulled out of Paris–Nice, but this was due to a case of bronchitis. Ullrich rode the Tour of Murcia and finished ninety-third, almost an hour behind the winner, David Cañada. The message from the T-Mobile team regarding Ullrich was *alles ist in ordnung* [everything is in order]. Late in February Pantani entered and retired from the Tour of Valencia. Ominously, his doctor started talking openly about stress and made it clear that Pantani's mental condition wasn't ideal.

When March came Ullrich entered the Tirreno–Adriatico stage race. He was so fat that his team managers tried to keep photographers away from him. The team said he had to lose about 3 kilos. Other racers said Ullrich had to shed at least 10 kilograms to be competitive. All the talk about Ullrich now centered on his weight and lack of conditioning. By late March Pantani was still postponing the restart of his racing season. Meanwhile Armstrong was testing his legs in spring races and getting top placings.

On May 13, after a long series of yes-and-no signals about his riding the Giro, Pantani announced he would indeed ride the Italian national tour. Ullrich attempted to ride the Midi Libre but abandoned after a poor time trial and a shelling in the mountains. Pantani ended up finishing the Giro an hour down and in twenty-eighth place, helping his friend and teammate Stefano Garzelli win. Pantani showed improving form in the Giro's latter stages with a second place in the mountainous stage 19.

In the drug war, a test for synthetic EPO had been developed, but because there were too many questions about its reliability, it was decided not to implement it for the Tour.

At the end of June it looked like Ullrich might have pulled a rabbit out of his hat when he took a fifth place in the Tour of Switzerland, finishing only 2 minutes behind the winner, Oscar Camenzind, and beating Virenque by 15 seconds. So at the start of the Tour, Armstrong looked to be rock-solid and his 2 main challengers were really unknown quantities. It was hard to know exactly what kind of fitness they would bring to the race. There were 2 other potential challengers, Escartin and Zülle, who had both prepared carefully.

The other important character in this, the Millennium Tour, was the route. The Prologue was lengthened to 16.5 kilometers, perhaps putting it out of reach of the short-distance men who specialized in doing well in the usual pure-power start-up to the race. For the first time since 1995, the Tour included a team time trial. Armstrong said he relished the addition, as well he should, given the strength of his team. The team time trial also favored ONCE with Olano and Jalabert, and Ullrich's Telekom squad. There was only 1 extended individual time trial, 58.5 kilometers coming on the third to last stage. To honor the history of the Tour, stage 14 would go over the historic route last used in 1949 and won by Gino Bartali that took in the Allos, Vars and Izoard. After the Pyrenean stages, there was only a short respite before 3 days of hard climbing in the Alps, a schedule that would favor the climbers. If Pantani had recovered both his physical form and his mental well being, he could be thought to be the favorite. That being unlikely, the race was really Armstrong's to lose.

The Tour started at the Futuroscope amusement park. Scotsman David Millar squeaked past Armstrong by 2 seconds to take the win and the first Yellow Jersey. Signaling fair-enough form, Ullrich was fourth, 14 seconds slower than Millar. Millar kept the lead until the stage 4 team time trial. Spanish racing had certainly changed a lot from the early days when Spaniards were only interested in and good at climbing. By the 1990s Spaniards were among the most accomplished time trialists in the world. Jalabert and Olano's well-drilled ONCE squad won the stage, even after a 20-second penalty for using a team car to tow a dropped rider back up to the squad. Jalabert was now in Yellow, a fact that did not displease the other contenders since it was assumed that Jalabert would not be able to hold the lead in the mountains, and yet his powerful team would be responsible in the short term for controlling the race.

During the team time trial Armstrong showed that he had more to learn about being a team leader. As Postal crossed a giant bridge over the Loire River, Armstrong took a hard pull. With the steep climb that crossing the big bridge entailed and the day's strong crosswinds, Armstrong's efforts blew the team apart. They struggled to get back together but it showed that even a team that has done the most careful practice and preparation can make serious mistakes in the heat of competition. Even with that error, the US Postal team came in second, only 26 seconds behind ONCE.

For Zülle, it was almost like 1999 again. His Banesto team lost 4 minutes, a time gap that would be almost impossible for him to take back from Armstrong. Again, his Tour was almost over before it started. Escartin was in even worse shape: his Kelme team came in fourteenth, almost 5 minutes slower than ONCE. In truth, barring a catastrophe in the mountains, the Tour for him was largely over.

The General Classification after the stage 4 team time trial:

1. Laurent Jalabert
2. David Cañada @ 12 seconds
3. Lance Armstrong @ 24 seconds
4. Abraham Olano @ 35 seconds
5. Viacheslav Ekimov @ 43 seconds

Jalabert was able to keep the lead for only 2 days. Early in stage 6, while Jalabert was taking a "natural break", a group of 12 riders rolled off the front and quickly formed a smooth working group. ONCE, Pantani's Mercatone-Uno team and US Postal chased but the 12 men would not be denied and were able to preserve a lead of over 7 minutes by the end of the stage. ONCE showed that they had higher ambitions than Jalabert's surely temporary time in Yellow by shutting down their own chase efforts after only a few kilometers. The man with the good fortune to have snagged the Yellow Jersey after the day's successful break was one of the oldest men in the peloton, 36-year old Alberto Elli of Telekom. Now, how much energy would Telekom expend defending Elli's lead? Telekom's manager predicted that Elli would keep the Yellow Jersey until the climbing started in stage 10.

The next day answered some questions. Telekom did work, albeit not too hard, to defend Elli's lead when French rider Christophe Agnolutto went on a successful solo break (the first one for a French rider in the Tour since 1997). Near the end of the stage Elli got into a break and US Postal jumped to the front of the pack and shut it right down. They didn't want things to get out of hand. The next day when Dutch rider Erik Dekker escaped it was US Postal and Mercatone Uno who did the work of keeping the gap manageable.

So, at the end of stage 9 with hard Pyrenean climbing coming the next day, here was the General Classification. Most of the higher ranking riders were beneficiaries of the stage 6 break:

1. Alberto Elli
2. Fabrice Gougot @ 12 seconds
3. Marc Wauters @ 1 minute 15 seconds
4. Pascal Chanteur @ 2 minutes 56 seconds
14. Laurent Jalabert @ 5 minutes 40 seconds
16. Lance Armstrong @ 5 minutes 54 seconds

Stage 10, the only major Pyrenean stage, with its hilltop finish at Lourdes/Hautacam would certainly sort things out. 205 kilometers long, the real climbing didn't start until kilometer 111 with the Col de Marie-Blanque followed by the Aubisque and then its little brother the Soulor before the final ascent. The day started in Armstrong's favor with cold, rainy weather, which Armstrong preferred and Ullrich loathed. It had now rained 9 out of the first 10 stages. Escartin's Kelme team sent several riders up ahead and they carved out a good-sized lead. Postal started to assert themselves on the Aubisque and rode hard enough to drop most of the peloton including Jalabert. Kelme rider Javier Otxoa went over the Aubisque first. Following him were 8 riders in an Escartin/Virenque group. About 3 minutes further back were the main contenders, Armstrong, Zülle, Ullrich and Pantani among them. Telekom rider Giuseppe Guerini did a lot of the work in the Armstrong/Ullrich group on the upper slopes of the Aubisque.

Very soon into the final climb Pantani attacked. Armstrong and Zülle were the only ones who could go with him. Then, in a move that astonished all who were watching, Armstrong jumped and dropped first Zülle and then Pantani. He then went after the others up the road and caught all but Otxoa, who was too far ahead. Otxoa won the stage after being away for about 160 kilometers. Armstrong came charging in 42 seconds later. Then the beaten and damaged former contenders crossed the line, Virenque and Escartin at 2 minutes, Zülle at 3 minutes, 47 seconds. Ullrich's poor preparation was clear, he finished thirteenth, 4 minutes behind Otxoa. Pantani was twenty-first, almost 6 minutes back. In a single day on a single climb Armstrong had put his rivals in a very dire position. Like Merckx 30 years before, once Armstrong gained time, it was almost impossible to take it back. Christophe Moreau, grasping for any silver lining, thought Armstrong might be vulnerable because his team wasn't as strong as in 1999.

The new General Classification:

1. Lance Armstrong

2. Jan Ullrich @ 4 minutes 14 seconds

3. Christophe Moreau @ 5 minutes 10 seconds

4. Marc Wauters @ 5 minutes 18 seconds

5. Peter Luttenberger @ 5 minutes 21 seconds

6. Joseba Beloki @ 5 minutes 23 seconds

The next day was a transition day of lesser climbs with a rest day to follow. Then they would have to contend with Mont Ventoux. Stage 12, which finished at the top of the dreaded "Giant of Provence" was held on the thirty-third anniversary of Tom Simpson's death in 1967. While the stage did have 3 second-category climbs, it was on the ascent to the top of Mont Ventoux that the action occurred. At the base of the climb Armstrong's teammates Tyler Hamilton and Kevin Livingston set such a hot pace that Zülle, Escartin and Moreau were dropped. So much for Moreau's being able to take advantage of the weaker 2000 Postal team. Eventually only 7 riders were left: Armstrong, Roberto Heras, Santiago Botero, Joseba Beloki, Richard Virenque, Jan Ullrich, and Marco Pantani. Pantani was yo-yoing on and off the back as Ullrich drove the group hard up the hill. Then, after the riders climbed past the tree line, with about 5 kilometers to go, Pantani surprised everyone and went to the front and delivered a series of hammer blows, the last of which were more than the others could withstand. The man who styled himself "the Pirate" was gone. But it wasn't over. Armstrong leaped out of the chasing group and took off after Pantani and caught him.

Armstrong wrote that as they fought the hard winds together near the top he tried to encourage Pantani and yelled, " *Vince*", for victory. Pantani misunderstood and thought Armstrong said " *Vitesse*" [go faster] and was trying to antagonize him. At the top, Armstrong wrote, he eased to let Pantani have the win (and that's exactly how it looked), the usual practice when the Yellow Jersey has worked with another rider and has gained a solid time increase with the other's help.

Pantani wins the Mont Ventoux stage.

The consequences of that act almost cost Armstrong the Tour. In a series of press conferences Armstrong indicated that he had indeed let

Pantani win the stage. Pantani was enraged and humiliated. He lashed back saying that he was the better rider and had fairly won the sprint. The dispute hit its nadir when Armstrong called Pantani "*Elefantino*", a nickname that Pantani detested because it made fun of his prominent ears.

Despite the sordid little episode Armstrong had delivered another punch to the peloton's solar plexus. The new General Classification:

1. Lance Armstrong
2. Jan Ullrich @ 4 minutes 55 seconds
3. Joseba Beloki @ 5 minutes 52 seconds
4. Christophe Moreau @ 6 minutes 53 seconds
5. Manuel Beltran @ 7 minutes 25 seconds
6. Richard Virenque @ 8 minutes 28 seconds

After a transition stage came stage 14, the stage which was to be a reminder of Tours past with its ascent of the Allos, Vars and Izoard, the first of 3 days in the Alps. One would have expected fireworks from those who knew they couldn't wait for the time trial to gain time. Again the Kelme team unleashed a storm of aggression and was rewarded with a solo stage win by Santiago Botero. The upper echelons of the General Classification remained unchanged.

When reviewing the final 2 Alpine stages, one can't help but think of that famous advice from Machiavelli's The Prince: "And let it be here noted that men are either to be kindly treated or utterly crushed, since they can revenge lighter injuries, but not graver." This has often been paraphrased as "Never do an enemy a small harm." Pantani had been stewing over Armstrong's post-Ventoux comments. Armstrong's needless tail-twisting had deeply angered the Italian who had been contemplating revenge.

Stage 15, from Briançon over the Galibier and the Madeleine with a hilltop finish at Courchevel was a climber's dream. Since the early kilometers on the Galibier there had been another Kelme-inspired break. The chasing peloton stayed together until the ride up to Courchevel. Pantani attacked early in the final ascent and only Armstrong could go with him. Then Pantani went again and Armstrong couldn't resist. Pantani went off up the road seeking the early breakaways. He caught them all and soloed in for a victory that could not be considered any sort of gift. Pantani made it clear that for him the win was a sort of revenge against Armstrong. Armstrong, who came in 50 seconds after Pantani ended up benefiting from the Pirate's move as he distanced himself still further from Ullrich and Beloki.

Now came the second of the 2 rest days before the final day in the Alps. Stage 16, from Courchevel to Morzine, had 4 big mountains, the Saisies, Aravis, Colombière and the Joux-Plane. Armstrong wrote that he expected this day to be the scene of certain war between Pantani and himself. War he may have expected, but he probably didn't count on the mutually assured self-destruction that ensued. On the Saisies, with over 120 kilometers of hard Alpine racing to go, Pantani exploded off the front. In a flash he was gone and the Postal team had no choice but to chase. Eventually Pantani made common cause with Escartin and a teammate of Virenque's, Pascal Hervé. The trio still had a lead when they went over the Colombière but by they time they had finished the descent the Postal-led peloton had caught them. It looked like Pantani's second day of trying to punish Armstrong had failed. On the Joux-Plane Pantani faded and lost contact with the Armstrong group. But the hours of relentless chasing had taken their toll on the others. The front of the peloton had come down to just 4 riders, Ullrich, Armstrong, Virenque and Roberto Heras. Armstrong had felt so good during the chase that he rolled right through the feed zone and didn't pick up any food; a failing he later called, "a feeble mistake, an unthinkable one for a professional."

On the climb, with 20 kilometers to go, Armstrong couldn't keep up with the others. 10 kilometers from the summit he bonked. For the second year in a row (see stage 15, 1999) Armstrong had not eaten enough and found himself in trouble. Seeing the opportunity, Ullrich started to pound up the hill for all he was worth. Armstrong, through an enormous effort of will, got himself up the final kilometers of the Joux-Plane and then hurtled down the other side of the mountain into Morzine. Because Ullrich had not come to the Tour with the body that had won the Tour in 1997, he couldn't capitalize on Armstrong's embarrassing failure to eat. Virenque won the stage but Armstrong lost only a minute and a half to Ullrich. Like Poulidor, Ullrich's career is strewn with these moments that could have been used to create a Tour victory. Armstrong was blessed in the quality of his competition. Pantani spent the evening suffering from terrible gastric problems and retired from the Tour the next day. Armstrong was deeply resentful of Pantani's kamikaze attack, but perhaps if the Italian had not been suffering from stomach problems he might have succeeded in winning the stage. In any case, he fulfilled, beyond his wildest dreams, his desire to "blow the stage up". Armstrong said that those agonizing minutes on the Joux-Plane were the worst in his cycling career.

Armstrong had a solid lead and had only the final time trial to worry about. Starting in Fribourg en Brisgau, Germany, and finishing in Mulhouse, France, Ullrich had the home-court advantage in the 2000 Tour's only long individual time trial. Armstrong, with a solid 5 minute, 37 second lead, didn't have to worry about losing the Tour to Ullrich unless misfortune struck. This is always a possibility in a time trial where the rider is going all-out. Over the first 10 kilometers, Ullrich was able to stay even with Armstrong, who started last, 3 minutes after the German. Then, after getting approval from Bruyneel, Armstrong upped the tempo and slowly forged a lead as he passed the crowds lining the road estimated at 1 million strong. At the end, Armstrong had gained his only stage win of the 2000 Tour, beating Ullrich by 25 seconds. It was the second fastest time trial in Tour history at 53.98 kilometers an hour, just off the 1989 mark of 54.545 set by LeMond. Winning the stage was terribly important to Armstrong who didn't want to take the ultimate victory by winning, as the Italians say, a la Balmamion.

The strength of the Postal team was made very clear when they were the only team to finish the Tour complete. None of the Postal riders had to abandon.

There was another race going on, the race for the Points Leader's Green Jersey. Telekom's Erik Zabel took his fifth *Maillot Vert*.

Final 2000 Tour de France General Classification:

1. Lance Armstrong (US Postal): 92 hours 33 minutes 8 seconds
2. Jan Ullrich (Telekom) @ 6 minutes 2 seconds
3. Joseba Beloki (Festina) @ 10 minutes 4 seconds
4. Christophe Moreau (Festina) @ 10 minutes 34 seconds
5. Roberto Heras (Kelme) @ 11 minutes 50 seconds
6. Richard Virenque (Polti) @ 13 minutes 26 seconds

Climbers' Competition:

1. Santiago Botero: 347 points
2. Javier Otxoa: 283 points
3. Richard Virenque: 267 points

Points Competition:

1. Erik Zabel: 321 points
2. Robbie McEwen: 203 points
3. Romans Vainsteins: 184 points

**2001.** The year started with what by now had become the normal press releases from Telekom, explaining that Ullrich's preparation was on track. He did train harder than the year before, but in March he was still responding to questions about his weight. By riding the Giro for training in May and June Ullrich was able to come to the Tour with his best form since 1997.

Armstrong, repeating the successful rehearsals of 2 previous Tours, had been carefully riding, reconnoitering and learning the 2001 route. He was tired of the constant sniping from the French press and lashed out in January, "It's unfortunate that the biggest bike race in the world is in France. We're living in an era of French innuendo and insinuation." This was churlish of Armstrong. It is the French culture and the French people who made possible the great race that Armstrong devoted himself to winning.

A French investigation into allegations of US Postal doping resulted in testing of archived urine and blood samples from the 2000 Tour. They were found to be clean.

While Ullrich was struggling to find competitive form Armstrong finished his training with a ride in the Tour of Switzerland. He used the stage 8 mountain time trial as practice for the stage 11 timed climb to Chamrousse in the upcoming Tour. Armstrong confirmed his superb condition by winning both the hill climb and the final General Classification, beating 2001 Giro winner Gilberto Simoni by a minute and a half. In addition to his personal meticulous preparation, Armstrong's team was improved, notably with the addition of Vuelta winner Roberto Heras.

Pantani, buffeted by 3 judicial investigations into doping allegations, raced a bit in Spain in February, but was not able to finish a race.
With Pantani's physical and mental form highly questionable and with
one of his teammates having been caught earlier in the season with a
high hematocrit, the Tour decided against inviting his Mercatone Uno
team. Sprint specialist Mario Cipollini's Saeco team also did not get an
invitation, partly because one of its riders was under the cloud of doping problems. After 1998 and 1999, the Tour wanted nothing to do
with any potential scandal. The result was a Tour that was heavily
weighted towards French teams.

    Just to let the world know that the doping in the pro peloton was
continuing unabated, Italian police raided the riders' hotel rooms during the San Remo stage in the Giro. Again the riders protested, causing
the cancellation of the next stage. The surprisingly large quantity of
drugs seized and the substantial number of renowned riders involved
generated a complete crisis within Italian cycling. It was clear that the
riders were not riding clean, but they were very skilled at evading doping controls.

    The 2001 Tour was a clockwise affair with the stage 7 entry into
the Vosges being the first climbing. After 2 Alpine stages the riders had
3 Pyrenean stages, all of which had hilltop finishes. At 3,453 kilometers
and 20 stages, the 2001 Tour was a bit shorter than the 2000 edition.

    Christophe Moreau, 2000's fourth place, won the 8.2-kilometer
Prologue in Dunkirk with Armstrong third, only 4 seconds slower, and
Ullrich fourth at 7 seconds. It looked like a good start to a good race.

    During the early stages as the Tour went into Belgium, the racing
was extremely aggressive. After stage 3, Credit Agricole rider Stuart
O'Grady was in Yellow. An extremely capable rider, O'Grady could be
expected to hold the lead at least until the mountains. The question
was, should the team defend the lead and burn themselves out or leave
O'Grady to the wolves in order to work for Bobby Julich who had been
third in the 1998 Tour? When a break went clear in stage 4, Credit Agricole was fortunate enough to have Julich in it. That put the onus on US
Postal and ONCE to bring back the break, which they did. With a team
time trial the next day, neither of the chasing squads wanted to expend
the energy, but Julich was too dangerous to be allowed any freedom.

    The team time trial was a surprise. Credit Agricole won it,
thereby giving O'Grady more time in the Yellow Jersey. US Postal had

a disaster when Christian Vandevelde slipped on the wet road and took down Roberto Heras. The team waited for them to remount and probably lost a full minute. Telekom also turned in a lackluster ride.

So, after the stage 5 team time trial and with the Vosges showing up in 2 days, here was the General Classification:

1. Stuart O'Grady
2. Jens Voigt @ 26 seconds
3. Bobby Julich @ 27 seconds
4. Igor Gonzalez de Galdeano @ 57 seconds
5. Joseba Beloki @ 1 minute 7 seconds
8. Christophe Moreau @ 1 minute 17 seconds
15. Lance Armstrong @ 1 minute 53 seconds
19. Jan Ullrich @ 2 minutes 20 seconds

When the hilly, twisty roads of stage 7 hit, Credit Agricole director Roger Legeay did the unexpected. Instead of defending O'Grady's lead, he sent another of his riders, Jens Voigt out on a break, a move which succeeded brilliantly. Voigt was now the leader.

The next day, stage 8, set the Tour on its ear. Bike racing strategy is almost always a gamble. In a 3-week stage race, the director always wants to minimize the work his team does. So when a break goes, he has to calculate whether or not to put his men at the front and start chasing. If the break is filled with riders who could not possibly be threats to the overall win, then they may be allowed to get away through the inaction of the top teams. Or, the sprinters' teams may decide that the break must be retrieved in order to bring the race together for a mass romp at the end. Early in stage 8 a group of 14 riders got away and amassed a lead of 35 minutes. In that break were O'Grady and good journeyman riders Andrei Kivilev and François Simon. O'Grady was back in Yellow and some good but unspectacular riders had made the coming 2 weeks of the race very interesting. The new General Classification:

1. Stuart O'Grady
2. François Simon @ 4 minutes 32 seconds
3. Bram De Groot @ 21 minutes 16 seconds

4. Andrei Kivilev @ 22 minutes 7 seconds

24. Lance Armstrong @ 35 minutes 19 seconds

So the stage was set for the first day in the mountains, and what a day it was! The day had 3 *hors catégorie* climbs: the Madeleine, the Glandon and a hilltop finish at l'Alpe d'Huez. Telekom decided to attempt to win the stage by going to the front and keeping the speed high. Over the Madeleine Armstrong moved back from the front of the peloton, looking uncomfortable and out of sorts. Encouraged by what they thought was Armstrong caught on a bad day, Telekom kept the pace very fast. On the Glandon Armstrong continued to appear on the edge of distress. At the base of the Alpe with the Telekom riders burning watts at a prodigious rate, Postal rider José Luis Rubiera went to the front and went full gas with Armstrong, Ullrich and Kivilev going with him. After Rubiera did his work and pulled off, Armstrong did a probing acceleration, slowed a moment and looked back, staring at the others, particularly Ullrich. Comfortable that they couldn't go with him he then rocketed off for a solo win. Stunned, Ullrich re-found his momentum and finished alone, second, almost 2 minutes later.

The entire stage with Armstrong's supposed trouble during the first 2 climbs had been a US Postal tactical set-piece. US Postal knew that the team directors all had televisions in their cars and could watch the race so that if Armstrong feigned difficulty, the other teams would know and act upon that information. Later it turns out that Telekom was suspicious but the opportunity to take back time from Armstrong doesn't occur every day. The chance had to be seized. Americans were ecstatic over what they saw was a challenging glare at Ullrich from Armstrong before he took off for the summit. Armstrong says that he didn't intend it to be the iconic "Do you feel lucky, punk?" type moment many thought it to be. In a later interview Armstrong said, "I wasn't being arrogant or cocky. I was looking to see [Ullrich's] condition and that of the riders behind him. I had to examine the situation. But when I saw it on TV, I could see why people were talking about it." Intentional or not, "The Look" has become a moment in sports that will always be remembered.

Things had changed dramatically. Armstrong voiced regret that Kivilev, an excellent rider, had been allowed to gain so much time.

1. François Simon

2. Andrei Kivilev @ 11 minutes 54 seconds

3. Stuart O'Grady @ 18 minutes 10 seconds

4. Lance Armstrong @ 20 minutes 7 seconds

5. Joseba Beloki @ 21 minutes 42 seconds

6. Christophe Moreau @ 22 minutes 21 seconds

7. Jan Ullrich @ 22 minutes 41 seconds

The next day was the time trial up to Chamrousse. With the race of truth, it is only a matter of speed and power. Armstrong had ridden the climb several times in his preparation for the 2001 Tour. His ride was superb. He won the stage and took another minute out of Ullrich. Kivilev was 6 minutes slower than Armstrong in this stage. While Simon was still in Yellow, the man thought to be the real danger, Kivilev, now had only 2 minutes on Armstrong in the Overall.

Next was a rest day and a transfer to Perpignan and the Pyrenees. Stage 12 had a first-category hilltop finish, the kind of stage that Armstrong had used over and over to gain time on his rivals. On the final climb to Plateau de Bonascre, the best of the Tour—Armstrong, Ullrich and Kivilev—were off the front. Ullrich attacked and Kivilev was dropped. Then, near the top Armstrong took off and took another 23 seconds out of Ullrich and brought himself to within 28 seconds of Kivilev. Simon remained in Yellow with a 9 minute lead on Armstrong.

The 2001 Tour's Queen Stage was next. The 194-kilometer stage 13 had 6 highly rated climbs starting with the second category Portet d'Aspet at kilometer 73. Then, crammed into the remaining 120 kilometers were the Menté, Portillon, Peyresourde, Val Louron-Azet (all first category climbs) and then the final *hors catégorie* ascent to Pla d'Adet/St.-Lary-Soulan. Laurent Jalabert had intelligently decided to forego chasing the General Classification, trying instead for the Polka-Dotted climber's jersey. At kilometer 25 he took off with a small group of non-contenders. Over each of the peaks, starting with the Col de Menté, Jalabert was first. By the time he reached the final climb he was exhausted and cramping, but the French crowds were delirious with joy over his exploit. Back in the peloton on the Peyresourde Telekom went to the front and upped the tempo. The increase in speed was too much for Simon who had dreamed of hanging on to his Yellow Jersey for another day. Along with most of the peloton, he was out the back. With the lead group down to just 23 riders Ullrich accelerated and only Armstrong could go with him. Together they went over the top of the

Peyresourde. On the descent Ullrich misjudged a corner and went tumbling off the road. In a very sportsman-like move Armstrong waited for Ullrich. Neither Ullrich nor his bike seemed to have suffered any real harm. The descent and the delay allowed for a small regroupment, with Postal riders Heras and Rubiera along with Beloki and Kivilev rejoining them. Rubiera set a hot pace up the final climb and after he pulled off it was again down to Armstrong and Ullrich. They traded hard pulls and when it was clear that Ullrich couldn't quite match Armstrong's speed, Bruyneel radioed Armstrong to deliver the *coup de grace*. Armstrong came in alone with Ullrich an even minute behind. Armstrong had taken the Yellow Jersey.

The new General Classification:

1. Lance Armstrong

2. Andrei Kivilev @ 3 minutes 54 seconds

3. François Simon @ 4 minutes 31 seconds

4. Jan Ullrich @ 5 minutes 13 seconds

5. Joseba Beloki @ 6 minutes 2 seconds

The final day in the mountains took in the Aspin, the Tourmalet and an ascent to Luz-Ardiden. At the base of the final climb there were remnants of an early break getting caught by the fast-moving Postal-led peloton. With about 10 kilometers to go Basque rider Roberto Laiseka exploded out of the Armstrong/Ullrich group and raced for the summit. Meanwhile Postal riders Heras and Rubiera chewed up what was left of the front chasing group leaving again only Ullrich and Armstrong. They raced together for the top and as Ullrich tried for the third place in play Armstrong didn't fight him. As they crossed the line Ullrich reached out for Armstrong's hand and they crossed together. Effectively, the Tour was over at this point and Ullrich acknowledged as much. Armstrong said that he was in the best condition of his life. It showed.

There was now only the 61-kilometer individual time trial in stage 18 to affect the results. Ullrich was clearly tiring as he lost 1 minute, 39 seconds to Armstrong, the stage winner.

There was still one battle left to fight, the ownership of the Sprinters' Green Jersey. Zabel had won the penultimate stage leaving Stuart O'Grady with 212 points and Zabel with 210. This would be settled on the Champs-Elysées. Czech rider Jan Svorada won the final sprint but Zabel was second and O'Grady third, giving Zabel his record sixth Green Jersey. Armstrong joined the elite group of Louison Bobet, Jacques Anquetil, Eddy Merckx and Miguel Indurain who were able to win 3 consecutive Tours.

Final 2001 Tour de France General Classification:

1. Lance Armstrong (US Postal): 86 hours 17 minutes 28 seconds
2. Jan Ullrich (Telekom) @ 6 minutes 44 seconds
3. Joseba Beloki (ONCE) @ 9 minutes 5 seconds
4. Andrei Kivilev (Cofidis) @ 9 minutes 53 seconds
5. Igor Gonzalez de Galdeano (ONCE) @ 13 minutes 28 seconds
6. François Simon (Bonjour) @ 17 minutes 22 seconds

Climbers' Competition:

1. Laurent Jalabert: 258 points
2. Jan Ullrich: 211 points
3. Laurent Roux: 200 points

Points Competition:

1. Erik Zabel: 252 points
2. Stuart O'Grady: 244 points
3. Damien Nazon: 169 points

**2002.** In January Ullrich traveled to the Tour of Qatar where his *directeur sportif* Rudy Pevenage said that "Jan is in excellent shape." But then on February 12, the bad news started. Ullrich started to feel pain in his knee and was told to reduce his training. In March, Ullrich's knee was still inflamed and it was announced that Ullrich would be out of action for 3 weeks. The injury continued to plague him all spring. In early May Ullrich was out driving one evening and hit a bicycle rack, and left without reporting the incident. The police suspended his license. Later it turned out that he was legally drunk at the time. That same week he announced that with his knee problem keeping him from racing, he could not ride the Tour. At one stroke the road to Armstrong's fourth win was made smoother. Armstrong wasn't happy, knowing that excitement is generated by healthy competition. He said that the Tour needed Ullrich in order to have a good race.

In early May it was finally decided to operate on Ullrich's knee. In June, in an out-of-competition drug test that all professional riders are subjected to, Ullrich was found to have amphetamines in his system. It wasn't a matter of his doping for performance enhancement, Ullrich wasn't racing. He had been at a clinic undergoing rehabilitation of his knee. The drug use was recreational. At a disco he had taken Ecstasy, which has an amphetamine content. His errant behavior was caused by depression over his inability to race. Ullrich's knee, even after the operation, wasn't getting better and he thought he might never race again. Telekom's boss Walter Godefroot had been angry about Ullrich's drunk driving. Now he was beside himself with fury. Because of the amphetamine use, the German cycling federation suspended Ullrich for 6 months. He underwent a second operation to the knee and this time he was able to resume training. Because of the suspension he could not begin racing until March 23, 2003. With no rider on the team capable of competing for the General Classification, Telekom was forced to build its team around Erik Zabel and his search for a seventh Green Jersey.

While Ullrich was imploding, Armstrong's preparations followed his proven model of hard training monitored by Chris Carmichael and Michele Ferrari and careful reconnaissance of the route so that Armstrong knew exactly what lay before him. The US Postal team was thought to be stronger than even the year before. With Pantani still in a deep mental crisis, there was really no one on the horizon who appeared to be capable of challenging Armstrong.

The 2002 Tour, at 3,276 kilometers, was shorter still than the short 2001 Tour. In fact it was the shortest Tour since 1905. With 20 stages and the usual 2 rest days, the average stage length of the 2002 Tour was down to 163 kilometers. The 2002 edition was counter-clockwise, starting in Luxembourg, heading west across Normandy and Brittany. Then after stage 10, the riders transferred to Bordeaux to ride south to the Pyrenees, then the Alps. To keep the suspense up, several of the key determining mountain stages were saved for the end of the Tour. While stage 16 was the last hilltop finish, stages 17 and 18 had serious climbs that could shake things up.

It was clear that Armstrong's preparation was on target when he won the Tour's 7-kilometer Prologue in Luxembourg. The highly technical course pushed the pure-power Prologue specialists like David Millar off the podium.

The first stage gave an excellent example of what happens when a strong rider takes an intelligent chance. Just before the final sprint Rubens Bertogliati took a flier and the sprinters looked at each other to see who would chase him down. The answer was no one, and Bertogliati became the new Yellow Jersey. Zabel allowed Bertogliati only 2 days in the lead. With the time bonuses accrued in the intermediate sprints and a second place in stage 3, Zabel was the new leader, his first time in Yellow since 1998.

The stage 4 team time trial was the first important stage of the Tour. For years ONCE had made this discipline their specialty. Riding a nearly flawless race, they were able to beat the ambitious-for-the-win US Postal team by 16 seconds. That made their Igor Gonzalez de Galdeano the Tour's new leader. Now, ONCE director Manolo Saiz had to ponder the future course of his team for the balance of the Tour. He had a true General Classification contender in Joseba Beloki who was third in 2001. Does he defend the Yellow Jersey for as long as possible and tire his team, or does he save his team's energy for Beloki?

The General Classification after stage 4:

1. Igor Gonzalez de Galdeano
2. Joseba Beloki @ 4 seconds
3. Lance Armstrong @ 7 seconds
4. Jörg Jaksche @ 12 seconds
5. Abraham Olano @ 22 seconds

Saiz was a banal, pusillanimous tactician. He answered the question early the very next day when a group of somewhat dangerous men broke away. ONCE quickly went to the front and shut it down. Effectively Saiz was conceding the race to US Postal, preferring to keep the Yellow Jersey they had for as long as possible rather than work for the Yellow they might get later. As the Tour raced at near record speed across northern France, ONCE worked with the sprinters' teams to keep the race together. US Postal was spared the need to waste energy policing the peloton. With the exception of a minor crash in stage 7 that cost Armstrong 27 seconds, coming into the first individual time trial US Postal had made no mistakes and suffered no serious misfortune.

Colombian rider Santiago Botero surprised everyone when he beat Armstrong by 11 seconds in the 52-kilometer time trial of stage 9.

Gonzalez de Galdeano rode well enough to preserve his lead, riding only 8 seconds slower than Armstrong. Writers looking for something to hang a story on started speculating that perhaps Armstrong might not be invulnerable. The answer would come in 3 days, on stage 11. With a rest day next, the General Classification stood thus:

1. Igor Gonzalez de Galdeano

2. Lance Armstrong @ 26 seconds

3. Joseba Beloki @ 1 minute 23 seconds

4. Sergey Gonchar @ 1 minute 35 seconds

5. Santiago Botero @ 1 minute 55 seconds

Stage 11, 158 kilometers long, went over the Aubisque at about the midpoint of the stage and then ascended part way up the Tourmalet to the La Mongie ski station. Jalabert was out trying to repeat his capture of the Polka-Dot jersey. On the Aubisque he joined and then dropped a small escaping group. None of them could keep up with him so he just went off on his own. Back in the peloton Postal set the pace. On the Aubisque the pace was tolerable and by the time the pack reached the base of the Tourmalet it was still about 70 men strong. It was here that Postal unleashed their twin JATO (jet assist take-off) bottles, Rubiera and Heras. First Rubiera pulled, setting a pace so fast that superb riders like Gonzalez de Galdeano, Christophe Moreau and Bobby Julich were dropped. Then Heras took over with about 5 kilometers to go. Only Armstrong and Beloki could hold the small Spanish climber's wheel as they roared by the now very tired Jalabert. Near the end of the ascent Armstrong jumped to take the sprint with Beloki only 7 seconds back. After the stage Armstrong said that it took all he had to hold Heras' wheel as he towed the duo up the mountains. Armstrong was now in Yellow.

After La Mongie the General Classification stood thus:

1. Lance Armstrong

2. Joseba Beloki @ 1 minute 12 seconds

3. Igor Gonzalez de Galdeano @ 1 minute 48 seconds

4. Raimundas Rumsas @ 3 minutes 32 seconds

5. Santiago Botero @ 4 minutes 13 seconds

The next day, stage 12, with its climbs over the Menté, Portet d'Aspet, Core, Port and then an ascent to Plateau de Beille, was almost a carbon copy of the day before. Jalabert went off looking for King of the Mountains points and US Postal kept the peloton working hard all day as they set a warm but not terribly high pace. On the final climb, again Rubiera started things going, then Heras took over and rocketed up the mountain at a white-hot pace. This time Armstrong escaped earlier and took a full minute out of Beloki, the only other rider who could stick with Heras. The days in the Pyrenees were done and Armstrong now had 2 minutes, 28 seconds on second-place Beloki.

Two days later, the stage 14 climb to the top of Mont Ventoux showed that even the Postal team was vulnerable. After Rubiera had done his usual set-up in the earlier part of the ascent, Heras, having a bad day, couldn't help. Armstrong was isolated without teammates. ONCE tried to take advantage of the situation and had Beloki attack. Armstrong not only closed up to him but counter-attacked, leaving the rest of the peloton behind. Up the road Richard Virenque had been in a break for almost 200 kilometers. He had shed all of his fellow escapees and was now laboriously turning the pedals, struggling to keep away from the hard-charging Armstrong. Virenque won the stage but Armstrong closed to within only 2 minutes, 20 seconds. Beloki had a terrible day on the hot slopes, losing almost 2 minutes in General Classification time. Even worse, Botero, who had been thought a likely contender for the podium, lost about 13 minutes. The tactics so far employed by the Spanish, who had at the beginning of the Tour had proclaimed that it would be "wide open" Tour and full of Iberian aggression, had been amateurish. Rather than try to put US Postal on edge, sending riders up the road, attacking at unexpected times, trying to isolate Armstrong, they were mostly content to sit on the Postal team and try to hang on for dear life on the final climb. Of course it was there at each hilltop finish that Postal's "murderer's row" would set the stage ablaze, destroy the peloton and release Armstrong for another win.

After a rest day the Tour faced 3 Alpine stages. The first one with its final climb to Les Deux Alpes didn't change anything in the top rankings. Botero, who had failed so dramatically on Mont Ventoux, rode to a solid solo victory.

In many ways, stage 16 with the Galibier, Madeleine and La Plagne climbs were just like the Pyrenean stages. Dutchman Michael Boogerd went off on a solo adventure at about the hundredth kilometer of the 180-kilometer stage. Early in the final climb Rubiera again lit the jets, leaving most of the remaining peloton in the dust. 5 kilometers from the finish Armstrong took off. He didn't catch Boogerd, but he put another 30 seconds between himself and Beloki.

The final Alpine stage, number 17, saw some epic riding as a break of 3 went away and held their lead to the end with Italian Dario Frigo taking the victory. The day had 3 first-category climbs but with the crest of the Colombière, the final one 20 kilometers from the end, it would be hard to hold any lead gained on the climb all the way to the finish. So the big guns rode tempo and no changes occurred at the top of the leader board.

The General Classification with the climbing completed:

1. Lance Armstrong
2. Joseba Beloki @ 5 minutes 6 seconds
3. Raimundas Rumsas @ 7 minutes 24 seconds
4. Santiago Botero @ 10 minutes 59 seconds
5. Jose Azevedo @ 12 minutes 8 seconds
6. Igor Gonzalez de Galdeano @ 12 minutes 12 seconds

Now only the 50-kilometer individual time trial could be reasonably expected to affect the Tour's outcome. Armstrong won the stage and avenged his stage 9 loss. He was fortunate in the misfortune of the man who came in second. Raimundas Rumsas was ahead of Armstrong at the first time check, but his aero bars came loose, surely costing more than the 53 seconds that Armstrong beat him by. That put the icing on the cake, giving Armstrong 4 consecutive Tour wins. He joined Anquetil (1961–1964), Merckx (1969–1972) and Indurain (1991–1995).

Again, the ownership of the Green Jersey came down to the final day in Paris. Australia's Robbie McEwen denied Erik Zabel his seventh sprinter's crown.

Final 2002 Tour de France General Classification:

1. Lance Armstrong (US Postal): 82 hours 5 minutes 12 seconds
2. Joseba Beloki (ONCE) @ 7 minutes 17 seconds
3. Raimundas Rumsas (Lampre) @ 8 minutes 17 seconds

4. Santiago Botero (Kelme) @ 13 minutes 10 seconds

5. Igor Gonzalez de Galdeano (ONCE) @ 13 minutes 54 seconds

Climbers' Competition:

1. Laurent Jalabert: 262 points

2. Mario Aerts: 178 points

3. Santiago Botero: 162 points

4. Lance Armstrong: 159 points

Points Competition:

1. Robbie McEwen: 280 points

2. Erik Zabel: 261 points

3. Stuart O'Grady: 208 points

Edita, wife of third-place finisher Raimundas Rumsas was arrested near Chamonix in the French Alps on the final day of the Tour, her car filled with various pharmaceuticals that a rational person would assume were doping products. She had been following Rumsas throughout the Tour. She was taken to jail where she insisted that these were medications for her mother. While Rumsas was accepting the award for third place in the Tour in Paris, he knew that his wife was in custody. Edita ended up spending several months in jail while her husband avoided going to France where he could be arrested. In 2006 the courts gave both husband and wife suspended sentences for importing illegal substances. Tested several times, Rumsas never failed a drug test in the 2002 Tour. But in the sixth stage of the 2003 Giro he was found to have taken EPO. Because Rumsas passed all drug tests given to him during the Tour, his 2002 third place, while highly suspect, remains official and on the books. In fact, all of the dope tests in the 2002 Tour were negative. All the riders were said to be clean and free of drugs. As Willy Voet—whose misfortune precipitated the 1998 Festina scandal—noted, the Tour's 141 drug tests merely show that the riders remained far ahead of the testers.

**2003.** In September of 2002, still under a racing suspension for his Ecstasy drug use, Ullrich announced that when his contract with Telekom expired at the end of 2002, he would not re-sign, preferring to find another team and a new beginning. This is usually a difficult time of the year to begin looking for a new team as most of the squads have their budgets for the following racing season settled and their rider contracts at least agreed upon. This late in the year few teams had the spare funds to take on a new and extremely expensive rider. But, a man who can compete for a Grand Tour victory is a rare commodity and the bidding was spirited with the CSC team, owned by Bjarne Riis, trying to bring him on board. Also Kelme, Phonak and the financially troubled Coast team tried for his services. He came close to a deal with a team sponsored by the German Postal Service. The deal was nixed when a new business plan for the German Post Office called for firing 40,000 postal employees. The politics of giving Ullrich a rich contract to ride bikes while tens of thousands of people were put out on the street killed the deal. The sagest advice anyone gave during this troubled time in Ullrich's life came from Armstrong, who advised Ullrich to ride for Riis for free. Armstrong understood that the difficult-to-coach rider needed direction, not more money. Riis had made it clear that if Ullrich came to ride for him, his free and easy ways were over. He would have to ride and train under Riis' instructions. Ullrich said that Riis wasn't exactly forthcoming about how much money he could pay Ullrich. In the end Ullrich chose Coast amid complaints from many of Coast's riders that they had not been paid their salaries for the second half of the 2002 season. Some surmised that Ullrich chose Coast over Riis because Ullrich wanted no part of the structured life and training that Riis would impose.

The UCI put the Coast team under a set of strict requirements regarding the payment of riders' salaries. On March 6, unhappy with Coast's foot dragging and endless excuses, the UCI suspended the team. Later in March the suspension was lifted but Alex Zülle, fed up with the turmoil and loss of racing time in March, bolted for the Phonak team.

In early May, Coast was suspended again. Team bike supplier Bianchi, who had assisted the Coast team with increased funding so that they could afford Ullrich, completely took over the team and its UCI license, thereby assuring Ullrich a place in the Tour.

Meanwhile super-sprinter Mario Cipollini's Domina Vacanze squad was not invited to the Tour. Noting that Cipollini always leaves the Tour before it hits the high mountains and that he had never finished a Tour, Tour boss Leblanc justified his decision by noting that in the 2003 Tour the mountains started after only a week of racing. Cipollini would surely ride only a few stages before abandoning.

It again looked to be a rematch between the troubled Ullrich and the perfectly prepared Armstrong. Armstrong rode a lighter race schedule but showed his good form when he won the Dauphiné. Wide speculation that Spanish rider Iban Mayo could challenge Armstrong for the Tour victory seemed optimistic at best. While the Spaniard might be able to match Armstrong in the mountains, he was incapable of time-trialing at Armstrong's level. Also, it was always dangerous to assess Armstrong's condition based on June races. His trainers Michele Ferrari and Chris Carmichael were always careful to bring him to his peak in the middle of the Tour in July, feeling that a rider could sustain a high level of form for only a few weeks. It later turned out that while Armstrong did win the Dauphiné, it was a pyrrhic victory because Armstrong had to go very deep into his reserves in order to win. Coming into the Tour he was still tired from the effort. Later Carmichael said that they should have let Mayo win the race.

Ullrich seemed to being doing better than had been predicted. While overweight, he still managed a fifth in the Tour of Germany.

Telekom's new General Classification protected rider was Alexandre Vinokourov, who had just won the Tour of Switzerland. Gilberto Simoni, victor in the recently completed Giro, boasted that with his superior climbing prowess, he would be able to take the Tour. Like the Spaniards the year before, Simoni was about to find out how hard it is to beat a supremely prepared and capable athlete. Speak softly and carry a big stick is very good advice.

Team selection was no longer based upon whomever the organizers chose to invite. Now the top 14 teams in the UCI's ranking automatically qualified to enter. Tour management had the ability to invite 8 other teams, called "wild cards".

This was the Centenary Tour. 100 years before, Georges Lefèvre and Henri Desgrange had cooked up the idea of a 6-stage race on the roads of France to help promote the ailing circulation of their paper, *L'Auto*. To commemorate the Tour's centennial at the October presentation of the 2003 route, 22 of the 23 living Tour winners were gathered together: Ferdy Kübler (1950), Roger Walkowiak (1956), Charly Gaul (1958), Federico Bahamontes (1959), Felice Gimondi (1965), Lucien Aimar (1966), Jan Janssen (1968), Eddy Merckx (1969, '70, '71, '72,

'74), Bernard Thévenet (1975, '77), Lucien van Impe (1976), Bernard Hinault (1978, '79, '81, '82, '85), Joop Zoetemelk (1980), Laurent Fignon (1983, '84), Greg LeMond (1986, '89, '90) Stephen Roche (1987), Pedro Delgado (1988), Miguel Indurain (1991, '92, '93, '94, '95), Bjarne Riis (1996), Jan Ullrich (1997), Marco Pantani (1998) and Lance Armstrong (1999, 2000, '01, '02 and eventually '03, '04 and '05). Only 1967's winner Roger Pingeon missed the gathering. To further solidify the historic nature of the 2003 Tour, the route visited the 6 original stage cities: Paris, Lyon, Marseille, Toulouse, Bordeaux, and Nantes with a complex series of prizes and competitions involving those who did well in those stages. As it had been the custom in earlier Tours, H.D., the initials of Tour father Henri Desgrange were returned to the Yellow Jersey.

The Prologue in Paris yielded a few surprises. Australian Bradley McGee won, but probably because David Millar's mechanic chose to lighten Millar's bike by removing the front derailleur. Millar got his chain jammed between the front chainrings and was forced to settle for a seething, furious second place. Ullrich showed that his spring preparation might have been good enough. He came in fourth, at 2 seconds. Armstrong was up to his usual performance, coming in seventh, 7 seconds slower. In addition to having some residual fatigue from the extreme effort it took to beat Mayo in the Dauphiné, Armstrong crashed in the Dauphiné and had to take antibiotics that didn't agree with him. To make things even worse, in the week leading up to the Tour Armstrong was suffering from gastroenteritis causing diarrhea that lasted right up until the start of the Tour. Given those handicaps, Armstrong's Prologue looks truly impressive.

In fact, Armstrong was having more problems than just a troubled gut. Armstrong changed shoes on the Thursday before the race start, causing a slight change in the pedal-cleat interface which caused an injury to his hip. He tried to mask the pain during the first week, but it contributed to his sub-par performance. Every rider has small and large problems along the way, but this was an unusual series of difficulties for a rider who usually came to the Tour perfectly prepared and in wonderful condition.

The first stage really showed how much depth Australian racing has acquired since the days in the 1920's when Hubert Opperman was the only competitive antipodean. Although Alessandro Petacchi won the stage, Aussie Robbie McEwen acquired the Green Jersey and his compatriot Bradley McGee remained in Yellow. As part of the Centennial, the Tour stopped for a moment at Montgeron, outside the restaurant *Le Réveil Matin* (The Alarm Clock) where the Tour started the very first stage in 1903. Just before Petacchi's final sprint victory, a nasty left turn caused a pile up that brought down several important riders including Armstrong. While Armstrong was unhurt, other riders including Rabobank's General Classification hope Levi Leipheimer, had to abandon. Tyler Hamilton broke his clavicle but decided to endure the pain and continue riding.

The first real sorting occurred in the 68-kilometer team time trial of stage 4. US Postal and its predecessor Motorola had always wanted to win a Tour team time trial. Frankie Andreu, who rode on both teams before retiring, said that the team time trial was Motorola director Jim Ochowicz's passion. Finally US Postal got their long desired victory, beating Beloki's ONCE by 30 seconds and Ullrich's Bianchi squad by 43 seconds. That put US Postal domestique Victor Hugo Peña in Yellow and Armstrong in second place, only 1 second behind with the mountain climbing commencing in 3 days. Over the next 3 days Peña kept the Yellow Jersey but US Postal came in for criticism when Peña went back to the Postal car to get water bottles for Armstrong. Many thought the Yellow Jersey deserved a bit more respect. What it showed was the absolute undeviating manner in which the entire Postal team viewed winning the Tour.

Stage 7 started the climbing. With several category 2 and 3 climbs to soften their legs, the riders' last major ascent was the Col de Ramaz, a category 1 summit that came 20 kilometers before the finish. Ridden in terrible heat, the day had a profound effect upon the Tour. Giro winner Simoni was exhausted from both his tough Italian Tour win and especially, he said, from the efforts of the stage 4 team time trial. He could not keep up with the contenders and lost 10 minutes. 2000 Giro winner Stefano Garzelli also had difficulty but didn't lose time. He also attributed his trouble in the stage to his efforts in the team time trial. About 40 kilometers into the stage Richard Virenque escaped and hooked up with several others who were already off the front, including teammate Paolo Bettini. Bettini bonked and had to let Virenque go. Virenque held his lead, taking off on the Ramaz and earning a solo victory. His beating the pack by almost 4 minutes earned him the Yellow Jersey with Armstrong still in second, now back by 2 minutes, 37 seconds. The tone of the Tour seemed to be clear. Postal set a moderate tempo for the peloton for most of the stage, and as in years past, the other teams were quite happy to sit on. It made for an easy ride, not having to do any of that messy racing stuff. By letting Postal dictate the race each year the other teams made the ultimate outcome nearly a foregone conclusion. Except for the Armstrong *tifosi*, the tactics the other teams had adopted in the face of Postal's strength since 2000 made for a boring race.

Stage 8 had a few category 2 and 3 climbs before the Galibier and a hilltop finish at l'Alpe d'Huez. While Armstrong may not have been quite at the top of his game, Ullrich was suffering with intestinal troubles as were several other members of the peloton. The real racers reached the base of the Alpe together. Then, in a shock to not only the peloton but also to the Postal team, new Postal recruit Manuel Beltran hit the bottom of the mountain with all jets blazing. His speed shattered the pack and put both Ullrich and Virenque out the back door. The other climbers, sensing that Armstrong and the Postal team had been riding easily over the Galibier for a reason started attacking. Beloki tried a couple of times to get away. Then Iban Mayo went and made it stick. Vinokourov attacked and made good his escape as well. Even Tyler Hamilton had a go but was brought back. Mayo won the stage, followed a couple of minutes later by Vinokourov. A half-minute later Armstrong led in the 6 other survivors. Armstrong was now in Yellow but it seemed as if the Tour, for the first time in years, was in play. Later Armstrong regretted not riding the stage harder because he feels he could have taken more time out of Ullrich.

It turns out that Armstrong's rear brake had been rubbing for much of the stage, including the climb over the Galibier. Armstrong wondered aloud about sabotage. It would not have been the first time in the Tour. The most famous occurrence of a rider's bike being vandalized was in 1937 and it almost cost Roger Lapébie the Tour when he tried to start a mountain stage and found that his handlebars had been partially sawn through. Nothing was proven in either case.

The new General Classification:

1. Lance Armstrong
2. Joseba Beloki @ 40 seconds
3. Iban Mayo @ 1 minute 10 seconds

4. Alexandre Vinokourov @ 1 minute 17 seconds

5. Francisco Mancebo @ 1 minute 37 seconds

6. Tyler Hamilton @ 1 minute 52 seconds

Stage 9 had the Lautaret and the Izoard, but both came before the 100-kilometer mark of this 184.5 kilometer stage. Late in the stage came the second-category St. Appollinaire and the third level Côte de La Rochette. They shouldn't have had too much effect upon the race, but affect the race they did. Armstrong had been unable to deliver a lethal coup de grace on l'Alpe d'Huez. The others had hit Armstrong with all they had and Armstrong was still the man in Yellow, but the sense that he could be challenged gave new life to the race. The day was characterized by constant aggression. Most of the good riders were together for the final climb when Vinokourov blasted off the front and drew no reaction. Further up the Rochette Armstrong hit the pack hard and took only a few riders with him, including Beloki, Mayo and Ullrich. They crested the Rochette only 15 seconds behind Vinokourov. It was on the descent that the race changed completely. On the serpentine road with its soft asphalt melted by the heat, Beloki went down hard. In a tight corner his rear wheel locked up, the tire rolled off the rim and blew up. Armstrong, who had been right on his wheel, went off the road, cutting across the switchback in a brilliant bit of quick thinking and excellent cyclocross riding. Beloki, in agony with a broken finger, elbow and femur, still wanted to get back on his bike. Just before the crash, his manager Manolo Saiz had told Beloki to let Armstrong take the lead. Now Saiz cradled the shattered racer in his arms, knowing that his Tour was over. With Beloki out, Vinokourov was in second place, 21 seconds behind Armstrong.

In intense heat the Tour rode stage 10 to Marseille; a day of rest followed. Postal's 43-second margin of victory over Telekom in the stage 6 team time trial was looking to be very important. Without that superb effort, Vinokourov would have been in Yellow at this point.

Stage 12 continued the drama. The day was a roasting 35° centigrade (95° Fahrenheit) and Armstrong suffered terribly from dehydration in the last leg of the 48.5-kilometer individual time trial. Ullrich won the stage with Armstrong, who had been going as fast as Ullrich for the first half of the stage second at 1 minute, 36 seconds.

The very tight General Classification stood thus:

1. Lance Armstrong
2. Jan Ullrich @ 34 seconds
3. Alexandre Vinokourov @ 51 seconds
4. Tyler Hamilton @ 2 minutes 59 seconds
5. Haimar Zubeldia @ 4 minutes 29 seconds
6. Iban Mayo @ same time

The Tour was now set for 3 days in the Pyrenees. Stage 13 had 2 tough climbs, Port de Pailhères and the hilltop finish at the Ax-3 Domaines ski station at the top of Plateau du Bonascre. While the other teams may have been guilty of using poor tactics during the Armstrong years, that accusation cannot be leveled at Postal's own manager Johan Bruyneel. He sent one of their best, José Luis Rubiera, up the road in a break. Eventually at the crest of the Pailhères he was one of a group of 4 that was a couple of minutes ahead of the Armstrong/Ullrich group and ready to assist Armstrong should he need help.

On the final climb Rubiera was caught by the Armstrong group but Carlos Sastre, who had been part of the break, managed to stay away and continued on to win the stage alone. Further back Postal had Roberto Heras attack the Armstrong/Ullrich group. That left just shattered remnants, several of whom took turns attacking: Zubeldia, Vinokourov and then finally Ullrich. Sitting in the saddle Ullrich was able to ride the others off his wheel and come in second behind Sastre. Armstrong closed to within 7 seconds of Ullrich. That left the General Classification still very close:

1. Lance Armstrong
2. Jan Ullrich @ 15 seconds
3. Alexandre Vinokourov @ 1 minute 1 second

The second Pyrenean day had 6 climbs categorized 1 and 2: Col de Latrape, Col de la Core, Portet-d'Aspet, Col de Menté, Portillon and the Col de Peyresourde, whose crest came 11 kilometers before the finish. On the Portillon Virenque, Laurent Dufaux and Simoni emerged from an earlier break and were able to stay away to the end. Simoni, recovering from his earlier efforts in the Giro and the Tour, won the stage, giving him some level of redemption. On the Peyresourde

Vinokourov joined a break that again generated no reaction from Ullrich and Armstrong. Vinokourov stayed away and narrowed the gap a bit more. Later Armstrong said that at this point he believed that his chances of winning the Tour were at best, 50 percent.

The General Classification podium now stood thus:

1. Lance Armstrong
2. Jan Ullrich @ 15 seconds
3. Alexandre Vinokourov @ 18 seconds

Stage 15, 159.5 kilometers from Bagnères-de-Bigorre to Luz-Ardiden, was the final Pyrenean stage with 3 big climbs. At kilometer 94 was the Col d'Aspin, at kilometer 135 the riders faced the Tourmalet. If Armstrong had recovered, his forte of grabbing serious time on stages with hilltop finishes would be well-served with the final ascent to Luz-Ardiden. On the Tourmalet Ullrich attacked hard but Armstrong came back up to him. On the descent Armstrong gapped Ullrich a few times on the tricky corners but the best riders were together for the final ascent.

With 9 kilometers to go Mayo put in a hard acceleration which Armstrong answered. Then, as the riders were going around a tight corner Armstrong took the shortest line and caught his bars in the straps of a spectator's musette. Down he went, taking Mayo with him as Ullrich swerved to avoid them. Armstrong and Mayo remounted and up ahead Ullrich slowed. The others weren't so interested in waiting for the Yellow Jersey so Tyler Hamilton went to the front and put his arm out to slow them. Armstrong, having trouble with his cleats, finally rejoined. Mayo took off again and then Armstrong jumped hard and no one could follow him. Ullrich, who is a momentum climber like Indurain, never did well when the speed changed on a climb. He had a hard time getting going again as Armstrong went by Mayo and took the stage beating Mayo, Ullrich and Zubeldia by 40 seconds. Mayo and Zubeldia were content to sit on Ullrich's wheel the remainder of the climb and try to take the cheap second place, which Mayo did. Ullrich did get his big body up to speed, taking 10 seconds out of Armstrong's gap in the upper slopes of the climb, but he ran out of mountain too soon. Waiting for Armstrong was a grand sporting gesture which probably cost Jan Ullrich the Tour. Comparisons have been made to the 2001 Tour when

Armstrong waited for Ullrich after he crashed on the descent of the Peyresourde. The situations are not comparable. Going into that stage Armstrong led Ullrich by 4 minutes. That race, in truth, even though François Simon was in Yellow, was over. The 2001 Tour was not in play for Ullrich. In 2003 it was.

The resultant General Classification:

1. Lance Armstrong
2. Jan Ullrich @ 1 minute 7 seconds
3. Alexandre Vinokourov @ 2 minutes 45 seconds
4. Haimar Zubeldia @ 5 minutes 16 seconds
5. Iban Mayo @ 5 minutes 25 seconds

After the awards ceremony where Armstrong donned the Yellow Jersey, Bernard Hinault greeted him with the simple and telling words, "Welcome to the club." Barring misfortune Armstrong had joined the 5-time Tour winner club.

Now a rest day, then the Tour was to be decided on the penultimate stage, a 49-kilometer individual time trial. That would have been it except that Tyler Hamilton, still suffering intense pain with a broken collarbone, took off in the mountains of the final Pyrenean stage and won a memorable solo victory.

The stage 19 time trial didn't disappoint for drama. It was raining hard in the morning. Ullrich loathed the cold and the wet while Armstrong thrived in it. Unlike Armstrong, Ullrich didn't go out on the course in the morning to familiarize himself with the roads, preferring to stay in bed and watch a videotape of the route. The race itself turned out to be fraught with danger. Several of the riders who had gone off before Ullrich and Armstrong crashed, one breaking some ribs. Understanding that the Tour would be decided during the coming hour Ullrich shook with anxiety in the start house. He took off cleanly and for much of the distance he was leading as he rode at the record individual time trial speed of 55.21 kilometers an hour. Perhaps in any other era Ullrich's effort would have won him the Tour. But at only a couple of seconds slower, Armstrong was nearly matching Ullrich's effort.

And then disaster struck. In a roundabout, as the weather was getting wetter and windier, a gust of wind caught Ullrich's rear disc wheel and sent him to the ground. The Tour was effectively finished. Armstrong slowed to avoid crashing himself, letting David Millar win the stage and Hamilton take second. Since Ullrich was ahead of Armstrong by only 6 seconds in the time trial when he fell, but down by 1 minute, 5 seconds in the Overall, the race was really already over and the crash didn't affect it.

Again, the Green Jersey's owner wasn't settled until the final stage in Paris. Robbie McEwen and Baden Cooke were separated by only 2 points. Cooke took second in the final sprint and McEwen was third giving Cooke the Points classification.

Armstrong joined Anquetil, Merckx, Hinault and Indurain in the elite club of 5-time Tour winners. Only he and Indurain had achieved their 5 wins consecutively. Virenque joined Bahamontes and van Impe as 6-time winners of the climbing competition.

Indicative of the intensity and the competitiveness of the 2003 Tour, it was raced at the record speed of 40.94 km/hr. It was also pointed out that if the peloton had really been riding clean they wouldn't be riding faster than during the 1990's, the glory days of EPO use.

Final 2003 Tour de France General Classification:

1. Lance Armstrong (US Postal): 83 hours 41 minutes 12 seconds
2. Jan Ullrich (Bianchi) @ 1 minute 1 second
3. Alexandre Vinokourov (Telekom) @ 4 minutes 14 seconds
4. Tyler Hamilton (CSC) @ 6 minutes 17 seconds
5. Haimar Zubeldia (Euskaltel) @ 6 minutes 51 seconds
6. Iban Mayo (Euskaltel) @ 7 minutes 6 seconds

Climbers' Competition:

1. Richard Virenque: 324 points
2. Laurent Dufaux: 187 points
3. Lance Armstrong: 168 points

Points Competition:

1. Baden Cooke: 216 points
2. Robbie McEwen: 214 points
3. Erik Zabel: 188 points

**2004.** Coming into the 2004 Tour there was a feeling that for the first time in several years the Tour de France was wide open. No one looking at the close results of the 2003 Tour thought that Armstrong was vulnerable now because of the weaknesses and errors of the previous year; it was generally understood that less than perfect preparation and several mistakes such as changing Armstrong's pedals and shoes just before the start of the Tour contributed to his difficulties. No one thought that these mistakes would be repeated.

There were 2 reasons for the feeling that the Tour was in play. The first reason was the improvement in the depth of the competition. Several riders seemed ready to really challenge Armstrong for supremacy:

1) Tyler Hamilton. His new team, Phonak, was generously funded with a $9.6 million budget. Hamilton got to have a purpose-built team to work for him for the Tour. The corporate, Tour-focused US Postal system seemed worthy of replicating. Hamilton's form looked nearly perfect. He won the Tour of Romandie and placed second in the Dauphiné, beating Armstrong in the time-trial up Mont Ventoux. His high placing in last year's Tour, accomplished with a broken collarbone, spoke well for his abilities.

2) Jan Ullrich. Ullrich was back with Godefroot, the team having changed its name from Telekom to T-Mobile. Godefroot had been very bitter about the 2002–2003 breakup. Even though Ullrich was welcomed back into the fold, Ullrich's personal trainer and good friend Rudy Pevenage was still *persona non grata* and was not allowed to travel with the team. He was forced to take care of Ullrich by traveling on his own at Ullrich's expense. This was an interesting window into Godefroot's psychology and why, after spending many millions of euros on superb talent, he had so little to show for it. He was willing to sacrifice the mental well-being of his most valuable and expensive rider to feed his anger. That, in a nutshell is the difference between Godefroot and Bruyneel and why Bruyneel always beat Godefroot. Bruyneel would never do anything that would in any way impair Armstrong's physical and mental well-being. The only point Bruyneel wanted to make was the one a victorious director makes when his rider wears Yellow in Paris.

Ullrich started training earlier than ever before for the Tour. His win in the Tour of Switzerland seemed to signal that his condition would be good. The only question mark was if his usual too-rapid weight loss in the weeks before the Tour would sap his strength. His teammate Alexandre Vinokourov would have been a second card for his T-Mobile team to play, both tactically to assist Ullrich and as a pure play for the Tour win. But Vinokourov crashed badly in the Tour of Switzerland and could not start. This was a hard blow for T-Mobile who had to re-think their strategy.

3) Iban Mayo. Always getting better. He won the Dauphiné, beating Armstrong in the time trial up Mont Ventoux and looked ready for the Tour. His question mark was the same as last year. Did he peak too soon? Last year he ran out of gas in the third week because he had tried to keep top form for too long.

4) Roberto Heras. When this erratic racer was firing on all cylinders, he was probably the finest pure climber alive. In the fall of 2003 he won the Vuelta. In the winter he moved from US Postal to the Spanish Liberty Seguros squad. His time spent as a domestique with US Postal was not wasted. Heras deepened his skills to become a competent though not world-class time trialist, demonstrated when he won the time trial in the Basque Country stage race. With only 61 kilometers of flat time trialing in the 2004 Tour, he had the chance of being the first pure climber to win since Marco Pantani in 1998.

There would be 1 tragic missing rider. In February Marco Pantani was found dead in a hotel room, a victim of his own terrible depression and an overdose of cocaine.

There were other riders with possibilities, but with the depth of the year's top-class field, any rider would have to rise to unusual heights to win.

The second reason for optimism among the other riders was Armstrong's age. Some think that upon having hit the magic number of 5 wins, since to date no one had exceeded that number, some insuperable wall arises. 5 wins is not a wall, it's just an arbitrary number of wins. The reason no rider has surpassed this number is that each of the previous 5-time winners, upon going for number 6, found younger, better riders, more capable of handling the abuse of a Grand Tour. I felt that at the beginning of the Tour, the race would be interesting and competitive because of Armstrong's age.

But there is a counter-argument. The other members of the 5-time club raced a full season. Eddy Merckx would suffer all winter in smoky six-day races. Then he would hurl himself onto the cobbles for the northern Spring Classics. When the time for the big stage races came around, he raced them.

Merckx did no special scientific preparation as we now understand it, no careful tune-up. Just constant, non-stop, intensive racing for most of the year at the highest possible level. Even when Merckx rode the post-Tour criteriums, he would race them with all the intensity he gave the hardest mountain stage in the Tour.

This unbelievable schedule gave us the legend of Eddy Merckx, who won an average of 1 race a week during his professional career. It also wore him out prematurely.

Armstrong carefully prepared for the Tour, prudently choosing his lead-in races. He rode the Tour de France and then quit racing for the season. His body got the optimal tune-up and recovery. For this reason, his career should (and did) last longer than the others.

To me, the proper comparison is Fausto Coppi. Because his bones were so fragile, Coppi was regularly laid up while he let his broken bones heal. It has often been remarked that because of the recovery these convalescences gave Coppi, he was able to attack the races he did ride with intensity and freshness. Sound familiar?

Let's look at the 32 and over Tour winners:
1903: Maurice Garin, 32 years old
1919: Firmin Lambot, 33
1921: Leon Scieur, 33
1922: Firmin Lambot, 36
1923: Henri Pélissier, 34
1926: Lucien Buysse, 34
1929: Maurice de Waele, 33
1948: Gino Bartali, 34
1952: Fausto Coppi, 32
1980: Joop Zoetemelk, 33
1996: Bjarne Riis, 32

In the last 50 years only Zoetemelk and Riis have been able to win the Tour after their thirty-second birthday. Hamilton was 33 on March 1 and Armstrong was 32 when the Tour started. Armstrong's birthday is September 18, so he was almost 33 during the 2004 Tour. Since World War II, more men have won the Tour 5 times than have won it after they turned 32.

The 2004 Tour was counter-clockwise, Pyrenees first. The route had some terribly difficult stages planned, and there was 1 interesting switch. The first time trial was up l'Alpe d'Huez. The Tour's climbing specialists would not lose as much time as usual in the time trials. They had only the Prologue and the Besançon time trial on the penultimate stage to cause them worry.

Another change was a "stop-loss" rule for the team time trial. The most a rider could lose in the team chrono event was 3 minutes. This harkened back to old Henri Desgrange who hated to see a weak rider get too much help from a strong team or a strong rider held back by a weak team. There was nothing new in this. We've noted that many previous Tours have awarded the winner of the team time trial only a small time bonification. Some Tours have allowed the team time trial to affect only the team standings, leaving the individual times unchanged. Some Americans, suspicious of French intentions and ignorant of Tour history, accused the Tour management of manipulating the rules to Armstrong's disadvantage.

The accusations of doping continued. Several members of the Cofidis team were found to have been habitual users of performance enhancing chemicals. The most notable of them was David Millar, the World Time Trial Champion. He wasn't found out through drug testing. He, like almost the entire pro peloton, had been able to finesse the testing regimen. It took the French police, who raided his home and found doping products, to extract a confession from the man who had for so long denied that he had cheated.

Armstrong had been at the center of accusations from almost the first moment when he showed that he could successfully contest the Tour. A French judicial inquiry into accusations of Armstrong and Postal team doping had been proceeding at a glacial pace. The investigators seemed to be convinced that if they looked long enough and hard enough they would find evidence of cheating. The inquiry took 21 months to complete. Finally, in September 2002 the investigation was closed for lack of evidence. In June 2004, a book titled *LA Confidential: the Secrets of Lance Armstrong* came out accusing Armstrong of systematically doping. It put together some rather plausible accusations, but to destroy a man's reputation, the book needed proof. Armstrong swore to bring the writers to account in court. Both sides failed. The truly compelling proof was missing and Armstrong did not pursue his accusers. To advance the story a bit more, in August of 2005 the French newspaper *L'Équipe* was able to discover the results of retrospective testing of frozen 1999 Tour urine samples. The newspaper said that 6 of Armstrong's samples were positive for EPO. Many arguments were mounted against the *L'Équipe* story, most of it silly francophobic spin. The one argument that Armstrong made that has legs was that no one could be sure of the chain of custody of the samples between 1999 and 2005. On that basis alone it is only fair to leave Armstrong's reputation intact. On the other side of the ledger, Armstrong was contemptuous of the few riders who either admitted to doping or spoke out against its use in the peloton. On several occasions he seemed to be helping to enforce the professional riders' *omerta*, the code of silence regarding dope.

The race:

The Prologue time trial was held in Liège, Belgium on wet, slippery streets. Both Ullrich and Hamilton chose to ride it conservatively, hoping to avoid a crash. Ullrich's teammate, Sergei Ivanov crashed earlier in the day so Ullrich's team boss Walter Godefroot instructed Ullrich to ride carefully.

Armstrong, being a superb bike handler, chose to ride the event all-out. The times showed the effect. Armstrong came in second and put 15 to 20 seconds between himself and his challengers before the first stage. Even with the cautious ride, Ullrich's time was slower than it should have been. Ullrich was coming down with a cold.

It was on the third stage that the first real drama of the 2004 Tour took place. 2 sections of pavé were included, the first being almost 3 kilometers long. As in Paris–Roubaix, each rider was desperate to be at the front as they approached the cobbles. The peloton accelerated to a near flat-out pace. Just before the first cobbled section, Iban Mayo and US Postal rider Benjamin Noval locked handlebars and went down. Also going down was the Yellow Jersey, Thor Hushovd. Postal hammered the front. When it didn't suit them, Postal had no trouble forgetting the traditional race courtesy of waiting for a fallen Tour leader. All of Mayo's Euskaltel team, including their number 2 General Classification man Haimar Zubeldia, dropped back to pace him back to the field. Before the Euskaltel team could rejoin the peloton, the race hit the cobbles. US Postal stayed at the front and rode the cobbled section blisteringly fast. First their George Hincapie and then more powerfully, Viacheslav Ekimov put in hard, long pulls. The field split into several groups under this onslaught. In the end, the front group with most of the top riders kept pulling away from a second chase group that contained not only Mayo, but top French hope Christophe Moreau.

They lost almost 4 minutes and saw their overall lead hopes dim on only the second stage.

The stage 4 team time trial was held in 64.5-kilometers of wet and sloppy conditions. US Postal executed their ride perfectly and won the stage, putting Armstrong in Yellow. Armstrong was impressive, taking kilometer-long pulls.

Having chosen narrow tires that were too light for the wet roads, tires that were required by their time-trial bikes' tight clearances, Hamilton's Phonak team suffered 5 flat tires as well as several mechanical problems. They were able to finish with the minimum number of riders, 5. In a team time trial, the team gets the time of the fifth rider across the finish line. Their ride was still impressive since they came in second after waiting twice for riders with problems and running a short team. They were denied the win, but it showed that Tyler's new team had real strength and could meet any need that would arise in the coming stages. With the new team time trial rules, Hamilton did not suffer the full 1 minute, 7 seconds that he lost to US Postal. Tour rules limited his loss to only 20 seconds.

Gilberto Simoni, the team leader of Saeco and multiple winner of the Giro, seemed to forget that he had to finish with his team to get the protection of the new rule. Coming into town, fearing a crash on the cobbles, he let himself get separated from his team. He lost 2 minutes, 42 seconds.

Armstrong made it clear that he would not defend his Yellow Jersey this early in the Tour. Early in stage 5, a break of 5 went off early and came in with a lead of 12 minutes, 33 seconds. Letting the break go was a considered judgment on Postal's part, but in the winds and bad weather and with a crash in the peloton, it became difficult to keep the break's lead from getting out of hand. This put the young French Road Champion, Thomas Voeckler of the Brioches La Boulangere team, in Yellow. This was not the result Postal wanted, as they remembered the trouble caused in 2001, letting a break containing Andrei Kivilev get a big lead.

The stages leading up to the first rest day after stage 8 were all run under wet and windy conditions across the north of France. Numerous crashes made the riders very nervous. It was said that more than 100 of the remaining 176 riders had been involved in at least 1 crash. At the 1-kilometer-to-go sign in stage 6 a terrible pile-up stopped most of the field. Tyler Hamilton went flying and landed on his back, breaking his helmet in the process.

Meanwhile, super-aggressive breakaway ace Jakob Piil had spent 551 kilometers of the first week in breaks.

By the rest day there were no real changes to the General Classification. Here were the standings before the Tour headed to the Massif Central for stage 9:

1. Thomas Voeckler

2. Stuart O'Grady @ 3 minutes 1 second

3. Sandy Casar @ 4 minutes 6 seconds

4. Magnus Backstedt @ 6 minutes 27 seconds

6. Lance Armstrong @ 9 minutes 35 seconds

7. George Hincapie @ 9 minutes 45 seconds

11. Tyler Hamilton @ 10 minutes 11 seconds

20. Jan Ullrich @ 10 minutes 30 seconds

The Tour management had put in 3 transition stages next. They were not pure climbing stages. Instead they were to be challenging with 'heavy' roads that would be tough on the peloton. Tour director Jean-Marie Leblanc said that he included these stages hoping that some of the Tour contenders would try to shake things up with tactical, aggressive riding rather than just sitting in Postal's wake, riding tempo and waiting for the mountains.

It was not to be. Each day, opportunistic, non-threatening breaks were allowed to go, then controlled. These stages across the Massif Central of France had no real effect on the General Classification. Thomas Voeckler did manage to hang on to his Yellow Jersey thanks to the hard working defense of his team.

Stages 12 and 13 were Pyrenean mountain stages.

Stage 12 started with a long, slow rise out of Castelsarrasin. There were 2 climbs, an assault on the Col d'Aspin and then a climb partway up the Tourmalet to La Mongie. It was an astonishing day that saw the hopes of most of Armstrong's challengers fade. Ullrich, Mayo, Zubeldia and Hamilton cracked very early on the final climb. The day turned cold and wet, the worst possible weather for an Ullrich who had become sick enough to require antibiotics. When asked over his radio if his team's number 2 man, Andreas Klöden should wait and escort him to the finish, Ullrich, knowing that he was going to lose real time that day, gave Klöden his freedom. In the end, only CSC's Ivan Basso could stay with Armstrong. In the final kilometers Basso actually looked better than Armstrong and beat the 5-time Tour winner to the line.

Stage 13 was more of the same. It was a 205-kilometer ride over Col du Portet d'Aspet, Col de la Core, Col de Latrape, Col d'Agnes and then up to Plateau de Beille.

Very early on in the stage Tyler Hamilton was forced to abandon the race. Injuries to his back from the crash in stage 6 kept him from being able to ride out of the saddle. He said that he was unable to apply any power to his pedals.

Later on, Euskaltel's Iban Mayo played out a repeat of Federico Bahamontes' attempts to quit the Tour 50 years ago. Suffering badly in his second day in the mountains, Mayo fell off the pace. At one point he got off his bike. His manager convinced him to get back on the bike and continue. After riding just a few meters he started to take his shoes out of the pedals. His teammates kept pushing him along, not letting him quit. Even Fabian Cancellara of the Fassa Bortolo team came up beside him and started pushing him along. He eventually finished the stage, 38 minutes behind the winners.

Armstrong's US Postal team completely controlled the race, keeping the tempo very high. By the penultimate climb, the Col d'Agnes, there were only 22 riders left in the Armstrong group, 7 of them Postal riders. This was a team domination that probably has no equal in modern Tour history. Within the first couple of kilometers of the final climb the Armstrong group was reduced to about a dozen riders. As Postal's Jose Azevedo increased the intensity, it was soon down to just 3: Azevedo, Armstrong and the young hero from the day before, Ivan Basso. After Azevedo had done his work for Armstrong and swung off, it was Basso and Armstrong trading pace to the line. This time, Armstrong was the better of the 2 while Basso was showing the strain of the 2 days in the mountains.

Plucky Thomas Voeckler looked like he was finally going to lose his Yellow Jersey as he struggled up the final kilometers to Plateau de Beille. He had fallen off the lead group on each of the climbs and chased back on the descents, fearlessly blazing down the mountainsides. As he passed under the 2-kilometers-to-go banner, his manager drove up next to him and told him that if he pushed it, he could keep the Yellow Jersey. Exhausted, Voeckler dug even deeper and kept his lead by a whisker-thin 22 seconds over second-place Armstrong; Ivan Basso was third at 1 minute, 39 seconds.

The utter collapse of nearly all the fancied challengers was a stunning result after only 2 days in the mountains. Armstrong and his team looked to be completely in charge before the Tour moved to the Alps.

Cyrille Guimard, the coach of van Impe, Hinault, Fignon and LeMond, called the day a massacre. He thought that only Ivan Basso had a chance at the final victory after stage 13. And that was doubtful because he was only as strong as Armstrong, not stronger. Armstrong was the better time trialist, making it very unlikely that Basso could take time out of Armstrong in the remaining days unless Armstrong were to have a very bad day.

After the Pyrenees and stage 13, going to a rest day and then the Alps, here were the standings:

1.  Thomas Voeckler
2.  Lance Armstrong @ 22 seconds
3.  Ivan Basso @ 1 minute 39 seconds
4.  Andreas Klöden @ 3 minutes 18 seconds
5.  Francisco Mancebo @ 3 minutes 28 seconds
8.  Jan Ullrich @ 7 minutes 1 second

On paper, the first Alpine stage, 15, was a challenging but not a crushing stage. It had a category 2 mountain to climb followed by the first category Col de l'Echarasson. There was some relatively minor climbing after that before the expected showdown. The stage's climax was foreseen to be the second category Côte de Chalimont, which crested just 15 kilometers from the finish. A quick descent was followed by a slight climb to the finish line.

Ullrich knew that he had to do something soon. He would run out of opportunities very quickly with all the climbing and time trialing packed into this last week. Riding with the Armstrong group on the Col de l'Echarasson, he heaved his big body up the road in a furious attack. In the Pyrenees he had pedaled with a ponderous, slow, ineffective cadence. Here he was turning over his big cranks at a high rate, looking fresh and as powerful as the old Ullrich. He crested the mountain with a lead of about a minute over the Armstrong group. He picked up some remainders of a fraying breakaway, Garcia-Acosta and Santos Gonzalez.

CSC hit the panic button. Not being confident that their Ivan Basso could challenge Armstrong for first place in the General Classification, Ullrich's attack could be a threat to the second place Basso currently held. Playing it safe, CSC's boss Bjarne Riis told Jens Voigt, who was up the road in an earlier break, to return to the small Yellow Jersey group that also had Carlos Sastre, Ivan Basso and 2 Postal riders. Together, CSC and US Postal brought Ullrich back to the peloton.

This group then came into the finish area. Armstrong sat in the back of the group in the big ring, cross-chained, ready to dump the gear for a sprint. Always prepared. He jumped, taking Basso with him and emphatically won the stage. Armstrong was now in Yellow.

Stage 16 was the wildly anticipated individual time trial up l'Alpe d'Huez. Before the collapse of almost of all of Armstrong's competitors, this was seen as a potentially electrifying stage that would showcase Armstrong, Ullrich, Hamilton and Mayo in a terrific, dramatic race. Given the lack of real competition left, the stage was expected to do nothing more than tighten Armstrong's grip on the lead.

Riding through a defile of race fans that were estimated between 500,000 and 1,000,000, Armstrong executed a convincing victory. He beat Ullrich by 61 seconds. His 2-minute man, Ivan Basso, was caught with about 4 kilometers to go. Nationalistic Germans showed their anger at their countryman Jens Voigt, who had been instrumental in chasing down Jan Ullrich the day before. Signs calling him "Judas" and catcalls from the crowd were his unfair reward. After the stage even Ullrich had to tell a press conference that was Voigt's job, to work for his team.

Stage 17, the 2004 Tour's Queen Stage was 204 kilometers of Alpine racing. The racers were to cross the Glandon, the Madeleine, the Tamié, the Forclaz and the Croix-Fry. T-Mobile had made it clear that this was an important opportunity to take the second and third places on the podium. They announced in advance that they would attack Basso.

As the racers rode kilometer after kilometer, US Postal set a fast pace causing all but the last few of the contenders to go out the back door without so much as a single attack. T-Mobile just sat behind Postal the entire way. Clearly the confidence had gone out of the legs of Ullrich and Klöden. As US Postal rider Floyd Landis, in an amazing display of power and endurance, led the leaders up the Croix Fry, the group was reduced to Armstrong, Ullrich, Klöden, Basso and of course, Landis. In the final descent into Le Grand Bornand, first Landis ("Run like you stole something", Armstrong told him) attacked and was brought back by Ullrich. Then T-Mobile's Klöden counter-attacked. Armstrong, upset at Ullrich for pulling back Landis, chased him like a fiend and caught him at the line. No change to the top placings still.

The penultimate stage, 19, was a 55-kilometer individual time trial. It consisted of an oblong loop over the rolling countryside starting and ending in Besançon. At every check point Armstrong was the leader. In the first time check, 18 kilometers into the stage, Ullrich had already lost 43 seconds. Ullrich had hoped to do well enough to make it to the podium but he fell far short of that goal. His teammate, Andreas Klöden, did beat Ivan Basso by a large enough margin to make it to second place in the General Classification.

And that's how it ended. Armstrong made history by winning his sixth Tour de France. He defied the calendar and his doubters.

Richard Virenque won his seventh King of the Mountains title, passing Federico Bahamontes and Lucien van Impe, who had 6 each.


Final 2004 Tour de France General Classification
1.  Lance Armstrong (US Postal): 83 hours 36 minutes 2 seconds
2.  Andreas Klöden (T-Mobile) @ 6 minutes 19 seconds
3.  Ivan Basso (CSC) @ 6 minutes 40 seconds
4.  Jan Ullrich (T-Mobile) @ 8 minutes 50 seconds
5.  Jose Azevedo (US Postal) @ 14 minutes 30 seconds
6.  Francisco Mancebo (Illes Balears) @ 18 minutes 1 second
7.  Georg Totschnig (Gerolsteiner) 18 minutes 27 seconds
8.  Carlos Sastre (CSC) @ 19 minutes 51 seconds
9.  Levi Leipheimer (Rabobank) @ 20 minutes 12 seconds
10. Oscar Pereiro (Phonak) @ 22 minutes 54 seconds

Climbers' Competition:
1.  Richard Virenque: 226 points
2.  Lance Armstrong: 172 points
3.  Michael Rasmussen: 119 points

Points Competition:

1. Robbie McEwen: 272 points
2. Thor Hushovd: 247 points
3. Erik Zabel: 245 points

**2005.** The 2005 route favored climbers a bit with only 74 kilometers of individual time trialing (2.6 kilometers fewer than in 2004) and 3 hilltop finishes. Instead of a short Prologue the 2005 started with a 19-kilometer individual time trial. This had the potential to change the complexion of the first week's racing. Normally the sprinters do reasonably well in the short, power-intensive Prologues. At worst they start the first road stage a few seconds out of the lead. Their hope is to accrue time bonuses along the way and gain the Yellow Jersey before they hit the mountains. With a long time trial the gaps between the better time trialists and sprinters would most likely put the lead out of time-bonus reach. One writer speculated that this might reduce the desperation and aggression in the early stages and make the racing a bit safer. Given the intensity of Tour racing, this was an unlikely outcome. The 2005 Tour went clockwise (Alps first), then headed to the Pyrenees and finished the climbing in the Massif Central before heading to Paris.

Professional racing was given a profound re-organization with the institution of the Pro Tour. The reigning president of the UCI, Hein Verbruggen, rammed through his vision of how the sport should be run. The 20 best teams were given a "Pro Tour" license good for 4 years. The most important races, which included the Grand Tours and the Classics, were given Pro Tour status. The Pro Tour teams would all have to send riders to all of the races that were on the Pro Tour calendar. The purpose of this reorganization was to give stability to the teams and a high quality peloton to all of the important races. Not happy with what they saw as a bald UCI power grab, the promoters of the Grand Tours pushed back finding many of the Pro Tour rules encroaching on their ability to run their races as they saw fit. While negotiations between the UCI and the Grand Tour organizers dragged on, both sides agreed to disagree for now and proceeded to run the season under a flag of truce. The result for the Tour was that all 20 Pro Tour teams had an automatic invitation to ride the Tour and the Tour organization could only choose 1 wild card. Facing a 200 rider limit to the peloton, there was some speculation that the Tour would have 8-man teams, allowing more small teams to compete. It didn't come to pass and only one discretionary invitation was issued, to the French Ag2R team.

There had been doubt as to whether Armstrong would ride the 2005 Tour and attempt to extend his winning streak to 7 consecutive Tours. In February he announced that he would, indeed, be on the line in July. His contract with his team's new sponsor, the Discovery Television Channel required him to ride another Tour, but he could choose to ride either the 2005 or the 2006 Tour.

Ullrich had already put in 2,500 kilometers by New Year's Day, announcing that unseating Armstrong remained his primary goal. When Armstrong announced that he would ride the 2005 Tour, Ullrich responded that this would make a better race. Also, he had made no secret of the fact that he longed to beat Armstrong.

The man who had given Armstrong such a scare both in 2003 and 2004, Iban Mayo, and who had suffered such a physiological crack-up in the mountains of the 2004 Tour turned out to have contracted mononucleosis. He wasn't ready to mount another challenge.

In the pre-Tour tune-up races, the Dauphiné Libéré and the Tour of Switzerland, both Ullrich and Armstrong did well enough. Neither wanted to be peaking in early to mid June. Ullrich led the Swiss Tour for a while and eventually came in third, only a minute and a half behind the winner, Aitor Gonzalez. Armstrong came in fourth in the Dauphiné while T-Mobile's other Tour hopeful, Alexandre Vinokourov was fifth in the Dauphiné, only 3 seconds behind Armstrong.

Armstrong's teams had been put together for a single purpose, to deliver Armstrong to Paris in Yellow. Ullrich's teams usually had split ambitions. Besides working for the General Classification, stage victories were highly important to the German team. In the pre-Armstrong years this had worked well for them. In 1997 they had won both the Yellow and the Green Jerseys courtesy of their successful dual-pronged Ullrich and Zabel attack of the Tour. For the 2005 Tour T-Mobile announced a team that was selected with the sole purpose of winning the Tour's General Classification. The team looked to be extremely strong, with 2004 second-place Andreas Klöden and 2003 third-place Alexandre Vinokourov. To make room on the team for another domestique who could help in the mountains, 6-time Green Jersey winner Erik Zabel was left off the roster. The T-Mobile team looked to be almost scary-strong. Still, the real question, given the rough parity Armstrong and Ullrich had in time-trialing, did Ullrich bring enough horsepower to the Tour to withstand Armstrong's explosive bursts of power near the final summit on stages with hilltop finishes? That was where the big time was lost, stage after stage, year after year. With the exception of 2003, Armstrong had about clinched each of his Tours with a rocket-like burst of irresistible speed at each year's first hilltop finish.

T-Mobile seemed intent upon confirming their image as the team that couldn't quite get things right. On the day before the Prologue, team director Mario Kummer was motorpacing Ullrich (driving a car or motorcycle with a rider right in the vehicle's slipstream) when he hit the brakes without warning. Ullrich crashed through the rear window and into the car. Everyone on his team went out of his way to say Ullrich was fine with only a few bruises and cuts.

Let's look at the first stage 19-kilometer individual time trial results. At 54.67 kilometers an hour, David Zabriskie's ride was the fastest time trial in Tour history, beating LeMond's fabled 1989 final stage record of 54.454 kilometers an hour. Zabriskie had been a member of Armstrong's Postal team but when they were uninterested in renewing his contract Riis picked him up for CSC. Armstrong, who started a minute after Ullrich, caught and blew by the slower moving German.

1. David Zabriskie: 20 minutes 51 seconds.

2. Lance Armstrong @ 2 seconds

3. Alexandre Vinokourov @ 53 seconds

12. Jan Ullrich @ 1 minute 8 seconds

Sports physiologists such as Michele Ferrari, Armstrong's training guru, noted that after a crash the body's diversion of precious energy and resources measurably impaired a racer. At the first stage Ullrich had given up a minute he shouldn't have, a minute he was unlikely to ever get back from Armstrong.

Zabriskie kept the lead until the fourth stage, a 67.5-kilometer team time trial going from Tours to Blois. CSC, having the Yellow Jersey, was the last team to ride. At each checkpoint throughout the ride they were ahead of Discovery by a few seconds. As CSC blazed the day's final 2 kilometers, Zabriskie had what can only be guessed to be a lapse of concentration. The team was in perfect formation and then Zabriskie went flying in a terrible crash. The team continued on and Zabriskie limped in a minute and a half later. Zabriskie had no memory of the crash and couldn't explain why it happened although a high-speed touch of wheels was the likely cause. Discovery won the stage by 2 seconds and Armstrong was now the Tour leader. Discovery's 57.325 kilometers an hour was the fastest Tour team time trial on record.

The next day's start (stage 5) was delayed a little because Armstrong, following an old tradition of not wanting to wear the Yellow Jersey the day after inheriting it from a rider who has lost it from misfortune, was told he would be ejected from the Tour if he did not put on the Yellow Jersey. That settled it and Armstrong was in Yellow. The early stages were the sprinter's private property with Belgium's Tom Boonen winning 2 stages and Australia's Robbie McEwen taking stage 5.

The finale to stage 6 made it clear that Alexandre Vinokourov would need to be watched. Just before the finish, as the pack was closing in on fading escapee Christophe Mengin, Vinokourov and Lorenzo Bernucci took off after Mengin and caught him. Mengin crashed in the dangerous final corner, forcing Vinokourov to slow, allowing Bernucci to take the stage. But with the 12 second time bonus for second place and the 7 second gap to the field, Vinokourov elevated himself to third in the General Classification.

Stage 8 took the Tour from the sprinters and gave it to the men of the Tour. Stage 7 had crossed into Germany and stage 9 took it over the Vosges as it headed back into France. It was a rare day in the Tour when T-Mobile out-raced Discovery. On the final climb, the second category Col de la Schlucht, Armstrong found himself isolated. The day's hot pace had forced his already tired team to be dropped. Vinokourov tried several savage attacks which were brought back. Then T-Mobile launched Klöden who caught an already escaped Pieter Weening. Their break stuck and Klöden moved to 1 minute, 50 seconds behind Armstrong, who remained in Yellow. Armstrong, knowing that he could not win the Tour without a working team to defend him, was clearly angry at being left alone and promised that there would be hard talk at the team's dinner table.

The next stage, looking to conserve energy and give the Discovery domestiques a rest from protecting the Yellow Jersey, a 3-man break containing CSC's Jens Voigt was allowed to go. This was exactly what

Discovery was looking for. They wanted to give the responsibility of the Yellow Jersey to a man who would not be a long-term threat. Voigt was just such a man and he now had the lead with a rest day next before the real climbing began. Again Ullrich crashed, this time at high speed early in the stage. He was able to rejoin the field with little trouble.

This Tour was shaping up to be a very fast, hard-fought race with an average speed of 46.22 kilometers an hour average over the 1,493.5 kilometers covered so far. The General Classification after stage 9:

1. Jens Voigt
2. Christophe Moreau @ 1 minute 50 seconds
3. Lance Armstrong @ 2 minutes 18 seconds
4. Michael Rasmussen @ 2 minutes 43 seconds
5. Alexandre Vinokourov @ 3 minutes 20 seconds
6. Bobby Julich @ 3 minutes 25 seconds
7. Ivan Basso @ 3 minutes 44 seconds
8. Jan Ullrich @ 3 minutes 54 seconds

Stage 10 was a simple enough stage with the category 1 Cormet de Roselend midway through the 180-kilometer stage, and then a hilltop finish at Courchevel. Simple though it may have been, Armstrong was again able to destroy the ambitions of several of his competitors on the final climb of the first high mountain stage of the Tour. This time there were no problems with his team. They were able to escort him until the final kilometers of the stage setting a very fast pace, especially from the end of the descent of the Roselend until the final climb. In the first 8 kilometers of the climb Roberto Heras, Alexandre Vinokourov, and Joseba Beloki were dropped. Then Ullrich came off and Floyd Landis (now riding for Phonak) was also shelled. T-Mobile decided to sacrifice Klöden and had him escort Ullrich up the mountain. Meanwhile Armstrong did the lion's share of the work as men who had spent almost a year preparing for the Tour were tossed and gored. With a kilometer to go Armstrong revved it up some more and only Alejandro Valverde could go with him. Valverde, being the better sprinter, took the stage and with that, the 2005 Tour was turned upside down. The new General Classification after several important riders had inexplicably failed their first test:

1. Lance Armstrong
2. Michael Rasmussen @ 38 seconds

3. Ivan Basso @ 2 minutes 40 seconds

4. Christophe Moreau @ 2 minutes 42 seconds

5. Alejandro Valverde @ 3 minutes 16 seconds

8. Jan Ullrich @ 4 minutes 2 seconds

16. Alexandre Vinokourov @ 6 minutes 32 seconds

Stage 11 was another day in the high Alps with the Madeleine, Télégraphe and Galibier before a long descent to Briançon. On the Madeleine Vinokourov joined a break of about 10 riders. As they rode over the 3 mountains almost all of Vinokourov's fellow breakaways dropped off until he was left with only Santiago Botero. Back in the reduced field, Discovery rode at tempo, not too worried about a rider with a 6-minute deficit in General Classification. Vinokourov outsprinted Botero for the stage win, and with the 1 minute, 15 second time gap to the field plus the 20 second stage-win time bonus Vinokourov moved up to twelfth, 4 minutes, 47 seconds behind Armstrong.

That ended the heavy Alpine stages. Now the very tired riders worked their way across Southern France in heat so oppressive that at one point the officials had a section of the road that had melted hosed down to cool it off.

Stage 13 saw a couple of racers lose their game of "poker" with each other and the peloton. Chris Horner and Sylvain Chavanel had a sustainable lead in the final kilometers when, jockeying for the stage win, first Chavanel and then Horner stopped working. Chavanel took the front but couldn't maintain the gap by himself and in the final meters they were swept up by the fast moving peloton.

Stage 14 was the first stage in the Pyrenees. In baking heat the stage started with a series of third and fourth category climbs and ended with the *hors catégorie* Port-de-Pailhères and a first category hilltop finish at Ax-3 Domaines. Again, an early break without any riders who could be considered trouble was allowed to get away. One of the riders, experienced pro Georg Totschnig, managed to drop the other breakaways and solo to victory. Back in the peloton T-Mobile decided to roll the dice and set a very fast pace up the Pailhères. T-Mobile's tactics seemed to be in a bit of disarray. Vinokourov rocketed away from the now very reduced group and Ullrich chased him down. In so doing he managed to gap Armstrong who was now without teammates. After waiting a few minutes Armstrong then calmly closed the gap up to the leaders. It was an impressive display of power and sangfroid.

Armstrong and Basso finish stage 14.

At the base of the climb to Ax-3 Domaines Vinokourov, who had been dropped after his earlier attack, rejoined and again tried to get away. This time Klöden brought him back and then dropped him. Now it was Basso, Ullrich, Armstrong, Levi Leipheimer and Landis. In the final kilometers of the climb it was down to Ullrich, Basso and Armstrong. Shortly before the end Ullrich was dropped and Armstrong jumped for a small gap on Basso, solidifying his hold on the lead.

Stage 15 was, without a doubt, the 2005 Tour's hardest mountain stage. 205 kilometers long, it included the Col du Portet d'Aspet, Col de Menté, Col du Portillon, Col de Peyresourde, Col de Val Louron-Azet and a hilltop finish at St.-Lary-Soulan/Pla d'Adet. On the Col de Menté a break of 14 went clear. Wanting to be up ahead to help Armstrong in the latter part of the stage, George Hincapie made sure he was in the break of the day. As they rode up and over the Pyrenees, one by one the others dropped off. By the time they were on the final climb it was down to just Oscar Pereiro of Landis' Phonak team and Hincapie. Pereiro, understanding that Hincapie was an Armstrong domestique and would not be allowed to help, did all of the work, dragging Hincapie along in his wake. After sitting on Pereiro for nearly the entire climb Hincapie jumped around the Spaniard for his first Tour stage win. Americans who generally loved the genial Discovery rider were enchanted by the win. Pereiro, however, was bitter about doing all the work and losing the stage.

The real race, of course, was back down the road. By the time the peloton went over the Peyresourde the Yellow Jersey group was down to 18 riders and the Hincapie/Pereiro break was long gone, being 14 minutes ahead. On the Val Louron-Azet Basso hit the front hard and gapped Ullrich who struggled back up but it was clear to Armstrong and Basso that the German was vulnerable. On the descent there was a small regroupment, but it was temporary. Early in the final climb Basso accelerated and only Armstrong could go with him, leaving Ullrich alone to suffer more time loss. Armstrong did not contest the sprint when Basso led him over the line. Clearly Basso and Armstrong were riding on a level well above the others.

The General Classification stood thus:

1. Lance Armstrong
2. Ivan Basso @ 2 minutes 46 seconds
3. Michael Rasmussen @ 3 minutes 9 seconds
4. Jan Ullrich @ 5 minutes 58 seconds

Now came a rest day and then a final day in the high mountains. Even though the stage included the Marie-Blanque and the Aubisque, the finish line was over 70 kilometers from the crest of the Aubisque so it was thought there wouldn't be any major change to the General Classification and that proved to be true. But Oscar Pereiro was still burning from his narrow loss to Hincapie. He managed to get into the winning break. This time Australian Cadel Evans did the lion's share of the work while Pereiro sat on and zipped around for the stage win. Selective indignation isn't very pretty.

The year's longest stage was the 239-kilometer run from Pau to Revel with a sawtooth profile of category 3 and 4 climbs. No one was giving up. Discovery's Giro winner Paolo Savoldelli was in the day's winning break and managed to win a very tactical sprint. Back in the Yellow Jersey group T-Mobile was not surrendering. On the final climb Vinokourov attacked hard. This effort was followed by an equally savage pull by Ullrich. The effect of these 2 attacks was to drop Christophe Moreau, Landis and Evans, who were caught unawares by the move. To make life still more miserable for the dropped trio, Armstrong and the rest of the remaining Discovery riders went to the front and drove the separated group hard. The result was to move Vinokourov from ninth to seventh place in the Overall. Armstrong collected his seventy-ninth Yellow Jersey, tying Bernard Hinault, but well behind Merckx's closet full of 96.

Stage 18 brought the Tour into the center of the Massif Central. Just before the end was a 3-kilometer climb with a 10% gradient. While the usual break of non-contenders was battling 10 minutes up the road, the peloton was being whittled down by the high speed of the pack as it rode over the region's relentless climbs. Just into the final climb Basso hit the front hard and then there were 4. Only Evans, Ullrich and Armstrong could go with the aggressive Italian. The losers of the day were Michael Rasmussen whose third place was now in jeopardy since Ullrich was only 2 minutes, 12 seconds behind him with the final time trial coming, and Vinokourov who could not go with the Basso move. Evans took back his seventh place, pushing Vinokourov to eighth.

The stage 20 time trial was important because there were so many positions in the General Classification in play.

Going into the time trial the standings stood thus:

1. Lance Armstrong
2. Ivan Basso @ 2 minutes 46 seconds
3. Michael Rasmussen @ 3 minutes 46 seconds

4. Jan Ullrich @ 5 minutes 58 seconds

5. Francisco Mancebo @ 7 minutes 8 seconds

6. Levi Leipheimer @ 8 minutes 12 seconds

7. Cadel Evans @ 9 minutes 49 seconds

8. Alexandre Vinokourov @ 10 minutes 11 seconds

9. Floyd Landis @ 10 minutes 42 seconds

10. Oscar Pereiro @ 12 minutes 39 seconds

11. Christophe Moreau @ 13 minutes 15 seconds

Moreau learned that his team, Credit Agricole, might want to replace him with Vinokourov as its protected Tour leader for 2006. He knew he had to do well and break into the top 10 in order to have a good negotiating position. Leipheimer wanted to take Mancebo's fifth place, Ullrich wanted to get on the podium. And so far Armstrong hadn't won a stage. He surely didn't want to win the Tour *a la Walko* (after Roger Walkowiak who won the 1956 Tour without winning a stage). The 55.5-kilometer course had a third-category climb and a descent that required care. Ullrich ripped the course, showing again that his preparation is always too late. His move to third place in the standings was aided by Rasmussen's catastrophe. First he crashed early in the stage. He then flatted and got an incompetent wheel change requiring several bike changes before he could continue. To add to his misery he crashed on the descent. Rasmussen finished seventy-seventh that day, 7 minutes, 47 seconds behind the day's winner Lance Armstrong, who chalked up his twenty-second career Tour stage win.

The results of the time trial:

1. Lance Armstrong: 1 hour 11 minutes 46 seconds

2. Jan Ullrich @ 23 seconds

3. Alexandre Vinokourov @ 1 minute 16 seconds

4. Bobby Julich @ 1 minute 33 seconds

5. Ivan Basso @ 1 minute 54 seconds

6. Floyd Landis @ 2 minutes 2 seconds

7. Cadel Evans @ 2 minutes 6 seconds

8. George Hincapie @ 2 minutes 25 seconds

This yielded a slightly changed General Classification. Note that now only 2 seconds separate Leipheimer and Vinokourov:

1. Lance Armstrong
2. Ivan Basso @ 4 minutes 40 seconds
3. Jan Ullrich @ 6 minutes 21 seconds
4. Francisco Mancebo @ 9 minutes 59 seconds
5. Levi Leipheimer @ 11 minutes 25 seconds
6. Alexandre Vinokourov @ 11 minutes 27 seconds
7. Michael Rasmussen @ 11 minutes 33 seconds

The final stage was a bit confusing because light rain made the streets a bit slippery. Not wanting to have a mass crash changing the final outcome the race, officials announced that because of the wet streets the winner's final time for the General Classification would be fixed when the Tour crossed the finish line on the Champs Elysées for the first time. But the time bonuses for the second intermediate sprint and final sprint were still in play. Leipheimer had to keep worrying about Vinokourov. Vinokourov, not one to ever give up, managed to take a couple of bonus seconds in one of the intermediate sprints despite the best efforts of Leipheimer's team to control the situation. Now he was behind Leipheimer by only a fraction of a second. Then a ruling seemed to come down saying that the stage's remaining time bonuses were cancelled.

In the final kilometer Vinokourov took off and managed to win the stage, securing the 20 bonus seconds which, to the surprise of Leipheimer, turned out to be up for grabs after all.

The final 2005 Tour de France General Classification:

1. Lance Armstrong (Discovery): 86 hours 15 minutes 2 seconds
2. Ivan Basso (CSC) @ 4 minutes 40 seconds
3. Jan Ullrich (T-Mobile) @ 6 minutes 21 seconds
4. Francisco Mancebo (Illes Balears) @ 9 minutes 59 seconds
5. Alexandre Vinokourov (T-Mobile) @ 11 minutes 1 second
6. Levi Leipheimer (Gerolsteiner) @ 11 minutes 21 seconds

Climbers' Competition:

1. Michael Rasmussen: 185 points
2. Oscar Pereiro: 155 points
3. Lance Armstrong: 99 points

Points Competition:

1. Thor Hushovd: 194 points
2. Stuart O'Grady: 182 points
3. Robbie McEwen: 178 points
4. Alexandre Vinokourov: 158 points

The 2005 Tour was run at the extraordinary speed of 41.654 kilometers an hour. This was an increase of about 4 kilometers an hour over Greg LeMond's 1989 Tour. This 10 percent increase in speed represents an extraordinary increase in rider energy output. Arithmetic increases in bicycle speed cause the cyclist's aerodynamic drag to go up by the square of the speed. Not all of a rider's efforts go into fighting the wind, there are other losses such as chain drag and tire rolling resistance, but the overall effect is to require perhaps a quarter again as much energy to ride the Tour at this higher speed. Better training?

Armstrong retired from professional racing after crossing the finish line in Paris. I think it is sufficient to say that he had done what no man in the Tour's 92 editions had been able to do, win 7 Tours and win them consecutively.

# Chapter 8

## 2006–2007. Cycling begins to really fight doping and the Grand Tours continue a turf war with the UCI.

**2006.** Armstrong had really retired. The giant who had dominated the Tour for the better part of a decade would not be on the line in 2006 to contest the Tour. The Tour organization seemed to be acutely aware of the new era. Tour boss Jean-Marie Leblanc had taken the doping accusations against Armstrong to heart and made it clear that he believed them to be true. When the 2006 route was unveiled he and his successor, Christian Prudhomme, said, "On the 24th of July we turned a page on a long, very long chapter in the history of the Tour de France. And 1 month later, current events made it clear to us that it was just as well that this was so." Leblanc was even more blunt in a later interview with the Associated Press, saying that "[Armstrong] was not irreproachable in '99. EPO is a doping product. So this tempers and dilutes his performances and his credibility as a champion." Armstrong replied with his usual vigor, saying, "Jean-Marie Leblanc says the Tour deserves a better fate, I believe it deserves a better leader." The dispute between Leblanc and Armstrong aside, Leblanc had done a wonderful job resuscitating a moribund Tour. Leblanc was responsible for remaking the Tour into an event that gave Armstrong his glorious renown.

Leblanc himself had been planning to retire for some time, originally hoping to turn over the reins of Tour leadership after the 2003

Tour. Daniel Baal, who had been the deputy director of the Tour, had been groomed as Leblanc's successor. As Leblanc hung on year after year, Baal finally resigned. Christian Prudhomme, a television journalist, was brought in as the new deputy to Leblanc with Leblanc retiring after the 2006 Tour.

There were several men poised to make the Tour perhaps the hardest fought race at least since 2003.

Jan Ullrich seemed to have banished his eating and training demons. He kept his weight under control over the winter and applied himself to his training with rigor. In spring he had a knee inflammation that kept him off his bike for a while, but he was recovered enough to ride the Giro for training. During the Italian Tour he never pushed himself except in the stage 11 individual time trial which he won, beating an on-form Ivan Basso by 28 seconds over the flat 50-kilometer course. He then went on to win the Tour of Switzerland, doing much better in the climbs than he had in the mountains of the Giro. Probably for only the second time since he had won the Tour in 1997, Jan Ullrich was in shape and really ready to contest the Tour. He was the only former Tour winner entered.

Ivan Basso had been maturing, showing that in 2005 he could stay with the best on the climbs. His 2006 Giro win was so complete that he made it look almost effortless. Backed up by the strongest team in the race he was able to pick his moments and deliver blow after lethal blow to his competitors. He reduced 2-time winner Gilberto Simoni to petulant accusations of Basso's trying to buy a stage win, accusations which Simoni later withdrew. The big question going into the Tour was whether Basso could hold his magnificent form over such an extended period of time.

Also a big question was Phonak's Floyd Landis. He had enjoyed a superb spring, winning 3 big stage races, the Tour of California, Paris–Nice and the Tour de Georgia. His trainers insisted that Landis had such an abundance of strength that he didn't have to dig too deeply for his spring victories. Landis had been part of the Armstrong machine for 3 years, but after the 2004 Tour Landis left the Discovery team for Phonak. As had happened with other riders who had gone from being his domestiques to competitors, Armstrong reacted to Landis' team change with bitterness.

Considered a serious challenger in 2005, by stage 11 Landis was already 4 minutes behind Armstrong. Some attributed Landis' final 12 minute, 44 second deficit to the psychological war Armstrong waged against him, an argument Landis says is wrong. But Landis seems to have lost a lot of his legendary fighting spirit after it became clear that the 2005 Tour podium wasn't to be his.

There were others waiting in the wings of what might be a wide-open Tour. Spaniard Alejandro Valverde, who showed he was a world-class climber, had matured and grown stronger. 2004 Giro winner Damiano Cunego rode a poor Giro but perhaps his preparation was just a bit late. He announced that he was just riding the Tour for the experience. But could a former Grand Tour winner and former world-ranked Number 1 rider resist the call of the Yellow Jersey? Alexandre Vinokourov had moved from T-Mobile in order to have a dedicated team behind him, but his climbing and inconsistency kept him a dark horse.

And what about the Discovery team? They no longer had Armstrong, but they were brimming with talent, talent that could help a great rider win the Tour. But were any of the remaining riders up to the task? Discovery didn't seem to have a Grand Tour man except Paolo Savoldelli who was probably still cooked from riding the Giro. Discovery director Johan Bruyneel refused to name a protected team captain. Instead, he said he would see how the riders performed as the race progressed.

The 2006 was a counter-clockwise race starting with a 7.1-kilometer Prologue individual time trial in Strasbourg. With 116 total kilometers of individual effort, the 2006 Tour placed a strong emphasis on time trialing. The race was loaded with big mountains at the end of the race with stages 15, 16 and 17 being very tough days in the Alps. With only 3 hill-top finishes, there were fewer opportunities than in some previous editions for the pure climbers to deliver a *coup de grace*.

Going into the Tour, once again the pall of a doping scandal hung over everything. On May 23, after a months-long investigation involving hidden cameras, the Spanish Civil Guard arrested 5 men who were accused of an assortment of doping crimes. Among them were the director of the Liberty Seguros team, Manolo Saiz, and José Ignacio Labarta, the assistant sports director of the Comunidad Valenciana squad. Immediately the Liberty Insurance Company withdrew its sponsorship. Because this was the team of Alexandre Vinokourov who was from Kazakhstan, a group of Kazakh businessmen replaced the missing funds and the team became Astana-Würth. Not being a Pro Tour team, Comunidad Valenciana was riding the Tour at the invitation (a Wild Card) of the Tour organization. With the doping scandal looming, the Tour organization withdrew the Wild Card invitation. At the same time, because the UCI had done nothing so far to change the status of the Astana-Würth team, Vinokourov's ride in the Tour looked to be safe.

The weekend before the start of the Tour is the traditional time for the National Championships. The countries' various champions can ride the Tour wearing their newly acquired national flag jerseys. On the Sunday morning of the Road Race Championships a Spanish newspaper leaked major details about the ongoing investigation, called *Operación Puerto*, showing that the riders and the teams had a deep involvement in systematized doping. The Spanish riders—as usual feeling that doping was their business and outraged at the publicity the story showered upon their illicit practices—staged a strike and refused to ride the Spanish Road Race Championship. Note that, as usual, the riders weren't outraged that there were cheaters amongst them. The anger was at the publicity. Nothing but the drugs themselves had changed.

It seemed that the second through fifth place finishers of the 2005 Tour were going to return in even better form than ever and fight an extraordinary struggle to be the first post-Armstrong Tour victor. And then on the Thursday evening before the Saturday, July 1 Tour start, the Tour organization gave dossiers to the team managers, documenting the growing case against the riders involved in the Spanish doping scandal. The Team managers and Tour organization met and decided that since the Pro Tour code of ethics said, "No team will allow a rider to compete while under investigation in any doping affair", the riders who were part of the inquiry would have to be excluded. Ullrich was in the team bus on the way to a Friday pre-Tour presentation when he was informed of his suspension by the team. CSC director Bjarne Riis had to tell Ivan Basso that he would not be able to ride the Tour. The other riders who were not allowed to start the Tour were Francisco Mancebo, Oscar Sevilla, Joseba Beloki, Isidro Nozal, Sergio Paulino, Allan Davis and Alberto Contador. For the first time since 1999 there would not be a former Tour winner on the start line.

Alexandre Vinokourov was collateral damage. Even though he wasn't suspended, his team lost too many riders because replacements weren't allowed when a rider is excluded for doping problems. Tour rules require 6 riders on a team and Vinokourov's Astana-Würth squad was now down to 5. In a stunning admission of a failure to perform even the most elementary due diligence, Vinokourov said that he only learned after he had signed for the team that team owner and boss Manolo Saiz had an ongoing war with the Tour. In 1998, at the height of the Tour's crises, Saiz pulled his ONCE team out of the Tour in order to…no, what he said he was doing to the Tour is unprintable. But Saiz had surely set up himself and his team for a fall by striking at the Tour at its greatest moment of difficulty.

The start list was now whittled down to 176 starters, the smallest field since 1984's 170 riders. First through fifth place of 2005 would not be competing. The highest-placed 2005 Tour finisher entered was Levi Leipheimer, sixth in 2005 at 11 minutes, 21 seconds.

The effect of the exclusion raised the hopes of many riders who were dreaming of only a place on the podium. Leipheimer, winner of the Dauphiné, voiced his feeling that he could win the Tour. Others such as Cadel Evans, Andreas Klöden and Bobby Julich were now thought to be potential winners. Damiano Cunego, who was originally said to be coming to the Tour just to learn said that he thought he now had a chance.

The opening Prologue had no surprises. Big, strong Norwegian Thor Hushovd (2005 Green Jersey) won, keeping George Hincapie out of Yellow by only three-quarters of a second. Just before the start of his ride, mechanics discovered a slash in Landis' rear tire. Not wanting to take a chance, they replaced it, forcing Landis to roll up the ramp late and take off immediately. The misfortune probably cost him 8 seconds.

After the Prologue, Discovery was the Team General Classification leader and in an effort to make that competition more visible, they were given yellow back numbers for the start of stage 1.

Stage 1 took its first casualty. Danilo Di Luca, overall 2005 Pro Tour winner, had been tormented with a prostate infection. Given a course of antibiotics, he was better, but was unable to stay with the peloton in the day's final high-speed kilometers. With a loss of over 2 minutes in the first stage, his chances of a Tour win were finished and he withdrew that evening. Riding right next to the crowd barriers while contesting the sprint, Yellow Jersey Hushovd was cut by a giant promotional cardboard hand being waved by a spectator. He finished the stage but television viewers were horrified to see blood gushing from his arm as he lay on the road after the sprint. The wound turned out to be minor and with some stitches he was able to start the next day. Earlier in the stage George Hincapie had bagged 2 bonus seconds in an intermediate sprint. That clever move was enough to give the likable rider his first Yellow Jersey in 10 Tour attempts. Maybe Discovery was starting its first post-Armstrong Tour well.

The next day Discovery director Bruyneel showed that he was looking for more than an early capture of the Yellow Jersey when he chose not to defend Hincapie's lead. He didn't want to exhaust his team chasing a short-term goal when what he really wanted was Yellow in Paris. That would require patience and a willingness to give the Jersey up for now. Which he did the very next day when Hushovd retook it.

Stage 3, another Northern European stage with some final category 3 and 4 climbs in Belgium and Holland, surely affected the outcome of the Tour. Several riders suffered race ending injuries, most notably Alejandro Valverde, a sure podium contender, who crashed and broke his collarbone in the final kilometers of the stage. The intense heat (35°C) and high speeds made for a fatigued peloton with riders susceptible to moments of inattention.

Laurent Fignon, who has replaced Bernard Thévenet as the race commentator of the France 2 television channel, explained why the carnage in a professional race crash can be so great. When a compact peloton (and the pros do ride closer together than amateurs) is racing hard, all the rider sees is the back of the rider in front of him and a peripheral view of the riders to his side. He really doesn't see much of what is going on up ahead as he fights to maintain his position while riding all-out. Then, when the helicopters following the race come down low and close to the bunch, if there is a crash, the riders can't hear the squeal of brakes and the riders' shouts and the sounds of folding and crashing bikes. The din of the helicopter's engines and rotors drowns that all out. So, the riders just continue down the road and into the waiting mess, blind and deaf to the carnage that awaits them.

The Spanish doping scandal continued to roil the waters. Würth pulled its sponsorship of the Astana-Würth team and the Comunidad Valenciana also withdrew its sponsorship. French sports minister Jean-François Lamour accused the UCI of failing to attack doping seriously. UCI president Pat McQuaid bristled in response, basically saying that the current state of the drug detecting art could not catch a modern, sophisticated doper.

This is true. This is why the riders caught up in *Operación Puerto* had never been caught in a drug test. As Lamour had said, only the naïve get caught in drug tests.

As the Tour moved across Normandy and into Brittany, the Tour remained the plaything of the sprinters. World Road Champion Tom Boonen wasn't able to win a stage, but by virtue of his consistent high placings and their attendant time bonuses he was able to secure the Yellow Jersey after stage 4 and hold it until the seventh stage 52-kilometer time trial. Boonen was the first man since Greg LeMond in 1990 to trade the Rainbow Jersey of the World Champion for Yellow.

The time trial in the Brittany town of Rennes was filled with surprises and heartbreak. The general expectation was that American riders or those sponsored by the American Discovery and the Danish CSC teams would emerge at the end of the day dominating the standings. Midway through the stage this hope received its first blow. CSC, which had already lost its premier General Classification man Ivan Basso to the Spanish doping scandal lost another of its best riders when Bobby Julich, a superb time trialist, crashed out of the Tour as he had in 1999. This time, going through an "S" curve at nearly full speed, he hit some gravel and went flying. David Zabriskie, usually one of the fastest men in the world against the clock, lost almost 2 minutes. Levi Leipheimer, who had won the Dauphiné only a couple of weeks before, was unable to find the strength to power his bike and lost 6 minutes. Barring a surprise, his quest for the podium was over. The Discovery riders, who are usually towers of power, lost out as well. George Hincapie lost 2 minutes, 42 seconds. Paolo Savoldelli, who depends upon his superior time-trialing to make up for weakness in the mountains, lost over 2 minutes.

The emergent winners? T-Mobile put 4 men in the top 10 in the stage with Ukrainian Sergey Gonchar—pounding a monstrous 55-11 gear—winning the day and the Yellow Jersey. T-Mobile ended up with 4 men in the top 6 of the General Classification (Gonchar, Rogers, Sinkewitz, Klöden). Floyd Landis again had a late start. This time officials forced him to modify the placement of his aero bars. After he started they came loose and he had to change bikes. Still, he came in second, losing only a minute to Gonchar. Discovery had no riders well-placed in the either the day's stage placings or the General Classification.

The General Classification after the stage 7 time trial:

1. Sergey Gonchar
2. Floyd Landis @ 1 minute
3. Michael Rogers @ 1 minute 8 seconds
4. Patrik Sinkewitz @ 1 minute 45 seconds
5. Marcus Fothen @ 1 minute 50 seconds
6. Andreas Klöden @ 1 minute 50 seconds
7. Vladimir Karpets @ 1 minute 52 seconds
8. Cadel Evans @ 1 minute 52 seconds
9. Denis Menchov @ 2 minutes
10. David Zabriskie @ 2 minutes 3 seconds

After he had seen the results, Discovery's director Johan Bruyneel said, "It's lucky Jan Ullrich is not here, otherwise the Tour would be over."

Behind the scenes of the Tour, the UCI and the Grand Tour organizers had been holding ongoing talks to see if the disagreements over the Pro Tour could be bridged. Patrice Clerc, spokesman for the Tour, announced that at this point the talks were dead and that the owners of the races would not participate in the Pro Tour.

Until stage 8 the sprinters' teams had been controlling the breakaways perfectly, letting a small groups of non-threatening riders go clear and bringing them back into the fold just before the end of the stage. In stage 8, their plans were foiled. With a bit more than 30 kilometers to go from the finish in the Brittany coastal town of Lorient, Sylvain Calzati jumped away from what remained of his break. Despite a vigorous chase, Calzati was able to stay clear, finishing over 2 minutes ahead of the peloton.

Now the Tour had a rest day and a transfer to Bordeaux for the run-in to the Pyrenees. During the rest day Landis announced that after the Tour he would have to undergo hip replacement surgery. Landis had broken his hip in 2003 and it had never healed correctly. The resulting extremely painful condition, avascular necrosis, prevented proper blood flow to the joint.

With the resumption of racing on Tuesday, first there was a flat stage to Dax, birthplace of the great sprinter André Darrigade. This time the break was caught just in time for a thrilling sprint, won by 3-time World Champion Oscar Freire.

Stage 10, from Cambo-les-Bains to Pau featured 3 major climbs, the third category Col d'Osquich, the *hors catégorie* Soudet and the first category Marie Blanque. It was rightly predicted that with the finish line 40 kilometers after the crest of the Marie Blanque, the day would be one of careful watching and perhaps one of attrition as the accumulated kilometers took their toll on the riders' legs. T-Mobile decided to do some work defending Gonchar's Yellow Jersey, thus giving Landis and the other true contenders a free ride. Juan Miguel Mercado and Cyril Dessel got completely clear on the Marie Blanque and drove their break all the way to the finish. They had been granted so much freedom that Dessel, who had been adventuring for climber's points, had gained enough time to take the Yellow Jersey. In the final kilometers Mercado tried to make a deal with Dessel, telling him that since Dessel would gain both the Yellow and Polka-Dot Jerseys, he should let Mercado take the stage win, a not unusual sharing of the spoils. Dessel was so sure of his strength and so desperately wanted the stage win that he refused the offer. Mercado immediately stopped working, forcing Dessel to pull the pair over the final 5 kilometers. Mercado easily won the sprint and Dessel took the Overall lead. Dessel's choice will have interesting consequences.

If the contenders had been keeping their powder dry, it was for stage 11. With the Tourmalet, Aspin, Peyresourde, Portillon and a hilltop finish at Pla-de-Beret, we would now have the clarity that had been lacking because of the best riders' conservative riding. On the penultimate climb, the Portillon, T-Mobile massed at the front and increased the tempo. The effect was to shell many riders who had been struggling all day. Over the top Klöden, Landis, Evans, Denis Menchov, Michael Boogerd, Michael Rasmussen, Cunego and Simoni were among the survivors. For Discovery, the news was bleak. Only Azevedo had been able to stay with the leaders. Hincapie, Savoldelli and Popovych had been dropped. Dessel, the Yellow Jersey also came off and he set himself to minimize his losses and hopefully, save his lead.

At the base of the final ascent, Rabobank had an embarrassment of riches with Rasmussen, Boogerd and Menchov having made the cut. Menchov told his teammates that he was feeling very good. In response, Boogerd and Rasmussen went to the front and set a pace that few could withstand. Only Evans, Landis, Leipheimer, Sastre and Klöden could stay with them. After Rasmussen sat up, depleted from his efforts, Boogerd continued to drive hard and dropped Klöden. The T-Mobile General Classification hope had cramped under the pressure of the withering heat and high speeds. With 8 kilometers to go, the lead group was down to Landis, Menchov, Leipheimer, Sastre and Evans. Leipheimer mounted 2 attacks and reduced the leaders to Menchov, Landis and himself. Menchov won the stage and Landis took the overall lead. But it didn't have to end that way. Dessel punished himself, racing for the finish line with all he had and ended the day 4 minutes, 45 seconds behind Landis, the exact difference in their General Classification times. Landis' 8-second time bonus for third place gave him the edge in time and levered him into the Yellow Jersey. If he had cooperated with Mercado the day before, Dessel would surely have arrived at the finish more than 8 seconds sooner and would probably have been in Yellow at least until the Alpe d'Huez stage the following Tuesday.

After stage 11, the General Classification stood thus:

1. Floyd Landis
2. Cyril Dessel @ 8 seconds
3. Denis Menchov @ 1 minute 1 second
4. Cadel Evans @ 1 minute 17 seconds
5. Carlos Sastre @ 1 minute 52 seconds
6. Andreas Klöden @ 2 minutes 29 seconds

That was it for the hard Pyrenean stages. The next day Discovery's Popovych got into the winning break and soloed home for a bit of salve on the open wound of the team's general collapse. That savvy move lifted Popovych to tenth in the General Classification, 4 minutes, 15 seconds behind Landis and made him the best-placed Discovery rider in the Tour.

The Spanish doping investigation continued. A German newspaper alleged that the records of Eufemiano Fuentes, the doctor at the heart of the scandal, showed that Jan Ullrich took insulin, cortisone, and various hormones including testosterone, as well as a unit of his own blood, in preparation for the 2005 Tour. If the allegations turned out to be true, it would put a nail in the coffin of the riders' defense that they were clean because they had passed every drug test. Ullrich had never had a positive drug test except for his out-of-competition test which had turned up the drug Ecstasy while he was recovering from knee surgery in 2002.

The relentless heat baked the riders. Saturday's stage 13 was the longest at 230 kilometers and possibly the hottest day of the 2006 Tour. A break of 4 strong riders low in the standings was allowed to gain a half hour. It appeared that Phonak wanted to let another team take and defend the lead. Oscar Pereiro of the Illes Balears team, who was the best-placed rider in the break, was perfect. He had lost a lot of time in the Pyrenees (he was sitting in forty-sixth place at the start of the stage) and could be expected to dutifully suffer badly in the Alps and surrender the lead, at this point only 1 minute, 29 seconds. Surely the Yellow Jersey was an unexpected development for the Spanish team and they would work like dogs to keep the lead for the next stage so that they could bask in it during the rest day. Phonak could take a rest and be ready for the real fight, Tuesday's stage 15 day in the Alps.

Indeed, Pereiro's team did work hard to defend his lead during stage 14, a transitional stage with 2 third category and 2 second category climbs, giving the Phonak team the planned bit of rest.

Stage 15, with the Izoard, Lautaret and hilltop finish on l'Alpe d'Huez, was the first of 3 days in the Alps. As usual, a break of non-contenders went clear early while the General Classification men stayed together until the base of l'Alpe d'Huez. T-Mobile started things rolling by sending their men to the front to whip up the pace. Then a Phonak rider went even harder and almost instantly it was down to Landis, Menchov, Evans and Klöden. Landis accelerated and dropped all but Klöden. But then others, including earlier dropees Leipheimer and Sastre regained contact. A later surge by Klöden dropped Sastre and Leipheimer. Up ahead, Luxembourger Frank Schleck, who had been away most of the day, managed to hang on to a slim 70-second lead for the stage win. Landis emerged from the stage back in the Yellow Jersey with a 10-second lead over Pereiro.

The General Classification after stage 15:

1. Floyd Landis
2. Oscar Pereiro @ 10 seconds
3. Cyril Dessel @ 2 minutes 2 seconds
4. Denis Menchov @ 2 minutes 12 seconds
5. Carlos Sastre @ 2 minutes 17 seconds

6. Andreas Klöden @ 2 minutes 29 seconds

7. Cadel Evans @ 2 minutes 56 seconds

After Landis' masterful performance in stage 15, the even more difficult stage 16 should have been a platform from which he could solidify his hold on the Yellow Jersey. The day included the Galibier, the Croix-de-Fer, the Col du Mollard and then a first-category hilltop finish at La Toussuire. Michael Rasmussen, who had such a disastrous final time trial in the 2005 Tour, took off from an early break on the Galibier with Tadej Valjavec and Sandy Casar. The peloton, knowing that worse than the Galibier was in store for them that day, continued to ride tempo. At this point Landis looked quite comfortable. On the Croix-de-Fer, Rasmussen was off alone, riding powerfully, having gained a 7-minute lead on the peloton.

When the Croix-de-Fer started to really bite, T-Mobile went to the front and lifted the pace. This attack cost Landis most of his team. For the first time, Landis was sitting further back in the peloton instead of his usual place near the front. On the second-category Col du Mollard, Landis rode at the back, starting to look truly uncomfortable. When the peloton arrived at the base of the final climb there had been some regrouping. The only teammate Landis had with him was Axel Merckx. Carlos Sastre, feeling good, took off on a solo flight. T-Mobile now lit the fuse in the largely diminished peloton and Landis's legs exploded. After displaying weeks of mastery, he was unable to stay with the leaders. He was soundly dropped and in the final kilometers to the summit, lost about a minute per kilometer.

Up ahead Rasmussen crossed the line first after being away for 173 kilometers. Sastre had been closing fast, but came up 1 minute, 41 seconds short. The big surprise was Oscar Pereiro, who came in third and retook the Yellow Jersey. Landis limped in twenty-third, 10 minutes after Rasmussen.

At this point, it was assumed that Landis' quest for the overall win was over. As to why he suffered a *défaillance* on this most crucial of days, Landis was less than candid, saying "I had a very bad day on the wrong day." Experienced riders like Bernard Hinault speculated that he had suffered a terrible hunger knock. In a later interview, 1988 Tour winner Pedro Delgado said that he had advised Pereiro to ride his own race and not let Landis dictate the terms of the contest. He told Pereiro to attack on the descents, which he did. That constant pressure probably kept Landis from eating, causing his stage 16 disaster.

That evening, instead of giving up, Landis and his team planned on getting back in the race. Eddy Merckx told Landis that the race wasn't over. Word got out to the other pros that he was going to do something spectacular early in the stage. Some of them asked him not to be so foolhardy. He told them to get a Coke because he was going on the first hill.

If possible, stage 17 was the hardest stage yet, with very few kilometers of flat road. It was almost all rising or falling terrain. For their final day in the Alps the exhausted riders had to climb first the Saisies, then the Aravis, followed by the Colombière, the Châtillon and finally the *hors catégorie* Joux-Plane. A break went clear in the first kilometers. On the Saisies, Landis' teammates massed at the front and drove hard. Klöden and Landis attacked and only a few could go with them. Then Landis attacked again and no one could hold his wheel. Up the Saisies he flew, riding as if he had never suffered any trouble at all the day before, lending credence to Delgado's explanation as to why Landis had collapsed the previous day.

Indicative of how complete Landis' recovery was, he ascended the 6.4% Saisies in the big ring. By the time he crested the Saisies he was over 3 minutes ahead of the peloton and within 3 minutes of the front break. He descended the Saisies hell-bent to make up his previous day's losses. He caught the remains of the front break on the lower slopes of the Aravis. He didn't wait or rest, but went right through them. Only Daniele Righi and Patrik Sinkewitz could stay with him. Over the top of the Aravis Landis had built his lead to 4 minutes, 31 seconds. Back in the peloton Pereiro was down to 1 teammate. By the base of the Colombière, Landis' lead was 5 minutes, 30 seconds.

Over the crest of the Colombière, Landis had an astounding 8 minutes, 30 seconds. So far, T-Mobile, CSC, Davitamon-Lotto and Ag2R, teams with riders in the hunt for the Yellow Jersey, had been playing a dangerous game of poker, depending on Pereiro's now 2 teammates to perform the chase. It wasn't working, but still they did nothing while Landis continued to ride away with the Tour de France.

On the descent of the Colombière Landis pushed his lead to 9 minutes. Finally the other teams woke up. CSC started to work to protect Sastre and eventually T-Mobile helped. That effort cut the gap. By the time Landis reached the base of the steepest climb of the day, the Joux-Plane, he still had 7 minutes, 25 seconds. Sinkewitz, who had been sitting on Landis' wheel all this time as the only one who could stay with the rampaging Phonak rider, was finally dropped. Landis was now alone. Behind, Sastre left the peloton and climbed strongly.

At the top of the terribly difficult Joux-Plane, Landis led Sastre by 5 minutes and Pereiro's group by 7. The descent down the Joux-Plane to Morzine is very technical and dangerous, perfect for a man with Landis' excellent descending skills. He dropped down the mountain as if his hair were on fire and extended his lead by another 30 seconds. He crossed the line 5 minutes, 42 seconds ahead of Sastre and 7 minutes, 8 seconds ahead of Pereiro. In addition, by virtue of his stage win, second intermediate sprint win and climber's bonuses for being the first over the mountains, Landis accumulated about 30 seconds in time bonifications. He was back in the race after performing an exploit that has, to the best of my knowledge, only 4 parallels:

1. Charly Gaul's 1958, stage 21 solo trip through the Chartreuse Mountains that left the Yellow Jersey, Raphaël Géminiani, in tears.

2. Hugo Koblet's 1951 stage 11 solo ride with Coppi, Bobet, Ockers, Robic and Bartali chasing for all they were worth, to no effect.

3. Gino Bartali's extraordinary 1948 stage 13, 14 and 15 rides in the Alps. When he soloed away on stage 13 he was over 21 minutes behind Louison Bobet. At the end of the day he was only 1 minute, 6 seconds down. Bartali then repeated the exercise in the next 2 stages, ending up with the Yellow Jersey and an 8-minute lead.

4. Lucien Buysse's epic 1926 stage 10 solo ride over the Aubisque, Tourmalet, Aspin and Peyresourde in conditions that can only be described as horrific. Through freezing rain he rode on muddy roads for hundreds of kilometers. He started the day 22 minutes down. He emerged from the hellish day that had begun at 2:00 AM with a 26-minute lead.

That was how extraordinary his ride was. Some compared Landis' ride with Coppi's 1952 stage 11 ride and Merckx's 1969 stage 17 ride. Both were amazing, but both riders had the lead at the time and had already demonstrated their superiority to a cowed peloton. Landis, like Gaul, Koblet, Bartali and Buysse before him, had performed his magnificent exploit when the Tour was in play. *Chapeau!*

The new General Classification:

1. Oscar Pereiro
2. Carlos Sastre @ 12 seconds
3. Floyd Landis @ 30 seconds
4. Andreas Klöden @ 2 minutes 29 seconds
5. Cadel Evans @ 3 minutes 8 seconds

The next day, anticipating the crucial 57-kilometer individual time trial, the contenders pulled back their claws. This would be settled on the penultimate stage.

T-Mobile announced that they had fired both Jan Ullrich and Oscar Sevilla. Both men had been given 30 days by the team to establish their innocence. Ullrich equivocated, refusing to take a DNA test that would exonerate him if he were innocent. His argument was that a man doesn't have to prove his innocence, others must prove his guilt. True in court, false in cycling. T-Mobile made it clear that even if Ullrich were eventually cleared, he would have to find employment with another team.

The Tour was settled during the final time trial, or so it seemed. While time-trial specialist Sergey Gonchar set the fastest time, over the first 14 kilometers Landis was only a second slower. But not wanting to blow up or worry about matching the speed of a man who was 2 hours down on the General Classification, Landis continued at his own pace. The surprise was how tenacious Pereiro was, losing only 10 seconds to Landis at the first time check. By the second time check at 34 kilometers, Pereiro had relented, giving up a full minute and the lead. There were 2 surprises: Sastre's meltdown costing him his podium placing, and Klöden's brilliant second-place ride, moving him up to third overall. Landis had now regained the lead with only the promenade to Paris left to go.

There were no surprises as the remaining 139 riders blistered the Champs Elysées. Thor Hushovd took advantage of the disorganization in the peloton from a series of hard attacks by the Discovery team. Without the lead-out trains keeping things together, it was every man for himself. Green Jersey Robbie McEwen was beaten by a stronger and faster Hushovd who had the distinction of winning both the opening Prologue and the closing sprint.

Final 2006 Tour de France General Classification. Landis' win made 11 American Tour victories in the past 21 years :

1. Floyd Landis (Phonak): 89 hours 39 minutes 30 seconds.
2. Oscar Pereiro (Illes Balears) @ 57 seconds
3. Andreas Klöden (T-Mobile) @ 1 minute 29 seconds
4. Carlos Sastre (CSC) @ 3 minutes 13 seconds
5. Cadel Evans (Davitamon-Lotto) @ 5 minutes 8 seconds

Climbers' Competition:

1. Michael Rasmussen: 166 points
2. Floyd Landis: 131 points
3. David de la Fuente: 113 points

Points Competition:

1. Robbie McEwen: 288 points
2. Erik Zabel: 199 points
3. Thor Hushovd: 195 points

That about seemed to be the end of it. On Monday the Spanish teams engaged in mutual recriminations over who should have taken the responsibility in reining in Landis during stage 17. Cyrille Guimard thought that if Dessel's team had ridden with greater intelligence Dessel could have won the Tour. The newspapers were filled with stories of the man with the bad hip who had tamed the European peloton. The other news about riders transferring to other teams and upheaval in T-Mobile was the usual sort of post-Tour fodder.

Then on Wednesday it was leaked that a rider high in the General Classification had tested positive for dope. Moreover, the positive, called an "adverse analytical finding", was for stage 17. Speculation was rampant as reporters tried to find out who the rider was. Because the national cycling federations are notified of a doping positive, riders from Germany, France, Spain, Italy and France could be eliminated when their federations said that they had not been so notified.

Reporters started to home in on Landis when he failed to show up for 2 lucrative post-Tour criteriums, races where he was to receive

$100,000 each in appearance money. On Thursday, with Landis still missing, his team confirmed that indeed he was the rider in question. Immediately, near hysterical reactions in the press filled the newspapers and the airwaves. By the next day there was some calming as people began to understand that the test that tripped up Landis measured the ratio between testosterone and epitestosterone and that Landis had shown an elevated level of the testosterone. The problem with this test as an absolute arbiter of intake of exogenous substances is that human variation renders this test nothing more than a guideline. Top pro bicycle racers, being by definition genetic freaks, regularly exhibit characteristics that are well off the far edge of the bell curve. So some have extraordinary hematocrits, such as former Giro winner Damiano Cunego's 53. Others have very high testosterone levels.

Landis surfaced Friday and began a series of public appearances, begging for patience while he mounted a defense to show that he had not cheated. The definitive test, called "Carbon Isotope Ratio Analysis" would have to be made to determine if the statistically excessive testosterone in Landis' system were synthetic or naturally secreted.

The test was performed and synthetic testosterone was found to be in Landis' system.

**2006 Postscript.** Landis mounted a million-dollar defense of his Tour title, forcing an arbitration hearing that was held in May, 2007. Landis argued that the doping lab's procedural errors were so substantial that his positive for testosterone was invalid.

It seemed as if things could not get worse. Then they did. Greg LeMond was called to testify in the arbitration hearing. The night before LeMond was to take the stand Landis' business manager made an anonymous call to LeMond, pretending to be LeMond's uncle. He threatened to reveal the secret of LeMond's childhood sexual abuse. Earlier, trying to convince Landis to admit to doping, LeMond had told Landis about being abused, telling him that holding secrets like this is very destructive.

The call was traced and the sordid episode came out. It turned out that Landis was present when the threatening call was made. Part of Landis' argument as to why he should be believed when he said he wouldn't cheat to win a race was that his character made him above that sort of thing. This episode certainly put that argument in a dim light.

On September 21, 2007, the arbitration panel ruled 2 to 1 that Landis had doped. The Tour stripped him of his title and awarded the 2006 Tour to Oscar Pereiro. As of this writing (winter 2007), Landis has promised to make a final appeal to the Court for Arbitration of Sport in Switzerland.

The new 2006 Tour de France General Classification podium:

1. Oscar Pereiro (Caisse d'Epargne) 89 hours 40 minutes 27 seconds

2. Andreas Klöden (T-Mobile) @ 32 seconds

3. Carlos Sastre (CSC) @ 2 minutes 16 seconds

**2007.** Doping news was all anyone could read about in the winter and spring leading up to the 2007 Tour.

Ivan Basso, who had so effortlessly won the 2006 Giro, looked to have skated past any problems with the Puerto scandal. It seemed to this writer that the Spanish judge examining the Puerto evidence was looking for a way to ignore as much of the case as possible and investigate as little of the dossier as would appear seemly. He ended up shelving the case, saying that at the time, while it appeared that doping had occurred, nothing that had happened was against Spanish law.

The Italian Olympic Committee (CONI) tried to investigate Basso. Since they couldn't get their hands on all of the evidence from the Spaniards, in October, 2006 they had to pronounce Basso able to sign for a team and ride. This non-exoneration clearance was all Johan Bruyneel needed to sign Basso to the Discovery team. Making matters worse, alone among the Pro Tour teams, Discovery signed several other Puerto riders.

The other Pro Tour teams erupted in fury over this because they had all agreed to avoid signing Puerto riders until the case was closed and the riders truly cleared. Because of this breach in the agreement, many of the teams combined against Discovery during races, making life hard in the peloton for the Discovery team.

It seemed that the Puerto inquiry was going to die, but it didn't. The big break came in early April 2007 when German prosecutors were able to match up Jan Ullrich's DNA with blood bags seized from Fuentes. In late April it was revealed that an Italian prosecutor had blood bags from Fuentes that were thought to contain Basso's blood. From then on, Basso's defenses came apart. Knowing what was coming, Basso requested and was granted release from his Discovery contract.

On May 7, 2007, faced with too much evidence, Basso confessed to being involved with Fuentes, but steadfastly refused to admit that he had ever doped. He said he had planned to dope in the 2006 Tour, but that so far, all of his wins were clean. Skeptical observers wondered why he had been paying Fuentes tens of thousands of euros since 2004. A doping program that really improves performance yet evades detection is very expensive.

The Giro organizers ruled that the 50 or so riders implicated in the Puerto scandal could not start the Giro. This meant Tyler Hamilton, Michele Scarponi and Jörg Jaksche, all potential contenders, would not be able to ride.

It's important to note that the race organizers had to get a handle on the doping and not just for reasons of common decency. In the wake of the Puerto scandal the television audience for the Vuelta fell 30%. When team sponsors Comunidad Valenciana and Liberty Seguros pulled out of the sport, they took millions of euros with them. Sales of racing related books and DVDs plummeted. It was absolutely vital to the economic health of pro racing that the cheating be brought under control.

At the end of April racing was hit with another blockbuster. Former Telekom *soigneur* Jef D'Hont alleged that during the mid 1990s Telekom team doctors administered EPO to the riders as part of a teamwide systematized program of doping. The usual denials were given. But the wall of silence started to fall. Telekom riders from that era, Erik Zabel, Rolf Aldag, Brian Holm, and Udo Bölts, among others, came forward and confessed. They said that with the pressure to win and to beat other presumably doped riders, they had to use the needle or risk losing their jobs.

On Friday, May 25, Tour de France winner and CSC team owner Bjarne Riis held a press conference. He finally came clean. The man who had the nickname of "Mr. 60%" because of his rumored extraordinarily high hematocrit when he won the 1996 Tour, admitted that he had used EPO, hormones and cortisone in his campaign to win the Tour. D'Hont said that Riis had run his hematocrit up to a scary-high 64%. Riis' incredible dominance in the 1996 Tour now became understandable. As more than one rider noted, the only way a rider could gain any semblance of competitiveness during the 1990s was to take the same drugs the other riders were taking. The Tour organization reacted to this confession by removing Riis from the winner's list. As far the Tour is concerned, 1996 has no winner.

Riis' confession left an important question unanswered. How could Riis, famous for his hands-on, close and careful management of his riders, not know about Basso's relationship with Fuentes and not wonder about Basso's extraordinary performance in the 2006 Giro, especially in light of his own dope-fueled performances?

The series of doping confessions made it clear that after 1998 many of the teams had continued with their institutionalized doping programs. The wounded denials coming from the accused managers sounded exactly like those that came from Roussel in 1998.

The effect of all this scandal was to create the third Tour in the last 30 years (1999, 2006, 2007) in which no former winner was on the line to contest the Tour. The Tour, wanting to make a symbolic gesture and not having the 2005 winner on the start line, decided not to give any rider the Number 1 back-number (or *dossard*). The riders' numbers would start with number 11, which was given to Valverde's Caisse d'Epargne team.

So, who was left standing to start the race? First of all, Alexandre Vinokourov was the favorite to win the Tour. At 33 he knew this was his last, best chance to win. His Astana team was superb with Andreas Klöden as part of a 1-2 punch that could be devastating in the hands of a good strategist. While he rode the Dauphiné for training, he showed that his form was excellent when he won the time trial.

With Basso tossed, Discovery fell back on their earlier signing, Levi Leipheimer. Leipheimer was a probable podium finisher, but an unlikely Tour winner, a view Bruyneel seemed to hold.

The 2 other major contenders were Alejandro Valverde and Cadel Evans. Valverde appeared to be riding under a Puerto cloud, but he denied any involvement and no firm evidence seemed to connect him. Valverde had shown over and over again that he was a gifted climber. Yet he had wilted under the assault of Vinokourov and his Kazakhs in the 2006 Vuelta. Evans seemed to quietly prepare for the Tour and made it clear that his condition was looking good when he came in second to Christophe Moreau in the Dauphiné.

The course itself seemed, like the 2006 route, good for a complete rider. The time trialing, at 117.4 kilometers was only a kilometer more than in 2006. There were 3 hilltop finishes. At 3,570 kilometers, the 2007 Tour's length was in line with recent Tours.

For the first time since 1996, the Tour visited Britain. This time, the Prologue was in London, and stage 1 was to be raced between London and Canterbury. Then the Tour was to cross the British Channel for a clockwise (Alps first) Tour. The riders had to confront the Alps earlier than usual, in stage 7 with an ascent of the Col de la Colombière. The next day the riders had to climb 3 first category climbs with a hilltop finish at the Montée de Tignes.

The Prologue in London was a smashing success with an estimated crowd of 1 million lining the streets to watch. World Time Trial Champion Fabian Cancellara won the stage convincingly. Most importantly, none of the major contenders lost any appreciable time. Andreas Klöden finished second, a bit ahead of the others who had ambitions of Yellow in Paris.

Late in stage 1 a crash took down several riders including Robbie McEwen. His team waited for him and agonizingly dragged him back to the fast-moving peloton. As the sprinters started to wind out the final meters, out of nowhere popped an amazing McEwen. He was bruised and battered, but moving far faster than any of the others as he nailed the stage convincingly.

The Tour crossed the English Channel and after a detour in Belgium, made its way south for the Alps. At the end of stage 3, still in Yellow, Cancellara surprised the sprinters who had a slight moment of hesitation before the sprint began. He jumped clear and earned the 20-second time bonus for winning the stage.

Vinokourov, who always seems to have a bottomless well of bad luck at his disposal, was again hit with misfortune, this time in stage 5. First, his teammate Andreas Klöden crashed and injured a previously fractured tailbone. Then, with about 25 kilometers to go, a slipped chain sent Vinokourov to the ground. Clearly hurt, it was a while before he restarted. His team sent back everyone but potential Tour winners Klöden and Andrey Kashechkin. Finally getting going, his team did all they could to get him back to the peloton. On the final climb Vinokourov left his teammates, chasing the raging pack all by himself. Because there was a break that threatened Cancellara's lead, CSC was at the front of the peloton chasing hard. Vinokourov never did make contact and lost 1 minute and 20 seconds.

After spending 5 hours in the hospital Vinokourov started the flat stage 6. Klöden was also able to start. But the effect of the crashes combined with the ultra-intense racing in stage 5 was to further open the Tour to others who were only dreaming of a shot at the podium.

The day's racing allowed the evergreen Erik Zabel to take the Green Jersey for the first time since 2002. The next day Tom Boonen won the last flat stage before the Alps and took the Green Jersey from Zabel.

Worse for Zabel, as a result of having confessed to doping in 1996, the Tour organization announced that they were stripping him of his Green Jersey for that year.

While I understand the Tour's outrage at the doping culture that has engulfed cycle racing and diminished the Tour, punishing the riders who cleared the air and confessed, no matter what their motivation, is a stupid way to motivate others to do the same. The biggest problem with doping is the code of silence and the Tour's move was surely counterproductive.

With the Tour scheduled to ascend the tough north-facing slope of the Col de la Colombière in stage 7, the General Classification stood thus:

1. Fabian Cancellara
2. Andreas Klöden @ 33 seconds
3. Filippo Pozzato @ 35 seconds
4. David Millar @ 41 seconds
5. Oscar Freire @ 43 seconds

T-Mobile's young Linus Gerdemann rode away from his breakaway companions on the climb of Colombière and came in alone after a very skilled descent into Le Grand-Bornand. Gerdemann was now in Yellow with a lead of 84 seconds over Spanish rider Iñigo Landaluze. While the stage may have removed the non-contenders from the top ranks, the day in the Alps had no real effect upon the relative positions of the best riders. The real racing would have to wait for Sunday's hilltop finish.

That evening both Alejandro Valverde and French champion Christophe Moreau said that that Vinokourov should be dealt a *coup de grace* while he was still suffering from his crash. With a rest day coming after the second alpine stage, the time to strike was now, before the Kazakh could take advantage of the day off to recover.

Well into stage 8, Michael Rasmussen left the peloton on the Cormet de Roselend. He rode away from a peloton that contained almost all of the big men and did so without the slightest challenge or marking from the other riders. They just let him go and go he did. He went through an earlier break and picked up T-Mobile's leader, former world time trial champion Michael Rogers. The fortunes of T-Mobile went from the high of Gerdemann's success the day before to the low of having Rogers crash out of the Tour on the difficult descent of the Cormet de Roselend. Doubling the pain of the injuries, when Rogers hit the railing on the descent he was the Tour's virtual Yellow Jersey, "I could see the Yellow, I could taste it, now it's gone," Rogers recalled.

The descent of the Cormet de Roselend took another casualty, but its true effect wouldn't be apparent until the end of the Tour. Leipheimer had problems with his chain, requiring him to freewheel down the mountain and lose contact with the lead riders. He switched bikes. After restarting he came next to his team car and got a good, long hard push. This probably would have been allowed in 2006 but in 2007 the judges decided to crack down on this abuse. Leipheimer was assessed a 10-second penalty.

Rasmussen continued on, riding powerfully and confidently to both the stage victory and the overall lead.

Behind him Moreau attacked the remnants of the peloton and managed to slightly distance himself from Vinokourov and Klöden. He tried desperately to get the others in his group, which included Evans and Valverde, to make a coordinated effort to get away from the Astana riders while the getting was good. Each of his accelerations was only matched. The others were content, until the final kilometer, to close up to him without helping him on the climb. The result was some damage to Vinokourov, but not the finality Moreau had sought.

The General Classification after stage 8, going into a rest day before the final alpine stage:

1. Michael Rasmussen
2. Linus Gerdemann @ 43 seconds
3. Iban Mayo @ 2 minutes 39 seconds

4. Alejandro Valverde @ 2 minutes 51 seconds

5. Andrey Kashechkin @ 2 minutes 52 seconds

6. Cadel Evans @ 2 minutes 53 seconds

7. Christophe Moreau @ 3 minutes 6 seconds

22. Alexandre Vinokourov @ 5 minutes 23 seconds

Stage 9 had the Iseran and the Galibier. After ascending the Galibier's little brother, the Télégraphe, Mauricio Soler of the wild-card Barloworld team took off and was never seen again. But back in the pointy part of the peloton, the speed on the ascent of the Galibier was too much for Vinokourov, who had to concede almost 3 minutes. This time Astana didn't have Klöden stay with Vinokourov, not wanting to destroy both riders' hopes. With the Alps behind them, the standings were thus:

1. Michael Rasmussen

2. Alejandro Valverde @ 2 minutes 35 seconds

3. Iban Mayo @ 2 minutes 39 seconds

4. Cadel Evans @ 2 minutes 41 seconds

5. Alberto Contador @ 3 minutes 8 seconds

6. Christophe Moreau @ 3 minutes 18 seconds

7. Carlos Sastre @ 3 minutes 39 seconds

8. Andreas Klöden @ 3 minutes 50 seconds

Stage 10 was a hot day and the baking temperatures only served to make Vinokourov more miserable. He said that during this day he actually considered abandoning. Possibly Vinokourov was not as unhappy as Bob Stapleton, the American brought in to manage the T-Mobile team under a regime of absolute intolerance to drugs. It was announced that T-Mobile's Patrik Sinkewitz, who had quit the Tour a few days earlier after breaking his nose in a collision with a spectator, had tested positive for testosterone in an out-of-competition test. Tired of the doping and fulfilling their threat to stop broadcasting the Tour if the scandals continued, the German public television network immediately pulled the plug on Tour coverage.

The next day there were rumors that some sort of move was afoot. After the feed zone, while Christophe Moreau was at the back of the pack following an earlier minor crash, the Astana team took advantage of the hot winds blowing across the peloton. They massed at the front and just detonated the race with a high-powered attack. The pack broke apart and Moreau, Zabel, and Hushovd were caught napping. Over half the field never saw the lead group again as the Kazakhs furiously hammered the front. The day had all kinds of effects. Zabel's chances for Green were profoundly reduced. Moreau's loss of over 3 minutes probably made it impossible for him to attain the podium in Paris. The Astana team had a new-found morale and had made it clear that they were there to race. The 2007 Tour was at least refreshing in its combativeness. It was turning out to be what old man Desgrange wanted his Tour to be, a contest using both heads and legs.

It was the universal wisdom that the 54-kilometer individual time trial would be Rasmussen's last day in Yellow. Further, it was thought that Valverde or Evans would take the lead. Nothing was going as planned in this Tour. Rasmussen delivered a superb ride, actually catching Valverde, his 3-minute man, shortly before the finish and retaining the lead. Vinokourov won the stage and took back more than 3 minutes, saying that he would set off fireworks in the Pyrenees. I am sure no one in the race doubted the veracity of that promise. The result of the day's competition was a tighter race:

1. Michael Rasmussen
2. Cadel Evans @ 1 minute
3. Alberto Contador @ 2 minutes 31 seconds
4. Andreas Klöden @ 2 minutes 34 seconds
5. Levi Leipheimer @ 3 minutes 37 seconds
9. Alexandre Vinokourov @ 5 minutes 10 seconds

The surprises kept coming. Stage 14, the first Pyrenean stage, ended with 2 *hors catégorie* climbs, the Port de Pailhères and a hilltop finish at Plateau de Beille. Saunier Duval, preparing for an attack by their Iban Mayo, threw everything they had into setting a scorching pace up the Pailhères. There were notable casualties: Mayo, who later finished the day over 9 minutes down, and Vinokourov. Clearly lacking power, whether from his injuries or from his extraordinary effort in the time trial, he couldn't stay with the favorites. To make matters worse, near the top of the mountain a zealous fan caused a teammate riding with Vinokourov to crash, forcing Vinokourov to land on his damaged

left knee. He conceded defeat and lost almost a half-hour. Later Cadel
Evans said that Saunier Duval's fast pacemaking left him tired.

The day's final showdown on the ascent to Plateau de Beille was
superb, exciting racing. The favorites took turns attacking and counter-
attacking. An early victim was Klöden, probably showing the effects of
having crashed in the time trial. Fate seemed to be unforgiving in her
treatment of the Kazakh team. From the series of savage blows the racers dealt each other, Contador and Rasmussen emerged and finished
together in that order. For a while it looked like Evans was going to be
able to match them, but he was shelled and lost almost 2 minutes.
Valverde's chances for a high placing were over when he came off the
Yellow Jersey group with 11 kilometers to go. Contador moved to second in the Overall and Rasmussen started to look like a man who might
wear Yellow in Paris.

But all was not well with Rasmussen. The UCI said that Rasmussen had missed several out-of-competition drug tests over the last 2
years. Worse, an American ex-racer alleged that in 2002 Rasmussen had
tried to trick him into smuggling a box of blood substitute into Europe
for him. In June the Danish Cycling Union kicked Rasmussen off the
National Team, meaning Rasmussen could not contest the World
Championship or the coming Olympics. The tardy timing of the release
of the news about his missing the required testing made many suspicious about the motives of the UCI, mired its ongoing war with the
Grand Tour organizers. It seemed to many that the UCI put out the
information about the Yellow Jersey wearer specifically to harm the Tour
de France.

As the Tour progressed, the other teams and the Tour organization became increasingly angry that Rabobank, knowing what they did
about Rasmussen, sent him to ride the Tour anyway. All of the Pro Tour
teams had signed a code of ethics that was clear and unequivocal. The
code barred all riders from competing who are even suspected of doping. Rabobank played dumb, saying that Rasmussen had not failed any
drug tests and therefore there was no reason to keep him off the team.
This explanation satisfied almost no one.

Stage 15 was still harder than the day before with the Port, Portet
d'Aspet, Menté, Balès and the Peyresourde on the day's menu. Early in
the day's racing Vinokourov joined a break that was allowed to go.
Vinokourov's nearly half-hour time loss the day before meant that the

General Classification men didn't have to worry about him. By the Peyresourde Vinokourov had managed to get entirely clear. He soloed over the crest and rode down the other side into Loudenvielle-Le Louron for what was a spectacular win.

Further back, the Yellow Jersey group was content to let Rabobank domestiques Thomas Dekker and Michael Boogerd set the pace. At about 2 kilometers from the top of the Peyresourde Alberto Contador delivered a series of 6 brutal attacks that only Rasmussen could answer. With each acceleration Contador was able to open a gap that Rasmussen struggled to close. It was clear the Rasmussen was weakening, but Contador had opened the hostilities too late in the stage. The 2 went over the top of the Peyresourde together. This made Wednesday (stage 16), the final day in the mountains with its hilltop finish on the Aubisque, the 2007 Tour's probable arbiter.

The next day was a rest day. Rasmussen had tried to avoid a question and answer session with the press, wanting only to play a video of himself. The press angrily rejected the proposal. When he did meet the press with an attorney along with team owner Theo de Rooy, the reporters' questions were given lawyerly answers that again, satisfied no one.

But there was bigger and more tragic news that Tuesday. It was announced that Vinokourov had tested positive for a homologous (from another human being) blood transfusion the day of his time trial win. The news staggered everyone. Vinokourov was out of the Tour and his Astana team was asked to leave with him, which they did.

There was still a race to be ridden, and what a race stage 16 was. But at the morning sign-in, the announcer had to stop talking for a moment when Rasmussen came forward because the crowd was whistling (the European way of showing contempt) and booing so loudly.

Rabobank's super combination of Denis Menchov, Michael Boogerd and Thomas Dekker kept the speed very high on the climbs. By the time the race was 10 kilometers from the summit of the Aubisque (the Tour's sixty-ninth visit to the big mountain), it was down to the Tour's best 4 riders: Rasmussen, Contador, Evans and Leipheimer. Contador tried to get away, but it was clear that he didn't have the same punch he had 2 days before. Rasmussen met each of the attacks and then with about a kilometer to go, soloed away for a 47-second time gain. Again the crowd booed and whistled. Later Contador revealed that he was coming down with a cold that blunted his attacks.

The situation looked sewn up. After the mountains were finished, the General Classification stood thus:

1. Michael Rasmussen
2. Alberto Contador @ 3 minutes 10 seconds
3. Cadel Evans @ 5 minutes 3 seconds
4. Levi Leipheimer @ 5 minutes 59 seconds
5. Carlos Sastre @ 9 minutes 12 seconds

That afternoon, it was announced that Cristian Moreni on the French Cofidis squad had tested positive for exogenous testosterone. He was thrown out of the Tour. In an interesting development that might have positive affects in the future, Cofidis pulled the entire team from the race and withdrew their cars from the publicity caravan.

And then Rabobank sobered up. They pulled Rasmussen from the Tour. It was a strange performance. Before, De Rooy had been adamant in his defense of his rider. Now, he was angry over Rasmussen's missed tests, claiming that the team had been lied to. It was an inexplicable overnight character transformation the sort of which one generally sees only in half-hour TV shows. My guess, and it is only a guess, is that Rabobank, the team's sponsor and an international financial powerhouse, decided that they didn't need the ongoing horrible publicity that Rasmussen was bringing them. Again, perhaps a good sign for the future.

But, while it was looking like the Tour and cycling was indeed cleaning up, 2 Cassandras spoke up with a hard truth. Both Greg LeMond and writer Joe Lindsey noted that the mountain ascension times in the 2007 Tour were as fast as or faster than Marco Pantani's. It is hard to square that information with a clean Tour.

Now there were 2 flat stages before the final time trial. The new General Classification with Rasmussen removed:

1. Alberto Contador
2. Cadel Evans @ 1 minute 50 seconds
3. Levi Leipheimer @ 2 minutes 49 seconds

4. Carlos Sastre @ 6 minutes 2 seconds

5. Haimar Zubeldia @ 6 minutes 29 seconds

It looked like the Tour was still in play. In the first time trial Evans had taken about a minute out of Contador. Almost 2 minutes would be a tall order. He would have to take back an average of 2 seconds every kilometer. The bigger problem for Evans would be fending off Leipheimer, a good time trialist who was clearly riding into shape during the Tour. Leipheimer had won 4 time trials so far this year.

The time trial made things thrilling and closer, but the top 5 placings were unchanged. Here are the time trial's results:

1. Levi Leipheimer: 1 hour 2 minutes 44 seconds

2. Cadel Evans @ 51 seconds

3. Vladimir Karpets @ 1 minutes 56 seconds

4. Yaroslav Popovych @ 2 minutes 1second

5. Alberto Contador @ 2 minutes 18 seconds

At 53.068 kilometers per hour, Leipheimer had uncorked the fourth-fastest individual time trial in Tour history. This yielded the following General Classification:

1. Alberto Contador

2. Cadel Evans @ 23 seconds

3. Levi Leipheimer @ 31 seconds

4. Carlos Sastre @ 7minutes 8 seconds

While the top 3 were now very close in time, with the Green Jersey competition still unsettled, it was unlikely that Evans could grab enough bonus seconds by outsprinting the specialists in the final stage to take the lead. Leipheimer said that he would not "pull a Vinokourov", remembering how the Kazakh had taken a placing from him in the final stage of the 2005 Tour.

And remember Leipheimer's 10-second penalty for the push in the Alps? He was now 8 seconds behind Evans. Without that penalty he might have been 2 seconds ahead. Leipheimer says that the push was necessary to help him regain contact. Without it, he might have suffered a catastrophic time loss.

And that's how the 2007 Tour ended, with the 24-year-old Spaniard taking the victory and the 31-second time spread for the podium being the closest in Tour history. That made the ninth Tour victory for Spain, previous Spanish winners having been Bahamontes, Ocaña, Delgado and Indurain.

The press, perhaps looking to sell papers more than anything else, started calling for a halt to the Tour after Vinokourov's positive, claiming that the scandal-plagued Tour was hopelessly mired in dope. I hope that the patient reader by now understands that the dope has always been there. What the 2007 Tour was undergoing was a crisis generated by a somewhat successful enforcement of the rules. The average speed of the 2007 Tour was 38.98 kilometers per hour, the slowest speed since 1994. The relentless obscene increases in speed that had been going on year after year had been halted, at least for now. I am not so naïve as to believe that this Tour was clean. But clearly there were changes afoot.

For Discovery, it was an amazing turnaround of fortune after their 2006 showing. They captured first and third in the General Classification, the Young Rider (Contador) and 2 stage wins.

Yet, again we had a winner with whom questions remain. There are suspicions that he was involved with Fuentes, suspicions that were not eased by Contador's truculent refusal to give clear answers at press conferences. When asked why he didn't just give the DNA samples that would surely clear him, he gave the tired response that he was innocent and "I don't have to prove everything to everyone." He also gave the meaningless defense that he had passed all of his dope tests.

The Tour organization, furious with the UCI over its continuing attempts to grab power and money from the Grand Tour owners, announced that they would withdraw from the UCI and set up a new cycling organization with the World Anti-Doping Authority. "There can only be one answer for the UCI, either they are incompetent or want to damage the Tour de France," said Tour director Prudhomme after the strange occurrences of July.

Making the UCI's feeling on the subject clear, UCI president Pat McQuaid said, "I don't think the Tour de France belongs to the ASO [the Amaury Sport Organization, owner and organizer of the Tour], I think the Tour de France belongs to the cycling family and I am president of the cycling family. I think in that context they should accept that and we should be sitting down together to work out plans for the future." I'm sure the ASO could feel McQuaid's hand in their pockets.

As the youngest winner of the Tour since Ullrich in 1997 (who was 23), the possibilities open to Contador seem almost unlimited. But the Tour seems to have a way of fooling us. The first winner in this volume, Felice Gimondi, crafted an effortless win in 1965 at 22. He never won the Tour again.

It's clear that a new era of organization governance and possibly doping enforcement is coming. As with any form of change it will be noisy and likely ugly. We'll all be forced to be in the position of watching sausage being made. Let's hope cycling puts something good on our plate.

Final 2007 Tour de France General Classification:

1. Alberto Contador (Discovery) 91 hours 26 seconds
2. Cadel Evans (Predictor-Lotto) @ 23 seconds
3. Levi Leipheimer (Discovery) @ 31 seconds
4. Carlos Sastre (CSC) @ 7 minutes 8 seconds
5. Haimar Zubeldia (Euskaltel) @ 8 minutes 17 seconds

Climbers' Competition:

1. Mauricio Soler: 206 points
2. Alberto Contador: 128 points
3. Yaroslav Popovych: 105 points

Points Competition:

1. Tom Boonen: 256 points
2. Robert Hunter: 234 points
3. Erik Zabel: 232 points

# Chapter 9

## The Greatest Tour Winner

Who is the greatest Tour de France rider? If the definition is limited to merely who is the most successful, the question is easily answered. By that standard, with 7 consecutive victories, Lance Armstrong is unquestionably the greatest Tour rider in history.

But I am looking for a more sublime and meaningful definition that accounts for the changes to the sport and the event that have occurred over the last 100 years. By great I am asking who is the giant, the man who whose victories were larger than life? The greatest Tour rider of all time must display an imposing superiority to all others of his age and those of all other ages. His Tour wins must be characterized by duration, quantity, quality and above all eminence.

Cross-generational comparisons are very dangerous. We must be alert to the trends and changes in cycling in order to make this judgment.

There is a core fact of Tour history: The basic tendency over the last 100 years in stage racing has been to increase the chances for the superior rider to be the winner and for him to win ever more consistently. Here are a few of the reasons for this evolution.

1. The bicycle has become a more reliable machine. Metallurgical advances make the broken forks that crushed Christophe's chances almost unheard of.

2. Roads are better. The first racers competed on dirt roads and climbed ascents that were little more than goat-paths. Broken wheels such as the one that kept Philippe Thys from winning the 1922 Tour are a thing of the past.

3. The rules that magnified the consequences of mechanical difficulties have been relaxed. Christophe had to walk to a blacksmith shop and repair his own fork. Even Koblet had to wait mid-race while his mechanic glued on a new tire to the spare wheel before it could be mounted on his bike. Today a flat tire is fixed in seconds. Thys' broken wheel that cost him $3\frac{1}{2}$ hours would have been replaced on the spot.

4. Teams are unified and dedicated to bringing a chosen athlete to Paris in Yellow. Bobet and Anquetil had to contend with intra-team feuds that sapped their strength, morale and hurt their chances. Gaul never really had a team. Coppi rode in fear that his team and director would betray him.

5. Early Tour riders were forbidden to ride in pace-lines. Today a team captain like Armstrong might see the front of the race for only a few minutes (individual time trials excepted) during the entire 3 weeks of the Tour. The rest of the time he, like other team captains, is surrounded, coddled and protected by a dedicated team. Earlier racers had a much more rugged time of it.

6. Time trials, which improve the superior rider's chances by isolating each rider's efforts and allowing him to gain time without fighting the unified efforts of the peloton, were not introduced until 1934.

7. Tour contenders now have the privilege of being more specialized. Gone are the days when Eddy Merckx would win Milan–San Remo in March, race the Classics in Belgium in April, contest the Giro, the Tour of Switzerland and then race the Tour. In 1974, after riding the spring Classics, Merckx raced almost nonstop from the start of the Giro on May 16 until the end of the Tour on July 21, winning the Giro, the Swiss Tour and the Tour de France and having surgery performed between the Swiss and French Tours. A modern stage race contender can start an important race fresh, at an optimal level of fitness.

8. Modern training techniques as well as advances in sports medicine allowed Armstrong to start a Tour Prologue with only about 25 days of racing in his legs. His chances of a race-induced injury in the run-up to the Tour are reduced. Thys' broken collarbone from a crash in the 1920 Milan–San Remo and Coppi's 1950 broken pelvis come to mind here.

9. Armstrong's entire season and his team were built around and ended with the Tour. He wasn't the first; he was only the culminating result of a 2-decade long tendency. This is in no small way a consequence of big-time sponsors who need the major-event win to get the mass media coverage they covet. In years past a bike manufacturer wanted his riders racing as often as possible, showing the bike and the equipment in every city and village. The crushing expense of team sponsorship has the unexpected effect of helping the better rider consistently win the Tour.

The trajectory of these tendencies can be seen in the Tour results. After Philippe Thys won 3 Tours in 1913, 1914 and 1920 no one won 3 Tours again until Louison Bobet did it in 1953, 1954, and 1955.

Then, Anquetil began his 5 wins in 1957. Merckx then won 5, starting in 1969. Hinault began his streak soon thereafter in 1978. Indurain won 5 in a row starting in 1991. Armstrong began his 7 wins in 1999. Barring his hunting accident LeMond would surely have slotted himself between Hinault and Indurain.

The trend is clear. Consistency became possible with the evolution and improvement of the bike, rules, teams, sponsor's goals and roads.

Therefore, the threshold by which a racer is judged changes over the passing years. Indurain's 5 consecutive wins are remarkable, but they do not stand out from the age.

So who is the Giant of the Road? To me it is very clear. One man stands heads and shoulders above the rest: Philippe Thys with his 3 victories spanning the First World War.

He showed his mastery of the nature of stage racing in his 1913 win.

In 1914 he won the first stage and was one of the rare riders to hold the lead from the beginning all the way to the end. All Tour winners from 1905 (Trousselier) to 1923 (Pélissier) started the 1914 Tour except René Pottier, who was dead. In addition, Lucien Buysse, the 1926 winner, also started. That made 11 men at the line who were either past or future Tour winners. Thys emerged supreme. I know of no other racer who has mastered competition with that much depth.

Thys didn't take the lead in 1920 on the first stage, he took it on the second and held it all the way to the end.

This start-to-finish stranglehold on a Tour doesn't happen often because it is considered suicide to expend so much energy keeping the lead for weeks on end. Often a rider who fancies himself in Yellow in Paris will purposefully relinquish the lead if he finds himself in Yellow too early in the Tour. Roger Walkowiak did this in 1956. Thys showed no such fear.

The writers at *L'Auto* (and presumably Desgrange) thought it likely that Thys would have won 7 Tours if the war hadn't intervened. Given his consistent performance in the Tour over such a long period of time this seems a very likely possibility.

Thys' 3 victories stand out from those of his age. All the post World War Two multiple Tour winners, while all wonderful and magnificent athletes, were fulfilling the predictable expectation of the trends of the Tour. Thys did not. His 3-Tour achievement would not be equaled again until 1955.

Maurice Garin won both the 1903 and 1904 Tours, holding the lead in both from start to finish. His second victory was taken from him in the aftermath of the 1904 cheating scandal. Might he have been the greatest? He had the physical ability but he didn't ride and win enough Tours to enter our elite club.

Coppi, like many great Italian riders, seems to have been intimidated or at least reluctant to ride the Tour. Given his prodigious talent he could have made a much larger mark on the Tour even with the war taking away so many of his best years. Like Garin, his Tour footprint is too small to be considered.

If Merckx had won all 5 of his Tours the way he won 1969 the judgment would be much harder. His 1969 Tour was won with startling ease. He rode it with complete tyrannical control over the race. But in the context of the era, he was, if one may be so bold, just another of the 5-time winners. If Merckx had slowed only a little to allow his body to recover between seasons, he would not have been worn out prematurely. He would surely have won more Tours with even greater authority and would probably be the greatest Tour rider of all time. But that pushes us into the realm of hypotheticals, not the facts.

Armstrong's 7 wins are a magnificent accomplishment. But they in no way contradict the expectations of the era. With each passing decade one expects greater consistency from the best riders and Armstrong was far and away the best of his time. While no one had won 7 before, no one had won 5 before Anquetil.

So here's to you Philippe, The Tour's true Giant of the Road.

## *Epilogue*

## Why the Tour de France is the
## greatest sporting event in the world

The Tour de France is the greatest sporting event in the world. No annual sports event has the television viewership that the Tour has. The Olympics and soccer's World Cup come along every 4 years and don't have the same impact on our consciousness. Only the most extraordinary Olympic accomplishment stays with us. Franz Klammer's insane skiing at Innsbruck, Mark Spitz's total domination of the swimming events at Munich or Abebe Bikila's marathon at Rome are remembered but most of the rest of the myriad Olympic events are forgotten. The World Cup mesmerizes the planet for a while and then we move on for another 4 years.

But every July the world knows that a struggle of epic proportions will occur and the man who emerges victor will have achieved truly lasting fame and glory. The Tour's consistent yearly intrusion into our lives gives the race an iron grip on us. And being 3 weeks long, it is a marvelous, gigantic event that has time to develop like a giant novel. While we can become captivated or repulsed by its players, we don't ignore them.

Over the years there have been many wonderful stories of courage, where a brave and talented athlete has triumphed over some terrible adversity. But the reason Lance Armstrong's story made him one of the most famous and acclaimed athletes of all time is that after beating a life-threatening disease, it was the Tour de France that he won.

The world's judgment was clear in choosing Armstrong's accomplishment as one of the most incredible stories of all time.

But why the Tour? Spain and Italy have their national tours and there are other important races. Why have we devoted years of our lives chronicling this race? The reasons are several and most go back to the vision, methods and authoritarianism of its founder, Henri Desgrange.

1. Desgrange was originally looking for a cheap sales tool to promote his newspaper's circulation. As he grew into his task of running the Tour he wanted more from his race. He wanted it to be a true test of the mind and body of the competitor. The Tour had to be so difficult that just finishing it was a monumental accomplishment. But he wanted more than that from his Tour. After her defeat in the Franco-Prussian war, France went through a long period of self-doubt and self-examination. Like all educated Frenchmen, Desgrange was aware of this. He wanted the Tour to be a tool to promote French industry and sport, to lift his countrymen to a higher economic and physical plane and wipe away the miasma of the war loss. He implemented this vision with an iron fist that infuriated many riders. Yet it was his race that they wanted to win.

2. The Tour has always been adaptable. From the very start, the Tour has shifted nimbly when the occasion demanded. This gave a life and vitality to the Tour and made sure it never grew old.

3. The Tour has been reasonably fair. It hasn't been perfect in its judging (the 1937 victory of Lapébie must be considered tainted and in the 1970s it seemed that drug penalties were not enforced as stringently against French riders), but overall, it has treated its riders justly. For that reason, the Tour has always been an international affair. Early in the Tour's history there were foreign winners and they were acclaimed. In contrast, for a host of reasons, the Giro didn't have a non-Italian winner until 1950.

4. Both Desgrange and Goddet could write. They could get their readers excited about the riders and the race. Also, they skillfully exploited the attention of the growing media (including films, radio and eventually television) to their event and the resulting exploding commercialization of the Tour.

5. The Tour was the first major stage race and being the senior Tour matters. Marketers know that being the first into a niche creates a lasting advantage that late-comers must struggle to overcome.

6. The Tour has been run consistently since 1903, interrupted only by the 2 wars. Spain's Vuelta had a late start and wasn't run consistently until 1955.

It's a combination of all the above that make the Tour a well-run, fair race of unbelievable difficulty with a gloriously rich history. For those reasons, in July, we race fans have our 3 weeks already marked on the calendar.

# *Glossary*

@: In English language race results an asperand (or "at" sign) is used to denote the amount of time or number of points behind the winner. In the example below Luis Ocaña won the race, taking 6 hours, 51 minutes, 50 seconds to complete the course. Joop Zoetemelk was behind him and crossed the finish line 15 seconds later. Pollentier was still further behind and crossed the line 3 minutes and 34 seconds after Ocaña. Van Impe and Thévenet were with Pollentier but slightly behind him. The "s.t." means that they were given the same time as Pollentier. If a rider finishes close enough to a rider who is in front of him so that there is no real gap, he will be given the same time as the first rider of that group. French or Spanish results will use often use "m.t." to denote same time. If no time is given, same time is assumed.

1. Luis Ocaña: 6 hours 51 minutes 50 seconds
2. Joop Zoetemelk @ 15 seconds
3. Michel Pollentier @ 3 minutes 34 seconds
4. Lucien van Impe s.t.
5. Bernard Thévenet s.t.

à : French for @ in race results

Abandon: To quit a race. See also broom wagon

Arc-en-ciel: French for rainbow. See Rainbow Jersey

Arrivée: French for the finish line

Arrivée en altitude: French for hilltop finish.

Attack: Generally a sudden acceleration in an attempt to break free of the peloton. On flat roads it is usually done by riding up along the side of the pack so that by the time the attacker passes the peloton's front rider he is traveling too fast for the pack to easily react. In the mountains it is usually enough to accelerate from the front.

Autobus: French. In the mountains the riders with poor climbing skills ride together hoping to finish in time to beat the time limit cutoff. By staying together in a group they hope that if they don't finish in time they can persuade the officials to let them stay in the race because so many riders would otherwise be eliminated. It doesn't always work. Often the group lets a particular experienced racer who knows how to pace the Autobus lead them in order to just get in under the wire. This risky strategy minimizes the energy the riders have to expend. Synonyms include Grupetto (Italian) and Laughing Group. See time limit.

Azzurri: Italian for the Men in Blue. The Italian National team wears blue jerseys, hence the name.

Bell Lap: If the riders are racing the final meters of a race on a velodrome or on a circuit in a town, a bell is rung at the start of the final lap.

Bidon: Water bottle. Now made of plastic, early ones were metal with cork stoppers. Until 1950 they were carried on the handlebars, sometimes in pairs. Around 1950 riders started mounting bottle cages on the downtube. The trend to dispensing with the bar-mount cages started in the early 1960s and by 1970 they were a thing of the past. In the early 1980s, as a result of the sport of Triathlon, builders started brazing bosses on the seat tube allowing mechanics to attach a second cage so that riders could again carry 2 bottles.

Bonification: Time bonus (actually time subtracted) awarded to a rider. Stage races vary and the Tour is always tinkering with its rules. Bonifications can be earned several ways: winning or placing in a stage, winning or placing in an intermediate sprint, being among the first riders over a rated climb. The rules have changed over the years. At one time in the early 1930s the Tour awarded a 4-minute time bonus for winning a stage. In 2005 that bonification was 20 seconds.

Bonk: To completely run out of energy. Sometimes a rider will forget to eat or think he has enough food to make it to the finish without stopping to get food. The result can be catastrophic as the rider's body runs out of glycogen, the stored chemical the muscles burn for energy. Famously José-Manuel Fuente didn't eat during the long stage 14 in the 1974 Giro. He slowed to a near stop as his body's ability to produce energy came to a crashing halt. Merckx sped on and took the Pink Jersey from the Spaniard who had shown such terrible judgment. It's happened to many great riders including Indurain and Armstrong but not always with such catastrophic results. The French term is défaillance but that term can also mean exhaustion or mental failure, such as when Gaul attacked in the Cévennes in the 1958 Tour. Bobet was unable to respond, mostly because he suffered a loss of confidence. This also would be a défaillance.

Break: Short for breakaway.

Breakaway: One or more riders escaping from the front of peloton, usually as the result of a sudden acceleration called an "attack". Riders will work together sharing the effort of breaking the wind hoping to improve their chances of winning by arriving at the finish in a smaller group. This can also be called a "break". Some riders do not possess the necessary speed to contest mass sprints and therefore try very hard to escape the clutches of the peloton well before the end of the race. Franco Bitossi was a master of the lone break even though he possessed a fearsome sprint. Hennie Kuiper won many famous victories this way as well. Sometimes a break will escape during a Tour stage and no team will take responsibility to chase it down. Sometimes the gap results in an unexpected winner as in the case of Roger Walkowiak in 1956. See Chapatte's Law.

Bridge: Short for bridge a gap. To go from one group of cyclists to a break up the road.

Broom Wagon: When Desgrange added high Pyrenean climbs to his 1910 Tour he thought it would be necessary to have a rescue wagon follow the riders in case the mountain roads were beyond their ability to ascend, hence the Broom Wagon to sweep up the exhausted racers. It is still in use, following the last rider in a stage. Today when a rider abandons he usually prefers to get into one of his team cars.

Years ago the Broom Wagon had an actual broom bolted to it but today this wonderful bit of symbolism is gone. In the 1910 Tour if a rider could not finish a mountain stage he could restart the next day and compete for stage wins but he was out of the General Classification competition. Today an abandonment sticks: the rider is out of the Tour for that year. Before a rider enters the broom wagon an official removes the dossard or back number on the rider's jersey. In French the broom wagon is called the voiture balai.

Bunch: When preceded by "the", usually the peloton. Far less often a group of riders can be "a bunch".

Cadence: The speed at which the rider turns the pedals.

Caravan: The long line of vehicles that precede and follow the racers.

Caravan publicitaire: The line of cars and trucks that precedes the race, promoting various companies' goods and services. When Henri Desgrange switched the Tour to using national instead of trade teams, he became responsible for the racers' transport, food and lodging. By charging companies money for the privilege of advertising their goods to the millions of Tour spectators along the route he was able to help pay the new expenses. When the Tour reverted to trade teams the publicity caravan remained.

Category: In European stage racing it is a designation of the difficulty of a mountain climb. This is a subjective judgment of the difficulty of the ascent, based upon its length, gradient and how late in the stage the climb is to be ridden. A medium difficulty climb that comes after several hard ascents will get a higher rating because the riders will already be tired. The numbering system starts with "4" for the easiest that still rate being called a climb and then with increasing severity they are 3, 2, 1. The most challenging are above categorization, or in the Tour nomenclature, "hors catégorie", HC. In the Giro the hardest climbs are rated a Category 1.

Chairman Bill McGann: A man mad about bikes. A harmless drudge.

Chapatte's Law: Formulated by former racer and Tour commentator Robert Chapatte, it states that in the closing stages of a race a determined peloton will chase down a break and close in at the rate of 1 minute per 10 kilometers traveled. If a break is 3 minutes up the road the peloton will need to work hard for 30 kilometers to catch it. It is now calculated by computer on French television. TV race commentator Paul Sherwen regularly uses Chapatte's Law to come up with his often surprisingly accurate predictions of when a break will be caught.

Chrono: Short for time-trial. See also cronometro, time trial.

Circle of Death: In 1910 Desgrange introduced high mountains into the Tour. The big stage with the Peyresourde, Aspin, Tourmalet and Aubisque was called the "Circle of Death" by the press who doubted that the riders could perform the inhuman task that was asked of them. Now the hardest mountain Tour stage is still occasionally called the Circle of Death.

Classic: One of 7 one-day races whose history and prestige will make the career of its winner. They are: Milan–San Remo, Tour of Flanders, Gent–Wevelgem, Paris–Roubaix, Flèche Wallonne, Liège–Bastogne–Liège and the Tour of Lombardy. Gent–Wevelgem is traditionally held mid-week between Flanders and Paris–Roubaix. Only Rik Van Looy has won them all. Some writers include a few other races in their list of Classics: Omloop Het Volk, Amstel Gold Race, Rund um den Henninger Turm, San Sebastian Classic, Championship of Zurich (also called "Züri Metzgete"), Paris–Brussels and Paris–Tours.

Col: French for mountain pass.

Combine: The Tour has had a competition that uses an aggregate of General Classification, Mountains and Points competitions to arrive at the winner of the Combine category.

Commissaire: A race official with the authority to impose penalties on the riders for infractions of the rules. A common problem is dangerous or irregular sprinting. The commissaire will usually relegate the offending rider to a lower placing.

Contre-la-montre: French for time trial.

C.L.M.: French abbreviation for contre-la-montre or time trial.

CLM par équipes: French for team time trial.

Criterium: A bike race around and around a short road course, often a city block. Good criterium riders have excellent bike handling skills and usually possess lots of power to enable them to constantly accelerate out of the corners. The Dutch and the Belgians are the masters of the event.

Cronometro: Italian for time trial. Cronometro individuale is individual time trial and cronometro a squadre is team time trial.

Départ: French for the start line of a race.

Défaillance: French for a total mental or body collapse. See bonk for more.

Directeur Sportif: The on-the-road manager of a bike team. Although French, it is the term used in English as well.

DNF: Did not finish. Used in results to denote that the racer started but did not complete the race.

DNS: Did not start. Used in results to denote a racer who was entered in a race but failed to start. Often seen in results in stage races where the rider abandons after the completion of a stage.

Domestique: French but used in English as well. Because bicycle racing is a sport contested by teams and won by individuals a man designated to be the team leader has his teammates work for him. These men have been called domestiques since Tour founder Henri Desgrange used it as a term of contempt for Maurice Brocco whom he believed was selling his services to aid other riders in the 1911 Tour. Today the term has lost its bad connotation and serves as an acknowledgement of the true nature of racing tactics. Domestiques will chase down competitors and try to neutralize their efforts, they will protect their team leader from the wind by surrounding him. When a leader has to get a repair or stop to answer nature his domestiques will stay with him and pace him back up to the peloton. They are sometimes called "water carriers" because they are the ones designated to go back to the team car and pick up water bottles and bring them back up to the leader. In Italian the term is "gregario".

Dossard: French for the rider's race number on the back of his jersey.

Drafting: At racing speed a rider who is only a few inches behind another bike does about 30% less work. Riding behind another rider in his aerodynamic slipstream is called drafting. This is the basic fact of bike racing tactics and why a rider will not just leave the peloton and ride away from the others, no matter how strong he is. Only in the rarest of cases can a racer escape a determined chasing peloton. To make an escape work he needs the pack to be disinterested in chasing for some length of time so that he can gain a large enough time gap. Then, when the sleeping pack is aroused they do not have enough time to catch him no matter how fast they chase. Hugo Koblet's wonderful solo escape in the 1951 Tour is one of the rare instances when a solo rider outdid a determined group of elite chasers. A rider who drafts others and refuses to go to the front and do his share of the work is said to be "sitting on." There are a number of pejorative terms for a rider who does this, the best known is "wheelsucker".

Drop: When a rider cannot keep up with his fellow riders and comes out of their aerodynamic slipstream, whether in a break or in the peloton, he is said to be dropped.

Échappée: French for breakaway.

Echelon: When the riders are hit with a side wind they must ride slightly to the right or left of the rider in front in order to remain in that rider's slipstream, instead of riding nose to tail in a straight line. This staggered line puts those riders further back in the pace line in the gutter. Because they can't edge further to the side, they have to take more of the brunt of both the wind and the wind drag of their forward motion. Good riders then form a series of echelons so that all the racers can contribute and receive shelter. Although this is a French word, it is not used in this sense by the French, who call it an éventail or bordure.

Équipe: French for team.

Escape: When used as a noun it is a breakaway. When used as a verb it is the act of breaking away.

Étape: French for stage.

Feed zone: The specific point along a race route where the riders pick up food and drink. Racing etiquette generally keeps racers from attacking at this point, but there have been some famous initiatives that have started while the riders were having musettes (bags) of food handed up. In 1987 a carefully crafted plot to attack Jean-François Bernard who was then in Yellow was executed by Charly Mottet and his Système U team. They informed Stephen Roche and Pedro Delgado of their plans so that there would be enough horsepower to carry it through, which they did.

Field: See Peloton.

Field Sprint: The race at the finish for the best placing among those in the peloton. The term is usually used when a breakaway has successfully escaped and won the stage and the peloton is reduced to fighting for the remaining lesser places.

Fixed gear: A direct drive between the rear wheel and the cranks. The rear cog is locked onto the rear hub so that the rider cannot coast. When the rear wheel turns, the crank turns. Because this is the most efficient of all possible drive trains riders in the early days of cycle racing preferred fixed gears to freewheels. When the Tour added mountains in 1905 the riders had to mount freewheels so that they could coast down the descents; otherwise their velocity was limited by their leg speed. Track bikes use fixed gears.

Flamme Rouge: French. A red triangular flag hung at the beginning of the final kilometer of a race.

Flyer: Usually a solo breakaway near the end of a race.

Fugue: Romantic French for breakaway.

GC: see General Classification.

General Classification: The ranking of the accumulated time or placings, whichever basis the race uses to determine its winner. The Tour (since 1913) and the Giro use time. Lance Armstrong was the winner in the General Classification for all Tours between 1999 and 2005. See stage race.

Giro d'Italia: A 3-week stage race, like the Tour de France. It is held in Italy, traditionally in May. It was first run in 1909.

Grand Tour: There are 3 Grand Tours, all lasting 3 weeks: the Tour de France, the Giro d'Italia and the Vuelta a España.

Grande boucle, la: French. The big loop, a nickname for the Tour de France that has existed since the earliest days of the Tour.

Green Jersey: In the Tour, awarded to the leader of the Points Competition (except 1968 when the Points Jersey was red). In the Giro, the leading climber wears a green jersey.

Gregario: Italian, see domestique.

Grimpeur: French for a rider who climbs well. Italian is scalatore.

Gruppo: Italian, literally, "group". In road racing it is the peloton. When they are all together without any active breakaways, it is "gruppo compatto". When referring to the bicycle, "gruppo" means the core set of components made by a single manufacturer, such as a Campagnolo Gruppo.

HD: 1. The initials of Henri Desgrange, the father of the Tour de France. For years the Yellow Jersey had a stylized "HD" to commemorate Desgrange's memory. Sadly, to make room for commercial sponsors for several years Desgrange's initials were removed from the Yellow Jersey. For the Tour's centenary and since, the initials have been replaced. 2. Hors délais, or finishing outside the time limit. See time limit.

Hilltop finish: When a race ends at the top of a mountain, the rider with the greater climbing skills has the advantage. It used to be that the finish line was far from the last climb, allowing the bigger, more powerful riders to use their weight and strength to close the gap to the climbers on the descents and flats. The Tour introduced hilltop finishes in 1952 and did it with a vengeance ending stages at the top of l'Alpe d'Huez, Sestriere and Puy de Dôme. In order to reduce Anquetil's advantage in the time trials and flatter stages the 1963 Tour moved the finish lines closer to the last climbs of the day, further helping the pure climbers.

Hook: To extend an elbow or thigh in the way of another rider, usually during a sprint, to impede his progress while he is attempting to pass. Often it is said that a rider "threw a hook". Means the same thing.

Hors délais: French. See time limit.

Hot Spot: See intermediate sprint.

Individuel: French. Independent rider in the Tour. See touriste-routier.

Intermediate sprint: To keep the race active there may be points along the race course where the riders will sprint for time bonuses or other prizes (premiums, or "preems"). Sometimes called "Hot Spots".

Isolés: A class of independent rider in the Tour. See touriste-routier.

ITT: Individual time trial. See time trial.

Jump: A rider with the ability to quickly accelerate his bike is said to have a good "jump".

Kermesse: A lap road race much like a criterium and associated with a city fair. Bill Kund, one of the first modern-era Americans to race in Europe says that the course can be longer in a kermesse, as long as 10 kilometers.

King of the Mountains: Winner of the Grand Prix de la Montagne. In 1933 the Tour de France started awarding points for the first riders over certain hard climbs, the winner of the competition being the King of the Mountains. In 1975 the Tour started awarding the distinctive Polka-Dot jersey or maillot à pois to the leader of the classification. The first rider to wear the dots was the Dutch racer Joop Zoetemelk. The classification has lost some of its magic in recent years because of the tactics riders use to win it. Today a rider wishing to win the KOM intentionally loses a large amount of time in the General Classification. Then when the high mountains are climbed the aspiring King can take off on long breakaways to be first over the mountains without triggering a panicked chase by the Tour General Classification contenders.

KOM: King of the Mountains.

Lanterne Rouge: French for the last man in the General Classification. In earlier years riders competed to be the Lanterne Rouge because of the fame it brought and therefore better appearance fees at races.

Laughing Group: See Autobus.

Loi Chapatte: See Chapatte's Law.

Maglia Rosa: Italian, see Pink Jersey.

Maillot à Pois: French, see Polka-Dot Jersey.

Maillot Blanc: French, see White Jersey.

Maillot Jaune: French, see Yellow Jersey.

Maillot Jaune Virtuel: French, see Virtual Yellow Jersey.

Maillot Vert: French, see Green Jersey.

Massed Start Road Race: All the riders start at the same time. This is different from a time trial where the riders are set off individually at specific time intervals. Known in French as course en ligne.

Mechanical: A problem with the function of a racer's bicycle, usually not a flat tire. Because rules have sometimes been in place that prevent riders' changing bikes unless a mechanical problem is present mechanics have manufactured mechanicals. In the 1963 Tour de France Anquetil's manager Géminiani cut one of Anquetil's gear cables so that he could give him a lighter bike to ascend the Forclaz.

Minute Man: In a time trial the rider who starts a minute ahead. It's always a goal in a time trial to try to catch one's minute-man. See time trial.

Musette: A cloth bag containing food and drinks handed up to the rider in the feed zone. It has a long strap so the rider can slip his arm through it easily on the fly, then put the strap over his shoulder to carry it while he transfers the food to his jersey pockets.

M.T.: in French, même temps or same time; in Spanish, mismo tiempo. See "@".

National Team: From 1930 to 1961, 1967, and 1968 the Tour was organized under a National Team format. The riders rode for their country or region. See trade team.

Natural or nature break: Because races can take over 7 hours the riders must occasionally dismount to urinate. If the riders are flagrant and take no care to be discreet while they answer the call of nature they can be penalized. Charly Gaul lost the 1957 Giro when he was attacked while taking such a break so he later learned to urinate on the fly.

Off the back: To be dropped.

Paceline: Riders riding nose to tail saving energy by riding in each
    other's slipstream. Usually the front rider does the hard work for a
    short while, breaking the wind for the others, and then peels off to go
    to the back so that another rider can take a short stint at the front.
    The faster the riders go the greater the energy saving from riding in
    the slipstream of the rider in front. When the action is hot and the
    group wants to move fast the front man will take a short, high-speed
    "pull" at the front before dropping off. At lower speeds the time at
    the front is usually longer. See echelon.

Palmarès: French for an athlete's list of accomplishments.

Parcours: The race course.

Pavé: French for a cobblestone road. Riding the pavé requires skill and
    power. Some riders such as the legendary Roger de Vlaeminck can
    seem to almost glide over the stones knowing exactly what line to
    take to avoid trouble. De Vlaeminck, who won the Paris–Roubaix 4
    times, rarely flatted in this race famous for its terrible cobbles because
    of his extraordinary ability to pick his way over the tough course
    while riding at high speed.

Peloton: The main group of riders traveling together in a race. Breaks
    leave the front of it, dropped riders exit its rear. Synonyms: bunch,
    group, field, pack.

Piano: Italian for soft. It can mean slow or easy when riding. The Giro
    often has "piano" stages where the riders intentionally take it easy
    until the final kilometers leading up to the sprint.

Pink Jersey: Worn by the rider who is currently leading in the General
    Classification in the Giro d'Italia. The color was chosen because the
    sponsoring newspaper *La Gazzetta dello Sport* is printed on pink
    paper.

Podium: The top three places, first, second and third. Many racers
    know that they cannot win a race and thus their ambition is limited
    to getting on the podium. In major races such as the Tour and the
    Giro, attaining the podium is such a high accomplishment that it
    almost makes a racer's career.

Poinçonnées: Riders in early Tours who had their bikes hallmarked or stamped so that the officials could know that the competitors started and finished with the same bike.

Point Chaud: French for Hot Spot. See intermediate sprint.

Points: The usual meaning is the accumulation of placings in each stage. Today the Tour gives more points to the flatter stages so the winner of the points competition is a more likely to be sprinter. See General Classification. In the Tour the Points leader wears a green jersey, in the Giro he dons a purple jersey.

Polka-Dot Jersey: Awarded to the King of the Mountains.

Prologue: An introductory stage in a stage race that is usually a short individual time trial, normally under 10 kilometers. The Tour has also used a team time trial format in the Prologue.

Pull: A stint at the front of a paceline.

Rainbow Jersey: The reigning World Champion in a particular cycling event gets to wear a white jersey with rainbow stripes. The championships for most important events are held in the fall. A former World Champion gets to wear a jersey with rainbow trim on his sleeves and collar. If a World Champion becomes the leader of the Tour, Giro or Vuelta he will trade his Rainbow Jersey for the Leader's Jersey. In the 1975 Tour after Thévenet defeated Merckx on the climb to Pra Loup, Merckx gave up his Yellow Jersey to Thévenet and wore his Rainbow Jersey the rest of the Tour.

Ravitaillement: French for taking on food and drink, usually in the feed zone. Zone de ravitaillement is French for the feed zone. Often shortened to ravito.

Rouleur: French for a rider who can turn a big gear with ease over flat roads. Rouleurs are usually bigger riders who suffer in the mountains.

Routier: French for road racer.

Same time: See "@".

Scattista: Italian for a climber who can explode in the mountains with a devastating acceleration. The most famous and extraordinary of these pure climbers were Charly Gaul and Marco Pantani.

Soigneur: Today a job with many duties involving the care of the riders: massage, preparing food, handing up musettes in the feed zone and sadly, doping. Usually when a doping scandal erupts the soigneurs are deeply involved.

Souvenir Henri Desgrange: A prize to the first rider of the highest summit of the Tour. In 2005 the Tour awarded Alexandre Vinokourov a 5,000 euro purse when he was first over that year's highest point, the 2,645-meter high Galibier. In 1974 it was also the Galibier and the prize of 2,000 francs was won by Spanish climbing ace Vicente Lopez-Carril.

Sprint: At the end of a race the speeds get ever higher until in the last couple of hundred meters the fastest riders jump out from the peloton in an all-out scramble for the finish line. Teams with very fine sprinting specialists will employ a "lead-out train". With about 5 kilometers to go these teams will try to take control of the race by going to the front and stepping up the speed of the race in order to discourage last-minute flyers. Sometimes 2 or 3 competing teams will set up parallel pace lines. Usually the team's train will be a pace line organized in ascending speed of the riders. As the team's riders take a pull and peel off the next remaining rider will be a quicker one who can keep increasing the speed. Usually the last man before the team's designated sprinter is a fine sprinter who will end up with a good placing by virtue of being at the front of the race in the final meters and having a good turn of speed himself.

Squadra: Italian for team.

S.T.: Same time. See "@".

Stage race: A cycling competition involving 2 or more separate races involving the same riders with the results added up to determine the winner. Today the victor is usually determined by adding up the accumulated time each rider took to complete each race, called a "stage". The one with the lowest aggregate time is the winner. Alternatively the winner can be selected by adding up the rider's placings, giving 1 point for first, 2 points for second, etc. The rider with the lowest total is the winner. The Tour de France used a points system between 1905 and 1912 because the judging was simpler and cheating could be reduced. Because points systems tend to cause dull racing during most of the stage with a furious sprint at the end they are rarely used in determining the overall winner. Because points systems favor sprinters most important stage races have a points competition along with the elapsed time category. In the Tour de France the leader in time wears the Yellow Jersey and the points leader wears Green. In the Giro the time leader wears pink and the man ahead in points wear purple or more accurately "cyclamen". The race's ranking of its leaders for the overall prize is called the General Classification, or GC. It is possible, though rare, for a rider to win the overall race without ever winning an individual stage.

Stayer: A rouleur.

Switchback: In order to reduce the gradient of a mountain ascent the road engineer has the road go back and forth up the hill. The Stelvio climb is famous for its 48 switchbacks as is l'Alpe d'Huez for its 21. In Italian the term is tornante.

Tappa: Italian for stage.

Team time trial: See time trial. Instead of an individual rider, whole teams set off along a specific distance at intervals. It is a spectacular event because the teams go all out with the most advanced aerodynamic equipment and clothing available. To maximize the slipstream advantage the riders ride nose to tail as close to each other as possible. Sometimes a smaller front wheel has been used on the bikes to get the riders a few valuable centimeters closer together. With the riders so close together, going so fast and at their physical limits, crashes are common. Some teams targeting an overall win practice this event with rigor and the result is a beautifully precise fast-moving team that operates almost as if they were 1 rider. Sometimes a team with a very powerful leader who is overly ambitious will shatter his team by making his turns at the front too fast for the others. Skilled experienced leaders take longer rather than faster pulls so that their teammates can rest.

Technical: Usually refers to a difficult mountain descent or time trial course on winding city streets, meaning that the road will challenge the rider's bike handling skills.

Tempo: Usually means riding at a fast but not all-out pace. Teams defending a leader in a stage race will often go to the front of the peloton and ride tempo for days on end in order to discourage breakaways. It is very tiring work and usually leaves the domestiques of a winning team exhausted at the end of a Grand Tour.

Tifosi: Italian sports fans, sometimes fanatical in their devotion to an athlete or team. The term is said to be derived from the delirium of typhus patients.

Time bonus: see bonification.

Time limit: To encourage vigorous riding the Tour imposes a cutoff time limit. If a racer does not finish a stage by that time limit, he is eliminated from the race. This prevents a racer's resting by riding leisurely one day then winning the next. The time limit is a percentage of the stage winner's time. Because it is the intention of the Tour to be fair, the rules are complex. On flat stages where the riders have less trouble staying with the peloton and the time gaps are smaller, the percentage added to the winner's time to arrive at the cutoff is smaller. On a flat stage it can be as little as 5% of the winner's time if the speed is less than 34 kilometers an hour. In the mountain stages it can be as high as 17% of the winner's time. The faster the race is run, the higher the percentage of the winner's time allowed the slower riders. The Tour has 6 sets of percentage time limits, each a sliding scale according to the type of stage (flat, rolling, mountain, time trial, etc.) and the stage's speed. If 20% of the peloton fails to finish within the time limit the rule can be suspended. Also riders who have unusual trouble can appeal to the commissaires for clemency. More than once Paul Sherwen, now a television racing commentator, was given special dispensation for riding courageously when he had suffered misfortune but bravely continued and finished outside the time limit.

Time trial: A race in which either an individual or team rides over a specific distance against the clock. It is intended to be an unpaced ride in which either the individual or team is not allowed to draft a competitor. The riders are started at specific intervals, usually 2 minutes. In the Tour the riders are started in reverse order of their standing in the General Classification, the leader going last. Usually the last 20 riders are set off at 3-minute intervals. If a rider catches a racer who started ahead of him the rules say that he must not get into his slip-stream but must instead pass well to the slower rider's side. This is one of the more often ignored rules in cycling. The Tour's first time trial was in 1934.

Touriste-Routier: A class of riders in early Tours who did not ride on a team and were entirely responsible for their own lodging, food and equipment. Various classes of independent or "individuel" and "isolé" riders persisted through 1937. As with all aspects of the Tour, the rules and designations regarding the riders constantly changed. Generally the best riders rode on teams. The best independent performance was Mario Vicini's second place in the 1937 Tour.

Track: See velodrome.

Trade team: A team sponsored by a commercial entity. Until the mid-1950s, cycle team sponsorship was limited to companies within the bicycle industry. That changed in 1954 when Fiorenzo Magni's bicycle manufacturer fell into financial difficulty. Magni was able to supplement the shortfall by getting the Nivea cosmetics company to sponsor his team. The move was initially resisted but it is now the standard. Bicycle companies do not have the monetary resources to finance big-time racing teams. Because the Tour organization suspected collusion between the various trade teams the Tour banished them from 1930 to 1961, 1967, and 1968. During those years the teams were organized under a national and regional team format. Riders rode for their country, such as France or Italy, or if need be to fill out the race's roster, regions such as Ile de France.

TTT: See team time trial

Transfer: Usually a Tour stage will end in a city one afternoon and start the next morning from the same city. When a stage ends in one city and the next stage starts in another, the riders must be transferred by bus, plane or train to the next day's starting city. This schedule is normally done so that both the finish and start city can pay the Tour organization for the privilege of hosting the Tour. The racers loathe transfers because this delays their massages, eating and resting.

UCI: The governing world body of cycling, the Union Cycliste International-nationale.

Velodrome: An oval bicycle racing track with banked curves. It can be sited either indoors or outdoors. Olympic tracks are usually $333^{1}/_{3}$ meters around but indoor ones are smaller and have correspondingly steeper banking. Some road races like Paris–Roubaix have the riders ride into the velodrome and finish after a couple of laps on the track. In the past the Tour would regularly do this, often with the rider's time being clocked as he entered the velodrome. With a 200-man field in modern Tours this is impractical.

Virtual Yellow Jersey: Not the leader of the Tour in fact. When a rider has a large enough lead on the Tour leader, so that if the race were to be ended at that very moment he would assume the leadership, he then is called the Virtual Yellow Jersey.

Voiture Balai: French. See broom wagon.

Washboard: A rough riding surface with small bumps or irregularities. Like the pavé, riding on washboard requires a lot of power and puts the smaller riders with less absolute power at their disposal at a disadvantage.

White Jersey: Currently worn by the best rider under 25. In the 1970s white was worn by the Combine leader.

Yellow Jersey: Worn by the rider who is leading in the General Classification in the Tour de France. Traditional history says that Eugène Christophe was awarded the first Yellow Jersey on the rest day between stages 10 and 11 during the 1919 Tour. It is further believed that yellow was chosen because the pages of the sponsoring newspaper *L'Auto* were printed on yellow paper. Both may not be true. Philippe Thys says that he was given a Yellow Jersey by Tour founder Desgrange during the 1913 Tour and yellow may have been chosen because jerseys of that color were unpopular and therefore cheap and easy to get.

# Bibliography

Books marked * are highly recommended.

*Lance Armstrong: *It's Not About the Bike: My Journey Back to Life*. New York, Berkley Books, 2000

Lance Armstrong: *Every Second Counts*. New York, Broadway Books, 2003

Samuel Abt: *Breakaway, On the Road with the Tour de France*. New York, Random House, 1985

Samuel Abt: Up the Road: *Cycling's Modern Era from LeMond to Armstrong*. Boulder, Colorado, Velopress. 2005

David Armstrong: *Merckx: Man and Myth*. Silsden, England, Kennedy Brothers Publishing, undated

Don Alexander and Jim Ochowicz: *Tour de France '86 The American Invasion*. South Pasadena, Alexander and Alexander Publishers. 1985

Philippe Brunel: *An Intimate Portrait of the Tour de France, Masters and Slaves of the Road*. Denver, Colorado, Buonpane Publications. 1995

Daniel Coyle: *Lance Armstrong's War*. New York, Harper Collins, 2004

Eric Delanzy: *Inside the Tour de France: the pictures, the legends, and the untold stories of the world's most beloved bicycle race*. USA, Rodale, Inc. 2006

Martin Dugard: *Chasing Lance*. New York, Little, Brown and Company, 2005

Jacques Duniecq: *1972 Tour de France*. Silsden, England, Kennedy Brothers Publishing, Ltd.1972

Peter Duker: *Tour de France 1978.* Silsden, England, Kennedy Brothers Publishing, Ltd. 1978

Graeme Fife: *Tour de France. The History, the Legend, the Riders.* Edinburgh, Mainstream Publishing Company. 1999.

William Fotheringham: *A Century of Cycling.* St. Paul, MN. MBI Publishing. 2003

Godaert, Janssens, Cammaert: *Tour Encyclopedie* (7 volumes) Gent, Belgium, Uitgeverij Worldstrips. 1997

*L'Équipe: *The Official Tour de France Centennial 1903–2003.* London, UK. Weidenfeld & Nicolson. 2004

N.G. Henderson: *Continental Cycle Racing.* London, England. Pelham Books. 1970

N.G. Henderson: *Fabulous Fifties.* Silsden, England. Kennedy Brothers Publishing, Ltd. Undated

N.G. Henderson: *Yellow Jersey.* Silsden, England. Kennedy Brothers Publishing, Ltd. Undated

*Marguerite Lazell: *The Tour de France, An Illustrated History.* Buffalo, NY. Firefly Books. 2003

Eddy Merckx: *The Fabulous World of Cycling.* Belgium, Editions André Grisard. 1982

Pierre Martin: *The Bernard Hinault Story.* Keighley, UK, Kennedy Brothers Publishing, Ltd. 1982

Pierre Martin, Sergio Penazzo, Daniel Schamps & Cor Vos: *Tour 82.* Keighley, UK, Kennedy Brothers Publishing, Ltd. 1982

Pierre Martin, Sergio Penazzo, Daniel Schamps & Cor Vos: *Tour 83.* Keighley, UK, Kennedy Brothers Publishing, Ltd. 1983

Pierre Martin, Sergio Penazzo, Daniel Schamps & Cor Vos: *Tour 84.* Keighley, UK, Kennedy Brothers Publishing, Ltd. 1984

Pierre Martin, Sergio Penazzo, Daniel Schamps & Cor Vos: *Tour 85.* Keighley, UK, Kennedy Brothers Publishing, Ltd. 1985

Pierre Martin, Sergio Penazzo, Daniel Schamps & Cor Vos: *Tour 88.* Keighley, UK, Kennedy Brothers Publishing, Ltd. 1988

*Owen Mulholland: *Uphill Battle*. Boulder, Colorado, Velopress. 2003

Owen Mulholland: Various essays published over the years

Svend Novrup: *A Moustache, Poison and Blue Glasses!* London, UK. Bromley Books. 1999

*Peter Nye: *Hearts of Lions*. New York. W.W. Norton Company. 1988

*Jean-Paul Ollivier: *Maillot Jaune*. Boulder, Colorado, Velopress. 2001

Bob Roll: *The Tour de France Companion*. New York, Workman Publishing. 2004

Jacques Seray: *1904, the Tour de France Which Was to Be the Last*. Boulder, Colorado, Buonpane Publications. 1994.

James Staart: *Tour de France—Tour de Force*. San Francisco, Chronicle Books. 2003.

David Saunders: *1973 Tour de France*. Silsden, England, Kennedy Brothers Publishing, Ltd. 1973

David Saunders: *Tour de France 1974*. Silsden, England, Kennedy Brothers Publishing, Ltd. 1974

Pascal Sergent: *100 Anni di Storia del Tour de France*. Milan, Italy, SEP Editrice, 2003

Pascal Sergent: *Paris–Roubaix*. London, UK. Bromley Books. 1997

J.B. Wadley: *Eddy Merckx and the 1970 Tour de France*. Silsden, England, Kennedy Brothers Publishing. Undated

*Christopher S. Thompson: *The Tour de France: A Cultural History*. Berkeley and Los Angeles, University of California Press. 2006

*David Walsh: *From Lance to Landis*. New York, Ballantine Books, 2007

Geoffrey Wheatcroft: *Le Tour. A History of the Tour de France*. London, UK. Simon & Schuster. 2003

John Wilcockson: *23 Days in July*. Cambridge, MA, Da Capo Press, 2004

*Les Woodland: *The Crooked Path to Victory*. San Francisco, Cycle Publishing, 2003

*Les Woodland: *The Unknown Tour de France*. San Francisco, Van der Plas Publications, 2000

*Les Woodland: *The Yellow Jersey Companion to the Tour de France*. London, UK, Yellow Jersey Press, 2003

Les Woodland: *This Island Race*. Norwich, UK, Mousehold Press, 2005

Magazines: Various issues of *Velonews, Procycling, Cycle Sport, Bicisport, Bicyclist*

## Websites

www.memoire-du-cyclisme.net

http://homepage.ntlworld.com/veloarchive/races/tour/index.htm

www.dailypeloton.com

www.letour.fr

www.bikeraceinfo.com

www.cyclingnews.com

www.velonews.com

www.radsport-news.com

www.gazzetta.it (the website of La Gazzetta dello Sport)

Conversations, letters and e-mails over the years with the following generous people, not in any particular order: Owen Mulholland, Les Woodland, James Witherell, Fiorenzo Magni, Giorgio Albani, Greg LeMond, Brian Robinson, Marcel Tinazzi, Felice Gimondi, Frankie Andreu, Joe Lindsey, Steve Lubanski, Celestino Vercelli, Paolo Guerciotti, Valeria Paoletti, Antonio and Mauro Mondonico, Faliero Masi, Rene Moser, Derek Roberts, Franco Bitossi, Ferdy Kübler, Bill Kund, Gianni Bugno, Pietro Piazzalunga, Bruce Hildenbrand. Thank you all so much.

Memories of stories told to me over the years of my career by the many people in the bike industry whom I have had the good fortune to meet.

# Index

Moser, Francesco, 20, 89-91,
96, 97, 145, 376
Motta, Gianni, 7, 9, 10, 12, 13,
32, 33, 58
Mottet, Charly, 156, 173-179,
199, 200, 202, 221, 362
Mugnaini, Marcello, 18-22
Mulholland, Owen, 28, 97, 168,
171, 217, 375, 376
Mulhouse, 50, 54, 57, 130, 270
Museeuw, Johan, 185, 196, 210,
216, 218
Naquet-Radiguet, Jean-
François, 171, 178, 185
National team formula, 24
Nelissen, Wilfried, 211, 217
Nencini, Gastone, 8, 20
Nice, 15, 41, 55, 66, 81, 88, 93,
98, 104, 110, 111, 129, 146,
163, 172, 192, 262, 318
Nijdam, Henk, 21
Nijdam, Jelle, 173, 179
Nilsson, Sven-Ake, 119, 120,
122
Noirmoutier, 257
Normandy, 8, 40, 47, 229, 237,
278, 323
O'Grady, Stuart, 238, 246, 252,
258, 261, 272-277, 283, 300,
316
Ocaña, Luis, 40, 48, 53, 55-81,
89-92, 98, 101, 102, 105,
110, 126, 132, 182, 260,
346, 355
Ochowicz, Jim, 218, 287, 373
Olano, Abraham, 230-232, 236,
238, 239, 242, 257-259, 261,
263, 264, 279

Ollivier, Jean-Paul, 129, 240,
375
Omerta, 14, 298
ONCE team, 196, 203, 211,
216, 225, 227, 228, 251,
255, 261, 263, 264, 272,
277, 279, 281-283, 287, 321
Operación Puerto, 320, 323,
334-336
Orcières-Merlette, 59, 61, 70
Orléans, 87
Pailhères, port de, 290, 310, 341
Pambianco, Arnaldo, 10
Panasonic team, 147, 161, 179,
197, 204
Panizza, Wladimiro, 44, 84, 85,
86, 88, 103, 123
Pantani, Marco, 217, 219-225,
236-244, 247-256, 261-269,
272, 278, 286, 295, 344, 367
Parc des Princes velodrome, 31,
95
Paris, 1, 6, 12, 13, 15, 22, 33,
36, 40, 41, 46, 47, 53, 55,
66, 67, 74, 81, 82, 87, 88,
95, 98, 104, 110, 111, 118,
127, 129, 136, 140, 142,
146, 163, 169, 170, 172,
175, 177, 189, 191, 192,
193, 227, 229, 233, 236,
242, 243, 262, 282, 283,
286, 293, 294, 298, 305,
306, 316, 318, 322, 331,
337, 341, 342, 349, 351,
359, 366, 372, 375
Paris–Nice, 6, 27, 47, 172
Paris–Roubaix, 81, 88, 359

Vandekerkhove, Bernard, 8, 9, 25
Vandenberghe, Georges, 32-35, 48
Vandenbossche, Martin, 44, 45, 52-54, 70
Vandenbroucke, Frank, 241
Vanderaerden, Eric, 140, 153, 155-157, 170
Vandevelde, Christian, 273
Vandevelde, Johan, 127, 128, 137
Vanwalleghem, Rik, 55
Vars, col de, 12, 43, 70, 94, 166, 214, 263, 268
Vasseur, Cédric, 237-239
Vélocipède Illustré, le, 1
Velodrome, 31, 47, 52, 57, 89, 119, 140, 356, 371, 372
Verbruggen, Hein, 305
Vercelli, Celestino, 60, 61, 103, 376
Versailles, 12, 53, 80, 189
Viejo, José-Luis, 100
Vietto, René, 89, 133
Vinokourov, Alexandre, 285, 288-293, 295, 306-316, 319, 320, 336-346, 368
Virenque, Richard, 101, 204, 210, 217, 219-243, 247, 249, 255, 257-261, 263, 265, 266, 268-271, 281, 287, 288, 290, 293, 304
Virlux, 40
Visentini, Roberto, 162
Vittel, 33
Voeckler, Thomas, 299-302

Voet, Willy, 245, 246, 252, 283
Voigt, Jens, 273, 303, 308, 309
Vona, Franco, 207, 209
Vosges, 3, 25, 26, 28, 40, 42, 67, 72, 99, 100, 120, 156, 157, 237, 242, 272, 273, 308
Vuelta a España, 7, 55, 74, 80, 82, 89, 98, 112, 129, 139, 143, 172, 217, 223, 236, 255, 271, 295, 335, 336, 354, 363, 367
Wagtmans, Marinus "Rini", 20, 43, 46, 52, 53, 55, 56, 60
Walkowiak, Roger, 285, 314, 351, 357
Wambst, Ferdinand, 47
White Jersey, 32, 89, 365, 372
Wiels Affair, 9, 69, 249
Winnen, Peter, 131, 132, 137, 143, 144
Winterberg, Guido, 192
Wolfshohl, Rolf, 35-38, 48, 57
World Road Championship, 41, 81, 133, 191
Wright, Michael, 8
Yates, Sean, 187, 218
Yellow Jersey, 7-10, 12, 16-18, 25, 33, 36, 39, 42, 49, 56, 59, 63, 65, 67, 75, 83, 93, 94, 102, 105-108, 112, 113, 115, 116, 118, 119, 123, 125, 126, 130, 134, 137, 140-143, 146, 147, 149, 151, 156, 159, 161, 164, 173, 174, 177, 179, 180, 189, 193-195, 198, 200, 203, 206, 207, 217, 218, 223, 224,

CPSIA information can be obtained
at www.ICGtesting.com
Printed in the USA
LVHW042100121218
600189LV00001B/82/P

9 781598 586084